The Seventeenth Century
The Intellectual and Cultural Context
of English Literature, 1603–1700

Rhetoric → prose 47
Moral influence of arts 48

Architecture 100

Gardens 55

Art & states 49

Longman Literature in English Series

General Editors: David Carroll and Michael Wheeler
University of Lancaster

For a complete list of titles see pages x and xi

The Seventeenth Century

The Intellectual
and Cultural Context
of English Literature,
1603–1700

Graham Parry

Longman

London and New York

Longman Group UK Limited,
Longman House, Burnt Mill, Harlow,
Essex CM20 2JE, England
and Associated Companies throughout the world

*Published in the United States of America
by Longman Inc., New York*

First published 1989

BRITISH LIBRARY CATALOGUING IN PUBLICATION DATA
Parry, Graham.
   The seventeenth century: the intellectual and cultural
   context of English literature 1603–1700. (Longman
   Literature in English series)   1. English literature, 1558–
   1702 — Critical studies.
   I. Title. II. Series.
   820.9'003

ISBN 0-582-49377-3 CSD
ISBN 0-582-49376-5 PPR

LIBRARY OF CONGRESS CATALOGING IN PUBLICATION DATA
Parry, Graham.
   The seventeenth century: the intellectual and cultural
context of English literature, 1603–1700/Graham Parry.
   p.   cm. — (Longman literature in English series)
   Bibliography: p.
   Includes index.
   ISBN 0-582-49377-3. ISBN 0-582-49376-5 (pbk.)
   1. English literature — Early modern, 1500–1700 —
— History and criticism. 2. Literature and society — England
— History — 17th century. 3. England — Intellectual life
— 17th century. 4. England — Civilization — 17th
century. I. Title. II. Series.
PR438.S63P37 1989   820'.9'004 — dc19 88-1130

Produced by Longman Singapore Publishers (Pte) Ltd.
Printed in Singapore.

Contents

List of Plates

Between pages 114 and 115.

Acknowledgements

We are grateful to the following for permission to reproduce illustrations: Wilton House (cover picture); the National Trust (Plate 3); the Louvre Art Gallery (Plate 9); the Tate Gallery (Plate 10); the Duke of Buccleuch (Plate 11): the National Portrait Gallery (Plate 13); and the Scottish National Portrait Gallery (Plate 14).

Editors' Preface

The multi-volume Longman Literature in English Series provides students of literature with a critical introduction to the major genres in their historical and cultural context. Each volume gives a coherent account of a clearly defined area, and the series, when complete, will offer a practical and comprehensive guide to literature written in English from Anglo-Saxon times to the present. The aim of the series as a whole is to show that the most valuable and stimulating approach to literature is that based upon an awareness of the relations between literary forms and their historical context. Thus the areas covered by most of the separate volumes are defined by period and genre. Each volume offers new informed ways of reading literary works, and provides guidance to further reading in an extensive reference section.

As well as studies on all periods of English and American literature, the series includes books on criticism and literary theory, and on the intellectual and cultural context. A comprehensive series of this kind must of course include other literature written in English, and therefore a group of volumes deals with Irish and Scottish literature, and the literature of India, Africa, the Caribbean, Australia, and Canada. The forty-seven volumes of the series cover the following areas: pre-Renaissance English Literature, English Poetry, English Drama, English Fiction, English Prose, Criticism and Literary Theory, Intellectual and Cultural Context, American Literature, Other Literature in English.

David Carroll
Michael Wheeler

Longman Literature in English Series

General Editors: David Carroll and Michael Wheeler
University of Lancaster

Pre-Renaissance English Literature

★ English Literature before Chaucer *Michael Swanton*
English Literature in the Age of Chaucer
★ English Medieval Romance *W. R. J. Barron*

English Poetry

★ English Poetry of the Sixteenth Century *Gary Waller*
★ English Poetry of the Seventeenth Century *George Parfitt*
English Poetry of the Eighteenth Century 1700–1789
★ English Poetry of the Romantic Period 1789–1830 *J. R. Watson*
★ English Poetry of the Victorian Period 1830–1890 *Bernard Richards*
English Poetry of the Early Modern Period 1890–1940
English Poetry since 1940

English Drama

English Drama before Shakespeare
★ English Drama: Shakespeare to the Restoration, 1590–1660
Alexander Leggatt
★ English Drama: Restoration and the Eighteenth Century, 1660–1789
Richard Bevis
English Drama: Romantic and Victorian, 1789–1890
English Drama of the Early Modern Period, 1890–1940
English Drama since 1940

English Fiction

★ English Fiction of the Eighteenth Century 1700–1789 *Clive T. Probyn*
★ English Fiction of the Romantic Period 1789–1830 *Gary Kelly*
★ English Fiction of the Victorian Period 1830–1890 *Michael Wheeler*
★ English Fiction of the Early Modern Period 1890–1940 *Douglas Hewitt*
English Fiction since 1940

English Prose

English Prose of the Renaissance 1550–1700
English Prose of the Eighteenth Century
English Prose of the Nineteenth Century

Criticism and Literary Theory

Criticism and Literary Theory from Sidney to Johnson
Criticism and Literary Theory from Wordsworth to Arnold
Criticism and Literary Theory from 1890 to the Present

The Intellectual and Cultural context

The Sixteenth Century
★ The Seventeenth Century, 1603–1700 *Graham Parry*
★ The Eighteenth Century, 1700–1789 *James Sambrook*
The Romantic Period, 1789–1830
The Victorian Period, 1830–1890
The Twentieth Century: 1890 to the Present

American Literature

American Literature before 1880
American Poetry of the Twentieth Century
American Drama of the Twentieth Century
★ American Fiction 1865–1940 *Brian Lee*
American Fiction since 1940
Twentieth-Century America

Other Literatures

Irish Literature since 1800
Scottish Literature since 1700

Australian Literature
Indian Literature in English
African Literature in English: East and West
Southern African Literature in English
Caribbean Literature in English
★ Canadian Literature in English *W. J. Keith*

★ *Already published*

Author's Preface

This book is divided into two sections, the first devoted primarily to the arts as an expression of cultural attitudes, the second to intellectual movements. It is selective rather than comprehensive in its approach to the age, since I believe that concentration on certain significant themes permits one to trace the continuity of ideas and attitudes within the period with greater clarity than an overall treatment would allow. I have been inclined to emphasize the importance of court culture throughout the century, because for most of the period the court was the focus of the nation's cultural energies. It was certainly the centre of artistic life and the great source of patronage. For much of this time, the court was the main cultural exchange for fashion and taste, and was a remarkably open place. Since the Stuart kings were all assertive men, who imposed their taste enduringly on court circles, I have thought it instructive to view the cultural activities of the different reigns in the light of the character of the monarch, and to look also at the iconography that was constructed for each ruler. Each reign was culturally distinct (even the Commonwealth period, so often dismissed as a time of desolation for the arts, turns out to have had a remarkably vigorous character), so I have tried to make those distinctions clear and explain how they arose.

The second part of the book looks at developments in the areas of science, religion, and political theory. I have also included a brief chapter on antiquarianism, for one of the notable features of seventeenth-century intellectual life was the resourcefulness with which the national past was explored and the findings applied to the present. Throughout the book I have interspersed short biographical sketches of representative individuals, hoping in this way to humanize the perspectives and remind the reader how the ideas, beliefs, and artistic enterprises of the period affected the lives of people who were themselves contributors to the national life.

In the note sections at the end of each chapter, some book titles are shortened, with minimum publishing details. Full titles and publishing details for these titles can be found in the General Bibliographies on pp. 255–62. The place of publication is, unless otherwise specifically stated, London.

Graham Parry
University of York

Introduction

No scene that turns with engines strange
Does oftener than these meadows change.

Like the meadows of Appleton House, like the versatile scenery that
Inigo Jones invented for the masques, the cultural and intellectual land-
scapes of the seventeenth century are subject to frequent change, and
each change seems to enhance the depth and variety of the view. Over
the past decade or so, the emphases and highlights have notably
altered. Recent interpreters of the seventeenth-century scene have had
a greater political awareness than their predecessors, and have shown
an interest in previously neglected aspects of the eventful panorama.
Accordingly, works of literature in this period are now viewed to best
effect when seen in the setting for which they were originally intended,
and this means that we should be mindful of their original audiences,
and that we should know something of the political, religious, and
social conditions that prevailed when they were composed. No work
can wholly evade its context of time and place. Choice of subject,
convention, style, even the resonance of particular words, will give
some indication of the author's allegiance or beliefs, and retain some
faint markings from the force of contemporary events. There has been
in recent years a pervasive curiosity about how works of literature
interact with the society that produced them. Perhaps as a consequence, there has been less regard for beauty of expression, less respect
for moral worth, and more attention to the social commentary that is
implicit in a poem, a play, a sermon, or a masque.

Those classes of literature that engage most closely with specific
social circumstances have benefited most from this shift in approach.
So, for example, masques have become the subject of intensive and
rewarding investigation, since D. J. Gordon and then Stephen Orgel
and Roy Strong have taught us how to read their coded language and
recognize the political dimension of the genre. Even the stage technology of the masques has been shown to derive from an intellectual
tradition of classical mechanics that was allied to a system of aesthetics,

transmitted through the Roman theoretician, Vitruvius. All kinds of festival, including ceremonial entries and coronations, have attracted attention because their language and imagery tell us so much about the ideology of princely power and the ways in which unseen forces were believed to operate upon the hierarchies of men. Panegyric, elegy, and all poems of occasion have enjoyed a revival of esteem, because such poems take us into the process of assessment of men and events by writers who were closely involved or were well placed to judge. Country-house poems have been assigned an importance out of all proportion to their number because they permit the scrutiny of social relationships and economic forces at work in a specific estate, and allow us to uncover the assumptions about the function and responsibilities of the gentry in an age when this class was the critical group in politics. Thus it is that Appleton House, the seat of a major figure in the Civil Wars, Lord Fairfax, has come to be the most trespassed-upon literary property of the century.

Drama offers a special challenge to reconstruct the context in which a piece was first performed, and because a play contains within itself a complete society, it is more than likely that the society of the play will be a distorted but still recognizable image of the society outside and around the play. By covert commentary, allusion, and jokes, by ancient actions or by novel fables, a Stuart play is likely to be engaging with its own times. Recent books by Margot Heinemann, Jonathan Dollimore, Jonathan Goldberg, and Martin Butler, among others, have greatly enlarged our understanding of the interaction between stage and society in this period.

Religious verse tends to be read these days with attention to the devotional techniques employed, and with a sensitivity to the doctrinal position of the writer. In both cases it becomes helpful to know the direction in which the writer was moving through the religious currents that agitated the seventeenth century. Pastoral now no longer appears as a genre of escape, set in some timeless arcadia. Pastoral has been contextualized, and its rural scenes are now understood to be far from innocent; upon closer inspection the shepherds' complaints have much to do with their anxieties about religion, politics, and sex. As David Norbrook has shown, there is a subversive strain in the shepherds' pipes, and their songs often use the language of opposition politics. Only love poetry has been overlooked by this tendency to reread works in a historical light, but this neglect may not endure, for the poetry reflects fashions in love, and these fashions represent shifts in the balance of power between men and women, and indicate adjustments of view about marriage and the status of women, as well as changes in the psychology of affection.

A good deal of the impetus to establish a more specific context for

literary productions in the seventeenth century is due directly or indirectly to the work of Christopher Hill. The many books of his long
career have explored the political, economic and religious developments of the century in intricate detail, and have had a profound influence over literary scholars as well as historians. Time and again he has
used literary sources to document deeply held beliefs or changing
opinion, to make a point about economic conditions or articles of faith;
in turn, writers about literature have been motivated to use Hill's findings to give a greater contextual depth to works of the imagination.
As Hill observed in a recent essay: 'It does not seem to me possible
to understand the history of seventeenth-century England without
understanding its literature, any more than it is possible fully to
appreciate the literature without understanding the history.'[1] The result
of this dialogue has been a succession of books on seventeenth-century
studies that have reinterpreted the character of the three major phases
of the period. One of Hill's enduring concerns has been to re-create
the appeal of many of the forgotten or discredited movements in the
political and religious life of Stuart England, and restore dignity to a
number of populist causes that had been largely ignored by other
historians. As he remarks, it is the victors who write the history of
events, and they usually succeed in diminishing the ideals of those who
lost. So 'The Good Old Cause' of the Puritans became 'The Great
Rebellion' for Clarendon when he wrote the 'authorized version' of the
events of the Civil War. Christopher Hill has managed to redress the
balance over a large front. His sympathetic advocacy of the radicalism
that caused so many men to act to bring about a more just society or
a more godly state – the two were often synonymous – has made
students of this period take a fresh and more admiring view of the long
tradition of Protestant activism that persisted from the early days of
the Reformation and appealed to the aspirations of plain Englishmen.
The Levellers and the Diggers have had their case reheard, and the
impassioned Winstanley now has a wider audience than ever he had
in his lifetime. Hill has inspired a fresh interest in the radical religious
movements of the age. The prophetic spirit, which was so urgent in
the first half of the seventeenth century, and which still flickered on
after the Restoration, has been given its due as an energizing power
over men's minds. Hill has also been the historian of Antichrist in the
seventeenth century, and has reminded us how broadly the current of
millenarianism ran through post-Reformation Britain. The belief that
men were living in the last age of the world, when history might reach
its golden climax with the return of Christ, profoundly affected the
behaviour of men and women at all levels of society and stirred them
to actions that took on a heightened importance because people
believed they were living in providential time. Many of these radical

strains contributed to the most complex of the ardent revolutionaries of the mid-century, Milton, and Hill's account of how Milton drew on so many activist traditions in the course of formulating his own solutions to the crisis of the time should stand as an imposing achievement of late-twentieth-century scholarship.[2]

Works of literature may record how people reasoned, speculated, and felt, but the visual arts are also an indispensable part of the mind of the past. The styles of painting and architecture reveal how men and women chose to be seen, and how they desired to frame their lives. Portraits form a record for posterity, for they offered the sitter a chance to project his appearance, character, and interests down to other generations; but the choice of artist determines the style of presentation, and style, which contains so much of the indefinable, conveys something of the spirit of an age, or at least of a certain class. A number of well-mounted exhibitions at the Tate and National Portrait Galleries over the last fifteen years have served the seventeenth century very well. Most of these exhibitions have benefited from the expertise of Sir Oliver Millar, the Surveyor of the Queen's Pictures; they have brought together many scattered works of art which have enabled us to appreciate the high quality of painting maintained throughout the century, and they have shown how painting supplements the literary record as a register of taste and sensibility. The architectural developments of the century have also been extensively reviewed. Inigo Jones's *œuvre* has been studied in detail, even though much of it has had to be re-created from drawings because so much has been destroyed. Such was the inventiveness of his long career, which extended over half the century, that Jones has rightly been seen as the man who was continually enlarging the possibilities of architecture and design, and offering his patrons the chance to live amid Roman settings and Italian décor, and feel they were coming into their proper inheritance of a classical culture. Jones's influence, however, was limited by his lack of assistants. After the Restoration, the sense of having attained a classical level of civilization – a concept that includes notions of balance, correctness, proportion, reasonableness, and civil order – was greatly intensified. (The significance of the historical parallel of the Augustan age of Rome following after a period of civil war was not lost on contemporaries.) Wren was the dominant architect of the later Stuart age, but by this time the values of classicism had been disseminated throughout society, no longer the perquisite of the court, so the 'Wrenaissance' style spread broadly across the country and was adapted and developed on a national scale.

Architecture, painting, music, and literature remain to tell us much about the civilization of Stuart England. We should, however, bear in mind that 'literature' is really a false category that we employ with too much facility in our discussions of the seventeenth century. The notion of 'literature' could not be said to exist then: *bonae litterae* or *litterae humaniores* perhaps might be used of classical studies, but 'literature' in the sense we understand was an invention of the next century. Men wrote poetry or plays, composed meditations, or devised treatises on one subject or another, but their writings had a function, which was specific and addressed particular issues and problems that exerted pressure on the time. Writers were conscious of genres and conventions (without using such terms), as well as of the innumerable tropes of rhetoric, but these were means to an end, serviceable instruments that allowed access to the large subjects that exercised men's imaginations. The subjects that attracted comment and discourse were large: the life of the spirit and the fortunes of the soul; the many forms of love; power and authority; the advancement of learning and the liberation of reason. Men wanted to write about civil behaviour and their apprehensions of the divine, they wanted to improve man's estate and his dignity, they wanted to assert their own perceptions of truth. In order to recover something of the immediacy of their thoughts, and to develop some sense of the complex of ideas that animated men and women three centuries ago, we try to re-create here some of the vistas of the mind as they existed in the Stuart age.

Notes

1. Christopher Hill, 'The Pre-Revolutionary Decades', in *Collected Essays* (1985), I, 3.

2. Christopher Hill, *Milton and the English Revolution* (1977).

Part One

Part One

Chapter 1
The Character of Jacobean Kingship, 1603–1625

In the seventeenth century, the character of the King had a determining influence on the religious and political events of his reign, and on the political philosophy that evolved in his time. Equally, the taste of the King, refracted through his court, conditioned the main lines of expression in the literary and visual arts. The first three Stuart kings were all forceful personalities, who pursued controversial religious aims and quarrelled with their parliaments more than they agreed with them. All three tried to extend the powers of the crown beyond limits that their parliaments considered tolerable, tempted as they were to take up the absolutist position that they saw successfully maintained by the kings of France and Spain and by the Holy Roman Emperor. Throughout the century the arts were deeply involved in this process of royal aggrandizement, painting and architecture serving to add splendour to the King's authority, literature creating adulatory myths to glorify the Stuart scheme, or inventing critical fictions to warn against excessive power. In an age of patronage, when virtually all writers and artists were associated with some prominent figure or faction, politics and religion were almost invariably dyed into the grain of the finished product, so that few works can be viewed or read profitably without some understanding of their context, and that context generally includes the monarchy.

King James's accession was welcomed by most Englishmen. (See Plate 1). He was the natural candidate for the throne, being Queen Elizabeth's kinsman, descended from Henry VII, the founder of the Tudor line, and he had the experience of a lifetime of kingship behind him, for he had been crowned King of Scotland at the age of one, in 1567. His articles of faith were Calvinist, but in matters of church government he favoured bishops rather than the Presbyterian system of ministers chosen by the congregation, believing that the hierarchical system strengthened his position as king; he was therefore in agreement with the Elizabethan church settlement, and few groups in England felt threatened by his coming in. His known tolerance for differing religious views was a considerable asset at this stage. There was a lot to be said too for an adult male on the throne of England after fifty-six years of minors and queens, and the old problem of succession was not merely solved but secured as the fertile Stuarts supplanted the barren Tudors. James was quite aware of the benefits he brought to his new kingdom, for he confidently spelt them out in the opening address to his first Parliament in March 1604, a speech that contains most of the major themes of his rule. He also took the occasion to expound some of his theories of kingship, about which he was highly articulate, having already devoted two books to the subject while he was King of Scotland. He spoke first of his lifelong commitment to peace as a policy of state, reminding his audience that he had already in his brief time as King of England put an end to the lingering war with Spain that had been draining the country's resources since the 1580s. 'I thank God I may justly say, that never since I was a King, I either received wrong of any other Christian Prince or State, or did wrong to any; I have ever, I praise God, yet kept Peace and amity with all.'[1] Given the belligerent nature of princes, James was exceptional in his desire for peace – 'no small blessing to a Christian Commonwealth' – which he was convinced added to the prosperity of the nation and allowed the sovereign to fulfil his duty to protect his subjects. Although his unwarlike policies were often criticized as evidence of weakness or cowardice, he held resolutely to them, attempting to mediate the international conflicts of his reign by diplomacy and conciliatory strategies of marriage, and being driven to a war with Spain only in the last year of his life when he had lost control of policy to his son and the Duke of Buckingham. His motto was 'Beati Pacifici', 'Blessed are the Peacemakers', from the Beatitudes, a fit ideal for a Christian king. In time, the peace of the Stuarts, extending almost uninterrupted until 1642, would become legendary.

The other benefit that James took especial pride in conferring was the union of the crowns. This was more than a political measure for the security of both England and Scotland, or an instant demonstration of James's success at ending ancient hostilities by peaceful means: union had an almost mystical significance for the King. The concept of kingdoms united by his will and in his person gave him a metaphysical pleasure, for it revealed the mysterious powers of kingship that he alluded to so often, while the historical fact of union was so remarkable that it could only be explained as an act of God's providence working through his chosen instrument, King James. Do not imagine, James told his Parliament in 1604, that this union of kingdoms is a mundane political event, when 'it is manifest that God by his Almighty Providence hath preordained it so to be'. He described 'that Union which is made in my blood' in terms of the marriage ceremony, which also 'signifies a mystical Union': 'What God hath conjoined then, let no

Lawful wife

man separate. I am the husband, and the whole Island is my lawful wife.'

The union could be exploited for imaginative effect. At his coronation he had adopted the style 'King of Great Britain' since he possessed the crowns of Scotland, England, Ireland, and Wales, and this title reflected a mysterious transformation in the condition of these countries, for they were now brought under one head for the first time since the legendary foundation of Britain by the Trojan Brutus, a figure who haunts the mythology of the Stuarts. James liked to figure his kingdoms in the North as a little empire with himself as emperor, a serviceable conceit that endowed his aspirations for the nation with inexpensive grandeur. Moreover, it was a Christian empire governed by one who professed the true reformed faith, who therefore enjoyed the goodwill and favour of God, with certain assurance of prosperity.

Having instructed Parliament in what he believed to be particular strengths and blessings of his rule, he turned to the question of how he should direct them to the advantage of his new realm, and this meant to most of his auditors how he would proceed in matters of religion. After assuring them that he would uphold the Church of England as he found it, he considered the position of the Puritans and Catholics in the State, and rather surprisingly he showed more favour to the Catholics, indicating that if only they could be persuaded to take an oath of allegiance that would recognize his sovereign power in England, they could continue to be profitable members of society. He took a tolerant view: 'I would be sorry to punish their bodies for the error of their minds, the reformation whereof must only come of God and the true Spirit.' The Gunpowder Plot in the following year 1605 would cause him to rethink his attitude towards the Catholics, but even so he never persecuted them, preferring to believe they could be more effectively converted by arguments in divinity that by force. James was less willing to extend toleration to the Puritans, whom he rightly saw as a greater source of trouble because of their reluctance to accept the hierarchical system of church government or the control of the State over the affairs of the spirit; he saved his most hostile words for 'the Puritans and Novelists, who do not so far differ from us in points of religion, as in their confused form of policy and parity, being ever discontented with the present government, and impatient to suffer any superiority, which maketh their sect insufferable in any well-governed Commonwealth'. It is clear here that James had in mind the extremist Puritans, the separatists who felt so strongly about their right to worship in their own way that they were prepared to emigrate to Holland and later to America to secure their freedom of conscience. His experience in Scotland had already warned him about the fractious nature of the sects, which would continue to increase in strength and clamorousness as the imperatives of the spirit worked among them.

In this first address to Parliament, James, like most politicians taking up power, was optimistic. He confessed that his highest ambition was 'that it would please God to make me one of the members of such a general Christian Union in religion as we might meet in the midst, which is the centre and perfection of all things'. This ideal of general Christian union persisted through his reign, having in view a *modus vivendi* for the Western nations around an acceptable body of Christian doctrine; it was to be accomplished by toleration, constructive debate, and a policy of marriage alliances, all of which might moderate the religious antagonisms of Europe. James had a noble design in view, even though it was decried by his opponents as impossible or unpatriotic, and he himself lacked the means and the diplomatic skills to shape events to his plan. Tragically, however, religious divisions grew more bitter all across Europe throughout his reign, resulting eventually in the Thirty Years War, the most devastating European war before 1914; James's policies came to look quite unseasonable, and he gained the reputation of an ineffectual meddler in the continental scene, when in fact he had cautious and humane policies in mind, and civilized and humane ideals of national and international concord to propose. The times required force, but James had a principled objection to the use of force, and was left to suffer taunts such as 'the wisest fool in Christendom' from Henri IV. In 1604, though, these challenges were yet to come, and as he described his political character to the newly assembled Parliament, he could take a confident view of his abilities.

Many of the themes that James sounded on this occasion had been given visual expression in the pageant of welcome that the City of London staged to celebrate the King's appearance in his capital, a few days before he opened Parliament. This was a grand ceremonial entry of a kind common in European states throughout the sixteenth century but never fully enacted in England before now, involving a series of triumphal arches often with accompanying dramatic tableaux to enlarge on the significance of the images that the arches displayed. The King's Entertainment, as it was called, was essentially an emblematic theatre that furnished an iconography for the new reign. Ben Jonson and Thomas Dekker had been chosen as the inventors of the tableaux, and it is clear that part of their purpose was to transfer to King James much of the symbolism that had been associated with Queen Elizabeth, and to invest him with additional insignia distinctive to a Stuart prince. Jonson and Dekker were unlikely to have had any contact with the King at this stage, but they would have found a clear mirror of the royal mind in his writings; their choice of themes, so close to James's own presentation to Parliament, shows how well they studied their

man. Central to the Entertainment was James's reputed descent from
Brutus, and much play was made of the Trojan origins of Britain and
the unity that James had reimposed on the long divided kingdoms.
Troy provided an illustrious ancestry for the King (one much easier
to praise than his descent from the troublesome Mary, Queen of
Scots), and also enabled propagandists of the new regime to strike the
note of imperialism, for the Trojans were the source of empire in the
West, as Virgil had described at length, and Britain, like Rome, was
settled from Troy. So at least the ancient chroniclers maintained, and
neither poets nor kings were anxious to disturb so serviceable a legend.
With James's accession a new Brutus takes the throne, and with him
a new cycle of British history begins. The first arch that the King
approached was decorated with a panorama of London, entitled Troy-
novant, in front of which the Genius of the City declaimed:

> When Brutus' plough first gave thee infant bounds,
> And I, thy Genius, walked auspicious rounds
> In every furrow; then did I forelook,
> And saw this day marked white in Clotho's book.
> The several circles, both of change and sway,
> Within this isle, there also figured lay:
> Of which the greatest, perfectest and last
> Was this, whose present happiness we taste.[2]

The character of the new era was unfolded by the imagery of the
succeeding arches: James would restore the Golden Age, which would
endure in the Fortunate Isles of Great Britain until the end of time.
(Here the royal fertility could be praised: James was a great cedar with
many branches canopying the realm.) Peace was the precondition of
this happy state, and James was a votary of Peace. Justice, so long
absent from the earth, would return: the figure of Astraea, the goddess
of Justice, stood on the summit of two of the arches, being now identified with James's rule as she had earlier been with Elizabeth's. James's
presence at another triumphal arch caused the Fount of Virtue to revive
and fertilize the land with its blessings: the arts also would flourish
under his encouragement. The image of England as a paradise of the
arts was most attractively figured in a rustic arch leafy with fruit-
bearing trees (Plate 2), where Peace and Plenty sat at ease, flanked by
the nine Muses and the seven Liberal Arts, who formed a consort of
musicians, and who were all animated into speech and song by the
arrival of the King, whose spirit gave vitality and harmony to the
scene. The music that broke out wherever the King went was clearly
understood to signify the harmony of his rule. In addition to these
attributes, two higher qualities made up the perfection of the Jacobean

Golden Age: Divine Wisdom, who was seen to counsel and support the King, and Divine Providence, whose presence indicated that all was in accordance with God's will. The last of the festive arches abounded with allegorical figures expressive of the civil blessings expected of the new reign, with the motto 'Redeunt Saturnia Regna', 'Out of Virgil, to show that now those golden times were returned again, wherein Peace was with us so advanced, Rest received, Liberty restored, Safety assured, and all Blessedness appearing'.[3] As James left the City, beneath a rainbow across the Strand (suggestive of a new covenant between King and people), he was hailed as a new Augustus destined to lasting glory. The character of Roman Emperor is imposed over that of Trojan Prince to herald a great imperial reign.

Such an abundance of congratulatory and optimistic symbolism had been tumbled out in the course of the King's procession that it could hardly be assimilated by the audience in the tumult of the occasion, but the themes that were proposed then would endure throughout the reign, and many would be carried over into Charles's time. No English monarch, not even Queen Elizabeth, has enjoyed such a fully orchestrated mythology as that which sustained James, and he derived considerable political benefit from it, for it surrounded him with potent images of authority and benevolence on a scale which owed something to the need to introduce and establish a new dynasty as favourably as possible, but which also reflected the high confidence and expectation that attended the new reign.

We should not overlook King James's own contribution to his cult, for his writings provided a structure of ideas on which artists and image-makers could build. He had already written several political treatises, an extensive body of poetry, both religious and secular, and a book on witchcraft (*Daemonologie*, 1597). He was proud of his reputation for learning – all the Tudors and Stuarts showed a love of learning that was exceptional in the history of the English monarchy, but James was undoubtedly the most erudite – and he was happy to be compared with Solomon for his wisdom and with David for his poetic inspiration. He had expounded his convictions about the divine right of kings in *The True Law of Free Monarchies* (1598) (to be discussed later in Chapter 9) and his most rounded book of statecraft was *Basilikon Doron*, literally 'the Gift of the King', which he had written in 1599 for his eldest son Prince Henry, and which had been reprinted in London in 1603 to give his new subjects access to his principles and ideals of government. Here he described the two natures of the monarch: the divinity that is inherent in kingship, and the humanity that belongs to the person of the King. Ideally, he tells the Prince, his human nature should be in every way exemplary to the nation, in conduct, action, and in qualities of mind, but it is the sacred character of the King that most occupies James's thought. Kings, he insists, are chosen by God, who invests them all with some measure of his own qualities of wisdom, authority, and sanctity, which are conferred by the rituals of consecration. The magical virtues of kingship are most fully revealed in the Hebrew kings of the Old Testament, and even though kings no longer walk so close to God, their divinity remains, for the institution of kings was appointed by God and he will sustain it still as a visible sign of his authority on earth. Kingship is patriarchal, for the King is father of his people as God is father of all men. The King's especial care is for his people, who in turn must render to him the total obedience that children owe their father. The King's own obedience lies to God, to whom he is responsible for all his actions and policies, and by whom he will ultimately be judged. The sonnet at the beginning of *Basilikon Doron* expressed in simple terms the outlines of James's political creed:

God gives not Kings the style of Gods in vain
For on his throne his sceptre do they sway:
And as their subjects ought them to obey
So Kings should fear and serve their God again.

A cardinal point (or a notorious piece of mystification) in James's elevated system of kingship was the conviction that God bestowed on kings a divine wisdom that controls what he calls their 'secretest drifts', the deep strategy of state policy; ordinary mortals have no capacity to penetrate the secret operations of this royal wisdom, although they are expected to marvel at the results when they become evident. The union of the crowns and the policy of reconciling the Western nations were examples of such deep designs. James was at pains to stress the solitary, exposed nature of kingship, its immense privileges and responsibilities, its ultimate mysteriousness. Evidently there would be little room in this scheme for Parliament, for that body of men could only be expected to offer advice, never to instruct or compel the King in important matters, and certainly not to sound out his 'secretest drifts'. There would be a long history of disagreements between James and his parliaments, and worse to come under Charles, because the concept of a sacred monarchy did not mix well with elected assemblies. This issue of royal prerogative, the King's privilege to act in his own way, would become one of the major battlefields between the Stuarts and their parliaments.

James worked harder than any English monarch to hedge himself with divinity, and to assert his unique privileges, but how far was he believed? Probably many of the bishops accepted his claims, for they too were in the business of magical authority, receiving their own spiritual power from a divine source. A large portion of the clergy must have assented for similar reasons. One may assume that there was some willingness among common people to believe in the divine powers of royalty in an age when magical practices were still wide-spread: certainly the sacred function most directly relevant to them, the service of healing (when the King touched those suffering from the disease known as 'the King's Evil') was always crowded with suppliants. It is impossible to judge how far the educated classes responded seriously to monarchical propaganda, but the credibility of James's claims was never really tested, for during his reign no one directly challenged the sacred powers of majesty. It is equally difficult to gauge James's own degree of belief in his semi-divine status, for he was quite conscious that kings act out their role on a public stage – he used the theatrical metaphor several times in *Basilikon Doron*, and well understood the need in politics for artifice and compelling imagery. Two of the leading commentators on his reign remarked on this aspect of James: Sir Anthony Weldon wrote that James's private motto was, 'Qui nescit dissimulare, nescit regnare' – 'He who does not know how to dissimulate does not know how to reign', while Arthur Wilson noted that 'Some parallel'd him to Tiberius for dissimulation', a comparison rather less flattering than the ones frequently made with Augustus.[4]

When we look at the elaborate ideological framework that was constructed for the monarch in the early seventeenth century, we should recall that James came to the throne at a time when the arts had reached a remarkable height of theatrical expressiveness, which could be directed to promote the royal image. Architecture had become more grandiose, painting more dynamic and heroic, music was developing a richer texture, poetry and drama now attained an extraordinary imaginative splendour. On the Continent, these arts had been increasingly used to glorify monarchs or popes in ways that abetted the growth of absolute power, by means of grand, irresistible claims about the authority and divinity of princes. James reigned when these celebratory forms were gaining ground in England and his broad and generous patronage assured that he enjoyed their full benefit.

The principal vehicle for royal elevation throughout the reign was the court masque, in which all the arts combined to honour the King, praise the blessings of his reign, and reveal the secret powers of majesty by means of spectacular fables.[5] All of James's masques were devised by Ben Jonson, who understood the arts of panegyric better than any man in the kingdom, in collaboration with Inigo Jones, who had learnt the complicated techniques of presentation from continental sources (perhaps during his first visit to Italy, when he may have seen the Florentine festivals of the Medici). Jones was to develop his mastery of illusionist stagecraft to astonishing heights as he worked to create the atmosphere of wonder that was essential to the operation of the masque. The masques were performed annually for most of James's reign, forming the climax of the Christmas entertainments on Twelfth Night. They began in 1605, when Queen Anne commissioned a festive setting in which she and her ladies could appear in exotic costumes and dance before the court, but Jonson was quick to transform that fairly simple device into an occasion to glorify the King, turning a festive pageant into a theatre of mysteries. Jonson made the King the essential point of reference in the masques, feigning that the royal presence exerted over the action an influence that revealed and illuminated some aspect of majesty. Thus, the King could be represented as the principle of Harmony or the source of Ideal Beauty, as Wisdom or Heroic Virtue, whose secret yet benevolent operation on the nation or the court could be made visible through the symbolic events of the masque. The masquers themselves were always of noble birth; although they never spoke (the acting parts were taken by players), they were disclosed at the climactic moment in a magnificent constellation shining under intense light. They might represent queens or princes of antiquity, chivalric heroes, demigods, the Glories of the Spring, or the Spirits of the Fortunate Isles, but always they owed their power to the King, or they perfected their virtue through his presence.

So the courtiers too were glorified by the masque: their own identity, though still recognizable, expanded to display the sublime character bestowed on them by the fable. When they descended from their glory to dance, they moved in intricate patterns suggestive of the harmonious evolution of the court beneath the eye of the King. Music, dance, and song all expressed the concord and felicity that were aspects of the King's majesty. At the end of the performance the masquers stepped down into the body of the hall to dance with the spectators in revels that often continued for several hours. Not merely did the entertainment then become general, but all the audience were able to associate themselves with the ideal qualities that composed the noble soul of the court. Essentially the masque was a form of platonic theatre, illustrating the ideal influences that emanated from the King's divinity. It also had an intellectual element, befitting the character of the King it served, for it made much use of symbolic images in which moral truths were locked up, to be penetrated only by the finer minds capable of understanding the mysteries of kingship. It would, however, be unwise to overemphasize its esoteric nature, for a masque was always a marvellous spectacle, which gave pleasure to all who were privileged to watch.

To appreciate how a masque functioned socially and politically, we shall look briefly at Jonson's *Hymenaei*, performed at court on 5

January 1606, to celebrate the wedding of the Earl of Essex to the daughter of the Earl of Suffolk. Since this was also the annual masque, it had the dual aim of honouring the couple and the King. The masque takes the form of a Roman wedding ceremony, which Jonson reconstructed in scholarly detail, as the notes to his printed text amply document. The procession of a bride and bridegroom, accompanied by Hymen, the erotic spirit of marriage, and by musicians, approaches the altar of Juno, the deity who presides over marriage and who sanctifies the rite. Hymen pays homage to King James and Queen Anne, who also preside over this particular marriage; he is awed by the divine splendour of their presence:

> What more than usual light
>   Throughout the place extended
> Marks Juno's fane so bright!
>   Is there some greater deity descended?
>   (ll. 83–86)

A power above the gods themselves sheds influence on the scene:

> 'Tis so: this same is he,
>   The King and priest of Peace!
>   (ll. 91–92)

Now behind the altar is revealed a great globe or microcosm which rotates to release the first masque of men representing the Humours and Affections (or passions, as we would call them), gloriously attired, who dance to 'contentious music' as they try to interrupt the ceremony.[6] These are the discordant properties of 'the little world of man', which need to be beneficently controlled if they are to enhance life, not disrupt it. So the figure of Reason, which was seated upon the turning globe, now descends. She is the highest faculty of the mind, and she bears emblems and is dressed in colours that display her affinity with the celestial regions. She proceeds to restrain and chasten the tumultuous dancers, pronouncing that harmony depends on 'the binding force of Unity', the ideal that adjusts all discrete parts to a greater whole.

At this point of balance the main masque begins. The scene opens further to show Juno enthroned in the lower air, attended by her ladies and by spirits making music; above her appears the whirling region of fire, and above that the Empyrean where Jupiter stands. Reason now becomes the interpreter to explain that 'Juno, whose great name/Is UNIO, in the anagram' (ll. 231–32) represents the secret power of union whose spirit pervades the universe, and hereafter the meaning of the masque spreads out to illuminate political and philosophic truths. The union that is made in marriage is a type of innumerable forms of harmonious conjunction: the union of God with man, of heaven with earth, the King with his kingdom, and the pairing of creatures in the natural world. In particular, the masque praises the union of the kingdoms that James's wisdom has brought about, to the greater happiness of all parties. We begin now to understand what Jonson intended when he wrote in the introduction to this masque that though these 'transitory devices' 'be taught to sound to present occasions, their sense or doth or should always lay hold on more removed mysteries'. So in the climactic tableau Jonson links the marriage of Essex and Suffolk to the royal marriage of James and Anne, to the union of the kingdoms, to the union of the elements of human nature under the government of Reason, and to the union of heaven and earth effected by the love of God: 'Such was the golden chain let down from Heaven' (l. 320). The beauty of the informing idea of the masque is expressed by the union in dance of the male masquers (the Humours and Affections) with the female masquers, who represent the powers of Juno the goddess of marriage, one dance forming the letters of the bridegroom's name, another forming the links of a chain. At last the dancers form into 'a fair orb or circle', whereupon Reason turns to the throne to offer a thanksgiving to the King whose magical powers have achieved, Prospero-like, this spectacle of harmony. The aristocratic marriage takes its place in the larger context of Stuart statecraft, and the rightness of the Stuart order is vindicated to the court in splendour, poetry, music, and dance.[7]

So the masque has taken advantage of two of James's favourite metaphors, union and marriage, which he had introduced into his first speech before Parliament and would often return to in later speeches. During the early years of the reign the metaphors were frequently picked up and glossed by preachers who wanted to flatter the King and ingratiate themselves with him. Even the coinage helped to circulate these themes, for James introduced a new coin called the 'unite', and had a phrase from the marriage ceremony stamped on his crown pieces. Shakespeare's *King Lear*, staged in 1605, reflected the royal concern by dramatizing the tragic chaos that would follow on the disunion of the kingdom by a politically unwise king.

This political strain which almost invariably mingled with the arts of Stuart England was apparent also in Jonson's choice of a Roman setting for his marriage masque. The exact classical details of *Hymenaei* were not just an exercise in antiquarian reconstruction, but an aid to the conscious formulation of a Roman imperial style for King James and his court, a process that had already begun in the triumphal entry of 1604 and would be reinforced in many more masques, in the drama, and in the style of the new architecture. The Roman imagery was adopted too by clerical commentators, who liked to remark James's affinities with Augustus, on account of his commitment to peace, and with the Emperor Constantine, for James's accession was considered to mark a new age in church affairs, when after the defensive phase of the Tudor period, which saw the settlement of the Protestant religion, the Church would enter a new period of expansion, as the early Church had done under Constantine. Churchmen hastened to describe the similarities between the two monarchs, aided in their work by the fact that one of James's first moves had been to call a conference of the various parties within the Church of England to establish some uniformity of doctrine, comparable, many thought, to the Council of Nicaea that Constantine had presided over. The parallels were extensively worked out in a sermon preached by one of the royal chaplains, Joseph Hall, on the tenth anniversary of James's accession. James, he maintains,

> hath trod in the steps of that blessed Constantine, in all his
> religious proceedings. . . . Constantine caused fifty
> volumes of the scriptures to be faire written out on
> parchment, for the use of the Church. King James hath
> caused the Book of the Scriptures to be translated and
> published by thousands. Constantine made a zealous edict
> against Novatians. . . . King James besides his powerful
> proclamations and sovereign lawes hath effectually written
> against Poperie. Constantine took away the libertie of the
> meetings of Heretickes: King James hath by wholesome
> lawes inhibited the assemblies of Papists and
> Schismatickes. Constantine sate in the middest of Bishops,
> as if he had been one of them, King James besides his
> solemne conferences, vouchsafes (not seldome) to spend
> his meales in discourse with his Bishops and other worthy
> Divines. Constantine charged his sonnes . . . that they
> should be Christians in earnest. King James hath done the
> like in learned and divine precepts, which shall live till
> time be no more. Yea, in their very coynes is a
> resemblance: Constantine had his picture stampt upon his
> metals praying, King James hath his picture with a prayer
> about it; O Lord, protect the Kingdomes which thou has
> united.[8]

An additional link with Constantine was the belief that the Roman Emperor was of British origin, born in Britain of a British mother. Following the habit – natural to the seventeenth-century mind – of interpreting contemporary history in the light of classical or biblical precedent, it was hoped that as Constantine had made his new capital a centre of Christian empire, so James would reign over a revived Christian empire, one that would extend into the New World, where the Virginia Company and the New England Companies were already playing their part in this dream of a Jacobean Christian empire by carrying the gospel to the American Indians. Church historians liked to believe that the Church in Britain preserved something of a true primitive character, and were fond of recounting the legend that the island was first Christianized shortly after the death of Christ by Joseph of Arimathea, who had brought to England the Holy Grail and who lay buried at Glastonbury. This story had the attraction of presenting England as a country already Christian before the coming of the Roman missionaries, and offered a tradition of apostolic descent that bypassed Rome and linked the Church to the age of Christ.

A distinctive theme in Jacobean religious propaganda was the suggestion that the Stuarts were the dynasty that should rule in the last age of the world. Protestants generally were disposed to believe that they were living in the latter part of time, for the Reformation was held to be the grand sign that God was beginning to close up the accounts of history, and was purifying his church to receive the saints or true believers and preserve them amidst the desolations that would mark the end of time. The end would be characterized, as the Prophets and the Book of Revelation so vividly foretold, by wars and disasters and by a bitter struggle against Antichrist, whom most Protestants unhesitatingly identified with the Pope. James and his children were optimistically recognized as the kings of pure faith, in whose time the struggle against Antichrist would occur, and who would prepare the way for the return of Christ. As soon as James was crowned, preachers were prophesying that he and his heirs 'shall be continued to the end of the world, we trust',[9] and in *Macbeth*, too, Banquo's descendants (of whom James was one) stretch out 'to the crack of doom' (IV. i.117). The furious controversies between the Anglican and the Roman churches were seen as part of the campaign to overthrow Antichrist, and James's pre-eminence in these controversies (for he wrote copiously against Rome) was acclaimed on the English side as a series of tremendous blows which wonderfully demonstrated the justice of James's title of Defender of the Faith. The outbreak of a great religious war in Europe in 1619, which would last for thirty years, was regarded as an event of apocalyptic significance. Yet Stuart Britain remained an island of peace untouched by the violence so common elsewhere. James and his ministers liked to believe this peace was ordained by God, and some dared to hope that it might be the harbinger of Christ's Second Coming. As the great peace of Augustus had been the occasion of his birth, so the peace of James might herald his return. James, 'like another Augustus, before the second coming of Christ, hath becalmed the world and shut the gates of war'.[10]

All great men in the seventeenth century were regarded by their admirers as instruments of Providence, but James enjoyed this reputation in the highest degree. We have already seen how one of the triumphal arches that greeted his entry into London showed the figure of Divine Providence protecting the King, and James had experienced many evidences of this special relationship: he was fond of recollecting how he had been miraculously preserved from death in the Gowrie conspiracy and in the Gunpowder Plot, both of which were made the occasions for annual services of thanksgiving. (James's life was indeed a miracle of preservation when we remember that his father was murdered, his closest associate Buckingham assassinated, and his mother and son both executed.) His marriage, his accession to the English throne, the union and his peace were all achieved with the help of providence, and he did not doubt that all was directed to some great Christian end.

Strong though the conviction was that the last age of history was unfolding, it did not inhibit men from building durably and with splendour. The architectural style favoured by King James was Roman and imperial, in keeping with the fictions of Augustan rule that he encouraged, and here Inigo Jones, who was Surveyor Royal from 1615, served him admirably. Jones's architectural theory was ultimately derived from Vitruvius, a true Augustan of the first century AD, whose *De Architectura* was the bible of Renaissance practitioners. Jones in fact approached Vitruvius via Palladio, the sixteenth-century Italian architect whose buildings and writings made a decisive impression on him, and the influence of both is apparent in Jones's major work for King James, the Banqueting House at Whitehall. This was the ceremonial centre of the realm: the hall of state and audience chamber, the setting of the masques as also of that other rite that testified to the King's divinity, the service of healing. Jones modelled his design on a Roman basilica, a building with imperial, judicial, and religious associations, but he transformed the traditional apse of the basilica into a great coffered niche where the King could sit enthroned. The discipline, order, and proportion of the architecture provided an ideal structure in which to magnify the Stuart kings. The Banqueting House may well have been intended as the first building of a total restructuring of Whitehall. It has recently been suggested that such a plan had been drawn up by the early 1620s, and that in designing the new complex Jones followed a scholarly reconstruction of Solomon's Temple, such as had inspired Philip II's palace, the Escorial.[11] This suggestion would be entirely in keeping with the iconography of King James and with the style of the Banqueting House, for Renaissance theorists believed that the classical orders of architecture had originally been composed for the Temple of Solomon.

Biblical and classical analogies were vital to the imaginative extension of the Jacobean regime. Perhaps none pleased the King so much as that of the British Solomon, a title that drew attention to his wisdom and to his close relationship with the Almighty. When King James's *Works* was published in 1616, the preface by Bishop Montague unhesitatingly (and probably with royal direction) singled out this archetype for James. 'God hath given us a Solomon, and God above all things gave Solomon Wisdom; Wisdom brought him Peace, Peace brought him riches, riches gave him Glory.' Since Solomon was renowned for his wisdom, it was understandable that Francis Bacon, in dedicating his *Novum Organum* to James, should appeal to him in this character for support for his scheme to construct a new philosophy of the natural world on the basis of experiment and research:

> Surely to the times of the wisest and most learned of
> Kings belongs of right the regeneration and restoration of
> the sciences. Lastly, I have a request to make . . . that you
> who resemble Solomon in so many things . . . in the
> gravity of your judgements, in the peacefulness of your
> reign, in the largeness of your heart, in the noble variety
> of the books which you have composed, would further
> follow his example in taking order for the collecting and
> perfecting of a natural and experimental history, true and
> severe . . . such as philosophy may be built upon . . . [so
> that it might] rest on the solid foundation of experience of
> every kind.[12]

Presumably in naming his 'College for Experimental Philosophy' in *New Atlantis* as 'Salomon's House' Bacon was trying to activate James to the founding of such an institution – in vain, as it proved, for James showed no interest in the sciences. It was as Solomon too that Rubens depicted James when he came to memorialize his reign on the ceiling of the Banqueting House in the 1630s.

When King James died in March 1625, it was as the British Solomon that he was buried. Donne preached during his lying in state on the text 'Behold King Solomon Crowned', and the funeral sermon in Westminster Abbey by John Williams, Bishop of Lincoln, was entitled 'Great Britain's Salomon'. Here Williams enumerated for the last time the parallels and correspondences between James and the Hebrew kings. He then assessed the achievements of the reign:

> all kinds of learning highly improved, manufactures at
> home daily invented, trading abroad exceedingly
> multiplied, the borders of Scotland peaceably settled, the
> north of Ireland religiously planted, the Navy Royal
> magnificently furnished, Virginia, New-Found-Land and
> New England peopled, the East India well traded, Persia,
> China and the Mogul visited, lastly, all the ports of
> Europe, Afrique, Asia and America to our red crosses
> freed and opened.[13]

Finally, he touched on the imperial theme: 'Not a particular of his life but was a mystery of Divine Providence to keep and preserve those admirable parts, for the settling and uniting of some great Empire.' Reading Bishop Williams's sermon, one realizes that religion and empire had both been considerably advanced under James. The lavish figures of praise did bear some relation to certain large truths. In an age of religion, what other nation had so theologically profound a king, one so able to expound and defend the tenets of his religion? In an age disrupted by religious wars, what other nation enjoyed so unbroken a peace as Great Britain? The settlements on the American coast, though minute, had the air of some momentous beginning. Viewed in this large perspective, Great Britain might seem to be the Fortunate Isles, and the reign of James was a golden age of sorts.

Certainly the arts flourished with unprecedented vigour, and the King's character must have contributed in some measure to encourage this cultural vitality. In the theatre, his influence was immediate: one of his first moves was to extend his patronage to Shakespeare's company, the Lord Chamberlain's Men, turning them into the King's Men. Jonson, Middleton, Beaumont, and Fletcher were all writing for this company, which performed regularly at court, offering the most remarkable repertoire in theatre history. James did not impose his taste on his players, nor were plays specially written for him, though certain plays undeniably appealed to royal concerns – Macbeth most notably, with its Scottish themes, its witchcraft and theological interest, Measure for Measure, and Cymbeline. Jonson's tragedies of state, Sejanus and Catiline, are Roman plays filled with Jacobean politics and comments on behaviour at James's court.[14] The generally high level of political debate in the plays written for the King's Men may well have been a response to their intently intelligent patron.

The King's desire for intellectual stimulation was equally evident in the religious sphere, where he liked to surround himself with churchmen of a speculative and witty cast of mind. He found much satisfaction in the searching sermons of Lancelot Andrewes, whom he nominated Bishop of Winchester. He advanced the careers of the philosophic Godfrey Goodman, whom he sent to Gloucester, of the poetic Joseph Hall, who went to Exeter, and of the eloquent John King, who held the bishopric of London. He recognized John Donne's potential as a preacher, ensured that he entered the ministry, and then made him one of his chaplains and placed him as Dean of St Paul's. It is difficult to feel enthusiastic about James's choice for Archbishop of Canterbury: George Abbot was a compromise candidate, an uninspiring ecclesiastic, whose dubious merit was that he did not greatly antagonize the Puritan wing of the Church. But, surveying the major place-holders, one could believe that the Jacobean Church was generally led by men of some spiritual and intellectual distinction, and that the King had advanced some way towards his ideal of a learned clergy. To James's credit too lay the encouragement of the new translation of the Bible. This project was first proposed at the Hampton Court Conference in 1604 from the Puritan side, and immediately taken up by the King, who appointed the committees and closely supervised the progress of the translation, which was completed by 1611 and was found acceptable by all the parties within the Church.

King James's court, then, was central to the cultural energies of the nation. A monarch who could command the services of Shakespeare, Jonson, Bacon, Inigo Jones, and Donne presided over a scene of exceptional imaginative intensity. The King's openness, curiosity, and intellectual combativeness were excellent qualities for encouraging adventurous expression. Yet while the intellectual life of the court was invigorating in the highest degree, the moral tone was often remarkably seedy. God's vice-regent was in his person gross and in his manners unseemly. A contemporary view of the King presents a repellent picture:

> His tongue too large for his mouth, which ever made him
> speak full in the mouth, and made him drink very
> uncomely, as if eating his drink . . .; his skin was as soft
> as taffeta sarsnet, which felt so because he never washed
> his hands . . .; his legs very weak, . . . that he was not
> able to stand at seven years of age, that weakness made
> him ever leaning on other men's shoulders; his walk was
> ever circular, his fingers ever in that walk fiddling about
> his cod-piece.[15]

The succession of favourites that he fawned over, the love-affair with Buckingham that he carried on in public, his crude and often contemptuous behaviour towards women, did not go down well with observers. Complaints abounded about his drunkenness and slovenliness, and about his evasion of state business in favour of the hunt.

Prodigal spending, excessive reliance on favourites, indiscriminate creation of titles, all helped to make his court a byword for corruption in the drama and gossip of the period, and the long-term consequences of his overbearing style of government did much to undermine the authority of his son's rule. Did this wide discrepancy between the ideal image of the first Stuart and the tawdry actualities of the reign signify very much? As far as James was concerned, probably not. The arts carried the responsibility for projecting the ideals of kingship, and if life failed to live up to art, that did not discredit the ideals. These ideals announced the character of Stuart rule and gave it a conceptual framework which clarified the grand design that the Stuarts were engaged in: by myths, poetic fictions, and historical parallels, the nature of the mission entrusted to James and his successors, their place in providentially controlled history, was made known. Contemporary history was given a comprehensible shape. If the King were indeed the agent of Providence, as most people believed, then the main events of the grand design would be enacted, irrespective of personal behaviour.

Notes

1. James's speech to Parliament, from which this and the next three quotations are taken, is printed in Arthur Wilson's survey of his reign, *The Historie of Great Britain* (1653), pp. 13–25, and also in *The Political Works of James I*, edited by C. E. McIlwain, (Cambridge, Mass., 1918).

2. 'The King's Entertainment in passing to his Coronation,' in *Ben Jonson*, edited by C. H. Herford and P. Simpson (1941). vii, 92.

3. Ibid., p. 100.

4. See J. Goldberg, *James I and the Politics of Literature* (1983), p. 68. In the same passage of Wilson's history, he expresses the opinion that James was a conscious manipulator of his role, 'As in curing the King's Evil, which he knew to be a Device, to ingrandize the vertue of Kings, when Miracles were in fashion; but he let the World believe it, though he smiled at it.'

5. For recent discussions of the art of the masque, see Stephen Orgel, *The Jonsonian Masque* (1965), *The Illusion of Power* (1975); S. Orgel and R. Strong, *Inigo Jones: The Theatre of the Stuart Court* (1973), Vol. I; D. J. Gordon, *The Renaissance Imagination* (1975); G. Parry, *The Golden Age Restor'd* (1981); and *The Court Masque*, edited by D. Lindley (1984).

6. This first entry of masquers is in effect an anti-masque, that is to say a group of dancers whose character is antagonistic to the main masque. Later, the anti-masque would come to consist of recognizably negative or comic forces which would be banished by the main masque. Jonson first formally introduced this contrast in *The Masque of Queens* (1609), where the anti-

masque consists of witches whose wild dances are quelled by a chord of music that symbolises royal authority. In *Hymenaei* Jonson has not yet worked out a clear relationship between the two parts of the masque, for the Humours and Affections are danced by gentlemen, whereas later anti-masques would be acted by players.

7. The fullest interpretation of this masque is to be found in the essay by D. J. Gordon, '*Hymenaei*: Ben Jonson's masque of Union', in *The Renaissance Imagination*, edited by S. Orgel (1975), pp. 157–84.

8. Joseph Hall, *An Holy Panegyrick* (1631). Quoted from *Works* (1627), p. 479.

9. Andrew Willet, *Ecclesia Triumphans* (1604).

10. Hall, p. 482

11. See Roy Strong, *Britannia Triumphans* (1980), pp. 55–64. For an account of the designing of the Banqueting House and the symbolical implications of its architecture, see Per Palme, *Triumph of Peace* (1957).

12. Francis Bacon, Epistle Dedicatory to *The Great Instauration*, translated in *Works*, ed. J. Spedding, 1859, IV, p. 12.

13. John Williams, *Great Britains Salomon* (1625), p. 52.

14. See Goldberg, pp. 164–209.

15. Sir Anthony Weldon, *The Court and Character of King James*, in *The Secret History of the Court of James the First*, edited by Sir Walter Scott, (Edinburgh, 1811, 2 vols), II, 12.

Chapter 2
The Iconography of Charles I, 1625–1649

King Charles was the inheritor of the ideology of Stuart rule, not its founder, and consequently he took some time to develop distinctive images for his own style of kingship. The first few years of his reign offered little visual display. Charles had no coronation procession and no great ceremony for his marriage to Henrietta Maria of France; there were no masques until 1631. He was, however, ready to spend money on paintings, his especial passion, not simply for the gratification of his taste, but also to display his glory as a prince, for by the seventeenth century a great picture gallery had become an international status symbol.

It was through painting that he made the most comprehensive statement about the character of Stuart power ideally understood, when he commissioned Rubens to paint a sequence of canvases for the Banqueting House ceiling in 1629–30. Rubens had come to England in his capacity as diplomat to settle a minor, ineffectual war with Spain, and Charles lost no time in putting before him a project for the decoration of Whitehall. The scheme of the ceiling, which would have been worked out by Charles himself or by Inigo Jones, presented one final triumphant spectacle of the benefits of James I's rule (benefits that would also be appropriated by Charles himself). All the grand themes of the transient masques were fixed permanently in the baroque panels that were inserted in the gilded roof, making the hall a temple to the memory of King James: he sits in judgement like Solomon creating the union of Great Britain by the fiat of his divine wisdom; enthroned like a Roman emperor he imposes his will on the allegorical figures before him, raising up Peace and Plenty, banishing Discord and Rebellion. The side panels are filled with imagery evoking the Golden Age: troops of innocent putti play among animals incapable of harm, bearing garlands of fruit and sheaves of harvested corn. The central oval of the ceiling shows the apotheosis of James, who is borne serenely heavenwards on an imperial eagle, aided by Religion and Faith, to receive the crown of victory from the hands of Minerva, goddess of Wisdom. The convention of apotheosis had been evolved by the artists of the Counter-Reformation to depict the irresistible triumphs of the saints and martyrs; the scene invariably shows the inhabitants of the celestial regions rapturously welcoming the spiritual heroes as they rise through the empyrean to everlasting glory. That this essentially Catholic form of celebration should be applied to a Protestant monarch is a sign that Britain's cultural isolation from Europe had ended; this country was now joining with the mainstream, and its ruling class was learning, from continental sources, how to use the rhetoric of the arts to advance their own political and social interests.[1] Charles had already been to Spain (to seek the hand of the Infanta) where he had seen how a great autocratic monarchy conducted its affairs, and how the arts could create a setting of convincing authority. He had also had a glimpse of the court at Paris, and these lessons were not lost on him. In the 1630s, Van Dyck would be invited over, to transform the image of the King and the aristocracy. There would be commissions for Gentileschi, Simon Vouet, Guido Reni. Charles would have dealings with Bernini and would dream of a palace as vast as the Escorial or the Louvre. The Earl of Arundel would talk to the Holy Roman Emperor about painting as well as about the Palatinate. Even Milton would go to Rome, dine with Cardinal Barberini, and admire the way in which the arts strengthened the power of the State with heroic images and exemplary fictions.

The Whitehall ceiling also serves as an indication of the move towards absolute government that would accelerate during the 1630s. The deified James is shown to be approved by Heaven: he possesses in himself all the essential wisdom and knowledge required for good government; there is no need of any human aid or counsel. The Rubens paintings aim to sanction the unmoderated exercise of power by wise and benevolent Stuarts.

Having honoured the spirit of his father, Charles set about creating his own mythology, using, like his father, the masques as the main vehicles to display the royal iconography. As all the masques of the reign were presented during the period of personal rule from 1629 to 1640, they are much concerned to vindicate the autocratic style of government, not by any specific defence of Charles's political actions, but by an assertion of powers so sublime and beneficent that criticism is made irrelevant. The controlling myth of the Caroline court throughout the 1630s was that of the ideal love of the King and Queen, whose perfection ensured the happiness of the nation. The myth was embroidered in masque and poetry for a decade. The cult of platonic love that lay at its centre had been introduced by Henrietta Maria from the French court, where its affectations were fashionable: starry-eyed debate about the refining effects of non-sensual love were already conventional in the dramatic pastorals with which the Queen amused herself at court in the 1620s. After the death of Buckingham in 1628, when the royal couple grew much closer together, Charles began to exploit the idea of an equal partnership of love guiding the nation's destiny, attracting the approval of Heaven. King James had had little sympathy for Queen Anne (she was largely a dynastic accessory, and they lived apart for much of the reign), but Charles liked to present Henrietta Maria as his equal, her virtue complementing his own. They presented masques to each other and they had themselves painted together in double portraits, an unusual fashion for the time. The Queen was a trusted counsellor in state affairs: the rose of England and the lily of France flourished together. The son of the pacific James married to the daughter of the warlike Henri IV presented a combination of peace and strength united by love that was frequently praised in the masques. Charles's first masque, *Love's Triumph through Callipolis* by Ben Jonson, celebrated the presence of Ideal Love in Callipolis, 'the city of beauty or goodness' – an obvious allusion to the court. The Queen (to whom the masque is dedicated) reigns under the influence of Love, 'who was wont to be respected as a special deity in court and tutelar god of the place'. Her radiant influence banishes all impure sensuous loves from her sphere, preparing the way for a Triumph of Platonic Love. The masquers make their appearance as a troop of noble lovers, led by the King himself as a Heroic Lover, one possessed by a fine fury for the virtuous perfections of the Queen, 'who is the wonder in the place'. They perform a dance of adoration before the Queen, and then the scene transforms to display an emblem of Stuart concord: 'There shooteth up a palm tree with an imperial crown on the top, from the root whereof, lilies and roses twining together and embracing the stem, flourish through the crown.' The chorus then praise the elevating qualities of the royal marriage that will ensure harmony in the State and 'shall ever be propitious/To both the kingdoms'.

Throughout the 1630s a sequence of such optimistic visions was offered to the court. The Queen almost invariably appears as the embodiment of some high principle of Beauty, Virtue, or Love, the King as some dynamic force – Heroic Virtue, Secret Wisdom, or the renewal of the ancient ideal of the Virtuous Emperor. Charles is portrayed as a philosophic monarch whose triumphs – and many of the masques are entitled triumphs – were essentially of the spirit. The arts contribute to this elevation of the monarchy: poetry, painting, sculpture, and architecture are shown in the masques to ennoble the minds of their admirers, awaken a sense of idealism, strengthen virtue, and direct ambition to worthy ends. The Muses find Caroline England a congenial home, appearing in *Love's Triumph, Chloridia* and *Tempe Restored* to approve the high civilization that has developed here. The masques project an image of Albion as a land of white peace, a fragile paradise preserved by the untiring care of the royal couple from envious, disruptive forces. In Carew's *Coelum Britannicum* (1634), the landscape of the main masque changes from 'wild and craggy' scenes to a modern prospect 'shewing a delicious garden with several walks and parterres set round with low trees . . . fountains and grots, and in the furthest part a palace' to express the achievement of Caroline civility and order; the singers praise the demigods whose skill preserves this order:

> This royal pair, for whom Fate will
> Make motion cease, and Time stand still,
> Since Good is here so perfect, as no worth
> Is left for after-ages to bring forth.
>
> (ll. 1093–96)

Pastoral scenes were especially favoured in the masques of this period, as tending to show royal power in its most benevolent aspect, with no political strains admitted.

Yet those political strains could not be denied. In the last masque of the reign, Davenant's *Salmacida Spolia*[2] of 1640, the King and Queen appeared together on stage to enact a fable to vindicate their rule against acknowledged opposition. By this time the discontents of the decade were coming to a head. There was deep and widespread resentment against Laud's policies in religion, against the toleration extended to Catholics, and against the imposition of Ship Money as a measure of arbitrary taxation. Charles's attempt to impose a new Prayer Book on the Scots had led to war: the English army had been reluctant to fight, and now had to be paid off. A Parliament would soon have to be called to raise the money, and that Parliament would be angry and filled with grievances. Even before the masque began, the royal position was aggressively apparent, for Inigo Jones had packed the borders of the stage arch with allegorical figures defending the King's conduct, complex abstractions that show a desire rather to reassert the royal position than to clarify it. There were the personifications of Doctrine and Discipline (a conceit in favour of high Anglican religious policy), Intellectual Light (a god-like quality of the King's mind), Forgetfulness of Injuries (a sign of royal mercy); figures of Counsel and Resolution stood together with Fame, Safety, Prosperity, Innocence, Felicity, and 'Affection to the Country, holding a grasshopper'. The masque opened with a tempest urged on by furies envious of Britain's peaceful state: they were dispersed by the Good Genius of Great Britain, and Concord, who lamented the ingratitude of the people towards the blessings they enjoyed, urging that goodwill be offered to the King instead of rage. A long sequence of anti-masques of a topical, satirical nature followed, until a chorus of the 'Beloved People' entered to watch a spectacular revelation of the King enthroned in honour, surrounded by his masquing lords. Charles had cast himself as Philogenes, 'Lover of his People'. He sat surrounded by fictitious trophies symbolizing the victories of his reign, while a song praised his tolerance in not crushing his enemies, for he understood that their disaffection was temporary and would pass. (In effect, the King's weakness was being passed off as mercy.) Once more the audience heard of the heavenly wisdom that guided his rule, when suddenly the Queen was revealed, personating that very power. So the royal couple danced together as Virtue and Wisdom, to music that feigned to echo the sound of the spheres, and for one final time the divinity of kings was reaffirmed, and all was pronounced well with the State.

> All that are harsh, all that are rude,
> Are by your harmony subdued,
> Yet so into obedience wrought,
> As if not forced to it, but taught.
>
> (ll. 471–74)

The Stuart masques were a form of royal magic, revealing for a moment the supernatural powers that attended on the King. For Charles and Henrietta Maria, these spectacles offered the opportunity for an annual renewal of confidence in their roles, so we can understand why they put weeks or months into rehearsals, and paid out huge sums from their impoverished exchequer. But the masques were presented only to the restricted circle of the court, and during the ten years of personal rule the court had become ever more isolated from political reality and from social discontents. Charles was never so much the monarch as when on the Whitehall stage; his command was increasingly that of a player king.

A strong theatrical strain ran through Charles's character: he liked the grand gesture, the unexpected move. This trait was first exposed by his daring ride to Madrid in 1623, when he travelled in disguise across Europe with Buckingham, to woo the Infanta. In Spain he encountered that hauteur of manners that gave him a style for his own reign. The conscious self-possession that accompanied that style was well demonstrated when he received the news of Buckingham's assassination: he was at prayer in the Chapel Royal when the news came, but 'he continued unmoved without the least change in his countenance till prayers were ended, when he suddenly departed to his chamber, and threw himself on his bed, lamenting with much passion, and with abundance of tears, the loss he had'.[3] His audacious appearance in the House of Commons to arrest the five Members most hostile to him had a calculated dramatic air, and one might even regard as a determined piece of theatre his decision to raise his standard at Nottingham in 1642, thus announcing a state of war. After the failure of his campaigns, he laid down the part of Warrior King and learned the role of Saint and Martyr. It was as 'the royal actor born' that Marvell praised his performance in his death scene on the scaffold. In another poem which might reflect on Charles's history, 'The Unfortunate Lover', Marvell wrote of a hero 'forced to live in storms and wars' who 'in story only rules' – a comment most applicable to the King of the Masques.

Van Dyck caught this theatrical element in Charles's kingship most emphatically in his painting of the King riding through a triumphal arch almost as if coming on stage in one of his masques to enact his role as imperial hero. (Plate 8). The painting was intended to hang in the royal gallery at St James, in company with portraits of Roman emperors by Titian and Giulio Romano. Several of Van Dyck's royal portraits complement the themes of the masques: there is the King in a peaceful landscape, now in the Louvre; Charles on horseback, armed, yet in a musing, philosophic pose, personifying Heroic Virtue, hangs in the National Gallery; a double portrait of the King and Queen shows them as royal lovers, exchanging emblems of victory and peace. Portraits of courtiers consolidate our sense of a society concerned with lofty or refined gestures, or with escapist fantasies: several leading figures chose to be painted in pastoral or Arcadian costume to suggest their poetic nature or their sympathy with the idyllic fictions of the court. Lord George Stuart, Lord Wharton, Sir John Suckling, and Mrs Endymion Porter are all so dressed, as if to talk of love and sheep were the summit of felicity.

The superb double portrait of Charles, Elector Palatine, and his brother Prince Rupert, one of Van Dyck's finest productions, well illustrates the insidious, evasive idealism of the Caroline court (Plate 9). The pair had come to London to seek King Charles's help with money and men to regain the Palatinate from Catholic control, though he had neither the means nor the will to assist them. Instead, they were offered entertainments, the chief of which was a masque by Davenant, *The Triumph of the Prince d'Amour*, whose theme was the vanquishing of the martial spirit by Love; then Van Dyck painted the young men as elegant heroes of romance posing against a soft twilit landscape. These two tributes indicate how the princes with their urgent demands were offered instead the agreeable anodynes of the courtly world, works of art taking the place of political resolution. The Elector Palatine also received the dedication of a lengthy platonic love-poem by Marmion, *Cupid and Psyche*, while he was in England – further evidence of the desire to draw him into the romantic escapist mood of the court. In several of Van Dyck's military portraits we sense that the sensitive man overshadows the warrior: the Earl of Northumberland, the Lord Admiral, turns away from a sea fight with delicate aversion (he was indeed more interested in collecting paintings than in running the navy); Lord Arundel, the Earl Marshal and leader of the army against the Scots in 1639, has his severity modified by the company of his innocent grandson; the Marquis of Hamilton (another important collector of paintings) stands amid rocks and melancholy shades. Only the steel-clad Strafford looks uncompromisingly grim and capable of firm action, and even from the painted record one can understand why the Long Parliament acted so promptly to remove him from the scene.

Caroline poetry took much of its tone from the court circles that Van Dyck so finely observed. The cult of idealized love that centred on the King and Queen found many votaries among the poets in the 1630s. Waller had his Sacharissa, Herrick his Julia, Lovelace his Lucasta, Carew his Celia, Habington his Castara, each poet lyrically responsive to the perfection of his mistress, whose mind is a platonic abode of beauty, goodness, and truth. The high complimentary style that characterizes Caroline love-poetry, the smooth wit, the airy gesture, belong to a generous and spirited society enjoying a brief phase of accomplishment. For an example of how a Cavalier poet can transform his perception of a social moment into enduring artifice, consider Lovelace's 'Gratiana Dancing and Singing':

> See! with what constant motion,
> Even and glorious as the sun,
>   Gratiana steers that noble frame,
> Soft as her breast, sweet as her voice
> That gave each winding law and poise,
>   And swifter than the wings of Fame.
>
> She beat the happy pavëment
> By such a star made firmament,
>   Which now no more the roof envies,
> But swells up high with Atlas ev'n,
> Bearing the brighter, nobler heav'n,
>   And, in her, all the deities.
>
> Each step trod out a lover's thought
> And the ambitious hopes he brought,
>   Chain'd to her brave feet with such arts,
> Such sweet command and gentle awe,
> As when she ceas'd, we sighing saw
>   The floor lay pav'd with broken hearts.

So did she move; so did she sing
Like the harmonious spheres that bring
    Unto their rounds their music's aid:
Which she performed such a way.
As all th' enamour'd world will say
    The Graces danced, and Apollo play'd.

Through Lovelace's skilful contrivance, the arts combine to honour
love and beauty in a world of pleasure.

In retrospect, it is evident that Caroline court culture was excessively distracted by sophisticated game-playing, insufficiently aware of
its dangerous isolation, and indifferent to the growing bitterness in the
world outside. Early in the 1630s Carew had expressed the happiness
of those who lived in the sheltered purlieus of the court, when he
attempted to compose an elegy on the Swedish King Gustavus Adol-
phus, the head of the Protestant cause in Europe. He found it hard to
engage with the unpleasant political and religious issues raised by his
subject:

Then let the Germans fear if Caesar shall,
Or the United Princes, rise and fall;
But let us, that in myrtle bowers sit
Under secure shades, use the benefit
Of Peace and Plenty, which the blessed hand
Of our good king gives this obdurate land.
Let us of revels sing . . .

Tourneys, masques, theatres, better become
Our halcyon days. What though the German drum
Bellow for freedom and revenge, the noise
Concerns not us, nor should divert our joys.
        ('In Answer of an Elegiacal Letter . . .,' ll. 43–49, 95–98)

The poem recoils from the ugliness and urgency of politics into
pastoral and romance. Carew shows an almost desperate desire to be
absorbed into the delicate fantasies of the court, into the gallantries of
love, where life is 'one continued festival'. This attitude too is a pose,
but a pose that he adopts with some conviction. Carew comes across
in his poems much like Lovelace's Cavalier grasshopper, playing
contentedly through the long summer, heedless of the threatening
sickle and the 'green ice' of winter.

Not all Cavalier writing was so complacent about royalty or the
state of the nation. At the very end of the time of peace, Sir John
Denham wrote a poem full of premonition, 'Cooper's Hill' (1641–42),
in which he accurately sensed the rising tension in the country. His

initial intention was to write a topographical poem that would enable him to trace the course of English history and praise the present King and Queen as he surveyed the landscape of the Thames from his well-situated hill. London, Windsor, and Runnymede were all in view, and the flow of the river suggested the flow of time; the subject-matter like the landscape was very fertile. Praise of the royal lovers at Windsor, and of the chivalric Order of the Garter that gave such distinction to their court, comes easily to Denham. But contemplation of a neighbouring hill where once a chapel stood until the Reformation swept it away gives him a tremor of apprehension as he reflects that the Church in his own time may be destroyed by another wave of zealous reformation. After a reassuring passage about Britain's prosperity, prompted by the Thames that receives the riches of the earth in trade, the poet's anxieties return as he surveys the riverside meadows where the King likes to hunt. What begins as a landscape picture of a royal hunt turns into a political allegory as the hunted stag takes on a disturbing resemblance to the Earl of Strafford, who, pursued by the parliamentary pack, finally has his death approved by his master the King.

> So the tall stag, amidst the lesser hounds,
> Repels their force, and wounds returns for wounds,
> Till Charles from his unerring hand lets flie
> A mortal shaft, then glad and proud to die
> By such a wound, he falls. . . .
>   (1642 version, ll. 295–99)

Then the poet's eye falls on Runnymede, where Magna Carta was signed, 'wherein the Crown/All marks of arbitrary power lays down'. The scene inevitably evokes thoughts about the long history of contention between King and Parliament. As a royalist, Denham believes that the King's authority has been too much trespassed upon – 'Thus all to limit Royalty conspire/While each forgets to limit his desire' – and in a moment of prophetic insight and wit, he links royal power to the flowing Thames, and recognizes that if men try to constrict its channel it will overflow and cause devastation all around. He foresees that the King will be forced to reassert his authority against the encroachments of his subjects; he prays that there will be restraint on both sides, but he fears the worst:

> But if with Bays, and Dammes they strive to force,
> His channell to a new, or narrow course,
> No longer then within his bankes he dwels,
> First to a Torrent, then a Deluge swels;

Stronger, and fiercer by restraint, he roares,
And knowes no bound, but makes his powers his shores;
Thus Kings by grasping more then they can hold,
First made their Subjects by oppressions bold,
And popular sway by forcing Kings to give
More, then was fit for Subjects to receive,
Ranne to the same extreame; and one excesse
Made both, by stirring to be greater, lesse;
Nor any way, but seeking to have more,
Makes either loose, what each possest before.
Therefore their boundlesse power let Princes draw
Within the Channell, and the shores of Law,
And may that Law, which teaches Kings to sway
Their Scepters, teach their Subjects to obey.[4]

'Cooper's Hill', however, is exceptional and late. As a rule,
throughout the 1630s, the Cavalier poets uncritically supported the cult
of the King and Queen as deities who assure the felicity of the realm.
This was habitually done in terms of religious ritual. Carew, for
example, could open a poem to the King with these 'pious rites':

> In stead of sacrifice, each brest
> Is like a flaming Altar, drest
> With zealous fires, which from pure hearts
> Love mixt with loyaltie imparts.
> ('To the King at Saxham' ll. 5–8)

Or he could address the Queen:

> Thou great Commandresse, that doest move
> Thy Scepter o're the Crowne of Love,
> And through his Empire with the Awe
> Of Thy chaste beames, doest give the Law,
> From his prophaner Altars, we
> Turne to adore Thy Deitie.
> ('To the Queene' ll. 1–6)

Herrick, whose ceremonious poems invite us into a world where
almost all the actions of life have become ritualized, approaches the
King and Queen with all the august decorum of an antique priest, 'as
to a still protecting Deitie', who is 'our Fate, our Fortune and our
Genius.'[5]

What is striking about all these acts of worship is their freshness and
their frequency. They are the tributes of men who responded to the

Magie

mysterious divinity of kingship as feelingly as other men did to the reality of religious power in their lives. As long as the divine right of kings remained credible, the cult of the King's supernatural powers would have its many followers. Charles encouraged this worship, this deification in effect, as a means of setting his rule beyond criticism as a kind of providential dispensation. He had caused his father to be deified on the ceiling of the Banqueting House, and in a sense his reign was protected and vitalized by the numinous powers that James had generated around the throne. When the Civil War broke the power of the King, his mystique was almost irretrievably injured. The parliamentarians recognized how valuable was royal magic to make the nation offer allegiance to a sovereign power for reasons beyond rationality: 'What we need is a King with plenty of holy oil about him' was an opinion of 1659,[6] but when Charles II was restored, both his character and the new perceptions about how power is gained and exercised made it very difficult to sustain the myth of the divinity of kings, for the climate of belief had changed, and a sceptical knowingness about politics, epitomized in the work of Hobbes, had replaced the old deference. Without the mysterious light of the monarch at the centre of the court and nation, the character of the arts changed markedly: the felt presence of the supernatural began to recede, and idealized modes of social expression became more difficult to sustain as aristocratic life lost the lustre it had derived from the King.

Charles's final image was far removed from the heroic and chivalric poses of the happier years of his reign. These earlier presentations were made to the limited audience of the court, which was not entirely a closed society, for any gentleman or wealthy merchant could gain access to its outer areas if they applied to the proper quarters, but it was obviously a very selective place, and its entertainments and its cultural life were the preserve of those privileged to haunt the inner circles. So the masques, court drama, poetry, and painting made their primary appeal to the powerful, influential, wealthy élite whom Charles and Henrietta Maria favoured. The King himself led a fairly secluded life, and his major public appearances really began on the battlefields of the 1640s. The misfortunes of these last years gave rise to a striking new image of the King, for he took on a Christ-like aura, suffering for the sins of his people. A few days after his execution on 30 January 1649, a book called *Eikon Basilike: the Portraiture of his Sacred Majestie in his Solitudes and Sufferings* was published. This was put forward as the King's book, written during his imprisonment in defence of his actions, though it is now known to have been the work of the cleric John Gauden, who seems to have used some of the King's private papers as a basis for his compilation[7] It sold in enormous numbers, running through thirty-six editions in its first year, and

probably doing more good for the King's cause than all the propaganda
of the 1640s, for at a time when people were shocked by his execution
and apprehensive of the rule of the army, it presented a most sympathetic and benevolent image of a misunderstood king, not a 'man of
blood' as Parliament denominated him, but a man of sorrows. The
Greek title is a poignant allusion to *Basilikon Doron*, for the book tells
of the tragic fate of a king who carried out his duties to God, the
Church, and the people as James had enjoined, yet who, in fulfilling
these duties of kingship, met with persecution instead of love.

In *Eikon Basilike* Charles appears in a role not far removed from
Philogenes, the Lover of his People in the last masque. As he reflects
on the various episodes that led up to the war, and on his fortunes in
that war, Charles habitually presents himself as a well-intentioned king
whose constant care has been for the well-being of his people, who
have failed to understand his motives or who have been adversely
affected by the malice of factions in Church and Parliament. In truth,
he had 'no other design but the General Good of my Kingdoms'; his
intentions were 'to give all just satisfaction to modest and sober desires,
and to redress all public grievances in Church and State'. He confesses
that he thought he had reigned 'with such a measure of Justice, Peace,
Plentie and Religion, as all nations about either admired or envied'. He
is distressed by the ingratitude of his people: 'Thou, O Lord, knowest
how hard it is for Me to suffer much evil from my subjects, to whom
I intend nothing but good.' This sentiment recalls that expressed in
Salmacida Spolia:

> . . . and much I grieve that, though the best
> Of kingly science harbours in his breast,
> Yet 'tis his fate to rule in adverse times,
> When wisdom must awhile give place to crimes.
>   (ll. 168–71)

As in the masque, there is no attempt to fathom why the people
were so discontented, only a complaint that envy of the King's peace,
malice, faction, and similar abstractions have made a tumult in the
realm. As in the masque, too, he extends mercy and forgiveness where
he cannot exert authority; a typical prayer runs, 'Let not thy Justice
prevent the objects and opportunities of my Mercie: yea, let them live
and amend who have most offended me in so high a nature, that I may
have those to forgive. . . .' There is no sense that Charles's own
policies or character might be at fault: all is lofty and magnanimous
protestation. One element that had been prominent in the masque has
vanished from *Eikon Basilike*: the divinity of the king's rule. This
concept has clearly been a casualty of the war, replaced instead by the

divinity of the King's sufferings, which are now seen to be Christ-like. 'Is there no way left to make me a glorious KING, but by my sufferings?' he asks. 'I may (without vanitie) turn the reproach of my sufferings . . . into the honor of a kind of Martyrdom', he avows, and notes in his meditations the parallels between himself and Christ. He has been sold by his enemies (the Scots) into captivity: 'I am only sorry . . . that my price should be so much above my Saviour's', and in his concluding thoughts he reflects, 'My enemies will, it may be . . . seek to add (as those did who crucified Christ) the mockerie of Justice to the crueltie of Malice.' He resigns himself to exchanging his crown of gold for one of thorns.

There is a peculiar fatality in the events of history. Charles's destiny had been linked with Christ's from the days of his accession, when an imperfect anagram of his royal name gained currency (Charolus Stuartus = Christus Salvator), the common inference being simply that Charles was a man of peace. That he would become persecuted, reviled, and executed was hardly to be imagined, yet these acts confirmed the prophetic nature of the anagram. *Eikon Basilike* exploited tbe resemblance to evoke a saintly picture of the suffering King. The frontispiece (Plate 7) shows Charles kneeling in a pose that recalls the Agony in the Garden, as he takes up his crown of thorns. His earthly crown is lost, but he sees a heavenly crown of glory shining through the window of his church, which is still the church of Tudor Anglicanism, as the roses and crosses woven into the altar-cloth confirm. Immediately after his death, a cult of Charles the Martyr sprang up, and relics of his person and of his blood were treasured by royalists. *Eikon Basilike* fanned the flames of this cult. Not surprisingly, the parliament men tried to discredit it, by getting Milton to smash the image of the King. This he did in *Eikonoklastes* (1649), where he went through the *Eikon Basilike* section by section, demonstrating the falseness of the King's professions, in an attempt to prove that 'he hath offered at more cunning fetches to undermine our liberties, and put tyranny into an art, than any British king before him'. Significantly, however, Milton picks on the engraved frontispiece for special scorn: 'The conceited portraiture before his book, drawn out to the full measure of a masking scene, and set there to catch fools and silly gazers . . .'; 'quaint emblems and devices, begged from the old pageantry of some Twelfth Night's entertainment at Whitehall, will do but ill to make a saint or martyr'. Milton's recognition of the theatrical strain in Charles's character is quite accurate. Indeed, it must have been widely recognized, for the engraver of the frontispiece and the composer of *Eikon Basilike* both responded to the drama of Charles's situation. But it is a measure of the transformation of the

times that the masque which had formerly been the great triumphal
vehicle of Stuart kingship, should now provide the imagery through
which Milton sought to expose the sham and frippery of royal
pretensions.

Notes

1. The apotheosis as a kind of posthumous panegyric began to be applied to
   English subjects in the 1620s. Milton made early use of the device in his
   'Elegy on the Death of Bishop Andrewes' in 1626 and Rubens painted his
   Apotheosis of the Duke of Buckingham in 1628. There is a fine print by Hollar of
   the *Apotheosis of the Earl of Arundel*, from 1646.

2. The title alludes to a fountain, Salmacis, whose pure waters reduced the
   fierceness of barbarian natures 'to the sweetness of the Grecian customs'. As
   such, it serves as an allegory of the King's power, which 'seeks by all means
   to reduce tempestuous and turbulent natures into a sweet calm of civil
   concord'. (William Davenant, *Salmacida Spolia* (1640), ll. 90–1.)

3. Earl of Clarendon, *History of the Rebellion* 6 vols (Oxford 1704), I, 30.

4. 'Cooper's Hill' (1642 version), ll. 337–54. Brendan O'Hehir, in his book
   Expans'd Hieroglyphicks, (Berkeley, 1969), prints the successive versions of
   'Cooper's Hill' and examines in depth the literary and political contexts of the
   poem.

5. Herrick, 'To the King upon his Welcome to Hampton Court', pp. 16–17.

6. In a letter to the Earl of Manchester, quoted by Christopher Hill in *Some
   Intellectual Consequences of the English Revolution* (1980), p. 28.

7. See F. F. Madan, *A New Bibliography of the Eikon Basilike* (Oxford, 1950), and
   H. A. Trevor-Roper, 'Eikon Basilike: the Problem of the King's Book', in
   Historical Essays (London, 1957) pp. 211–20.

Chapter 3
The Arts in Stuart England

In Elizabethan England the monarchy had not been prominent in its support of the arts. The Queen was reluctant to spend money in this way, though she encouraged her courtiers to undertake great works at their own expense. So we find that the Renaissance passion for magnificent building was exuberantly indulged in by her principal courtiers and by the provincial magnates, while Elizabeth appreciatively visited their houses but built nothing herself. In palaces such as Hardwick, Burleigh, Longleat, and Wollaton we can still sense the vast confidence of the Elizabethan aristocracy, whose houses were designed for successive ages of peace, their great block-like structures glinting with innumerable windows and crested with festive decoration. Around them lie formal gardens often edged with arbours and small banqueting houses, while beyond lie the vast parks.

The cultural life of these great households was sustained by music, poetry, and theatrical performances. On the panelled walls hung portraits of the monarch, the family and its allies in marriage and politics, and the great men of state. Although remarkably vigorous, this was by and large an insular culture, which had developed during the half-century of isolation from Catholic Europe; its strongest foreign links were with the Low Countries, which provided many of the artists and much of the architectural fashion of late Elizabethan England. The accession of James I seemed hardly likely to change this situation greatly, for he came from an impoverished and peripheral throne, and was not known to have any marked interest in the visual arts. The transformation of taste that occurred in his reign owed much to his queen, Anne of Denmark, who had the same love of courtly magnificence as her brother, Christian IV, and who rapidly began to introduce novelties into the cultural scene. Her most significant act of patronage was to attract Inigo Jones into her service in 1604, drawing him back to England from her brother's court where Jones seems to have had his first experience of working for royalty. Jones was already skilled as a theatrical designer, and appears to have made at least one journey to Italy where he probably had the opportunity to observe the staging of the extravagant intermezzi that were the high points of the festive year in certain courts. We do not know where he went or what he saw, but he had enough expertise in stage design and mechanics to mount the *Masque of Blackness* for Queen Anne in 1605, after which, year by year, with ever increasing virtuosity, he entertained the courts of James I and Charles I with dazzling illusory spectacles in which perspective scenery, magical effects of light and motion, and rich, fantastic costumes combined with music, poetry and dance to glorify the monarch and cast an idealizing radiance over the whole court. An important side-effect of these masques was to familiarize the courtly audience with Italianate architectural designs, and with baroque mythological scenarios which until now had not formed part of the experience of cultivated Englishmen.

Queen Anne was also an active collector of paintings, not only of portraits but of mythological and religious subjects as well: she had Marcus Gheeraerts the Younger in her service, and Isaac Oliver, the miniaturist. Later she would attract Paul van Somer from Holland. She was willing to experiment with the new architecture, getting Inigo Jones to design for her the Queen's House at Greenwich in a pure Palladian style. She was interested in fashionable interior decoration, as her remodelling of Somerset House (again by Inigo Jones) showed. Both these locations were the setting of her personal court, which she maintained independently of the King. She laid out her gardens at Greenwich and Somerset House in the Mannerist style, which was just reaching England in the early 1600s, employing for this purpose the Frenchman Salomon de Caus, who first introduced the Italian concepts of garden design here – programmes of mythological statuary, large-scale hydraulic effects of fountains and cascades, and gloomy, fantastic grottoes. De Caus's construction at Somerset House, of a great, rocky Parnassus fountain, with statues of Apollo and the Muses on top, and river gods pouring their urns below, marked a new sophistication in garden ornament, and this combination of the arts and technology to create effects of wonder and admiration was obviously part of the same movement in taste that inspired Inigo Jones's designs for masques.

Anne transmitted her interest in the arts to her two sons, Prince Henry and Prince Charles, encouraging them to develop their judgement in the arts to a remarkable degree. The precocious Prince Henry inherited his mother's taste at an early age, with the result that in his brief life he became an outstanding patron, and established an unprecedented level of connoisseurship which was rapidly emulated by certain members of the aristocracy. He soon built up the most varied collection of paintings in the country, showing a particular preference for Venetian art. He understood the need for agents abroad to negotiate for pictures, asking the English Ambassador in Venice, Sir Dudley

Carleton, to search for paintings on his behalf in 1610, and making similar arrangements in the Netherlands. Foreign states recognized his enthusiasm: on the occasion of his investiture as Prince of Wales in 1610 (when he was sixteen), the Dutch states presented him with a series of marine pictures, and Venice also sent paintings as diplomatic gifts. The Grand Duke of Tuscany sent him a valuable group of Florentine bronzes from the workshop of Giovanni da Bologna in 1612.· He made a fine collection too of coins and medals. Within his household, painters were welcome and respected. His preference was for Robert Peake, who worked in a characteristically stiff late-Elizabethan style which gradually grew more animated and fluent in response to his patron's desire for a more modern manner. The brilliant miniaturist Isaac Oliver entered the Prince's service after being limner to Queen Anne, executing a number of wonderfully delicate, well-observed portraits; his later work shows a movement towards softer modelling and muted harmonious tones that suggest an assimilation of the Venetian qualities favoured by the Prince, qualities much in evidence in Oliver's finest miniature. Henry, in chased armour, is set against a background of military preparation, and the sensitively modelled features framed in a flaring lace ruff present the perfect image of a Renaissance warrior prince, intelligent, cultivated and tough. One might couple this miniature with another image, a large equestrian portrait, very probably by Peake, with the Prince in full armour against a twilit landscape: he appears as a romantic figure of legend, almost a character out of Sidney's *Arcadia*. The association would be appropriate, for Prince Henry had a marked desire to revive Elizabethan traditions of chivalry, and his model for style, conduct, and (not least) Protestant zeal was Sir Philip Sidney.

Henry cultivated the character of the chivalric prince. He liked tilting and other martial exercises (in great contrast to his father's peaceful inclinations) and he gathered around him the survivors of the Sidney circle and the friends of the Earl of Essex, who was Sidney's successor in the role of charismatic Protestant hero. Henry's military bearing was reflected in the works of art produced in the setting of his personal court, which occupied the palaces of St James's and Richmond. His portraits emphasize his readiness in arms: to those already mentioned should be added the splendid anonymous painting at Dunster Castle showing him in the richly decorated tournament armour given to him by Henry IV, (Plate 3), and the etching, after Isaac Oliver, of the Prince wielding a pike, which was printed at the beginning of Drayton's patriotic poem *Poly-Olbion*, a book dedicated to the Prince. George Chapman translated Homer's *Iliad* with Henry's encouragement and dedicated it to him, associating him thereby with the glories of the ancient heroes of Troy. The masque for his investiture as Prince of Wales, *Prince Henry's Barriers*, depicted him reviving the spirit of Chivalry, and culminated in a display of feats of arms. The masque *Oberon*, of 1611, by Jonson and Jones, presented him as 'The Faerie Prince', a figure of romantic chivalry. Paintings, literature, and masques consolidated the image of a resolute, noble-minded prince.

Like most great Renaissance princes, Henry had architectural ambitions too, and of a forward-looking kind. He favoured the Italianate style, and his desire to advance the understanding of that style is evident in the fact that the first English translation of a Renaissance treatise on architectural theory was produced in his household, when Robert Peake translated Serlio's *Booke of Architecture* in 1611. The Prince also appointed Inigo Jones as his Surveyor of Works in 1610, although no details survive to indicate what work he carried out. Jones was probably the only man in England at this time who could command the vocabulary of the Palladian style, but even so, Prince Henry aspired to greater authenticity, inviting over an architect from Florence, Constantino de Servi. Whether any buildings by him were erected we do not know, but he designed fountains, summer-houses, and galleries, and helped to mount festivals. He collaborated with Salomon de Caus, who had moved from Queen Anne's service into Prince Henry's, and who was proposing grand schemes of ornamental waterworks and garden design; there was every indication that they would have created at Richmond Palace a princely ambience of a most sophisticated kind, with galleries for the display of the Prince's pictures, Palladian loggias for social encounter, and formal gardens with cascades and hydraulic devices such as water-organs and *jeux d'eaux*. All was in prospect, but, to the universal dismay of the nation, Henry died suddenly of typhoid in 1612 at the age of eighteen. The many writers he had favoured sent up a great chorus of lamentation, and their hyperboles were justified, for Henry was that rarity, a generous, conscientious patron with high standards and an eagerness to encourage the whole spectrum of the arts. In the few years that his court flourished he established an admirable style of life in which love of the arts came to be associated with distinction of mind and fineness of spirit.[1]

This combination of qualities was perpetuated by Prince Henry's close adviser and friend, Thomas, Earl of Arundel, the premier earl of England. He too felt the lure of the arts of Italy, and in order to sharpen his taste he twice visited Italy, on the second occasion inviting Inigo Jones as a companion for a stay of eighteen months. They spent a long time in the Venetian Republic which was then on friendly terms with England. Here they could study at first hand the buildings of the leading modern architects, Palladio and Sansovino, inspect the collections of the great Venetian families, and engage in the cultivated life of the State. They could see how a humanist architecture of symmetry and proportion contributed to the dignity of the civic life, and appreciate the amenity of the classical manner. They visited Rome and Naples, places almost inaccessible to Englishmen who were not Catholics, where they could form an estimate of classical civilization that must have been a revelation to men accustomed to the towns of the Gothic North. It was here that Arundel's passion for antique sculpture was kindled, as he saw the collections of princes, cardinals, and senators. He coveted these marbles as tangible evidences of the ancient world and as monuments of classic beauty. He obtained a licence to dig, and began his own excavations, unearthing several statues that were carefully crated and sent home. For the first time, an Englishman was digging in classical soil, with the conviction that Roman culture was also his culture, and with a desire to share an inheritance that was more than literary.[2]

Upon his return, he commissioned Inigo Jones to build a two-storied gallery at Arundel House on the Strand to house his collections (Plate 4). These galleries can be seen in the background to the portraits of the Earl and his Countess painted in 1618 by Daniel Mytens, the Dutch artist whom Arundel had attracted to England that same year. The soberly clad Earl turns his long, dispassionate, aristocratic face to the viewer, and points with his marshal's baton into the sculpture gallery, an elegant, restrained hall, styled completely in an early sixteenth-century Italian manner, open at the far end where an arch leads through to a balcony over the river. The statues, raised on plinths, include a Diana and a Minerva. The Countess is seen sitting before the lower gallery, which is lined with portraits and which leads out into a formal garden terminating in a pergola. These two paintings present Arundel as a new type of Englishman, able to invite comparison with the sophisticated *cognoscenti* of the continental aristocracy.

Arundel continued to enlarge his sculpture collections throughout his life. He was particularly eager to acquire Greek marbles, asking the Ambassador in Constantinople to act for him, as well as sending out his own agent, William Petty. Over the years these men combed the eastern Mediterranean for Greek statuary and inscriptions, visiting places such as Ephesus, Pergamon, Troy, Corinth, Samos, and Scio. Their activity involved considerable expertise and expense in negotiating, packing, and transport, but the results were rewarding. Authentic fragments of Hellenistic art began to appear, to be displayed at Arundel House and to stimulate the interest in Greek studies that was a developing feature of scholarly life. George Chapman, whose translations of Homer, Hesiod, and the Homeric Hymns made a new world of the imagination accessible to Englishmen, was one of those who could appreciate what Arundel was doing; another was John Selden, the Jacobean polymath who eventually published a description of the statues and antique inscriptions for the benefit of classical scholars throughout Europe in his *Marmora Arundelliana* (1628). This work attempted to provide a historical context for the objects of the collection, and was the first direct study of classical archeaological material by an Englishman, a notable piece of scholarship for its time, and a book which did much to spread the fame of Arundel as a collecter to an international audience.

Paintings flowed into Arundel House from all over Europe. The inventory of 1655, drawn up after the death of the Countess, lists over 600 paintings, with a notable strength in Venetian paintings from the hands of Titian, Tintoretto, Veronese, and Giorgione; there were 12 paintings attributed to Raphael, 11 Caravaggios, and no less than 25 attributed to the mannerist, Parmigianino. Besides 5 paintings attributed to Leonardo, Arundel owned the famous collection of Leonardo drawings now at Windsor. Outside the Italian school, he possessed a remarkable collection of Holbeins, 43 works in all, and of Dürer, an artist so esteemed by the Earl that he interrupted his embassy to the Holy Roman Emperor in 1632 several times in order to seek out works by this master. Even more important than his role as collector was his function as patron. Not merely did Arundel commission large numbers of paintings; he was also active in bringing over to England major continental painters, who came because of Arundel's reputation as a lover of art and artists, and so helped to involve England in the currents of contemporary European art. A recurring concern of the cultural avant-garde in the earlier seventeenth century was the desire to draw leading European painters to England, to counter the common assumption that this was an insignificant country in matters touching the fine arts, provincial to the point of banality in its attachment to the old fashion for flat, icon-like images. So Prince Henry angled for Miereveldt, Queen Anne brought over Paul van Somer in 1617, and Arundel introduced Mytens in 1618. More ambitiously, Arundel established relations with Rubens, and tried to lure his outstanding pupil, Van Dyck, to London. The Earl was painted at least twice by Rubens, and the Countess once in a large vigorous baroque composition filled with the rhetoric of power that makes Mytens's portrait of her two years before look timid and demure. Van Dyck did come to London in 1620, when he painted Arundel and Buckingham, but he was then persuaded to go to Italy to improve his style. Always one senses this concern for quality in Arundel's dealings with artists.

During the 1620s and 1630s, Arundel House occupied a unique place in London's cultural life. It became in effect an academy of the arts, a gathering place for artists and gentlemen of taste. The collections formed a kind of semi-private museum, frequented by the more refined members of the aristocracy, diplomatic visitors and the curious. Arundel's household in itself was more impressive than the body of Fellows at most colleges of Oxford or Cambridge. His librarian and curator was the German Francis Junius, a philologist, Anglo-Saxon scholar, and author of a book on painting in the classical world that made high claims for the moral influence of the arts on public and private virtue: *De Pictura Veterum*. Henry Peacham, the poet, artist, and emblematist, was tutor to the Earl's children; his much reprinted book *The Compleat Gentleman* (1622), detailing the attainments expected of a Stuart gentleman (including a good deal of aesthetic expertise) reflects the dignified and cultivated life-style of Arundel House. The Earl's chaplain was William Oughtred, the deepest mathematician of the time; his physician (not resident) was William Harvey. Artists in residence included the Dutch painter van der Borcht and the Bohemian etcher Wenceslaus Hollar, whom Arundel had taken into his service on his German embassy of 1636. Hollar was the most delicate etcher in Europe, an exquisite landscapist and a tireless recorder of the contemporary scene; his post at Arundel House, however, primarily required that he make an engraved record of the treasures of the collection for eventual publication. With Inigo Jones a frequent visitor, and later Van Dyck, here was a centre of international distinction where the arts were seen as essential to the good life and where antiquity and modernity coexisted in an ethos of scholarship and discrimination.[3]

The aristocratic life-style that recognized in the arts the fullest expression of nobility of spirit was adopted by increasing numbers of noblemen from the second decade of the century onwards. The royal favourite, Somerset, began early, but shed his collections at his fall, when other courtiers gratefully picked up the pieces. As might be expected, the Earls of Pembroke were among the foremost in this field, both the third Earl, William, and his brother Philip, the fourth Earl, using their large resources to buy pictures and statuary abroad to fill their house at Wilton, which was splendidly rebuilt and enlarged in the 1650s by Inigo Jones's pupil John Webb. The Earls of Rutland and Northumberland became enthusiastic about the fine arts, building up respectable collections. Sir Dudley Carleton, later Lord Dorchester, who was Ambassador at Venice and at The Hague, had plenty of opportunities to put together an interesting collection, as did his fellow diplomat, Sir Henry Wotton. All these were overshadowed by the Duke of Buckingham, the royal favourite, whose collections mushroomed with his rapid growth in status. By about 1620 Buckingham already recognized that a great art collection and a profession of connoisseurship were indispensable to distinction at home and abroad. Amid the innumerable transactions of his meteoric career, he urged on his agents across Europe to purchase the best paintings available, and he competed rancorously with Arundel for Greek and Roman statuary in Italy and the Levant. The core of Buckingham's collection was a remarkable display of Venetian pictures, dominated by Titian, and his greatest coup was the purchase of Rubens's personal collection of paintings, drawings, and statues in 1627, the climax of a long relationship with Rubens as patron and friend. Rubens had painted several portraits of the Duke with lavish baroque accessories, turning him into one of the demigods of the West. Although Buckingham's collection was highly impressive, it did not rival Arundel's, but no doubt would have done so if the favourite's life had not been cut short.

King James expressed little interest in the visual arts, at least in his recorded conversations and written works, which are disappointingly void of comment upon such matters. There is no evidence that he ever bought a work of art in his life. King Charles, in contrast, was one of the most discerning patrons of the arts ever to occupy the English throne. His courtiers hastened to share his tastes, with the result that by the 1630s Whitehall could be considered among the most sophisticated courts in Europe. Charles had inherited Prince Henry's collections, and then his mother's many portraits came to him on her death in 1619. He bought avidly, using discreet and efficient agents. A famous catch was the Raphael cartoons of the Acts of the Apostles, bought in Genoa in 1623 and now in the Victoria and Albert museum. In 1627 the King astonished the art world by purchasing the collection of the Dukes of Mantua after patient secret negotiation. The Gonzaga family had patronized many great painters, including Mantegna, Leonardo, Perugino, Caravaggio, and Giulio Romano; they had accumulated wonderful Venetian masterpieces by Titian, Giorgione, and Tintoretto; now all their treasures were removed to London, to give substance to a theme often sounded in the masques and poetry: the westward migration of the Muses, the movement of culture from its ancient haunts to the welcoming territory of Great Britain. The impoverished Duke of Mantua held on to his most prized item, Mantegna's great sequence 'The Triumphs of Julius Caesar', but in 1628 Charles swept those away as well. 'The Triumphs of Caesar' became Charles's triumphs too, for he had outmanoeuvred the Emperor, Cardinal Richelieu, and the Duke of Tuscany for possession of Mantua's riches.

The Mantegnas and the set of twelve Roman emperors by Titian, also from the Mantua Collection, held a particular significance for Charles, for, as we have seen, he was increasingly disposed to cast himself in an imperial role as Emperor of Great Britain, a style already adopted by King James but more grandiosely assumed by Charles. In this guise he appeared in court masques, and was painted by Van

Dyck. Most books dedicated to him during the 1630s allude to his imperial qualities. His three kingdoms, distant Virginia, and a scattering of islands provided some substance for the claim, his governance of the Church of England strengthened it, and the memories of Britain's Roman past suggested that the seeds of empire had been planted long ago. Charles encouraged an iconography that amplified his imperial style or gave additional dignity to the nation; 'The Triumphs of Caesar' and the Titian Emperors were therefore strategically displayed at Whitehall to impress ambassadors and courtiers with their aura of power.

Most of Charles's important commissions involved an enhancement of the royal image for political purposes, to emphasize the King's authority or wisdom, or his chivalric nature or philosophic elevation. We have already observed how he had Rubens fill the Banqueting House ceiling with images of the divinely sanctioned power of King James that projected ideas of benevolent absolutism. Charles then commissioned a painting from Rubens, showing him and Henrietta Maria in a fantasy of royal romance: in an idealized English landscape, the King as St George delivers the Queen from the dragon, which lies slain. The painting draws together many strands of Caroline mythology, including the King as heroic lover (whose devotion to his virtuous queen has beneficial consequences for the whole nation, as the King's influence, tempered by love, extends its harmonious influence over the State), the King as lover of his people (prefiguring the Philogenes figure of the masque *Salmacida Spolia*, for Rubens depicts a grateful nation happy at their deliverance from the dragon). The painting depicts the bold, resolute spirit of the King, and by the character of St George it reminds its audience of Charles's special devotion to the Order of the Garter as the mainstay of honourable aristocratic conduct in the realm. The landscape suggests the flourishing condition of the country under Charles, and the painting as a whole offers an optimistic view of his complete control of events.

With Van Dyck the King's relations were very close, for he must have recognized what an asset the painter was to his reign. He knighted him, and loaded him with gifts and honours, a situation reflected in the artist's portrait of himself pointing to a sunflower, a symbol of royal favour, and fingering the heavy gold chain he had been given by the King. In return, Van Dyck painted a series of royal portraits that idealized the King and Queen and glorified their court. In particular, three great canvases capture important aspects of the monarch: heroical, as he rides through a triumphal arch hung with cloth of state; philosophic, as he sits pensively upon horseback, in armour, recollecting himself before action; and peace-loving, when, dressed as a country gentleman, he surveys, with casual elegance, the fertile landscape of his estates.[4]

In the decade of the 1630s most of the leading courtiers sat to Van Dyck, who created through these portraits a vision of an exquisitely refined and intelligent society that forms our enduring image of the Cavalier world. Alert and responsive as they face their companions or the viewer, almost all of Van Dyck's subjects seem possessed of an exceptional fineness of spirit, conveyed by their confident poses, their beautifully textured silks and lace or highlighted armour, and by the smooth vitality of the artist's brushwork. Whether Sir John Suckling chooses to be painted in Arcadian dress reading Shakespeare among the rocks, or the Earl of Denbigh in Indian costume reflecting on his travels, or, more conventionally, if Mistress Anne Killigrew agrees to pose in fashionable silks against brown curtains and a clouding sky, we know we are in a society where style is paramount, and role-playing an instinctive habit.

To see Van Dyck at the height of his powers, and to appreciate how his art could add nobility to even the most distinguished subjects, one should look at the portrait of the Pembroke family that he painted c. 1634 (see cover picture). This is the largest piece he executed in England, and it hangs in the Double Cube Room at Wilton, where it is beautifully incorporated into the decorative scheme which John Webb created in the 1650s. The younger members of the family are elegantly grouped around the Earl and the Countess, who sit in state on a dais beneath a great escutcheon of the Pembrokes, with its many quarterings which tell of their illustrious lineage. The children hold a variety of casual poses which admirably convey their aristocratic breeding; each maintains a balance between natural ease and conscious grace, which was an aspect of Cavalier style in the 1630s. The parents, in contrast, in their sombre black costume, inhabit a different dimension of space and time by virtue of their authority and age: they sit formally, almost regally, their power implicit in the dignity of their pose, the grandeur of their coat of arms and the sweeping background of their black cloth of state. The group is held together by a wonderful rhythmic movement from left to right, their heads being placed almost like notes of music on a stave to create a visual melody. The tawny silks of the young men harmonize with the white silks of the women, yet the parental black subdues the colour range and imposes an air of distinction and restraint upon the scene. The overall composition of the painting might have suggested to a seventeenth-century connoisseur other great family groups – the Gonzaga family of Mantua by Mantegna, for example, or the Vendramin family of Venice by Titian – and the comparison would not be lost on the Earl of Pembroke, who was himself a collector of repute.

To contemplate this picture is to see a brief chronicle of the power, the glory, and the tragedy of seventeenth-century England. Here are the representatives of some of the greatest families of the land: Philip, fourth Earl of Pembroke, the head of the ancient family of the Herberts; his wife Anne, descended from the even more ancient Cliffords, Earls of Cumberland, and one of the richest heiresses of England; in the foreground stands Mary Villiers, the Pembrokes' daughter-in-law, and herself the daughter of the most recent and resented member of the aristocracy, the Duke of Buckingham. The Earl of Pembroke was Lord Chamberlain of England, and holds the delicate white wand of office, a slender token of considerable political force. His relaxation was hunting – 'it was in his Lordship's time that Hunting was at its greatest Heighth that ever was in this Nation', thought Aubrey – and the hunting dog in the left-hand corner of the painting is a reminder of this passion. But there was another side to Pembroke, for he was one of 'the most Noble and Incomparable Pair of Brethren' to whom Shakespeare's First Folio was dedicated, and the large volume carried by one of the children on the left may well commemorate this honour. Lady Anne Clifford, the Countess, had been a close companion of Queen Anne, and a participant in the first masques of court. She had married the Earl of Dorset and been mistress of Knole: by the 1630s she had become devoutly religious and inclined to retire from the world. She did not get on with her second husband, which is perhaps why Van Dyck paints her as a self-contained figure, arms folded as she gazes straight ahead, while the Earl, divided from her by his wand of office, turns slightly aside to regard his children by another wife. On the right stands their ward, Robert Dormer, the Earl of Caernarvon. When the Civil War broke out, he was to raise a company of horse for the King and to be killed at the first Battle of Newbury, and he would be eulogized by Clarendon as a dextrous commander, 'an excellent Discerner and Pursuer of Advantage upon his Enemy' and 'a great Lover of Justice'. The Earl of Pembroke would side with Parliament, while the Countess's loyalties would be with the court and the suppressed Church of England. Thus this great family group of Van Dyck, when seen in the perspective that history supplies, yields a surprisingly diverse record of the various energies of the age.

It is remarkable how many of Van Dyck's subjects were themselves collectors of art and sculpture. Arundel, Pembroke, Northumberland, Strafford, Danby, and gentlemen such as Endymion Porter, George Gage, Nicholas Lanier, and Thomas Hanmer, as well as the many members of the House of Stuart, all professed a high level of judgement in the arts. Within two generations the English court had advanced from a misty ignorance about the fine arts to an impressive level of connoisseurship. The royal gallery at Whitehall became one of the sights of Europe, and its contents were steadily enlarged by diplomatic gifts. The King of Spain offered Titians and Correggios in compensation for the failed match with the Infanta; Rubens's *Peace and*

War came as a gift from the artist at the conclusion of the peace treaty with Spain in 1630; the Dutch states gave seascapes to help resolve the dispute over the herring fisheries in the North Sea; the city of Nuremberg presented Charles with a Dürer as a token of esteem.

Charles should have been wary of nuncios bearing gifts, however, and he would have been well advised to turn some of them away. In the mid-1630s the Pope tried to persuade Charles to liberalize the position of Catholics in England and he sent him offerings of works of art, including paintings by Leonardo, Andrea del Sarto, and Giulio Romano. Philistine English Protestants smelt a rat among these expensive consignments. When the Pope gave permission to Bernini to carve busts for the King, suspicion grew in England that Charles was going soft on Catholicism in exchange for a few marble vanities. The whole cult of Italian painting that pervaded the court seemed damnable to strict Protestants, who saw Catholic religious works coming back into England and being praised as objects of beauty and virtue. The cherishing of pictures and statues was to them a form of idolatry, and there was widespread complaint that (in notable contrast to our own times) the King could always find money for the arts, while neglecting the defence of the realm. The royal navy decayed, troops could not be raised to help the Palatinate, but masques and paintings were somehow paid for. The aesthetic tastes of Charles I in the end did much to alienate stolid Protestants, who suspected that the course of the Reformation was being subverted. It was not at all surprising that after the execution of Charles in 1649, Parliament ordered the sale of the royal collections, and that much of the proceeds was used to pay military expenses. The profits from the sale of Hampton Court, for example, were 'lent unto the treasurers of the navy, for supply and present uses of the navy'.

Architecture was a less contentious matter. A new restraint and decorum had become fashionable as a result of Inigo Jones's advocacy of the Italianate style, but his work was on the whole limited to the royal family and the inner court circle. Jones was a purist, who had a thorough command of the neo-Classical vocabulary derived from Palladio and from direct observation of buildings in Italy; his work appealed to those who wished to associate themselves with international standards of correctness. Unfortunately he was allowed relatively few occasions for the full display of his powers, as he was usually asked to design units of buildings such as galleries, chapels, or lodges rather than complete ensembles. His masterpiece, the Banqueting House, survives, as does the Queen's House at Greenwich, which he designed for Queen Anne and completed for Henrietta Maria. Much, though, has been lost. His work on St Paul's, which involved recasing the cathedral and adding a giant portico to the west end, so much admired by contemporaries, went up in the Great Fire; the elegant range of rooms he designed at Somerset House for Henrietta Maria was demolished in the eighteenth century. His development at Covent Garden, where he laid out houses with colonnaded ranges and a simple chapel on one side to produce a piazza in the Italian style (the first example of modern civic planning in London), has been rebuilt beyond recognition. His grandest scheme, for a completely rebuilt Whitehall to fulfil Charles's dream of a palace that would rival the Louvre, never got beyond the drawing-board.

A number of pre-Civil War country houses claim to be associated with Inigo Jones, such as Castle Ashby, Ashton Court, Stoke Bruerne, or Kirby Hall, but firm evidence is not available. For the most part they are good 'artisan' houses, built by competent designers who borrowed their details from Serlio or Palladio, but they betray a faulty architectural grammar, making mistakes (though often very pleasing ones) in their handling of the orders, their spacing of the windows or their understanding of the pediment, and they lack the purity and rigour of Jones's classicism. An eclectic Italianate style did achieve a certain currency in the 1620s and 1630s, helped along by an engaging and widely circulated discourse *The Elements of Architecture* by Sir Henry Wotton, published in 1624. Wotton had spent years in Venice as ambassador, so he was well qualified to expound the beauties of the Italian manner. This is the first architectural treatise by an Englishman, and although it is concerned mainly with the siting and design of a country house, and is not illustrated, it communicated the values of the Classical style to an audience far beyond the court. Drawing much on Vitruvius, Alberti, Palladio, and the contemporary French master Philibert de l'Orme, Wotton stresses the practical and pleasurable aspects of architecture, with epigrammatic felicity: 'Well-building hath three conditions: commodity, firmness and delight.' 'Let all the principal chambers of delight, all studies and libraries, be towards the east: for the morning is a friend to the Muses.' The book is a brief education in the humanist principles of architecture, and he writes well about the psychology of Classical architecture, how its forms are designed to please and elevate the mind. He explains, for instance, the principles of musical intervals that should regulate the proportions of architectural detail throughout, 'reducing symmetry to symphony, and harmony of sound to a kind of harmony in sight'. He conveys the aesthetic satisfaction of a fine design, describing 'that agreeable harmony between the breadth, length and height of all the rooms of the fabric, which suddenly, where it is, taketh every beholder by the secret power of proportion'.[5]

There were a few identifiable architects who worked in the Italian style before the Civil War, notably Balthazar Gerbier, who designed the additions to York House for the Duke of Buckingham, and Nicholas Stone, who seems to have been responsible for Kirby Hall, Northamptonshire, and who probably designed Lindsey House in Lincoln's Inn Fields. But most English gentlemen still preferred to build in a recognizable English idiom, showing a preference for picturesque groupings, with high-pitched roofs, plenty of gables, and imaginative skyline effects produced by towers, chimneys, cupolas, and finials. Not for them the chaste rectangular blocks of the new classicism. The vernacular style of this period, as it developed from Elizabethan precedents with importation of Dutch detail (satisfyingly Protestant), can be viewed at houses such as Blickling Hall (Norfolk), Swakeleys (Middlesex) (Plate 5), Audley End (Essex), Aston Hall (Birmingham), or Bolsover (Derbyshire). The decades of the 1640s and 1650s, with all their political uncertainty, were not good times for building, but work did go forward, with Jones's solitary pupil John Webb as the most active practitioner. He designed Gunnersbury House, Middlesex, in the 1650s, and worked at Wilton, where the series of staterooms in the Jonesian style survives to give an idea of the rich decorative interior schemes of this time.

Almost inseparable from architectural planning in the seventeenth century was garden design. Roy Strong's book *The Renaissance Garden in England* has explored this area in a most revealing way, marking out the stages of fashion in gardening up to the Restoration. He traces the change from the Elizabethan formal garden with its knotbeds and intricately patterned borders to the emblematic gardens which enjoyed a vogue in Jacobean and Caroline times. In this latter phase, conceits of a witty or philosophic nature could be laid out in herbs and shrubs and flowers. Since a garden was considered a primary example of art imposing order on nature, and was also a place of pleasure, it should present to the spectator a set of noble ideas or convey motifs that suggested the intelligent mind at play. Many gardens were designed to a theme, such as the Countess of Bedford's at Twickenham, the setting of one of Donne's better-known poems, where part of the garden was laid out as a model of the Ptolemaic universe in concentric walks and borders representing the planetary orbits. The gardens of Sir Henry Fanshawe at Ware Park and of Lord Fairfax at Appleton House both had military schemes which imitated the arts of fortification with banks and escarpments in plants and flowers. One Caroline garden at Packwood House, Warwickshire, figured the Sermon on the Mount with clipped yews as the Apostles and the attendant crowd.[6] Patterns of symbolic geometry expressed theological or moral ideas: triangles for the Trinity and pentangles for the virtues, for example. There were gardens of love, with appropriate statuary, gardens that drew their inspiration from classical legend or from Sidneyan romance.

Distinctive additions to the repertory of garden ornaments in the first decade of the century, remaining fashionable until the Civil War, were hydraulic effects, automata and grottoes. This complex of amenities was yet another case of importing Italian taste, for this combination of mechanical wonders and artificial grottoes was a famous feature of the Duke of Tuscany's pleasure gardens at Pratolino, and also of the Villa d'Este at Tivoli, where the owners imagined they were re-creating types of classical garden ornamentation of the kind described by Pliny the Younger, and incorporating mechanically operated wonders derived from the *Pneumatics* of Hero of Alexandria, a technical writer of the second century BC.

The engineer who was responsible for introducing these 'Inventions for refreshment, and Alexandrian delicacies' as Wotton called them, was the Frenchman Salomon de Caus, whom we have already mentioned in connection with Queen Anne and Prince Henry. De Caus had investigated the Duke of Tuscany's gardens at first hand, and under royal patronage in England he set out to introduce here gardens of mythological fantasy. He began at Somerset House, the Queen's residence, where as a centrepiece he constructed the rocky Mount Parnassus described above. De Caus also provided mythological compositions and fountains at Greenwich for the Queen, before he began to develop the grounds of Prince Henry's palace at Richmond for a spectacular sequence of Mannerist garden fantasies. He also worked for Robert Cecil, helping to plan the gardens at Hatfield. He left England in 1613 to serve Prince Henry's sister Elizabeth when, after her marriage to the Elector Palatine, she moved to Heidelberg, where de Caus proceeded to lay out the most extraordinary garden of seventeenth-century Europe, the Hortus Palatinus, that masterpiece of geometrical fantasy and technological skill. In the 1620s Salomon's brother Isaac de Caus came to England to continue the hydraulic tradition, designing for the Earl and Countess of Bedford at Moor Park, and most ambitiously for the Earl of Pembroke at Wilton.[7] The appeal of these water-gardens was to the sense of wonder that was readily aroused by unexpected spectacles and ingenious devices; it is possible too that the mythological statuary gave visual expression to ideas about the order and vitality of the natural world, following the lines suggested by Francis Bacon in his *Wisdom of the Ancients*, where he speculated that the myths of the Greeks and Romans were in effect parables of natural science or of moral philosophy.

Grottoes, often lined with limestone fragments and decorated with sea shells, were held to be suitable places for meditation or for philosophic discussion, perhaps because they induced the melancholy humour which was thought to be propitious to elevated thought. They had their hazards: Aubrey reports that the Earl of Arundel and his mathematical friend William Oughtred were nearly killed when the grotto in which they were discoursing collapsed.[8]

In an age instinctively given to moralizing and accustomed to seeing everywhere links between the natural and the divine, gardens, whether great or small, were valued as places for contemplation and religious musing as well as for the pleasures they afforded. The habit of daily meditation was common, and gardens provided much material for reflection. Plants and trees had their particular significations, such as

> The Cedar of high Contemplation, the Cypress of
> odoriferous Fame and sanctitie of life, the Laurel of
> Constancie, the Palm of glorious Victorie, the Mulberie of
> Patience, the Myrtle of Mortification, the Olive of Mercie,
> the Almond of Fruitfulness, the Figtree of Deliciousness,
> the Planetree of Faith.[9]

William Drummond's medications in *A Cypress Grove* (1623) carried him through the veil of death to glorious intimations of immortality; George Herbert could find in the orderly rows of fruit-trees an image that seemed to promise him a place in paradise:

> I bless thee Lord because I Grow
> Among thy trees, which in a row
> To thee both fruit and order ow.
> ('Paradise' ll. 1–3)

Ralph Austen enlarged on such speculations in his meditative work The *Spiritual Use of an Orchard* (1653), in which he too found a promise of being transplanted to heaven by the Universal Gardener. The network arrangement of fruit plantations gave rise to Sir Thomas Browne's baroque meditation *The Garden of Cyrus* (1658) in which, inspired by that 'Lord of Gardens' 'the splendid and regular planter' King Cyrus, Browne traces the persistence throughout history and the natural world of the lozenge-shaped pattern, incorporating the figure of the cross, which Cyrus had used in his plantations. It is a discourse that arises in paradise and fades into eternity, all times and all nations being drawn together on the axes of that 'emphaticall decussation' the mystical letter X.

Imaginative men in the seventeenth century almost invariably associated gardens with Eden. 'God Almighty first planted a garden', wrote Bacon, and Milton described the art with which he landscaped it in *Paradise Lost*, IV. 132–53. Gardening was the most innocent of pleasures, the nearest approximation to the paradisal state that most fallen men could hope to attain. During the 1650s, for so many men who had been forced out of public life by the swing of political events, gardening became a refuge and a solace of the first order. Its innocence and order contrasted tellingly with the confused circumstances of society. Nor was it only royalists who took this course. Lord Fairfax had been general of the parliamentary armies until he resigned in 1650 over the plan to march against Scotland, and retired to his estates at Nun Appleton in Yorkshire, where 'he did, with his utmost skill,/Ambition weed, but conscience till':

> The gardener had the soldier's place,
> And his more gentle forts did trace.
> The nursery of all things green
> Was then the only magazine.
>
> ('Upon Appleton House', ll. 337–40)

Marvell's garden poems, which were probably written during his time with Fairfax in 1651–52, all suggest that the retiredness of the garden life has such pleasures and exaltations that it renders all other vocations vain, shallow, and wearisome.

In the minds of its most enthusiastic advocates, then, gardening could be envisaged as the summit of human felicity, gratifying the mind and senses in equal measure. John Evelyn imagined the creation of a vast ideal garden centred on a country house, where a group of choice spirits might lead a life of innocent fulfilment; he communicated his dream to Sir Thomas Browne, who he knew would give it sympathetic audience:

> Our drift is a noble, princely, and universal Elysium,
> capable of all the amenities that can naturally be
> introduced into gardens of pleasure, and such as may stand
> in competition with all the august designs and stories of
> this nature, either of ancient or modern times. . . . We
> will endeavour to show how the air and genius of gardens
> operate upon human spirits towards virtue and sanctity, I
> mean in a remote, preparatory and instrumental working.
> How caves, grots, mounts and irregular ornaments of
> gardens do contribute to contemplative and philosophic
> enthusiasm; . . . for these expedients do influence the soul
> and spirits of man, and prepare them for converse with
> good angels; besides which, they contribute to the less
> abstracted pleasures, philosophy natural and longevity.
> And I would have not only the elogies [= inscriptions]
> and effigy of the ancient and famous garden heroes, but a
> society of the *Paradisi Cultores*, persons of ancient

simplicity, Paradisean and Hortulan saints, to be a society of learned and ingenuous men. . . by whom we might hope to redeem the time.[10]

The elect society of garden 'saints' would engage in a kind of Christian Epicureanism, in which horticultural exercises would be combined with recreational pleasures and philosophic contemplation, remote from the disturbing influences of political conflict or social distraction. Evelyn nurtured this fantasy throughout his life, and his vision of a garden that is part Eden, part English country house, informs his most extensive work, the still unpublished manuscript 'Elysium Britannicum'.

The Commonwealth period, when so many gentlemen devoted themselves to their estates, was in fact a time of considerable improvement in horticulture and husbandry. The propagation and cultivation of fruit-trees were intensively studied, techniques of grafting refined (satirized by Marvell in 'The Mower against Gardens'), the fertility of the soil improved, and many new species of plants and vegetables introduced. There was much planting of new trees to replace the timber lost in the Civil Wars. By the time of the Restoration, England was becoming an efficiently cultivated country.[11]

Music of all kinds received encouragement under the Stuarts. In the time of James I, most great houses had their musical establishment to provide entertainment at dinner and for dancing afterwards, or to play at services in the private chapel. At court the King's Musick was a large and important department of the royal household. King James employed 40 musicians on average at his court; Queen Anne had a group of 15, playing viols, lutes, virginals, and the various wind instruments. Charles had even greater resources, with the King's Musick numbering 78 at the beginning of his reign, falling later to about 65 members in the 1630s. Their functions were extensive: the King's Musick provided ceremonial music at court for royal entries and for the reception of ambassadors; small groups played for the King and Queen at dinner, and would provide accompaniment to the court dancing that often filled up the evenings. When a masque was staged, the King's Musick was responsible for the musical part, and often needed to have their forces supplemented for the really grand productions. Soloists or small consorts of lutes and viols played to the great men of the court to indulge their humours or assuage their melancholy; they played too at sick-rooms to compose the souls of mortal men, and the frequent funerals of the court involved them in elaborate musical obsequies.

The monarch also maintained a sacred music establishment in the

Chapel Royal. The forces there in Jacobean and Caroline times usually comprised twenty-four singing men and twelve singing boys, some of whom had been specially trained for the Chapel, others recruited or often impressed from cathedral service elsewhere. There were groups of instrumentalists here too, which were reinforced by members of the King's Musick for important occasions. The Chapel Royal held daily services at Whitehall or at the other palaces in the London region where the court was in session. The great tradition of post-Reformation church music flowed through the Chapel Royal, and much of the music composed for services there was later taken up by cathedrals and collegiate churches. Thomas Tallis had been appointed to the Chapel in 1540 and William Byrd had followed in 1570, keeping up his association well into James's reign. Byrd was immensely prolific in all sacred forms – the great English master of polyphony, whose motets, anthems, psalm-settings, and litanies, with their exquisite vocal line, contributed so much to the establishment of a complete music for the English Church. Byrd was in fact a Catholic, but, like so many artists at court, he was too valuable to dismiss on such grounds. In addition to his compositions for the Anglican service, he wrote several fine masses for recusant families which should remind us of the vigour of the Catholic culture that was unobtrusively maintained in some of the great houses of the old faith. Byrd was succeeded by John Bull and Orlando Gibbons, who were both organists in the Chapel Royal, the latter literally dying in the royal service, as he collapsed as he prepared to offer a musical greeting to the newly arrived Henrietta Maria in 1625. Thomas Tomkins continued the line. All these men were keyboard virtuosi as well as highly inventive composers; from all of them, the regular demand of the Chapel Royal for new settings of the liturgy drew a succession of remarkable compositions, and the presence of men of such high musicianship maintained the excellent standards of performance for which the Chapel was famous.

Secular music too received a fertilizing influence from the court. There the demand for novelty was most urgent, and fashionable courtiers liked to show off the pieces that had been composed for their pleasure by musicians in their patronage. The lute, virginals, and viols were the popular instruments in James's reign, when the outstanding secular composer was John Dowland. Dowland spent many years abroad, for some time in the service of the King of Denmark, returning in 1606 to become the lutenist of Lord Howard de Walden, eventually gaining a court post as one of the King's Lutes in 1612. His pieces for solo lute and his songs with lute accompaniment are the final flowering of the expressive polyphonic manner that had been evolving throughout Elizabeth's reign. The chromatic fantasias, the intricate dance forms of the almains, galliards, and pavans, the haunting songs, had a delicacy and spirit which testified to the aesthetic sophistication of English musical taste in the early seventeenth century. His works have an affinity with the miniatures of Hilliard and Oliver, though it must remain an open question whether some of Dowland's pieces were in fact musical portraits of the men and women whose names they bear. Dowland's intellectual depth makes it quite likely that he might have sought to achieve an impressionistic relationship between his music and the character of the person honoured by it. To some extent the names in titles must have conjured up the presence of the dedicatee when the dances were played in company, and it is not difficult to believe that pieces such as 'The Lady Clifton's Spirit', 'My Lady Mildmay's Delight', 'Sir Robert Sidney His Galliard', 'Sir John Langton His Pavan', and 'Mistress Winter's Jump' came to be seen as aspects of those persons' characters, and their dances were played to honour them when present, or to call them to mind when absent or dead, in the way that miniatures also served.[12]

Dowland's outstanding publication was the volume entitled *Lachrimae or Seaven Teares*, of 1604, dedicated to Queen Anne. The melancholy of the title was a mood congenial to the composer, as one might guess from his motto, 'Semper Dowland Semper Dolens' (which inspired both a lute solo and a setting for a consort of viols), and from the habitually gloomy comments of his surviving letters. The *Lachrimae* were written for a consort of five viols plus lute, and take the form of pavans, slow stately measures to which the repeated falling cadences give a deep tragic tone. Their complex structures are created by devices of daring ingenuity: 'Suspensions, false relations, and the clash of parts moving against each other at temporarily discordant intervals are combined in a musical texture of extraordinary emotional intensity.'[13] Following the melodious tears comes the meditation on the composer's name and character already mentioned, 'Semper Dowland Semper Dolens', which might be regarded as a musical self-portrait, then a funeral pavan for Sir Henry Unton that extends still more the mournful nature of the collection. At last the mood brightens with 'The King of Denmark's Galliard', the first of a number of galliards and almains. The compass of moods and emotions in the *Lachrimae* volume makes it a not unworthy music book for the Shakespearean world, and with its mixture of introspective melancholy and fitful gaiety it would be an apt object of study not only for the King but also for the Prince of Denmark himself.

Dowland had the misfortune to see musical taste change at court in his lifetime, moving away from the rich polyphonic manner in which he excelled to a simpler style that emphasized the melody at the expense of the intricacy of setting. Polyphony gradually gave way to harmonically conceived melody over a supporting bass. The cause of change was most probably King James's taste and the dominance of masque in court entertainments, for which firm, vigorous, linear writing served best. Dowland was not asked to compose music for masques; instead the names we meet with are those of Alphonso Ferrabosco, Thomas Campion, Robert Johnson, and Nicholas Lanier. They were prolific composers of masquing tunes and ready to take account of the new fashion for French corantos and voltes, sprightly, stylish affairs of great gaiety; they were more willing to let their music be an accompaniment to the increasing exhibitionism of the vocal soloist. The intellectuality of Dowland's art told against him in the festive world of court pleasures.[14]

In the sociable musical circles of Jacobean England, madrigals kept the popularity they had enjoyed in Elizabethan times, and fresh invention flowed steadily from John Wilby, Orlando Gibbons, and Thomas Tomkins, though their compositions have a more homophonic character than their predecessors'. In the Caroline period, the art song began to gain favour and the finest exponent of this new genre was Henry Lawes, most famous these days for having written music to *Comus*, in which he also played the part of the Attendant Spirit. Lawes set the lyrics of many of the Cavalier poets – Carew, Suckling, Lovelace, Waller, and Herrick, among others – in a wonderfully limpid style which gave the words a high prominence on a clear line of harmonically sustained melody. Lawes also developed the distinctive form of the 'declamatory ayre', a form of continuous recitative which owed much to Italian operatic techniques. It had a vocal line of one or two parts, with a relatively simple accompaniment that 'humoured' the text, as contemporary usage put it.[15] This method gave prominence to the words and offered the singers the opportunity to display their skills in ornamentation and emotive delivery. Recitative had been introduced into the masque as early as 1617 in Jonson's *Lovers Made Men*, where 'the whole Maske was sung (after the Italian manner) *Stylo recitativo*, by Master *Nicholas Lanier*; who ordered and made both the Scene, and the Musicke'.[16] Lanier's cantata *Hero and Leander*, which enjoyed a vogue in the 1630s, was composed entirely in this recitative style (which is better known to us perhaps in its original and more accomplished form, in the works of Italian composers such as Monteverdi). In order to emphasize the expressiveness of its single vocal line, Lanier called his work a monody, a term that evoked the stylized delivery of an ode in Greek tragedy, and which in the seventeenth century was used to indicate the recitative manner, which was thought to resemble the Greek usage. (Milton applied the same term to 'Lycidas' and this suggests something of the heightened affective utterance Milton might have had in mind for the delivery of his poem.)

Lawes's *Ariadne Deserted* of *c.* 1640 is a fine example of a lament using this manner of musical declamation that Lawes believed was a revival of the ancient Greek mode of half-sung enunciation, in which words and rhythms had priority over the musical line. This style seems also to have been applied to the musical settings of Davenant's 'opera' *The Siege of Rhodes*, when it was performed in 1656, one of the composers of its vocal music being Henry Lawes.

The Interregnum years saw a considerable decline in the public performance of music, and as court entertainments effectively ceased, and with the Chapel Royal and playhouses closed, the stimulus to composition declined. However, with the fall of the monarchy, the monopoly on music publishing that had existed since Elizabeth's time was broken, with the result that books of music from earlier years could be readily reprinted and sold more cheaply, and here John Playford served the musical community well, for he published all manner of musical scores, madrigals, psalms, keyboard music, music for viols, lutes and consorts of wind instruments, collections of catches, as well as books of theory, so that he made music available to a wider audience than at any previous time. Domestic playing flourished, with friends gathering to play their viols together or sing. Matthew Locke and John Jenkins were the prominent string composers at this time. Thomas Tomkins, whose posts at the Chapel Royal and at Worcester Cathedral had disappeared, gave himself over to the composition of keyboard music that could be played in the private setting of the home. The virginals were still the preferred keyboard instrument, but gradually in the 1660s the spinet would become more fashionable.

Cromwell, as is well known, had a musical disposition, and maintained a modest musical establishment at his court for ceremonial and state occasions, employing a number of musicians for his private pleasure. (Eight masters of music walked in his funeral procession.) His requirements, however, were not sufficient to give the public side of the musical profession of London much support. Nor did the first attempts at staging opera, under Davenant's initiative (see pp. 93–5), improve the musical scene, for the performances were intermittent and hardly capable of providing regular employment.

The Restoration caused an immediate revival in musical fortunes. The secular and sacred centres of music reopened as the court reassembled, the Chapel Royal was reconstituted, cathedrals regained their choirs and organs, and the playhouses provided entertainment once again. Music and musicians were everywhere in request, with many players coming over from France and Italy to meet the sudden demand. Charles II loved music and dancing and during his exile had developed a pronounced French taste, with a penchant for the style of Lully. Following the model of Louis XIV, he established a band of twenty-four violins as the nucleus of the King's Musick soon after his return, so putting an end to the old pattern of consorts of related instruments of viols, lutes, recorders, and wind bands, which had been the characteristic grouping of music at the earlier Stuart court. By the end of 1662 the band of violins made their appearance in the Chapel Royal, to enliven the proceedings there.

> His Majesty, who was a brisk and airy Prince, coming to the Crown in the flower and the vigour of his age, was soon, if I may so say, tired with the grave and solemn way, and ordered the composers of his Chapel to add symphonies etc. with instruments to their anthems; and thereupon established a select number of his private music to play the symphonies and ritornellos which he had appointed.[17]

Not everyone approved, least of all the conservative John Evelyn:

> One of his Majesty's chaplains preached, after which, instead of the ancient, grave and solemn wind music accompanying the organ, was introduced a concert of twenty-four violins between every pause, after the French fantastical light way, better suiting a tavern or playhouse than a church.[18]

Charles encouraged a new generation of English composers, urging John Blow to develop his talents, and sending Pelham Humphrey to France and Italy to improve his style. The unquestionable genius to emerge from the nursery of the restored Chapel Royal was Henry Purcell, who was appointed Composer to the King's Violins in 1667 after the death of Matthew Locke. Purcell was also employed in the Chapel Royal, and he was active too in composing for the stage, so that all the dominant kinds of Restoration music lay within his scope. Many of his verse anthems for the Chapel Royal exploited the French manner still in fashion, having a sprightly overture, parts of which might be repeated as a sinfonia between the verses. The vocal parts tended to be exceptionally florid and melodious, the whole being driven by an energy of invention and resulting in a splendour of sound that gives the distinctively Purcellian tone. Purcell was able to achieve striking effects of sonorousness through his rich orchestration, his use of dissonances, and his attention to the bass line; in consequence his music seems to gain a special eloquence and authority. Such qualities were heard to best advantage in the court music he wrote for Charles II, James II, and William and Mary. The 'Birthday Odes', which became a feature of later Stuart court flattery, and the 'Songs of Welcome' to Charles and James on their periodic returns to Whitehall drew from Purcell the most splendid acclamations, even when he had to work with the deplorably banal texts provided by Shadwell, D'Urfey, Lee, and Tate. (These ornate and confident acts of royal worship could be said to form the musical complement to the baroque theatricality of Thornhill's frescoes in honour of William III on the ceilings at Greenwich.) Purcell's celebratory manner reached its height in the 'Odes for St Cecilia's Day' in the 1690s, when the purpose of the occasion, the praise of music's patron saint, gave him every incentive to provide the most richly textured scores for orchestral work yet heard, and to explore the range of the principal instruments in passages of virtuosity unprecedented in English music.

In the later years of his career, Purcell turned more and more to music for the theatre, writing incidental music for large numbers of Restoration plays. He wrote his one complete opera *Dido and Aeneas* in 1689, a chamber opera not for one of the public playhouses or the court, but for amateur performance. Even with the limited resources imposed by this occasion, however, there is a power of feeling which is new in Purcell as he phrases the emotional relationships between the lovers. The work follows the lead given by John Blow's small-scale court opera *Venus and Adonis* (*c.* 1682), which could claim to be the first English opera free from the masque elements of dance sequences, entries of interlude players, and special effects. *Dido and Aeneas* still retains its place in the theatre as fluent, integrated opera, with a unity of mood and passionate dramatic interaction. Purcell was not encouraged to write more operas, however, for the taste of the London audiences did not respond to this whole-hearted adoption of the recitative style. They retained their preference for the traditional use of spoken dramatic dialogue, though now increasingly interspersed with musical interludes and songs, and this 'mixed-media' approach became in effect the English alternative to opera. (We see here an indifference to consistency which has frequently characterized English divergence from the academic orthodoxies encouraged in the arts of France and Italy, where the tragedies of Corneille and Racine would never have suffered the intrusion of a comic fool, and the porticoes of Palladio could never have been coupled with a spire.) Purcell contributed extensively to such productions, but despite his genius, any sustained expressiveness is inhibited by the awkwardness of the form, and the works are rarely performed today.

With the re-establishment of the court at the Restoration, and the full resumption of aristocratic life, all the arts enjoyed a great renewal of patronage. The prospect of a settled future encouraged men to build, the restored royalists wanted portraits to record the recovery of their fortunes, and the compelling desire for pleasure in social life required music, fine settings, and more splendid fashions. The new society was very susceptible to French taste, for many of the exiled royalists had had some experience of France and the French court under the young Louis XIV. Costume was most obviously affected by French models, and the general adoption by gentlemen of the periwig was a new kind of cultural indebtedness. Intellectually, there was a vogue for methodizing the arts, by giving rules to them in the French Academic way, exemplified in Dryden's critical essays on satire, dramatic poesy and the like, or in the discussions about the purification of the language that we find in Dryden and Sprat, centring on what vocabulary was acceptable and what not, and on the need for consistency in levels of style. Following the French trend, gardening too became methodized, with the emphasis now on formal terraces and parterres, and a fondness for symmetrical floral patterns and long, clear vistas. The symbolical suggestiveness of the older gardens was lost on a society that preferred precision and explicitness in form and meaning. Architecture was also in danger of regularization: in 1664 Evelyn published his translation of Fréart's *Parallel between Ancient and Modern Architecture*, with many illustrations to enforce a correctness of neo-Classical detail and composition. Louis XIV's new buildings excited admiration in England; Wren went over in 1665 to study the new work at Versailles and the Louvre, and elsewhere in the Ile-de-France, meeting Bernini and also probably Mansart, the royal architects. Charles II envied Louis's absolutist regime, and its visual expression in stone, and while reluctantly aware that he would never achieve the same position in England, he was strongly drawn to grandiose building schemes that would show the power of the restored monarchy. Towards the end of his reign this tendency became stronger, resulting in the design and partial construction of a new palace by Wren at Winchester, in imitation of Versailles, and the erection of Chelsea Hospital along the lines of Les Invalides in Paris. Charles was always contemplating a splendid reconstruction of Whitehall, and he embarked on a huge new palace at Greenwich, of which one massive block designed by John Webb was raised in the 1660s, in a much more monumental style than anything previously erected by the Stuart kings.

A modified neo-Classical style in architecture gained rapid acceptance across the country, with a concession generally made to the English climate in the form of a pitched roof and prominent chimneys. The artisan tradition of gabled picturesque houses collapsed with surprising suddenness. There were still few professional architects, for there was no academy for training, so most of the new houses were designed by talented gentlemen amateurs such as Hugh May, who was responsible for Eltham Lodge in Surrey, and Cassiobury Park in Hertfordshire, and who undertook the remodelling of the staterooms at

Windsor. Sir Roger Pratt was another gifted amateur; his two outstanding houses have unfortunately been lost, Coleshill in Berkshire, destroyed by fire in 1952, and Clarendon House, Piccadilly, (Plate 6) demolished not long after the fall of its owner by the even more ambitious Duke of Albemarle, who built his own house on the site. Robert Hooke has been similarly mistreated by time and accident. This friend and associate of Wren was a most handsome designer: his Royal College of Physicians was a rich piece of Restoration work with a fine courtyard and an octagonal theatre over an arcaded base. This was all pulled down in the nineteenth century, as was his most famous building, Bethlehem Hospital, known as 'Bedlam,' in Moorfields (Plate 20). If architecture can have an elevating and harmonious influence over the spectator, Hooke's buildings at Bedlam should have cured more of the insane than any doctor's remedy. Hooke's other major work in London, Montague House, on the site of the British Museum, burned down in his own lifetime. Only the Monument to the Great Fire, and Ragley Hall in Warwickshire, survive as an unrepresentative record of one of the most imaginative of the Restoration architects.

The typical pattern of the Restoration great house was set by Clarendon House, begun for Lord Chancellor Clarendon in 1664. A large block of two main floors, with a central pediment peaking level with the roof line and usually framing three bays, projecting wings with firmly detailed quoins at the corners, a low-pitched roof often with a balustrade running the length of it, all topped with a cheerful cupola in the centre: this design can be found all over the country. It is exemplified to perfection at Belton House, Lincolnshire (begun 1684), whose architect is unknown, but whose design is a tribute to the excellence of a completely assured tradition of building.

Wren's emergence as the chief architect of the age (Plate 19) was almost accidental, for he was already Professor of Astronomy at Oxford before he started to try his hand at architecture. He began in the tradition of the gentleman amateur obliging his uncle Bishop Matthew Wren with a design for a chapel at Pembroke College, Cambridge, that the Bishop raised as a thanksgiving for having survived imprisonment in the Civil War days. He was then commissioned by his Oxford colleague Gilbert Sheldon, newly appointed Archbishop of Canterbury, to design the Sheldonian Theatre as a parting gift to the university, in 1663. This building emphatically established Wren's reputation. His original intention was to produce an archaeological reconstruction of the Roman Theatre of Marcellus, but his inventive spirit and eclectic habits led him to a distinctively original design, with an Italianate front rather like one of Palladio's church facades, a semicircular body consisting of a rusticated arcade with windows above, and a roof storey with rounded gable windows above that, surmounted by the obligatory cupola; there is an air of restrained festivity about the whole (Plate 19). The interior was quite surprising, one of the first baroque interiors in the country: an illusionist ceiling painted by Robert Streeter showed the canvas awnings that covered an antique theatre thrown back to reveal a clouded, crowded sky with an allegory of Truth descending on the Arts and Sciences ('the spirit of the Baroque descending on Oxford', perhaps).

It was of course the Great Fire that gave Wren the opportunity to stamp his character on the City of London. At first Wren was just one of the members of the rebuilding commission, along with Pratt and May, Hooke and Edward Jevons, and it was not until 1670 that he was given particular responsibility for the City churches. Forced to design for odd angles and inconvenient sites, he produced wonderful solutions to difficult problems in the fifty or so churches he rebuilt, their towers and spires being a free re-creation of their medieval antecedents. As one looks at them, one can appreciate Wren's freedom of invention, his evident pleasure in combining elements of the Classical style with his own fanciful motifs, and his aeriel ambitiousness. Yet one would not say that he was a fully baroque architect, for he shows always a certain intellectual restraint, partly from personal inclination, partly in deference to the Anglican mode. The Anglican influence is strong too in the plan of the churches, usually rectangular with no chancel as a sacred space set apart for priestly mysteries, but with large, well-lit auditoriums made for preaching and praying. The team of interior decorators brought together by Wren was, however, an innovation characteristic of the baroque spirit, whereby the various arts worked together to create an elevation of spirit through dynamic interaction. The highly carved woodwork, the exuberant plasterwork, and the elaborate wrought iron of these church interiors produced a buoyant atmosphere for the even-tempered worship of Restoration Anglicanism.

The building of the City churches was overshadowed in every respect by the erection of St Paul's. After several rejected designs, work on the cathedral began in 1675. The common feature of all the proposals was a vast dome, which represented to Wren the most formidable of constructional challenges which, if realized, would place London on equal terms architecturally with Rome, Florence, and Paris. The special significance of St Paul's for the arts in England, however, is that it forced into being a full architectural establishment and provided a training ground for craftsmen of all kinds who would spread out later to work on country houses and churches all over England and transmit their skills in a broad tradition of craftsmanship that would run throughout the eighteenth century until Regency times. Around Wren a new generation of architects grew up: Hawksmoor, who was his chief assistant at St Paul's, Vanbrugh, Gibbs, Talman, and Archer. The team of craftsmen that Wren assembled for St Paul's, most of whom also contributed to the decoration of the City churches, included that French master of wrought iron, Jean Tijou, Grinling Gibbons in wood-carving and sculpture, and his associates Edward Pierce, Jonathan Maine, and Caius Cibber, and the plasterers John Grove, Henry Doogood, and Edward Goudge: these were the masters who, with their apprentices, would produce the intensely civilized interiors of the later seventeenth century.

Once William and Mary settled into England, they lost no time in exploiting Wren's talents for their own building projects. Both rulers disliked Whitehall, preferring Kensington Palace and Hampton Court. Wren remodelled Kensington, giving it a pleasant domestic air with a suitably Dutch character. At Hampton Court he added a superbly designed courtyard to the existing Tudor courts. But it was at Greenwich that Wren achieved his greatest triumphs, when William and Mary agreed to allow the site to be used for a naval hospital. On this waterside setting Wren composed an open courtyard, where he incorporated John Webb's block for Charles II into his design; then, setting dome against dome, balancing hall with chapel, he contrived a deep perspective view from the river, leading the eye along the immense length of his colonnades to the terminus of the Queen's House, built long ago by Inigo Jones. It is a theatrical composition, and in its way a tribute to Jones as the source of the neo-Classical style in England.

Painting in the Restoration period did not undergo any major alterations comparable to those that affected architecture. Portrait remained the ascendant mode. Van Dyck's successor Peter Lely, who had maintained his appeal all through the Commonwealth years, continued to dominate the Restoration scene. Lely responded to the new society by adding a greater luxuriousness to his style, lingering over the richly tissued costume of his sitters, and enhancing the sensuous lines of their features. In an observant phrase, Alexander Pope remarked, 'the sleepy eye that spoke the melting soul' when he wrote of Lely; but there is also great pride and determination in many of his male subjects. He was an apt artist for an age of pleasure, yet he did not let the grandeur of the times pass unacknowledged. Although he had an enormous practice and numerous assistants, he kept up a remarkably high quality in his work. The same cannot be said of Godfrey Kneller who succeeded Lely (who died in 1680) as the fashionable artist of the last decades: his lacklustre portraits too frequently have a monotony of brown tones, similarity of facial types, and a deferential approach to the subject.

A new development in painting appeared in the late 1660s: the vogue for fresco, which no doubt owed much to French examples of

painted walls and ceilings at Versailles. The houses of the Restoration
aristocracy now included mythological or heroic fantasies that climbed
up the staircase and spread out along the ceilings of the staterooms.
These amplified the achievements of the family or advertised the
culture, magnanimity, or just the wealth of the owner. The most
sought-after artists were Antonio Verrio, an Italian who had worked
in France who came over in 1672, and Louis Laguerre, who came to
England about 1684. Both enjoyed extensive patronage.[19] Their work
has not stood up well to English conditions, where damp and lack of
light have a depressing effect, but its character is one of the revealing
signs of the heroic view of themselves and their age adopted by the
later Stuart aristocracy. Their sense of having recovered the nation
from a disastrous political lapse – a feeling vastly intensified after the
'Glorious Revolution' of 1688 – their pride in England's trade and prosperity, in her naval power, and in the high spirit raised by the wars
against the Dutch (which were generally disastrous) and against France
(usually victorious), their strong conviction of being firmly in control
of the country, all these emotions find expression in the heroic frescoes
on their walls. The passion for heroic drama during this period is
another manifestation of the same mood (see pp. 119–20).[20]

The work that Verrio and Laguerre did at Hampton Court may
serve as an example of the brief phase of baroque art that bloomed in
late Stuart England; it also gives us a glimpse of the iconography
employed to glorify William III, the last of the Stuarts to use the arts
effectively to impose his image. Verrio and Laguerre use as the central
motif of their design the figure of Hercules, long associated with the
House of Orange and now introduced into England as a royal ante-
type. On the walls of the grand staircase, William in his Herculean
lionskin performs his heroic tasks of maintaining the State and the
Protestant religion, under a ceiling in which the zodiacal sign of Leo
is ascendant. The *trompe-l'œil* columns that form the setting for the
scene rise immense upon a base painted with military trophies. Allegorical figures mingle with the heroes of the Revolution in a scene of
considerable vitality and confusion, rendered in powerful, heavy
colours. The Herculean motif extends throughout Wren's new block
at Hampton: sculpted lionskins drape the window frames of the Fountain Court, on one side of which the Labours of Hercules were painted
by Laguerre; the sculpture of the pediment facing the garden presents
William as Hercules conquering Superstition, Tyranny and Fury –
recollections of 1688 and William's wars against France – while Fame
leads him to the Arts of Peace.[21] Heroic decoration reached its height
at Hampton Court and at Greenwich, where Thornhill's ceiling paintings in the Painted Hall again glorify the reign of King William, and
heroic architecture attained its peaks in the early years of the eighteenth

century in the epic conceptions of Vanbrugh at Castle Howard and Blenheim.

Our impression of the late seventeenth century is perhaps too heavily coloured by the satirical literature of Dryden and Swift, intent on mocking and deflating their society or their political enemies; they had ample cause in the loose morals, peculations, and political viciousness of contemporary public life, but the visual arts bring before us a nobler idea of the governing class that exaggerates their merit as much as satire undervalues their ability.

Notes

1. For a detailed study of all aspects of Prince Henry's career, see Roy Strong, *Henry Prince of Wales and England's Lost Renaissance* (1986) and J. W. Williamson, *The Myth of the Conqueror. Prince Henry Stuart, a Study in Seventeenth-Century Personation* (New York, 1978).

2. One object that Arundel failed to secure was an Egyptian obelisk that was lying in Rome. Difficulties of transport proved insuperable, and eventually the obelisk was used by Bernini in his scheme for the Piazza Navona.

3. The fullest account of Arundel as a collector is by David Howarth, *Lord Arundel and his Circle* (1985).

4. The paintings are respectively in the Royal Collection, the National Gallery, and the Louvre. Roy Strong explores the iconography of Charles I in Van Dyck's portraits in *Charles I on Horseback* (1972). The most compendious account of the painter's English career is Oliver Millar, *Van Dyck in England* (1982).

5. Wotton's little treatise can be supplemented by Peacham's chapter on architecture in *The Compleat Gentleman* (1622) and Bacon's essay 'On Building' (1625). Bacon is primarily interested in the layout of the great house, and not much concerned with the style of the building.

6. Roy Strong, *The Renaissance Garden in England* (1979), pp. 120–22 (Twickenham), 123 (Ware Park), 211 (Packwood House).

7. Sir William Temple gives a long, plain, detailed account of the Countess of Bedford's garden at Moor Park in his essay 'The Gardens of Epicurus', but, writing two generations after its creation, he cannot retrieve the imaginative *raison d'être* of such a garden.

8. See Aubrey's life of William Oughtred in *Brief Lives*, edited by O. L. Dick (1949), p. 224. Given the philosophic associations of grottoes, it is possible, as Roy Strong suggests (*Renaissance Garden*, p. 103), that Prospero's cell might have been imagined as a grotto.

9. Henry Hawkins, *Partheneia Sacra* (1633), edited by Iain Fletcher (1950), p. 14. Quoted in Strong, *Renaissance Garden*, p. 210.

10. *The Letters of Sir Thomas Browne*, edited by G. Keynes (1946), p. 301.

11. See Charles Webster, *The Great Instauration* (1975), pp. 446–83, for a detailed account of agricultural improvement in this period, and for information about the practical treatises on the subject that appeared during the Commonwealth.

12. Consider for example how the popular coranto that Sir Bulstrode Whitelocke had composed was played whenever he attended the Blackfriars Theatre in the 1630s to acknowledge his presence in the audience.

13. Diana Poulton, *John Dowland*, second edition (1982), p. 347. This book provides a comprehensive account of Dowland's work and its social setting.

14. Ibid., pp. 72–73, for an account of the change of taste in the 1610s. For a detailed contemporary account of the character of music accompanying a Jacobean masque, see Campion's descriptions of the musical accompaniments to Lord Hay's Masque (1607) in *The Works of Thomas Campion*, edited by Walter R. Davis (New York, 1969), pp. 211–30.

15. See Richard Luckett's account of Lawes in the entry on 'Music' in *The Diary of Samuel Pepys*, edited by R. Latham and W. Matthews (1983), x, 270 (the companion volume). Luckett gives an admirable account of music in Pepy's lifetime.

16. From Ben Jonson's prefatory description of *Lovers Made Men*, in *Ben Jonson*, edited by C. H. Herford and P. Simpson (Oxford, 1941), 454.

17. Thomas Tudway, quoted in J. A. Westrup, *Purcell* (1980 edition), p. 199.

18. John Evelyn, Diary, 21 December 1662.

19. Verrio's major work was at Euston Hall, Arlington House, Cassiobury House, Montague House, Burghley House, Ham House, Chatsworth, Whitehall and Windsor. Laguerre's was at Chatsworth, Sudbury, Burghley, Hampton Court, Canons, Petworth, and Blenheim.

20. Sir William Temple, Swift's patron, could write an essay 'Of Heroic Virtue' (*c.* 1685) in the belief that it was a quality not irrelevant to his society.

21. See Judith Hook, *The Baroque Age in England* (1976), p. 138, for an account of these decorations.

Sir Henry Wotton

If we wish to appreciate the cultural and intellectual opportunities that were available in the earlier seventeenth century to well-educated, open-minded men and women who were advantageously placed in their society, we shall need to look at individual case histories. These brief surveys of the lives of Sir Henry Wotton, a diplomat, and Lady Anne Clifford, a great heiress, allow us to form an idea of Stuart civilisation as embodied in two notable figures.

Sir Henry Wotton is representative of those gentlemen of broad general culture who conducted the business of the Jacobean State with competence, and who had an international outlook that went together with a great love of the arts. Wotton was born in 1568 into a well-established Kentish family which had land and moderate wealth. He attended Winchester College, and then proceeded to New College, Oxford, and finally to Hart Hall, where he began a friendship with John Donne which would endure throughout their lives. From his student days he was fascinated by all things Italian, and when he came to undertake the foreign travels that enabled young men of good family to study statecraft, languages, and manners at first hand, it was to Italy that he gravitated. From 1589 to 1594 Wotton was abroad, travelling first through Germany to Vienna and then to Prague, where the eccentric Emperor Rudolph II lived in his great Gothic castle, fascinated by alchemy, clockwork, and the occult, and patronizing a flourishing Mannerist culture in the arts. From Prague Wotton went to Italy, where he remained for some two years, staying much in hospitable Venice and making three trips to Rome – disguised as a German, for the Papacy was at war with England. His experience there gave him a lasting dislike of Roman politics, for their ruthlessness and cunning, and made him for ever an enemy of the Jesuits who marshalled the forces of the Counter-Reformation. He ventured as far as Naples, where he may have met Tasso, before moving on to frequent the court of the Grand Duke of Tuscany at Florence. After his long perilous exposure to Catholic culture, Wotton fortified his Protestant beliefs by staying for nearly a year in Geneva, where he lodged with Isaac Casaubon, the Greek scholar and apologist for Calvinism.

By the time he returned to England, Wotton was well equipped to seek a diplomatic career or become a secretary to some great man. The Earl of Essex recognized his abilities, and Wotton entered his service; the Earl's political ambitions were leading him to construct what was in effect a private diplomatic service, in rivalry with that of Burghley. Essex, however, found direct action more attractive than diplomacy, and it was not long before Wotton found himself embarking on the Cadiz expedition of 1596, along with Donne and many other hopeful young aspirants to fortune. After that loyal exercise in buccaneering, he sailed the following year with Essex and Raleigh on the less effective Azores expedition. In 1599, being now one of Essex's secretaries, Wotton accompanied him to Ireland and endured his catastrophic mismanagement of the Irish campaign. Foreseeing the ruin of his patron, Wotton opportunely removed himself abroad before Essex raised his futile rebellion in 1601.

Wotton went to Florence, and before long was employed by the Grand Duke on secret business with James VI of Scotland, warning him of a Catholic plot. On this occasion, Wotton passed himself off as an Italian in Scotland, and James was so impressed with his conduct and his political *savoir-faire* that, when he came to the English throne in 1603, he soon appointed Wotton to a major diplomatic post, Ambassador to Venice.

Venice was at that time a liberal state, inclined to be friendly with England and hostile to Rome and Spain, both of which powers had designs on its territory and on its relatively tolerant policies, which they viewed as a betrayal of the militant Catholicism of the Counter-Reformation. (For example, Padua, a city in Venetian territory, had a university which accommodated many Protestant students, especially in its famous school of medicine which provided the best medical education in Europe.) To Venice then in 1610 came Sir Henry, and he was most favourably received, for Venice regarded England as a potential ally in any conflict with Spain or the Papal States. Once established in his Venetian palace, Wotton turned his residence into a kind of academy for his retinue of advisers and young English followers: they studied the classics together, read the books of the moment in English and Italian, engaged in debates, tried chemical experiments, and made music together, with Wotton playing the viola da gamba. They also worshipped together under the ministry of the Anglican chaplain. Wotton himself was attracted to the music of the Venetian palaces and churches – this was the time of Giovanni Gabrieli and of early Monteverdi. He was also developing a great responsiveness to Venetian painting and architecture. Titian, Tintoretto, Veronese, and the Bellinis worked their spell on him, and he had ample access to the palazzi where so many works of art hung in the settings for which they were originally intended. He collected paintings himself and also acted as an agent for Robert Cecil, Earl of Salisbury, the King's chief minister. Wotton's knowledge and advocacy of Venetian art was decisive in forming the taste of leading courtiers back in England. As the only official representative of England in Italy, he was in a uniquely favourable position to advise on works of art in the early years of the century, and he could obtain paintings on favourable terms. He sent paintings back for Cecil and also for Prince Henry, whom he admired beyond measure, and whose portrait hung in his study in Venice; later he would buy paintings on behalf of the Duke of Buckingham.

Wotton was a great beneficiary of Venetian culture; what he wished to give the Venetians in return was an experience of Protestantism. King James's policy and Wotton's personal desire ran together here. James hoped that the Venetians, who were at odds with Rome and who had expelled the Jesuits from their republic, might prove responsive to Protestant doctrines, and allow the practice of that religion in their state. Wotton had a discreetly evangelical tendency. He tried in private conferences to convert the theological counsellor to the Republic, Paulo Sarpi, to Anglicanism, but Sarpi remained faithful to the Catholic Church, even though he was no admirer of the Pope. Wotton circulated Protestant books among his acquaintances, and worked tactfully to establish a Protestant church in Venice, hoping to engage the services of the Italian Protestant Giovanni Diodati (whose son Charles would be one of Milton's closest friends). None of Wotton's schemes bore fruit. In 1610 he formally presented to the Doge King James's book *A Premonition to all most Mighty Monarchs, Kings, Free Princes and States of Christendom*, that offered a defence of Protestant principles and a warning against papal ambition, calling for a united front against Rome; but the Senate laid it by unread.

Having gained no ground in these religious manœuvrings, Wotton terminated his first embassy. But before he returned, in one of his last dispatches he notified King James of the remarkable discoveries that Galileo had made with his new telescope, detecting unknown stars in that region of the heavens hitherto believed unalterable. Most likely he also wrote to his friend John Donne about these developments and discussed them on his return to England, enabling Donne to work them into his long philosophic poem *The First Anniversary* (1611), which pondered on the signs of decay in the universe and expressed the bewilderment that men felt at the changing world-view: 'And new Philosophy calls all in doubt. . . .' Several verse-letters from Donne to Wotton survive, as do various private letters between the two men, testifying to their community of interest and closeness of spirit.

On his return to England, Wotton now became deeply involved in negotiations to arrange a marriage contract between Prince Henry and a princess of Savoy, a project that was encouraged by King James as part of his grand strategy for binding European states by marriage alliances that would help to harmonize Christendom. Off to Turin went Wotton to prepare the ground, but in 1612 Prince Henry died and the scheme unravelled. The same year had seen the death of Robert Cecil, Wotton's principal patron, and predictably, at a time when both his major supporters had gone, Wotton managed to run foul of King James who took offence at Wotton's notorious remark that 'an ambassador is an honest man sent to lie abroad for the good of his country'. He was out of favour for two years, until the King drew on his abilities again, sending him on a brief embassy to the Hague, and then back to Venice for another term as ambassador (1616–19). Here he renewed his contacts, and reverted to his old scheme of planting Protestantism in the Republic. Much energy went into attempts to set up a Protestant seminary on the borders of the State, but the Venetian senators had no intention of allowing such a contentious project to succeed.

More unrewarding service to the State followed when James

ordered him to undertake an embassy to the Holy Roman Emperor, Ferdinand II, at Vienna with the aim of securing a truce in the bitter religious war that had broken out over Bohemia's offer of its crown to the Protestant Elector Palatine from Heidelberg (whose wife was King James's daughter). No expedition could have been more futile, given the resolve of the Habsburgs to destroy the Protestant threat to their control of the Empire, and Wotton returned with all his pleas rejected. It was, however, typical of his intellectual curiosity that he should have broken his journey at Linz to meet the astronomer Kepler, and urge him to move to England where he promised an admiring reception.

Once again Wotton returned to Venice, on his third and final embassy, maintaining cordial relations between England and the Serene Republic. His main problem in this phase was coping with a visit from the less than serene Countess of Arundel, who came to reside in Venice in 1619 with a large train, and who became involved in a tangle of misunderstandings and cross-purposes with rumours of sedition and infidelity. Wotton and the Countess did not see eye to eye, and there was mutual irritation. Wotton had not got on well with the Arundels in the past, and the incident moved him to be more active in seeking out paintings and works of art for the Arundels' rival as a collector, the Duke of Buckingham, securing for him a number of desirable Titians.

At the end of 1623 Wotton's last Venetian embassy ended and he returned home. His combination of diplomatic skills and connoisseurship in the arts was one that was now becoming increasingly common in England's representatives abroad. Sir Dudley Carleton, who alternated with him at Venice, was a man of similar talents, active in the art markets for patrons at home or on his own behalf; Sir Thomas Roe at Constantinople was another such, and also Sir Isaac Wake in Holland. Part of their mission abroad, as they understood it, was to expand the cultural frontiers of England as well as represent her political interests.

One of Wotton's first acts on his return was to write and publish a short treatise on architecture which preserved his experience of living in the most modern and refined architectural region of Italy and communicated to Englishmen his knowledge of the theory and style of neo-Classical architecture, as well as his sense of the amenity of the buildings he admired. Wotton had purchased drawings by Palladio while in Venice, and loved the proportional grace of his designs. He writes enticingly in The Elements of Architecture of the civilized, elegant, and noble way of life that may be led in the setting of the architecture of humanism.

In 1624, at the age of fifty-six, Wotton was appointed Provost of

Eton, succeeding the classical scholar Sir Henry Savile. Here he settled down to a congenial life of academic routine. He contemplated more than he achieved: he thought of writing books on the arts of Ancient Rome, a history of the Reformation, a history of England, a life of Luther and a life of Donne. None was forthcoming. He did, however, exercise his political judgement by writing a comparison of two court favourites he had known, Essex and Buckingham. He put together a brief 'Survey of Education' in 1630, a piece of 'moral architecture' as he described it to the King, which offered an optimistic and aphoristic account of what might be achieved with young responsive spirits by apt tuition. He also wrote a 'Panegyric' of Charles I, which might have spoken for many committed royalists, praising the King for his devoted care for the doctrine and dignity of the Church of England, for the purity of his personal life, and for his attention to the business of state. The glory of his reign is in the flourishing of the arts: the royal collections are seen as a sign of distinction of mind and elevation of spirit. Wotton also now gave time to gathering together the poems he had written on various occasions, some formal, some witty, but most marked by a certain philosophic power of reflection.

One incident of Wotton's later days deserves to be recorded, and that was the visit that Milton paid him in 1638, when the two men talked of ancient authors and Milton asked for advice about his impending visit to Italy. Afterwards, Milton sent Wotton a copy of *Comus*, which Sir Henry acknowledged with a letter of high critical praise. 'I should much commend the tragical part of it if the lyrical did not so ravish me with a certain Dorique delicacy in your songs and odes: whereunto I must plainly confess to have seen yet nothing parallel in our language.' Milton was so gratified by the letter that he printed it in his *Poems* of 1645, where it stands as an act of recognition of the younger poet by a distinguished arbiter of the older generation.

In his Eton period Wotton developed a warm friendship with Izaak Walton, who incorporated many fond reminiscences of him both as fisherman and as 'easy philosopher' in *The Compleat Angler* (1653). It was Walton who eventually wrote the life of Wotton and acted as his literary executor, putting together a collection of his writings under the title of *Reliquiae Wottonianae* (1651) and prefacing it with a biography. Walton's 'Life' emphasizes Wotton's serene temperament and his lifelong fidelity to the cause of the Church of England, noting his tireless efforts to extend the influence of Protestantism in Venice. The character that Walton transmits is that of a secular saint of Anglicanism; but Walton had a special interest in manufacturing saints for an Anglican pantheon, as his other lives of Donne, Herbert, Hooker, and Sanderson reveal. A less partial estimate might judge Wotton to have been a highly civilized diplomat whose major initiatives were either mistimed or frustrated by circumstance; his more profound contribution to English society was to act as an important transmitter of Italian taste and experience. He was, everyone agreed, the perfect 'Englishman Italianate', but his love of Italy and Italian arts never compromised his Anglican faith. Wotton died in 1639.

Further Reading

Reliquiae Wottonianae (1651).
Logan Pearsall Smith, *The Life and Letters of Sir Henry Wotton* (Oxford, 1907; reprinted 1966).

Lady Anne Clifford

The long life of Lady Anne Clifford, which spanned much of the seventeenth century, provides a striking history of social interaction and cultural involvement that embraced both court and country. She was the daughter of George Clifford, the third Earl of Cumberland, the soldier and adventurer who was Queen Elizabeth's Champion, and whose brilliant image as the Knight of Pendragon Castle, in the annual tournaments before the Queen, survives in one of Hilliard's most famous miniatures. Her mother was Margaret Russell, daughter of the second Earl of Bedford. Born in the North in 1590, Lady Anne was brought up at the court of Elizabeth in the expectation that she would become a maid of honour to the Queen, and was given a broad humanist education under the guidance of her tutor, the poet Samuel Daniel. She entered fully into social life in the early years of the new reign, becoming a companion of Queen Anne and dancing as one of the principal masquers in the early masques of the Stuart court. In 1608 she embodied one of the elements of Ideal Beauty in Jonson's *Masque of Beauty*, a neo-Platonic entertainment attractively wrapped for court consumption in exquisite costumes, set amid symbolic architecture and, according to Jonson, danced to perfection by the Queen's ladies. Next year she appeared in *The Masque of Queens*, impersonating Berenice, Queen of Egypt, famous for her long blonde hair which, mythology recounts, became a constellation. Lady Anne's hair, she recalled in a diary, fell below her calves in her youth. Inigo Jones's design for her costume on this occasion survives to show her dancing, apparently bare-breasted, in tissues of green, carnation, and white. She danced too in the masque offered by Queen Anne to celebrate Prince Henry's creation as Prince of Wales in 1610, Samuel Daniel's *Tethys Festival*. In this masque, the rivers of England paid homage to the Prince, and Lady Anne danced the part of the River Aire that ran through her native Skipton.

In 1609 she married Richard Sackville, who shortly thereafter became Earl of Dorset. She moved to Knole, the house of the Sackvilles near Sevenoaks, and took on the duties of entertainment that fell to the mistress of a great house near to London. She now began to engage in prolonged litigation to try to secure the reversion of the vast Clifford estates in northern England which her father had improperly made over to his brother the new Earl of Cumberland and his heirs. The passion for lawsuits that was such a malignant feature of Tudor and Stuart England had depressing effects on Lady Anne's life, for she was entangled with suits over land inheritance for over thirty years. (This zeal for litigation helps to explain why so many gentlemen went to the Inns of Court as an essential part of their practical education, knowing they would inevitably need to protect their interests at law; conversely, the fact that so many gentlemen had been to the Inns of Court tended to encourage legal confrontations.) Eventually King James personally intervened in her case, acting as the English Solomon, and decided against her, but though temporarily checked, she never gave up her quest. In her private life, her relations with her husband alternated between affection and hostility. He was handsome, high-spirited, spendthrift, and unfaithful; addicted to gambling, he ran down the Sackville fortunes, and persistently tried to get his hands on his wife's estates and assets. She fought him off with even greater persistence. They had two children that lived, and several that did not. Increasingly, Lady Anne's diary tells of neglect, and she began to settle into the routine of embroidery and religious devotion that was the lot of so many women who were discarded by their husbands.

The Earl of Dorset died in 1624. Lady Anne lived a strict and prudent widow for several years before agreeing to marry again. As an heiress who might still inherit the Cumberland estates, and with two daughters to establish in the world, she felt the need to protect herself against exploitation and so allied herself to one of the noblest families in the kingdom by becoming the second wife of Philip, fourth Earl of Pembroke. She had known him for many years, from the time when they had danced together in the early masques. Philip was brusque, ill-tempered, devoted to hunting, but also a considerable connoisseur of the arts. It was probably a marriage of convenience on both sides. As Countess of Pembroke at Wilton she formed a close friendship with George Herbert, who had just entered holy orders and been appointed to the family living of Bemerton outside the gates of Wilton. Herbert must have acted as Lady Anne's chaplain, and probably as her spiritual adviser; the one letter from him to her that survives has an attractive, friendly tone that speaks of a familiar relationship between them. Of Lady Anne's piety there can be no doubt; she was a committed Anglican who maintained her devotional practices uninterruptedly throughout the Commonwealth years. In the 1630s she sat to Van Dyck for the great Pembroke family portrait that still hangs at Wilton (and which is discussed on pp. 51–2). She also involved herself in the rebuilding of Wilton, for which purpose she and her husband seem to have engaged Inigo Jones to design a new Italianate palazzo and Isaac de Caus to lay out the gardens in the Italian Mannerist style with extensive waterworks, grottoes, and mythological statuary. Whether Jones carried out his part of the work, or whether the whole enterprise fell to de Caus we do not know, because the building history of Wilton in the 1630s and 1640s is confused, and much of the house had to be rebuilt, this time by John Webb, Jones's assistant, after the fire of 1649. Given Lady Anne's long interest in architecture, she must have been closely involved in these projects.

Throughout her life Lady Anne was a great reader, and we are fortunate to have a painting of her, a triptych in fact (done in the mid-1640s, and now in Appleby Castle), depicting different phases of her life, which shows her surrounded by books and which enables us to form an idea of the scope of her reading, for the titles are meticulously marked. In one pile lie Camden's *Britannia*, Ortelius's maps of the world, and Cornelius Agrippa on the vanity of science. There are books of Roman history and philosophy. Castiglione's *Courtier* is there, with Montaigne's *Essays* and Gerard's *Herbal*. Among the works of imaginative fiction are Ovid's *Metamorphoses*, Chaucer's works, Sidney's *Arcadia*, Spenser's works, and *Don Quixote*, and her taste in modern poetry would be approved today: Donne, Jonson, and Herbert. The works of Fulke Greville make an unexpected appearance, but Henry Wotton's *Elements of Architecture* is altogether in character. There are books by Daniel and the Protestant poet Du Bartas, both of whom dedicated writings to her. In general, religious books predominate, however, and one notes particularly the Bible, Augustine's *The City of God*, Eusebius, Boethius, and the sermons of Joseph Hall and John Donne. The painting provides an excellent record of the intellectual horizons of a remarkable woman.

In 1643 her cousin the Earl of Cumberland died, and all the alienated estates reverted to her by default of a male heir. Suddenly she became the greatest lady of the North, owning large parts of Cumberland, Westmorland, and northern Yorkshire. But the Civil War was in progress, and she could not take possession of her inheritance. She was for the King, her husband for Parliament; political differences widened the temperamental division between them, and they spent much time apart. Not until 1649 was she able to travel north to survey her estates, and hardly had she arrived when she received the news that the Earl of Pembroke had died in London. She now determined to settle in the North and rule over her territory like a benevolent provincial monarch, which she did for more than a quarter of a century. Her dominant passion became building – or rebuilding. All the ruined castles in her domains were restored and made habitable: Skipton, Appleby, Barden, Brougham, Brough, and Pendragon. Indefatigably she travelled between her many residences, supervising the work of reconstruction, meeting her tenants, settling disputes, establishing herself as the supreme power. No one intervened in her remote activities, and it was as if the feudal days had returned to the North. She built churches too, in the 1650s when the Anglican Church was officially proscribed, and in the 1660s: two churches at Brougham and the church at Mallerstang are hers, and she partially rebuilt the church at Appleby. She favoured a plain Gothic style that expressed continuity with the late Middle Ages when the Cliffords had enjoyed their greatest exercise of power; her furnishings too were archaic in character, the woodwork being carved for the most part in a peculiar form of the Jacobean style. Throughout the 1650s she kept up the Anglican service in her chapels.

Her feeling for history was profound. She placed inscriptions on most of the buildings she built or restored to record her own sense of acting in history, and, as the last of the Cliffords, she went to considerable lengths to ensure that the greatness of her family would be remembered. The rebuilding of the castles was one form of memorial to the Cliffords, but she also commissioned elaborate books of genealogy and a grand family portrait. Monuments fascinated her: her early diaries record several visits to Westminster Abbey to admire the tombs that were then being installed in large numbers. She was moved to raise a monument there to Edmund Spenser, whose poetry evoked most eloquently the chivalric age she loved in her imagination. Naturally she buried her own family well. The effigy she commissioned for her mother's tomb in Appleby church is of the highest quality, owing something in style to Queen Elizabeth's memorial in London. Lady Anne's own tomb, erected in her lifetime, had no effigy, but above the black marble slab she placed a display of twenty-four coats of arms which chronicled the descent of the Cliffords from the time of King John. It was a final vindication of her right to inherit her great territories, for which she had fought so long, but it was also the last tribute to an ancient family made by a woman who was in love with the past. Lady Anne Clifford died in 1676.

Chapter 4
Cultural Life during the Civil Wars and the Commonwealth, 1642–1659

'A warlike, various, and a tragical age is best to write of, but worst to write in.' Such was Cowley's view as he looked back on the 1640s in the preface to his *Poems* of 1656. Yet these disturbed times were remarkably favourable to publication, if not to imaginative invention, and a glance at the volumes of poetry that came out in the decade following the outbreak of civil war in 1642 shows what a range of notable work first appeared in this period. Cavalier verse is prominent, with Carew's *Poems* published in 1642 and again in 1651, Waller's *Poems* enjoying two editions in 1645, Suckling's *Fragmenta Aurea* coming out in 1646, reprinted 1648, Shirley's *Poems* in 1646, Cowley's *The Mistress* in 1647, Herrick's *Hesperides* in 1648, and Lovelace's *Lucasta* in 1649. Crashaw brought out his volume of Laudian devotional verse, *Steps to the Temple*, in 1646, which met with such demand that it was reprinted in 1648. Vaughan published steadily through this period, with his *Poems* in 1646, *Silex Scintillans* in 1650, and *Olor Iscanus* in 1651. One of the great volumes of poetry of the century appeared in 1645, when Milton released his *Poems*. There are various reasons for this outpouring of verse, the most obvious being the collapse of censorship which freed poets from the obligation of official approval for their work: this must have encouraged many poets to seek a wider audience for their verse than polite circulation in manuscript allowed. The relative freedom of the press, then, must have been a factor, but in addition there must have been a widespread conviction among poets that the old safe Stuart world had gone for ever, and their true audience had been scattered by war, despoliation, and death. The poetry that had been composed for use at court, or for gentlemanly recreation, or as a devotional aid for worship in a now desecrated church, might as well be published to find what audience it could.

Milton's *Poems* definitely had the air of belonging to a finished phase of creativity. The latest poem was his Latin elegy for Diodati from 1639, while the last of the English poems was 'Lycidas', composed in 1637, whose closing promise of 'Tomorrow to fresh woods and pastures new' looked sadly unfulfilled in 1645. The majority of the poems date from Milton's college days, and from his years of intensive study in the early 1630s, and they reflect his engagement with a world where Caroline values are firmly established. There is much pastoral writing here of a kind fashionable at court: Milton appears sympathetic to a ceremonious Anglicanism in poems such as the elegy on Bishop Lancelot Andrewes and 'Il Penseroso', and the most substantial work in the collection is 'A Masque, presented at Ludlow Castle', otherwise *Comus*. The composition of a masque, the most celebratory and idealizing art form of the age, and one closely associated with the court and with the honour of the aristocracy, would have characterized Milton as a man hoping to make his career in court circles, an impression strengthened by the pastoral entertainment 'Arcades' that he wrote for the Countess of Derby, and by his collaboration with the musician Henry Lawes of the Chapel Royal. Milton in these early poems seems like a figure of the Caroline establishment, but with vaster ambitions and more philosophic elevation than any of his contemporaries. The voice of a Christian prophet preparing to pronounce on God's providence towards mankind is intermittently heard, and there is much evidence of Milton's aspiring to a mastery of neo-Platonic systems of thought through which he might apprehend the essential unity of the created world and intellectually perceive the operations of divinity. All these carefully planned ambitions and his establishment allegiances must have seemed part of a vanished world when the *Poems* were published in 1645, by which time Milton had been engaged for several years in radical pamphleteering against the royalist cause and in favour of a root-and-branch reformation of the Church. Some twenty years were to elapse before Milton again gave his full attention to poetry.

Many of the poems in the collections by Carew, Waller, and Herrick must also have had a somewhat dated air, for they belonged mainly to the 1630s, or even to the 1620s, and preserved the generous, civilized, complimentary manner that had prevailed in the courtly world. Discussions of the good life, of the niceties of love, of the virtues of friends or the excellencies of the royal family, which had sustained poetry through the serene Caroline years, must have had a considerable nostalgic appeal when they were published in the 1640s. Suckling's poems, gallant yet sardonic, amorous, and frequently erotic, have the modish air of a man who has grown impatient with the restraints and courtesies of ritualized wooing and wishes to let some fresh air into the system. The flair with which his poems are conducted recommended them to readers throughout the disordered times, and a third edition was called for in 1659.

The poet who most tellingly registered the effects of political division and war on the leisured and refined society of Stuart England was Richard Lovelace. His mistresses – Lucasta, Aramantha, Ellinda,

Althea – were perfections of their kind, and he observed their graces and their gestures, their slightest allurements, with an eye as sharp and appreciative as Herrick's: Aramantha's dishevelling her hair, Lucasta's breathtaking manipulation of her fan, her tantalizing descent to the bath, these are moments of Cavalier rapture; yet there are poems too when the honours due to love are set aside in favour of the imperatives of war, and when love becomes a memory which serves to counteract the misery of political imprisonment. The song 'To Lucasta, going to the Wars' perfectly catches the crisis of the times as the courtier, so long inured to peace, prepares to meet the challenge of war in a spirit of Cavalier gallantry, while 'To Althea from Prison' rises above misfortune to express the poet's royalist sympathies with a conviction that makes a victory of defeat:

> When, like committed linnets, I
>   With shriller throat shall sing
> The sweetness, mercy, majesty,
>   And glories of my King;
> When I shall voice aloud how good
>   He is, how great should be,
> Enlarged winds, that curl the flood,
>   Know no such liberty.
>
> Stone walls do not a prison make,
>   Nor iron bars a cage;
> Minds innocent and quiet take
>   That for an hermitage;
> If I have freedom in my love,
>   And in my soul am free,
> Angels alone, that soar above,
>   Enjoy such liberty.
>   (ll. 17–32)

Lovelace's ode to his 'noble friend' Charles Cotton, entitled 'The Grasshopper', advances to a new height of distinction the poem of friendship that had been so satisfying a feature of Caroline verse, for the adversity of the times now discloses the true value of that bond. The grasshopper as an image of the carefree Cavaliers is most aptly chosen, and the pastoral evocation of the Caroline summer now abruptly ended, overtaken by a political winter, is movingly and powerfully achieved:

> But ah, the sickle! Golden ears are cropt;
>   Ceres and Bacchus bid good night;

Sharp frosty fingers all your flowers have topt,
  And what scythes spared, winds shave off quite.

Poor verdant fool, and now green ice!

(ll. 13–16)

The retreat into private life that follows, where friendship, poetry, and wine provide the Horatian consolations for the loss of ascendancy, was the lot of many royalist gentlemen after the Civil Wars: the literary ideal of retirement took on a new significance for the losing side, as political circumstances forced them out of public activities, and poetry such as Lovelace's helped to mitigate the experience of defeat.

The popularity of Crashaw's poetry may come as a surprise, but it shows the strength of high Anglican sentiment throughout the 1640s, and suggests that many men and women found Crashaw's enraptured contemplation of the sacraments and mysteries of Christianity a valuable aid to their own devotions. As formal worship in the Church of England was closed down, it is probable that volumes of religious verse came to serve as a means of upholding the spiritual life of those who were deprived of their church and therefore had recourse to the private disciplines of meditation that poetry offered. The continuing availability of and affection for Herbert's *Temple* throughout this period (it was reprinted in 1641, c. 1647, and again in 1656) was an important factor in sustaining the faith of Anglicans in a time of adversity. King Charles's attachment to this book during his captivity is only the most eminent example of an attitude common to many thousands of members of the Church. For Henry Vaughan, *The Temple* became a surrogate church, providing the language and devotional inspiration for many of his own poems in *Silex Scintillans*. Of course, the appeal of *The Temple* was not restricted to Anglicans, for its piety and meditative practice were rewarding to Christians of almost any persuasion, but the formal beauty of its modes of worship recommended it especially to Anglicans who had been sympathetic to the Laudian discipline. Among such people too would be found the audience for Crashaw's verse, which perpetuated a florid and emotional style of devotion for years after it had been suppressed in church or college chapel services by the Puritan commissioners. Catholics too, denied the exercise of their religion, would have welcomed Crashaw's rich, intense celebration of the sacraments and saints.

The three volumes of Vaughan's verse form an interesting commentary on how a poet of moderate abilities made the uncomfortable transition from a stable, courtly society into war and then to some restoration of religious life independent of sect or society. His *Poems* of 1646 are full of gestures by which he tries to associate himself with

Caroline poetic life: affectionate remembrances of Ben Jonson, poems of friendship in the Cavalier mode, and a sequence of platonic love-poems of a kind that were in vogue at court in the 1630s. Vaughan had had no contact with the court milieu that sustained and validated Cavalier verse, so it is hardly surprising if his poems have a weak and imitative air; yet the fact that a young poet was drawn to these conventions shows how attractive the delicate, sophisticated wit of the court style remained even after its social setting had been swept away. In the preface to this volume, he acknowledges the untimeliness of his poems, deprecating 'that courage that durst send me abroad so late and revel it thus in the dregs of an age'. The last English poem of the volume, 'Upon the Priorie Grove', tacitly admits that a career as a social poet is a hopeless course in present times, and proposes retirement to innocence and love in the Welsh countryside. Vaughan's next volume, *Olor Iscanus* ('The Swan of Usk'), was ready for the press in 1647, but publication was deferred until 1651. Here the attempt to construct a quiet pastoral retreat is frustrated by the irruption of war and death which destroy his sanctuary and peace of mind. The structure of the volume reflects the disasters of the times. The opening idyll to the River Usk is shattered by the following poem, 'The Charnel House', which brings the disturbing presence of death into the happy land. The shock waves set off by this initial confrontation run all the way through the book, as poems proper to the pastoral world have their tranquillity destroyed by messages from the war-torn land outside: the elegies on Mr R. W. slain at Rowton Heath, and on Mr R. Hall slain at Pontefract, and the poem on the death of the King's daughter, dismally convey the violent disorder of the times and the difficulty of finding an adequate poetic response to the contemporary scene. Vaughan's dilemma was resolved in *Silex Scintillans* ('The Flashing Flint', 1650), which records the extraordinary spiritual experiences that had affected the poet in his rural seclusion. The death of friends may well have contributed to his new religious condition, but the haunting power of *Silex* derives undeniably from the profound transfiguring experience described in the first poem, 'Regeneration'. The mystical revelation that occurs within the sacred grove brings Vaughan into the presence of God in nature; thereafter the countryside of Wales becomes continuous with the landscapes of the Old Testament. Divinity blazes in the bushes, shines in the clouds, whispers in wind and stream:

My God, when I walk in those groves,
And leaves thy spirit doth still fan,
I see in each shade that there growes
An Angel talking with a man.

('Religion', ll. 1–4)

It would appear that in the absence of a formal church during the Commonwealth years, Vaughan fell back instead on to the numinous pastoral world that the Bible describes before the erection of the Temple, when God by lights and signs made known his presence in Israel. The landscape is alive with divine intimations and with the praise of the creatures. The pastoral harmonies of *Silex Scintillans* make the pastoral inventions of his earlier verse seem insubstantial literary fictions, devoid of experience or credibility. In *Silex* he had found his true vocation as a poet and as a religious figure of some originality. The way that Vaughan was moved to create a system that dispensed with formal church institutions, frequenting instead the temple of nature, evidently met with a broad approval, for *Silex* was reprinted and enlarged in 1655.

Vaughan's religious poetry possessed a genuinely innovatory quality, and innovation of a different order in religious matters came steadily from Henry More, whose books of Platonic poetry describing the philosophic progress of the soul towards the intellectual light of the divine mind appeared at intervals during the 1640s, sublimely oblivious of the disorders of the State. Yet the volume of new verse that seems to have enjoyed the warmest reception in these hard times was not religious but amorous: Cowley's *The Mistress* of 1647. This collection of witty and contentious love-poems owed something to Donne, although it had little of his metaphoric power and none of his personality. Cowley offered ingenious, smartly argued accounts of pursuit and entreaty; much abstract reasoning was set to catch the lady. What is striking is the absence of social setting in these poems: Cowley has dispensed with the courtly or pastoral backgrounds that gave Cavalier love-poetry much of its character and appeal, writing instead of unlocalized love – and unerotic love as well – in a way that was immediately successful. Perhaps because Cowley freed love from being the property of the Cavaliers and made it over to intelligent men of any party, he was admired beyond the understanding of all later generations; maybe his cool reasonable approach to love had the appeal of a new fashion after an era of courtly wooing; for whatever cause, Cowley was the coming man.

With all these examples in mind, it can be appreciated that the decade of warfare and political uncertainty, from the outbreak of civil war to the emergence of Cromwell as head of state, was unusually favourable to the publication of poetry of the most varied kind. The actual conflicts of the Civil Wars inspired relatively little poetry, almost all unmemorable. However, consciousness of the war is often betrayed by the language of poetry reaching instinctively for military or political idioms or using the vocabulary of destruction and waste. Marvell's lyrics are particularly suggestive in this regard. In his pastoral land-scapes and in his scenes of love we often catch the sharp gleam of armour: in 'A Definition of Love' 'decrees of steel' are enforced, 'iron wedges' crowd like armed companies into a weak place; 'the iron gates of life' threaten to close on the lovers in the 'Coy Mistress' like the portcullis of a beleaguered city. 'The Nymph Complaining' opens with a scene in which soldiers burst into the pastoral world:

> The wanton Troopers riding by
> Have shot my Faun and it will dye.

The mowers with their lethal scythes may speak of love, but they could at any moment be pressed into the nondescript armies of the Civil Wars, and the storm and 'rattling thunder' of 'The Unfortunate Lover' belong to the battlefield as much as to the Petrarchan fields of love.

The main literary instruments of aggression in the Civil Wars were pamphlets, backed by news-sheets and sermons. The most ambitious attempt to record the wars in poetry was made by Cowley, who saw in them the subject for a contemporary epic, hoping to emulate Lucan, whose *Pharsalia* had heroically treated the Roman civil wars. Cowley was a committed royalist, and he began his poem in the royalist stronghold of Oxford in 1643. His partisan feelings are never disguised. The epic machinery that propels the action of *The Civil War* involves God and his angels lending support to the righteous cause of King Charles, while a conclave in hell shows Satan and his devils extending aid·to the rebels.[1] Angels hover over the royal army at Edgehill in company with Loyalty, Religion, and the Arts, outfacing the fiends and their allegorical allies who urge on the parliamentary troops. Masque-like incidents assert that the powers of majesty that were so irresistible on the Whitehall stage will continue to prevail on the battlefield: the King's mysterious will conjures up vast armies and the Queen exerts her virtuous influence from afar. An ardent royalist, William Cavendish, Earl of Newcastle, enjoys the effortless conquests of the masque of war[2].

> How soon forc'd he the Northern Clouds to flight?
> And strook Confusion into Form and Light.
> So did the Power Divine in a few Days
> A peaceful World out of wild Chaos raise.
>
> (I. 519–22)

Nowhere does criticism fall on the King or on the royalist leaders; their every move wins Cowley's admiration. As a literary construction, *The Civil War* is an enterprising attempt to create a modern heroic poem. Within his epic framework, Cowley also incorporated several minor genres appropriate to his task. There is a great deal of panegyric of the royal family and the great royalists, in the extravagant manner common in court poetry of the 1630s; satire is witheringly aimed at the parliamentarians and at the profusion of religious sects engendered by the war, and elegy lends its tone of mourning for the noble dead. The poem in fact breaks down after the long and moving elegy for Lord Falkland, Cowley's friend and the paragon of his age, who was killed at the Battle of Newbury in September 1643. Falkland's death so dejected Cowley that he abandoned his poem and never published it, a decision that shows some critical sense, for the work has a laboured and uninspired character. Having to wait upon events deprived Cowley of the freedom of invention congenial to a poet, and prevented the formation of a satisfactory structure.

At the same time that Cowley was in Oxford registering the course of the Civil Wars in verse, the artist William Dobson was there painting the chief men on the royalist side as they conducted operations from their headquarters. Dobson was effectively the official painter to King Charles and his court during their occupation of Oxford from 1643 to 1646; his presence there and his relatively large output illustrate both the encouragement of art in the royalist camp even in wartime, and the compulsive need of the gentry to be painted in prosperity or in crisis. No doubt many portraits were ordered so that posterity should know that Sir Narcissus Sucklace or Lord Golightly had faith-fully served his king in the great division of the times. Dobson has left a remarkable record of the royalists at war. His subjects stand firm against pillars in their buff jerkins and steely breastplates, pistols at the ready; behind them turbulent skies hang over fields where scenes of conflict and pursuit take place, the rolling smoke of the guns merging into the low clouds. As Cowley had depicted his heroes assisted by allegorical figures reminiscent of the masques, and had in mind the Roman parallel of Lucan and his poem, so Dobson introduced into his portraits pieces of classical statuary that add a mythological resonance to this modern war. Behind Colonel Neville, Mercury rouses Mars to action; Minerva as Heroic Wisdom urges on the Marquis of Montrose; the fallen Medusa's head of Rebellion, with its snaky locks, is overlaid with royalist colours in the portrait of the young Prince Charles that probably commemorates his presence at Edgehill. The allusive statu-ary, as well as the pillars and drapery and confident poses, are part of Dobson's inheritance from Van Dyck, whom he succeeded, though he was never his pupil. He did not possess the full measure of Van Dyck's fluency, animation, or colouristic sense, nor did he have that psychological rapport with his subjects that made Van Dyck so sympathetic an interpreter of Stuart character, yet, for a native English painter, Dobson had a rare competence, and his paintings show the invigorating effect that Van Dyck's example had on English art. Although the repertoire of his poses is somewhat restricted, he had a robustness that was proper to the occasion of his work.[3]

If one has to select a painting that shows how Dobson adapted Van Dyck's style and fitted it to the changed circumstances of national life, it should be the portrait of the courtier and connoisseur Endymion Porter (Plate 10). Porter had been a close friend of Van Dyck, who had painted him several times in scenes of friendship and family life in the innocent years of the 1630s. Now, in the early 1640s, Porter appears stern yet forthright as he stands between a bust of Apollo and a relief showing the figures of Painting, Sculpture, and Poetry. Dressed in the fashionable clothes of peacetime, and flanked by testimonies to his love of antiquity and his patronage of the arts, he wishes to present himself also as a country gentleman (we may remember that he was the recipient of one of Herrick's fine poems on the country life), and here the gun-dog and dead game serve to remind us of this role; yet the large musket that he holds has an ambiguous function, both for sport and war, while the dark landscape with its black clouds encroaching on the sunset suggest a gathering storm. It is not the best of paintings, for the sculptural accessories are too heavy and intrusive, the foreground too cluttered, but it is a work that suggests very powerfully the transition of the Caroline age into war, and the firm determination of men like Porter to maintain the Caroline values, come what may.

Endymion Porter served his king, but by the end of 1645 he was in exile in France, as was Cowley. By the mid-1640s the Caroline cultural élite had crossed over to Paris, where they regrouped around Queen Henrietta Maria, who maintained an impoverished court at St Germain. Here were to be found Sir William Waller, Sir John Denham, Lovelace, Davenant, Killigrew, and Sir Kenelm Digby; Crashaw arrived in 1645, rejoining his Cambridge friends Abraham Cowley and John Cosin. Hobbes was there, and so was Sir Edward Hyde, the future Lord Clarendon. Intellectual life did not decay in exile: Hobbes wrote his *De Cive* and *Leviathan* during his Paris years; Davenant began his heroic poem *Gondibert* on new critical principles which he debated with Hobbes in the Preface that he published in 1650, encouraged by Cowley and Waller; Cowley composed his collection of love-poems *The Mistress* in Paris, and it may be that the absence of an authentic, well-established social setting caused by the circumstances of exile accounts for the cool tone that we have already noted and for the contrived relationships of these pieces. Crashaw channelled the experience of his recent conversion to Catholicism into the rhapsodic hymns of *Carmen Deo Nostro*. The poem that stands at the beginning of that collection, the verse-letter to the Countess of Denbigh

'Persuading her to Resolution in Religion, and to render herself without further delay into the Communion of the Catholick Church' confronts an issue that was insistently present for the exiled English community that had congregated around the Catholic Henrietta and enjoyed the protection of a Catholic state. With the suppression of Anglicanism at home, and the persecution of its most active supporters, and with no expectation of its re-establishment in the foreseeable future, the temptation to accept Catholicism as the closest form of worship was strong. Many did convert, and most of the Paris exiles would be suspected of being crypto-Catholics for the rest of their days; in many cases – as with Charles II and his deathbed avowal of Rome – that suspicion might be justified.

What the English learned in France about theatre, music, and poetic expression will be considered in the next chapter, which deals with the Restoration, when these French influences entered the mainstream of English practice. For the present it is enough to note the vigour of the exiled culture of the *ancien régime*, many of whose members would reconcile themselves to the new Commonwealth during the 1650s, and would eventually return to contribute their talents to the changed scene. The question that now arises is: what courses remained open for imaginative expression in the England of the Puritans?

Conditions were more favourable to the arts than might have been expected. The conventional view of the Commonwealth years is that they were hostile to the arts and the pleasures they aroused, but this is by no means the case upon investigation, especially after the rule of the Major-Generals gave way to Cromwell's Protectorate in 1653. Cromwell's installation as Protector brought in a more settled condition of national affairs. He now became one of the princes of Christendom, governing a nation that was becoming increasingly influential in European politics, and as such he was required to maintain a degree of state that confirmed his authority. In these circumstances, the arts revived a little, encouraged by Cromwell's civilized character. It seems proper to speak of a revival of the arts under Cromwell, because although England had endured a revolution, in which the monarchy and Church had been overthrown and the powers of the aristocracy restrained, yet when Cromwell took power in 1653 and ended the stalemate between Parliament and the army, the character of his rule soon took on a monarchical air. In spite of all the experimental political theories proposed in the 1640s, innovation yielded to practical considerations, and Cromwell's style of government was a reversion to a kind of princely authority, although he acknowledged that he derived his power from Parliament, and not, as the Stuarts had claimed, from God. The royal palaces were recovered for his use, and he set up his Protectoral court in Whitehall – on a modest scale undeniably, but in

plain
style.

structure it imitated the courts of the Stuart kings. Many of King Charles's paintings that had not been sold now enhanced the state of the Protector: Mantegna's magnificent sequence of paintings 'The Triumphs of Julius Caesar' now dignified Cromwell's receptions in the long gallery at Hampton Court, and appropriately so, for Cromwell's path to power resembled Caesar's in many ways. Raphael's cartoons for 'The Acts of the Apostles' provided a series of heroic religious images as a background to the godly Protector's transactions of state. Aesthetic considerations overcame religious prejudices at Whitehall, where paintings of the Madonna with Angels and the Assumption of the Virgin hung with a Judgement of Venus. The conviction that fine paintings were an essential part of the magnificence that should accompany a prince, which had only gained currency under the Stuarts, was accepted without question by Cromwell, whose gallery at Whitehall, though greatly depleted since Charles's time, was none the less impressive to foreign visitors.[4]

Although Cromwell showed no interest in collecting mythological or religious paintings, he was obliged to commission portraits of himself and his family for state purposes and as gifts. He patronized in particular Peter Lely, who perpetuated the suave traditions of Van Dyck through the Commonwealth years (albeit with a certain subdued air appropriate to the times), and Samuel Cooper the miniaturist, whose forthright manner seems to have appealed to Cromwell. It was probably to Cooper that Cromwell made his request to be painted with 'pimples, warts and everything as you see them'; at any rate, Cooper's famous miniature of the Protector carries out exactly this prescription, offering an unforgettable image of a bold, thoughtful man (Plate 11). It is noticeable from the many surviving portraits of Cromwell that he never allowed himself to be glorified by means of symbolism or by the elevating devices so frequent in the period. Plainness was his style.

Granted this personal preference for the unadorned, Cromwell was not averse to surrounding himself with the customary cultural splendours. The tapestries that hung in his private quarters at Hampton Court suggest a man who had no quarrel with the main traditions of Renaissance art: Mars and Venus and The History of Vulcan shared the walls with The Seven Deadly Sins. Even a Cupid and Venus tapestry was bought back from the man who had purchased it at the auction of the King's goods, and made over to the Protector.

Court entertainments too revived. When the Portuguese Ambassador came to London in 1653 to sign a treaty of alliance with England, he was received by Cromwell and, most improbably, regaled with a masque. This was *Cupid and Death* by James Shirley, who had been responsible for one of the most elaborate Caroline masques, *The*

Triumph of Peace, back in 1634. It had scenery that 'wanted no elegance, or curiosity for the delight of the spectator', its music was composed by Christopher Gibbons, the son of Orlando, and by Matthew Locke, and its dances were performed by a company of gentlemen. The survival of the 'Cupid' theme that had been so fashionable at King Charles's court is particularly intriguing, for it suggests a continuity of taste from the 1630s into the 1650s. However, the neo–Platonism that once lightly coloured the stories of Cupid has faded; now the action is played for its wit, and the higher harmonies of the masque have gone. In Shirley's entertainment, Cupid and Death both lodge at the same inn for the night and a chamberlain exchanges their arrows, so that thereafter Cupid's targets die, death's victims become rejuven-ated lovers, and mortal enemies become friends. Order is finally restored by Mercury, to the relief of distressed Nature, although the dead lovers are not revived but are seen in the closing tableau gloriously clothed and enthroned in the Elysian Fields. It is possible that there is an undercurrent of contemporary reference in this masque. Cupid's followers who are also victims may be an allusion to the Caroline court world undone by death, and the action may refer to the disruption of the nation by civil war and the subsequent return to order, ending with an honouring of the dead; but these political implications are certainly not strongly marked, only faintly suggested. The masque makes no attempt to glorify the State or to allude to the power of the Protector; it remains a modest and unambitious piece in comparison to its Stuart predecessors, yet the very fact of its production must have been encouraging to all who had an interest in the arts.[5] A novel feature of its musical style was its use of recitative throughout; one might infer from this development that as the masque in its revived form had shed most of the magical functions that belonged to a defunct social order, it was beginning to evolve towards a new secular genre, opera.

Opera proved to be the means by which the dramatic arts returned publicly to Cromwellian London despite the laws against dramatic performances. The man who achieved this feat was the enterprising Sir William Davenant, who had a talent for experiment and inno-vation. In the old reign he had been a playwright, masque-maker, and court poet; in exile he had concentrated (when not engaged in royalist intrigue) on the defence and illustration of a modern heroic poem, *Gondibert*, designed to challenge Bacon's criticisms of poetry as a mere 'fanciful deceiver of the mind'; now he introduced opera, presenting it in a way acceptable to the authorities who disapproved of drama. Davenant got away with it by professing to revive a lost classical art form: 'Entertainment and Declamations after the manner of the Ancients.'[6] He prudently prepared the ground by mounting in 1656 a preliminary debate with musical accompaniment, the first part of which was set in Athens, where Aristophanes and Dionysus argued for and against the new 'Public Entertainment by Moral Representation', followed by a modern scene with a citizen of London and a citizen of Paris exchanging their views of each other's city, manners, and customs. This rudimentary action concluded with two songs in praise of the Protector. The performance, staged in the great hall of Rutland House, the old city mansion that Davenant occupied, did not provoke any official complaint, so later that year, in the same place, Davenant produced a full-scale opera, *The Siege of Rhodes*.

The subject concerned the siege by the Turks of Christian Rhodes, an event of relatively recent history; the conflict focuses on Alphonso the Sicilian Duke who wishes to pursue honour and die in defence of the island, yet who is urged by the Grand Master of Rhodes to return to Sicily and the love of his wife. The character of the action has strong affinities with the concerns of French classical tragedy, and foreshadows the heroic drama of the Restoration stage. In order to ensure the opera's survival, Davenant in his Preface hastens to commend the morally elevated tone of his work: 'The story is heroical and is (I hope) intelligently conveyed to advance the Characters of Vertue in the shapes of Valor and Conjugal Love.' In several ways, *The Siege of Rhodes* retained features of the masque – it was in fact entered as 'a maske' in the *Stationers' Register* in 1656 – for it had entries 'prepared by instrumentall music' instead of acts, five changes of perspective scenery (designed by John Webb), and powerful lighting effects, while the action was moved along by recitative, aria, and chorus playing on a strong text. The floodlit scenes of revelation have gone, as have the dances, both of which had been vital parts of the masque. Symbolic action has given way to heroic drama. Yet the sense of cultural continuity is remarkable: Davenant, who wrote *The Siege of Rhodes* as well as producing it, had written the last of Charles I's masques, *Salmacida Spolia*; John Webb, who designed the scenery for the opera, had been Inigo Jones's assistant in the last masque; while of the opera's two composers, Henry Lawes and Matthew Locke, Lawes had provided the music for Milton's *Comus*, as well as for Davenant's masque *The Triumphs of the Prince d'Amour* in 1636, and had set many songs by Cavalier poets.[7]

The success of *The Siege of Rhodes* in semi-private performance encouraged Davenant to move his opera into a public playhouse. By early 1657 he was producing it at the Cockpit Theatre in Drury Lane, having squared the authorities by pleading that his 'moral representations' were entirely conducive to the public good. Thereafter he put together two more operas, both of which combined heroic drama with patriotic themes that lent support to Parliament's current concern in foreign policy, war with Spain. *The Cruelty of the Spaniards in Peru* dramatized Drake's South American expedition against the Spanish and reminded the audience how much better fitted to control this region Britain was, rather than Spain, and *The History of Sir Francis Drake* repeated the same theme. These works, with music, dancing, and songs, with stage machines and scenery and splendid costumes, were performed daily, and their production is evidence of the tolerant atmosphere of Cromwell's regime in the more settled years of the mid-1650s. They testify also to the unabated appetite for dramatic entertainment in London.

The common notion that the theatres were closed and acting suppressed from 1642 onwards is, upon investigation, only a half-truth, for there are many records of plays being performed during the 1640s, even though play-acting had become illegal.[8] The Globe was pulled down in 1644, but plays were frequently put on at The Fortune, The Bull, The Cockpit, and at Salisbury Court, and actors maintained a hole-in-the-corner existence throughout this time. Sometimes performances were allowed to run for several weeks, although invariably the soldiers were eventually sent in to put a stop to them and confiscate the players' costumes. In spite of attempts to fine the audiences, the actors never lacked popular support, but it was only when Davenant found an innocuous vocabulary to justify his enterprise and persuaded some influential political figures to recognize the merits of his 'representations' that a form of drama could once again be openly played.

It is clear that Cromwell was well disposed towards the arts, and one might imagine that had he lived longer they might have flourished in support of his increasingly king-like state. We have seen how he favoured musical–dramatic representations, and since there are two contemporary references to Davenant as Cromwell's 'Master of the Revels', it may be that there was more festivity at the Protector's court than we are aware of. Cromwell's fondness for music is well known: he had the organ of Magdalen College, Oxford, moved to Hampton Court for his own pleasure, and he retained a small musical establishment, including two singing boys, to provide music in his household. There is little evidence of music being specially composed for Cromwell, but Marvell's poem 'Music's Empire' may have been written and set to music for some Protectoral entertainment: its closing stanza would seem to be directed to Cromwell in praise of his modesty, his piety, and his love of music.

> Victorious sounds! Yet here your homage do
> Unto a gentler conqueror than you:
> Who though he flies the music of his praise,
> Would with you heaven's hallelujahs raise.

The theme of empire, harmoniously attained, would not have been irrelevant to Cromwell, whose own policies had a strong imperialist drift.[9]

The marriages of Cromwell's daughters in 1657 offer a glimpse of Commonwealth revelry. The wedding feast of Frances Cromwell, who married Robert Rich (grandson of the Earl of Warwick) was held at Whitehall, where, according to Sir William Dugdale's report, 'They had 48 violins, 50 trumpets and much mirth with frolics, besides mixed dancing (a thing hereto thought profane) until 5 of the clock.' When Mary Cromwell married Lord Fauconberg, Marvell provided two pastoral dialogues, which were very likely set to music for the occasion. The fictions of Caroline pastoral are once again enacted, but now before Cromwell, and Marvell even dares to reintroduce as a final gesture the motif associated with the masques of Stuart absolutism, the recognition of a godlike presence that orders and controls events:

> Joy to Endymion,
> For he has Cynthia's favour won.
> And Jove himself approves
> With his serenest influence their loves.

Cromwell had three major poets on his staff: Milton, Marvell and Dryden. Milton, who was Secretary for Foreign Tongues, gave his best energies in this phase to the ideological defence of the Republic, writing very little poetry, only some political sonnets. Dryden occupied a minor secretarial post, with little time to court the Muse. Marvell, who was Milton's assistant, was the outstanding poet of Cromwell's time: he was at the height of his powers in the 1650s, and was fascinated by the significance, both political and religious, of Cromwell's career. However, Marvell was the most reticent of poets, reluctant to publish and unwilling even to circulate his verse beyond his trusted friends. He can therefore hardly be considered as a significant voice of the decade – most of his poems were not published under his own name until 1681 – but because he served great men in humble capacities, he had the opportunity to apply his sharp and judicious observation closely to two of the parliamentary leaders whose actions were shaping contemporary history, Fairfax and Cromwell.

Marvell's distinction is such that it is worth pausing over his political poems of the 1650s to consider how a shrewd observer interpreted the drama of national life. The large religious context in which he set current affairs, as he attempted to understand the pattern of destiny, produces a disconcerting grandeur of effect in his poems, yet we should remember that very many Englishmen felt they were living in prophetic times, and expected miracles. Perhaps it was his association with the living heroes of the Civil Wars that encouraged him to offer himself, very discreetly, as an explicator of events. Marvell had spent two years in the household of Thomas, Lord Fairfax, as a tutor to his daughter. This was shortly after Fairfax had resigned as commander-in-chief of the parliamentary armies in order to avoid leading a campaign against the Scots, a move that he saw as an unjustifiable and aggressive extension of war. On his Yorkshire estates Fairfax led a life not dissimilar to that of many of the leading royalists who had retired into private life from the vicissitudes of politics: he laid out his gardens, practised husbandry, investigated local antiquities, read books, and wrote poetry. Marvell must have found him a most congenial patron.

In the long poem *Upon Appleton House,* which was the enduring memorial of his sojourn with Fairfax, Marvell was able not only to contemplate his patron's estates with civilized approval, but also to view there a re-enactment in miniature of recent occurrences in national history. The resolute Protestantism of the Fairfax family provides the background to the symbolic images of the poem, giving a powerful religious resonance to the pastoral activities at Appleton House. The central episode of the mowing scenes comments metaphorically on the Civil Wars that have scythed the flourishing estate of England, and its techniques of allusion make one aware that all the prospects of the poem have some dark significance. Marvell laments the desolations of the wars, yet seems disposed to feel that they form part of some divinely ordained scheme of history. As the general of the godly armies, Fairfax is characterized as a man destined to preside over an important phase of this scheme, but only for a time. The promptings of his conscience that cause him to withdraw from public life before the grand design of providence has been fulfilled are shown to be in harmony with the will of God: Fairfax 'makes his destiny his choice'. The gardens that he tends in his retirement recall in their discipline and colours the militia that he so lately commanded; the peacefulness and innocence of those gardens evoke the peaceable world of pre-war England, yet also suggest to the poet the qualities that Fairfax might have restored to England had he continued to exercise the genius of his command:

> And yet there walks one on the sod
> Who, had it pleased him and God
> Might once have made our gardens spring
> Fresh as his own and flourishing.
>
> (ll. 345–48)

But the magnanimous Fairfax was not to lead England into a new phase of history. That role would fall to the harder Cromwell. Marvell muses on the varied scenes of Appleton House, perceiving the shadows cast by political and religious events – reformation, revolution, regicide – until darkness sets in and familiar sights take on an eerie and supernatural air. Apocalyptic suggestions intensify as the poem proceeds: the mowing scenes and the flood hint at the harvesting of the earth and the cataclysm prophesied of the latter days; the darkness of the poem's end may be the night of time; there is mention of the Beast and of the Lord who delays, and the appearance of the young Maria is accompanied by phenomena associated with the Book of Revelation.[10] All this is most subtly handled; there is no sense of a rigid scheme being applied, but one becomes conscious of an insistent flicker of allusion to the momentous acts of expiring time.

In many of his political poems of the 1650s, Marvell is inclined to interpret contemporary events in terms of providential history. Like so many of his fellows, he liked to believe that the hand of God directed the course of English history, and that the chief actors in the movement of politics and religion were instruments of providence helping to shape the grand design of God's purposes towards his favoured nation. Marvell first displayed his sense of Cromwell's special calling in his 'Horatian Ode on Cromwell's Return from Ireland', written in the summer of 1650 after Cromwell had returned from crushing the Catholic Irish and was about to lead an army against the Scottish royalists, to carry out in fact the policy that had just caused Fairfax to resign his military command on grounds of conscience. Marvell recognizes that a critical stage of English history has been reached, as Cromwell now has sufficient power to subject Parliament, whose servant he is in principle, to his authority. The Roman allusion in the poem's title raises the question of whether Cromwell might not prove to be another Augustus, abandoning republican principles to become an emperor. The poem adopts an ambivalent attitude towards Cromwell. Marvell shows no warmth for the man or for his actions, for the poet's sympathies seem to lie with 'the Kingdom old' and the 'ancient Rights' of monarchy, and he deplores the violence that marks Cromwell's advance; yet Marvell responds to the idea of Cromwell as a providential force whose power is ordained and fateful. Even King Charles is represented in the poem as accepting the inevitability of Cromwell's power, complying with the force of events and acquiescing in his execution as a necessary act in the historical drama. The Stuarts have incurred the disfavour of God, yet Marvell remains assured that God's intentions towards England are benevolent, and that Cromwell will be the agent of their enactment. The poem looks forward to some triumph of the Protestant cause achieved by Cromwell, some conquest over the spiritual night.

Whereas Marvell was speculative and divinatory in the 'Horatian

Ode', in the poem he wrote to celebrate Cromwell's first year as
Protector he declares an unprecedented admiration for his rule, which
he now believes to be of apocalyptic significance. Throughout the
1640s the turbulent commotions of English politics had been widely
interpreted as evidence that history was moving rapidly towards the
fearsome termination that had been foretold by the Old Testament
prophets and darkly described in the Book of Revelation. The End
would be characterized by wars, upheavals, and desolations, and by
a climactic struggle against Antichrist which would be waged by a
Christian prince who would prepare the way for the return of the
Messiah to judge and reign over his elect. Protestants of every hue gave
some credence to these beliefs, and it was widely accepted that the last
age of history had begun with the Reformation, which was seen as a
divinely inspired movement to purify the Church to receive the elect.
Contemporary events were freely interpreted in the light of biblical
predictions concerning the latter days. In 'The First Anniversary'
(published anonymously in 1655) Marvell reveals himself to be one of
those who shared these expectations, for it is an excited, prophetic
poem that hails Cromwell as the divinely guided hero who will govern
the nation in conformity with the will of God and prepare for the
Second Coming of Christ. Cromwell's notable love of music is now
interpreted as a sign of his harmonious spirit which seeks to resolve
the discords of England into the concord of a godly state which enjoys
the entire approval of God:

> While indefatigable Cromwell hies,
> And cuts his way still nearer to the skies,
> Learning a music in the region clear,
> To tune this lower to that higher sphere.
>
> (ll. 45–48)

Marvell attributes Orphic powers to Cromwell, creative powers of
imaginative control characterized by metaphors of musical and architectural authority. Here we see him composing the fair structure of the
Commonwealth, directing the work until all is harmoniously set, the
tensions of opposing elements held in balance by his supreme mastery
as Protector:

> The Commonwealth does through their centres all
> Draw the circumference of the public wall;
> The crossest spirits here do take their part,
> Fastening the contignation which they thwart;
> And they, whose nature leads them to divide,

> Uphold this one, and that the other side;
> But the most equal still sustain the height,
> And they as pillars keep the work upright,
> While the resistance of opposed minds,
> The fabric (as with arches) stronger binds,
> Which on the basis of a senate free,
> Knit by the roof's protecting weight, agree.
>
> (ll. 87–98)

The poem proceeds to praise Cromwell's activism and Protestant zeal as he applies his heroic energies to the fulfilment of the prophecies associated with the end of time and the Second Coming: he seeks the conversion of the heathen and of the Jews, and is tireless in his attack on the Beast of the Apocalypse, commonly held by Protestants at this time to be the monster of popery 'in her Roman den impure' (l. 129). He treads 'the path where holy oracles do lead' (l. 108). He is unquestionably at the head of militant Protestantism in the West, and Marvell looks eagerly forward, anticipating that Cromwell will urge his fellow princes into the final crusade, against the Roman Antichrist:

> How might they under such a captain raise
> The great designs kept for the latter days!
>
> (ll. 109–10)

Yet Marvell stops short of absolute conviction. All the signs are present, the nation has struggled towards reform and renewal, Cromwell has every appearance of being the long-awaited Christian prince who will prepare the way for Christ – he himself had told Parliament 'You are on the edge of the promises and prophecies' – yet impediments continue to delay the Second Coming, and until the mysterious light breaks in the East, certainties cannot crown themselves assured.

> Hence oft I think if in some happy hour
> High grace should meet in one with highest power,
> And then a seasonable people still
> Should bend to his, as he to heaven's will,
> What we might hope, what wonderful effect
> From such a wished conjuncture might reflect.
> Sure, the mysterious work, where none withstand,
> Would forthwith finish under such a hand:
> Foreshortened time its useless course would stay,
> And soon precipitate the latest day.
> But a thick cloud about that morning lies,
> And intercepts the beams of mortal eyes,

That 'tis the most which we determine can,
If these the times, then this must be the man.

                                    (ll. 131–44)

'The First Anniversary' marks the high point of Marvell's millenarian expectations. Traces of it remain in the congratulatory poem
addressed to Cromwell on Admiral Blake's victory over the Spanish
at Tenerife, which is seen as a Protestant triumph in the universal
conflict of religions, achieved by the conquering force of Cromwell's
spirit that now controls events at a remote distance:

For your resistless genius there did reign,
By which we laurels reaped e'en on the main.
So prosperous stars, though absent to the sense,
Bless those they shine for, by their influence.

                                    (ll. 145–48)

When Cromwell died in 1658, however, Marvell's long elegy
(which he did not publish) preserved little recollection of the extravagant hopes that he had formerly entertained of the Protector. The
apocalyptic vision had faded as Cromwell's rule had settled down to
the business of state without the aid of divine intervention. The elegy
is, rather, an honourable, complimentary summation of Cromwell's
virtues and of the remarkable passages of his life; it emphasizes too his
humanity and the warmth of his domestic affections. The vast perspectives of the earlier poems have now narrowed to a more conventional
view appropriate to the death of a head of state.

The funeral of Oliver Cromwell closely followed the ceremonies
that had been enacted at the burial of James I. At his lying-in-state,
the crown and orb and sceptre were laid by the effigy, and his body
was entombed in the royal chapel in Westminster Abbey. This state
of all-but-kingship that enveloped Cromwell, especially after he was
reinvested with the office of Protector in 1657 in a ceremony that was
almost a coronation, should strengthen our impression that there was
more continuity between the Stuart court and the Cromwellian court
than is commonly acknowledged.

While Marvell wrote obscurely about great matters, rarely allowing
his name to catch the light of public scrutiny, Cowley, the other
significant poet writing of public affairs in the 1650s, published openly,
though preferring to clothe his opinions in biblical or classical dress.[11]
Cowley, like Davenant, is a good example of the royalist who returned
to England in the 1650s and determined to make an accommodation
with the Commonwealth. They find it difficult to be enthusiastic about
the new order, but they are willing to accept it without protest. In the

preface to his *Poems* of 1656, Cowley printed a formal recognition that the royalist cause was dead, and agreed not to stir up old quarrels by means of poetry. Rather than risk offence, he was even prepared to give up writing poetry:

> When the event of battle and the unaccountable will of
> God has determined the controversy, and . . . we have
> submitted to the conditions of the conqueror, we must lay
> down our pens as well as our arms, we must march out
> of our cause itself, and dismantle that, as well as our
> towns and castles, of all the works and fortifications of wit
> and reason by which we defended it. We ought not, sure,
> to begin ourselves to revive the remembrance of those
> times and actions for which we have received a general
> amnesty as a favour from the victor.

This submission facilitated the publication of his poems, but did not do Cowley's reputation any good when he tried to regain royal favour at the Restoration.

In this 1656 volume, the uncompleted epic *Davideis* shows the dilemma Cowley found himself in when trying to clarify his reaction to the Cromwellian regime after his long support for the crown. The incompleteness is itself a measure of the dilemma of allegiance. The poem is set amid the complexities of ancient Jewish strife, wherein the reader may observe a shadowy commentary on modern conditions. Indeed, given the habitual identification of post-Reformation England with Old Testament Israel as the theatre of God's providence, it would be improbable not to find connections between biblical antiquity and the English experience of the seventeenth century. Cowley's subject is the confrontation of David with the tyrant Saul. The position of neither party is entirely sound, for Saul's kingship is shown to be well established but poorly maintained, vitiated by his tyrannical character, and David is a vital, aspiring but unaccountable figure. Yet there is no one-to-one association with Charles and Cromwell here; Cowley is more concerned to depict and deplore the civil disorders that afflict a kingdom when two forces compete for supreme power. The poem prefers to turn away from the unsettled present and look forward to the time when Christ 'The great Mystick King' shall appear to impose true kingship on the restless nations, 'even Albion's stubborn Isle'. *Davideis* is a dutiful, responsible, non-controversial work, unlikely to provoke objections, and its grim neutrality enabled Cowley to take his place again among practising poets.

The 'Pindaric Odes' that were also published in the 1656 volume contain more contentious stuff. In particular 'Brutus' is transparently an occasion for praise of Cromwell, and its use of the Roman parallel gives it obvious affinities with Marvell's 'Horatian Ode'. As the personification of the ideal of republican virtue, Brutus is a reliable cult figure for those who oppose monarchical tyranny. His murder of Caesar may be represented as an honourable and principled act, although he will always suffer the detraction of those who cannot understand the fineness of those principles that entail the shedding of blood in a political cause.

> Th'heroic Exaltations of Good
>   Are so far from understood
> We count them Vice: . . .
>   Ingrateful Brutus do they call?
> Ingrateful Caesar who could Rome enthrall!
>
> (ll. 19–21; 38–9)

A notable sign of Brutus's integrity was his refusal to take Caesar's place – as Cromwell had refused the crown. Yet Brutus too is subject to 'Ill Fate' and is vulnerable in turn. Cowley turns the poem away from Roman politics with their English shadow to reflect that shortly the advent of Christ will transform our sense of virtue, and the temporary order that great men can impose on society will be redeemed by an order 'improved by Grace', when man's eternal good will be assured by the presence of Christ. Political expedients, no matter how nobly they are undertaken, will give way to the infinitely more desirable state of divine order.

The Pindaric ode 'Destinie' reflects condescendingly on the political campaigns of men, imaged here as a game of chess in which the pieces imagine they have 'Life, Election, Liberty', when in fact they are manipulated by an angelic power: 'An unseen Hand makes all their Moves.' Cowley regrets 'th'ill conduct of the mated King', but the strategy of the poem makes the King's failure due to the will of provi- dence, 'for Destiny plays us all'. From the facile and unprotesting fatalism of these lines, Cowley retires into a stoical self-possession, claiming that the same Destiny that disposes of states has made Cowley a poet, capable of transforming the tragic pageant of the times into harmonious verse.

Cowley's most detailed engagement with contemporary politics was *A Discourse, by way of Vision, Concerning the Government of Oliver Crom- well*, a prose treatise heightened by occasional poetic flights which seems to have been inspired by the death of the Protector, although it was not published until 1661. He used the occasion to attempt an assessment of the Protector's rule, trying to give credit for his personal qualities and political accomplishments as well as decry the impact of his destructive energies on 'the Kingdom old'. (In reading Cowley in verse or prose, one is always reminded that Marvell has covered the same ground with infinitely more skill and judgement, for one is inclined to paraphrase whole tracts of Cowley by the succinct phrases of the 'Horatian Ode', or of the 'First Anniversary'.) Cowley claims objectivity and balance as he takes the measure of 'this prodigious Man': 'Sometimes I was filled with horror and detestation of his actions, and sometimes I inclined a little to reverence and admiration of his courage, conduct and success.' Yet the whole experience of rebellion had been for Cowley a most miserable trial; his nature so loved order and tranquillity that he could never really forgive the instigators of revolt, no matter how severely they had been provoked. His nostalgic sentiment for the halcyon age of Charles's reign is poured into the poem:

> Ah, happy Isle, how art thou chang'd and curst,
> Since I was born, and knew thee first!

For all of his reasonable determination to conciliate himself to the upstart government of the Protectorate, he cannot restrain his deep conviction that the Puritan victory has been an immense and mysterious affliction upon England. He casts his discourse as a dialogue between himself and an Apparition representing the Idea of the Protectorate, who is given so violent and fearsome a character that one cannot fail to recognize that this spirit is a rebel angel. The spirit defends Cromwell with impressive arguments, but we know he speaks as devil's advocate; Cowley's own protestation of a kingdom violated by revolt, a church despoiled and replaced by an anarchy of sects, and a parliament subverted by the will of a dictator fills much of the discourse but fails to convince his supernatural antagonist. The dialogue is interrupted by a more sublime vision. The heavens reveal a figure who mingles attributes of Christ and a Stuart king. His glory transcends all human beauty:

> His Beams of Locks fell part dishevel'd down,
> Part upwards curl'd, and form'd a natural Crown,
> Such as the British Monarchs us'd to wear.

He wears the insignia of the Garter, and bears the English arms of a red cross on a white field, and pronounces the name Jesus. The Protectoral Spirit flees from this apparition, and the discourse ends.

It is notable that in all these works by Cowley from the 1650s there is some repeated hope of a divine intervention that will put an end to the present distracted phase of history and restore the mystic kingship of Christ. What we see here is a kind of forlorn millenarianism that entirely lacks the impassioned assurance of Marvell's 'First Anniversary'. Christ's return to rule over his British Israelites is a wishful dream in which Cowley indulges as an escape from the apparently interminable sequence of political patchings and contrivances through which he has had to live, a dream about as improbable as the restoration of Stuart monarchy that he also entertains as an ideal solution. Cowley's faint summoning of future events has the air of a man desperately conjuring without conviction, but the persistence in his works of this Messianic dream helps to put Marvell's hopes into some sort of perspective. The possibility of a universal deliverance by Christ was a belief held with varying degrees of optimism in the mid-seventeenth century: Cowley with a minimum of real hope foresees it as the most desirable termination of the present mess; Marvell looks forward with confidence to the Second Coming as the climax of a providentially ordered movement of history. Both feel that Cromwell is the critical figure whose extraordinary career provokes far-searching questions about God's intentions towards the English nation: he is a phenomenon that demands interpretation.

Cromwell died in 1658 on his fateful day, 3 September, the day of his victories at Dunbar and at Worcester – a coincidence that confirmed to many the supernatural patterning of his life. Cowley watched the funeral, Marvell probably walked in the procession; if this was the case it provides a nice demonstration of their relative degrees of engagement in Cromwell's affairs. Both would give a literary shape to their reactions, Marvell in his 'Elegy', Cowley in his 'Vision'. Milton and Dryden, too, walked behind Cromwell to his grave. Dryden's 'Heroick Stanzas' on the death of the Protector remain a remarkable tribute to his achievements – a rare case of an encomium that does not greatly exaggerate the truth. Cromwell's valour and clemency are justly praised, as are his political skills, which held the country together when the military failed, and which eventually made England a more formidable international force than she had been for a century. Dryden had no doubts that the arts had also flourished under Cromwell: when the Liberal Arts appear to praise him, they 'do an Act of Friendship to their own'.

Cromwell's death did precipitate a crisis of government, out of which arose what seemed to many the miracle of the Restoration. Cromwell had not been a bad caretaker of the arts, and his tolerant rule had permitted more cultural continuity than would have seemed possible to an observer of Cromwell the regicide in 1649. The firm conduct of his Protectorate had given rise to a poetry of political appraisal, and his relaxations had encouraged a revival of music and drama. When the Restoration came, with its flood of patronage, there was a broad and varied cultural life ready to be enlarged and transformed.

Notes

1. Cowley's *The Civil War* has been edited, with extensive notes, by Allan Pritchard (Toronto, 1973).

2. See *The Civil War*, Pritchard's introduction, pp. 37 and 38, for a discussion of the masque elements in the poem.

3. Dobson's career is traced, with many illustrations, in Malcolm Rogers, *William Dobson* (1983).

4. The Protector's establishment is described by Roy Sherwood in *The Court of Oliver Cromwell* (1977), and details of his pictures and tapestries are given there, pp. 25–31.

5. *Cupid and Death* was performed again in 1659, when it was described as 'a private entertainment'. It was probably produced by Luke Channon, the choreographer of the masque, who ran a dancing school in London.

6. This re-creation of what was believed to have been a classical form of composition combining music, poetry, and action had also motivated the first experiments in opera at Florence by Caccini and at Venice by Monteverdi and Cavalli.

7. See *The Siege of Rhodes*, edited by Ann-Mari Hedback, (Uppsala, 1972), pp. lxviii–lxxviii, for an account of the operatic character of this work. Davenant's career has been clarified and reassessed by Mary Edmond in *Rare Sir William Davenant* (Manchester, 1987).

8. The records of stage performances in London throughout the Civil Wars and Commonwealth period are extensively documented in Leslie Hotson, *The Commonwealth and Restoration Stage* (Cambridge, Mass. 1928).
   An interesting indication of the cultural tolerance of Cromwell's rule – and no doubt of the confidence in the regime's stability – was the publication in 1657 of Thomas Stanley's *Psalterium Carolinum*, which was a versification of King Charles's *Eikon Basilike*, set to music by Dr John Wilson, who was appointed Professor of Music at Oxford in 1656. The work is openly dedicated to Charles II. In 1656, Cromwell had permitted the burial of Archbishop Ussher in Westminster Abbey to the accompaniment of the full liturgy of the Church of England.

9. One might note that coins struck in 1656 and 1658 depict Cromwell with the dress and laurels of a Roman emperor.

10. See Margarita Stocker, *Apocalyptic Marvell* (1986), Chapter 2, for a thorough interpretation of 'Upon Appleton House' in the light of apocalyptic expectations.

11. For a comparable discussion of Cowley's poems of the 1650s, see Nicholas Jose, *Ideas of Restoration in English Literature, 1660–71* (1984), pp. 78–85.

Chapter 5
The Restoration Ethos, 1660–1688

The events leading to the Restoration moved so rapidly and surprisingly that the hand of Providence was widely perceived to be once again active in England's affairs, this time in favour of the Stuarts. Discontent against the Rump Parliament had grown strongly in February 1660. General Monck held the initiative as head of the army, and growing more inclined to bring in the King to resolve the political chaos that had developed since Cromwell's death, he forced into being a new Parliament which was negotiating with Charles by April, and by May the King had returned. A miracle of a kind had happened, so that royalists were inclined to view the Restoration as much as a religious as a political event, with Charles acclaimed as the saviour of his country's fortunes. The Christ-like imagery that had accompanied Charles I in his sufferings now glowed briefly around his son, until his emerging character effectively extinguished it. That Charles entered London on his thirtieth birthday, at the same age that Christ had begun his ministry, was a coincidence frequently remarked upon, and inevitably many poets and preachers recalled the unusually bright star that had shone at the time of Charles's birth, and which had seemed to augur some illustrious destiny.

> That Star, that at your birth shone out so bright,
> It stained the duller sun's meridian light,
> Did once again its potent fires renew,
> Guiding our eyes to find and worship you.

Such was Dryden's adoring response to the new prince of peace in *Astraea Redux* (1660) (ll. 288–91). Most of the poems of welcome that were written in the euphoric early days of the Restoration struck a religious note; many noted a Christ-like quality in the King, others saw him as a David, a Solomon, a new king in Israel, even a new Adam come to restore the perfections of innocence and peace. Cowley, for example, in his 'Restoration Ode', exclaimed that 'the very ground/Ought with a face of Paradise be found', for 'Felicity and Innocence' were come again.

The very term 'Restoration' carried with it a religious connotation, associated with the idea of a return to an original state of perfection, spiritual and intellectual, and it was related to the beliefs that permeated seventeenth-century English society in various forms that history was returning cyclically to a time of renewal. The millenarian expectation of the return of Christ was one of these engrained beliefs, and this in turn was allied to the Protestant conviction that the reformation of the Church in matters of doctrine and faith had as its ideal the return to the purity of the Primitive Church which Christ had left behind on earth. Only when that purity had been regained by the strenuous endeavours of the faithful could Christ's return be envisaged. 'Lord, wilt thou at this time restore again the kingdom to Israel?' (Acts 1. 6) was a question much repeated in this age, and the answer was widely imagined to be in the affirmative. However, although the English reckoned themselves to be the new Israelites, the means and the time of restoration were the subject of tireless debate. The Edenic state that would be the setting for the kingdom of Christ was an aspect of divine restoration that exercised an enduring spell over the English imagination in the seventeenth century, filling it with dreams of paradise and light. The advancement of learning of which Bacon was the theorist and spokesman took as its justification the need to regain the fullness of knowledge – 'a pure light of natural knowledge' – that had been instinct in Adam but had disintegrated after the Fall. Milton shared this sense that modern men should aim to recover a lost wholeness of knowledge: 'the end, then, of learning is to repair the ruins of our first parents', he stated in his tractate *Of Education*. The vast programme for the renewal of learning that Bacon proposed was entitled by him 'The Great Instauration', the word being synonymous with restoration. These themes of renewal flourished throughout the century. They were frequently present in the masques of the first two Stuarts that served as a theatre of ideas for the court; the titles were indicative, for a considerable number of masques dealt with the recovery in the present age of some lost harmony or perfection: *The Golden Age Restored, Love Restored, The Fortunate Isles, Time Vindicated, Mercury Vindicated* (where vindication has the force of restoration), *Tempe Restored*. Titles of antiquarian works such as Verstegan's *Restitution of Decayed Antiquity* or Inigo Jones's *Stone-Henge Restored* speak of a recovery and renewal of knowledge in line with the optimistic spirit of enquiry of the times. Notions of Christian and classical renewal came together in the concept of restoration. On the cultural side it included the prospect of a revival of the golden age of Augustus, when in the great peace of the Roman world, the civilized arts had attained their perfection under the patronage of an enlightened emperor. This Augustan golden age analogy was relentlessly applied to Charles II by the poetic well-wishers who greeted his return, eager to ensure a climate favourable to the arts.

The use of the term 'Restoration', then, to describe the events of 1660 drew on all this fertile complex of allusion to give every advantage to the yet untested monarch, who was almost universally welcomed in a vast upsurge of hope for a tolerant, benign reign. Poems on the Restoration abound with propitious images of cloudless days, perpetual spring, olives, bees, wine, calm seas, and halcyons. Images of reconstruction are also prominent: images of temples rebuilt (the Church of England was 'preserved from ruin and restored by you'[1]) and of cities re-edified, images which by their frequency and force suggest the deep desire for stability and lasting peace that lay behind the poems. Dryden's *Astraea Redux* was one of the most admired celebrations of the new King: its assured arrangement of symbolical figures and firm heroic measures gave clear indication of the poet's unusual competence. His title declared the theme. Astraea was the figure of Justice who would return to earth only when the golden age was renewed; the epigram from Virgil on the title-page reinforces the theme, 'Iam redit et Virgo, redeunt Saturnia regna' being the line from the Fourth Eclogue that proclaimed the golden age of Augustus (and deemed too by later commentators to have prophesied the opening of the Christian era). The Augustan motifs are strong: the poem announces that 'with a general peace the world was blest' after years of strife. From the security of the new reign, Dryden casts his eye along the scenes of war and exile which stretch like some grand fresco where men, gods, and allegorical figures combine, and he discerns the hand of providence guiding Charles through the confusions of the times to his triumphant return to Albion. The Christ-like power and mercy of Charles are invoked, after which the poem breaks into prophecy, inspired by its Virgilian original:

> And now Time's whiter Series is begun,
> Which in soft Centuries shall smoothly run;
>
> (ll. 292-93)

as history is understood to enter its final age in which the long-withheld blessings of the spirit shower down on the fortunate island. A vision of boundless empire succeeds: prosperity will be maintained by trade, with all nations resigning themselves to the felicity and justice of a British commonwealth. The Augustan note is struck one final time:

> Oh Happy Age! Oh Times like those alone
> By Fate reserved for great Augustus' throne!
>
> (ll. 320–21)

But, by a witty inversion, the glories of the Roman age are seen to have been only a foretaste of the time of true perfections, which commences now, with Charles, the 'happy Prince whom Heaven hath taught the way'.

The Augustan parallel derived additional force from the historical coincidence that Charles, like Augustus, began his reign after the disruption of a civil war, so that the achievements of peace seemed all the more admirable. Men looked to the King to heal the wounds of civil war by his clemency, and indeed, for the first two years of his reign, before the divisive religious Acts were issued, there was a sense of national unity unknown for decades. A prince 'Born the divided world to reconcile', sang the enraptured Waller, after having made the requisite Augustan gestures in his poem on 'His Majesty's Improvement of St James's Park' (which allowed him the sweet conceit of seeing paradise replanted). Lest one should imagine that all the extravagance of panegyric was gravely received by an approving monarch, one might recall the occasion when Charles complained to Waller that his congratulatory poem on his restoration was not so fine as his verses in praise of Cromwell, and had the reply 'poets, Sire, succeed better in fiction than in truth'. But no matter how improbable the visionary inventions of the poets, they served a valuable social function. They accentuated an already high state of national morale, and imposed a series of redeeming ideas over the confusion of political events. They helped to relate the present moment to the great structure of Western history, and to the providential purpose that was held to shape that structure. The poets provided too the heroic scheme that compensated for the not infrequent personal failings of the protagonists, for the roles and actions proposed in that scheme remained permanently valid on an ideal plane, and they would be upheld by all the arts that sought to interpret the higher significance of the age: poetry, painting, architecture, history, and the sermon.

The dominant themes of the Restoration were incorporated into the triumphal arches that were erected in the City of London along the path of Charles II's coronation procession in April 1661. These arches recall the series erected for James's London entry in 1604 (Charles I had had no public scenography at his coronation), but whereas those flamboyant Jacobean structures had been overwrought with curling ornamentation, tricked out with aspiring pinnacles, and dense with emblematic detail, the Restoration arches were much more cleanly designed on neo-Classic lines, their ornament restrained and their symbolical scenes fewer, clearer, and displayed with greater dignity. The advance of taste towards an accomplished Roman style was well documented by these arches, for the unknown designer handled the classical vocabulary of architectural detail with confidence and understanding, and we can see that the long career of Inigo Jones had left a firm impression on the architectural scene; no trace of Gothic or irregular Jacobean work survives upon these archways into the new age. The arches were illustrated and described by the publisher John Ogilby in his commemorative volume *The Entertaiment of his Most Excellent Majestie Charles II* in 1662; in his learned annotations on the triumphal arches he insisted on the thoroughgoing Romanness of the conceptual frame within which contemporary events were to be interpreted. The sustaining ideas were signalled by phrases from Virgil, the chief fabricator of the Augustan myth: 'Redeunt Saturnia regna' was inscribed on the first arch, dedicated to the glory of the Restoration, and another phrase, from the *Aeneid*, echoed the idea, 'volvenda dies en attulit ultro,' for what England now celebrated was 'Felix temporum reparatio', the happy renovation of the times.[2] The iron age of the rebellion was depicted as overthrown and replaced by the golden age of Charles. (Ogilby's notes make it clear that the bloodless nature of the change and its astonishing swiftness confirmed to many that the momentous event was a unique case of 'times trans-shifting', when God advanced the fortune of the State.) The alteration of the times was characterised through an image of architectural reparation: a painting on one side of the arch showed a scene of ruins, the disorder of the Commonwealth, contrasted with a prospect of finely styled buildings, the image of the new age. A relief over the arch showed Rebellion attended by Confusion, matched by a corresponding panel of Monarchy supported by Loyalty in a dignified tableau of serenity and order. In a brief theatrical scene enacted alongside the arch, Monarchy routed Rebellion after an exchange of strong speeches, and the people were praised for their instinctive loyalty to the King. Charles himself figured centrally on this first arch, depicted at the moment of his return, in the dress of a Roman emperor, about to assume his peaceful rule.

The second arch honoured the benign expansion of British influence, the new Augustan Pax Britannica to be achieved by world-wide trade and commerce, protected by an invincible navy. The dominion of the seas by British fleets was shown, the improvement of the sciences of navigation foretold, and the blessings of trade extolled. The implied theme is the aggressive enlargement of British naval power, but the overriding theme of a new golden age precludes the explicit praise of arms and force, so the banners of altruistic sentiment conceal the warlike stance. The arch of Concord that came next fortified the professions of benevolent rule once more. Glad figures sang a hymn of praise to Charles, 'The King of Peace', 'Converting Iron Times to Gold', while the concord was musically expressed by an orchestra of twenty-four violins set upon the arch, playing sprightly airs in the fashionable style of Lully. Finally there stood the Arch of Plenty, a rusticated structure with vines curling around the pillars, adorned with images representing England as a garden of plenty flourishing in the 'general peace' of the new Augustan age (Plate 12).

Such, then, were the elevating prospects through which Charles rode to his coronation. Poets, painters, architects, the court, and the King himself were all unanimous in finding the Roman parallel the perfect characterization of the times, and the confident adoption of Augustan motifs symbolized their conviction that a distinct new phase of national history had opened.

'In good King Charles's golden days' is a phrase that has remained in the popular memory. In practice, however, the gold proved gilt and soon tarnished. The general contentment at the King's return lasted well into 1662, when his marriage to the Portuguese princess, Catherine of Braganza, saw another Catholic queen and her retinue of priests installed in Somerset House. This unwelcome development was shortly followed by the imposition on the nation of a new Book of Common Prayer which destroyed the tolerant compromise of the Restoration settlement, caused the dispossession of many conscientious clergy who would not conform to the prescribed liturgy and rituals of the new service book, and began to close the doors of the Church of England against Dissenters. The same policy that had proved disastrous to Charles I, who was soft on Catholicism and harsh against Puritanism and dissent, and the same insensitivity towards the profound prejudices and convictions of the majority of Englishmen, were combining again to distance another Stuart king from his people.

The second Stuart age would in time develop a high and even heroic line of achievement in the arts, and in intellectual culture at large, but the immediate consequence of the Restoration was a reign of pleasure unlike anything experienced before in England. The King and his companions were young and had entered into times of good fortune and enjoyed the recovery of their estates. The country as a whole had endured two decades of war and of intense debate about religious and political principles, and had lived under a Puritan code of ethics that set a low value on the gratification of the senses. Now, encouraged from the top, the nation displayed an astonishing capacity for pleasure. London in particular became the centre of every kind of entertainment from the sophisticated to the lewd, as the nobility and gentry poured in from exile or from too many years of restraint on their rural estates to enjoy the social amenities raised up by the taste and money of the court. For the next generation, the pleasures of the town almost obliterated the attractions of rural retirement: the countryside became synonymous with dullness, there were no more country-house poems, and the natural world almost disappeared from view. To leaf through Pepys's Diary for the 1660s is to embark on the full tide of pleasurable life – even the church services are enlivened by fashionable music and by the stimulating presence of alluringly dressed women – yet we might reflect that during the 1650s, Pepys had shown a Puritan disposition in keeping with the times. Now, although he applies himself energetically to his business at the Navy Office, his life is diversified by theatre-going, musical gatherings, dinner parties, and drinking sessions, and by uninhibited discussions. More than any other contemporary document, Pepys's Diary conveys the sense of living in a new age and experiencing a renewal of time. He deliberately began the Diary as events in 1659 began to stir and signs of a miraculous alteration became evident. Every page in Pepys relays his sense of the freshness of life; each new day in the early years of the Restoration seems individually vivid and is savoured to the full. So many of the details of ordinary life feed his consciousness of the recent change: manners, dress, language, love, and religious observance all remind him of how different his world has become. He flirts and dreams of mistresses, he spends considerable sums on stylish clothes for himself and his wife, and on redecorating his house in the most modern taste, and acquiring the furnishings and luxuries of a society that was learning how to live comfortably and well.

The King (Plate 13) set the tone of the new society, and was himself a prominent figure on the London scene. He was a most accessible monarch, who might be encountered at the playhouse or riding down the street, stopping to chat with acquaintances, or taking a brisk walk in St James's Park with ministers or friends. His curiosity about inventions and novelties led him to attend the meetings of the Royal Society from time to time, to drop in on interesting citizens (as when he visited John Evelyn to inspect his new glass beehives), or to descend on his shipyards to see some new techniques of construction. His sexual curiosity took him all over London. Pepys one evening heard the King making love in the adjoining house, and Evelyn overheard 'a very familiar discourse' between the King and Nell Gwyn, 'she looking out of her garden on a terrace at the top of the wall, he standing on the green walk under it'; any gentleman with access to the court might watch the King kissing his mistress in some corner of Whitehall. The openness of his affairs was one of his engaging qualities, but his restless sexual adventures soon had a coarsening effect on court life.· 'His inclinations to love were the effects of health and a good constitution, with as little mixture of the seraphic part as ever man had', thought Lord Halifax in his 'character' of the King. Now, royal mistresses were officially acknowledged by titles and pensions, women of some beauty and little repute became duchesses, and royal bastards proliferated and grew up to be dukes. The King's example soon spread: his brother the Duke of York, a man of some sternness, with an honourable military record gained in exile, began to soften in this sybaritic world and to indulge in mistresses, wrecking his marriage to the daughter of the Earl of Clarendon (Plate 14). Many a noble mind was o'erthrown in the hedonistic excesses of the royal circle. The Duke of Buckingham was the most spectacular casualty: a gifted man of sharp political skills, with a talent for scientific as well as literary experiment, he had every advantage on his side. In 1657 his marriage to the daughter of General Fairfax was seen as a tactical triumph and heartening evidence of the reconciliation that could occur between great royalist and parliamentarian families. Instead of capitalizing on this position at the Restoration to make himself the leader of the forces of moderation and enlightened compromise in national affairs, he threw himself into a career of accelerating debauchery that wasted his immense fortune and dissipated his political assets, so that, at the end, the censorious Bishop Burnet could hold up his flayed character thus:

> He had no principles of religion, virtue or friendship; no
> truth or honour, no steadiness of conduct in him . . . he
> could keep no secret, nor execute any design without
> spoiling it. Pleasure and frolic, and extravagant diversion
> were indeed all he minded: by his eager pursuit of these he
> ruined one of the greatest estates in England, and perhaps
> one of the finest wits and finest personages that the world
> then knew.[3]

The Earl of Rochester ruined himself even more rapidly. He had 'a brightness in his wit to which none could arrive, and was not destitute of natural modesty till the Court corrupted him'.[4] Then, his spirits raised by lust and wine, he swam in seas of pleasure, until he went under in 1680, at the age of thirty-three, making last-minute gestures of repentance. Lord Buckhurst and Sir Charles Sedley were two more noble roisterers who did a good deal of damage to themselves, to their rivals, and to the reputation of the court by their drunken and frequently violent escapades. Yet all these wits had a remarkable sharpness of intelligence, literary flair, and an instinct for political action. They had too an irrepressible sense of the pretentiousness and hypocrisy of social life. With all their abilities, why did they

Around the arch: ✠ IACOBUS D.G MAGNÆ BRITANNIÆ/FRANCIÆ/SCOTIÆ/ET HYBERNIÆ REX ANNO MDCXIII

Qui regis imperio divisos orbe Britannos,
    Rex tot virorum fortium;
Qui terrore tui solius nominis Sostes

Qui pace ecclesiam, jus   *Ihs qui legibus ornas*
    Forum, scholas doctoribus;
Atq, inter vates pangis pia cármina, sceptro
    lunæ decenter lauream .

Plate 1. King James, engraving by Crispin van der Passe, 1613. The King wears a laurel wreath to celebrate his fame as a writer of divine poetry.

Plate 2. The Rustic Arch ('England's Arbour'), erected for King James's London entry in 1604. The arch images England as a garden of the arts.

Plate 3. Prince Henry, wearing armour given to him by Henri IV of France. Portrait by unknown artist at Dunster Castle.

Plate 4. Arundel House, etching by Wenceslaus Hollar. Situated between the Strand and the river, Arundel House was effectively an Academy of Arts during the 1630s, and housed the collections of paintings and sculpture accumulated by the Earl and Countess of Arundel.

Plate 5. Swakeleys, Middlesex. Built in the early 1630s, a good early Stuart house combining conservative features such as an Elizabethan window plan and Jacobean gables with fashionable Italianate pediments.

Plate 6. Clarendon House, Piccadilly. Designed by Sir Roger Pratt in the early 1660s for the new Lord Chancellor, it shows the typical characteristics of a great house of the Restoration.

Plate 7. Eikon Basilike, frontispiece, 1649. Engraved by William Marshall. An emblematic tableau portraying Charles I exchanging his earthly for a heavenly crown. The emblems on the left that illustrate Charles's condition show a rock unmoved amid a tempest, and the palm trees of Virtue that grow better under the weight of affliction.

Plate 8. Van Dyck, Charles I on Horseback, under a Triumphal Arch, 1637. The theatrical presentation of the King evokes the royal actor of the Whitehall masques. He is accompanied by his riding master, the Seigneur de St. Antoine.

Plate 9. Van Dyck, Prince Charles Louis and Prince Rupert, 1637. King Charles's nephews, the sons of Princess Elizabeth and Frederick, Elector Palatine, came to London to enlist Charles's help in the recovery of the Palatinate from the Catholic powers. Their mission was unsuccessful.

Plate 10. William Dobson, portrait of Endymion Porter. An image of a cultured Stuart gentleman painted close to the outbreak of the Civil War.

Plate 11. Samuel Cooper, miniature of Oliver Cromwell. Reputed to be the most accurate likeness of the Protector.

Plate 13. Charles II, a portrait after P. Lely.

Plate 12. Coronation Arch for Charles II. One of a sequence of neo-Classical arches erected for the coronation of the King in 1661.

Plate 14. Lely, Anne Hyde, Duchess of York. The daughter of Edward Hyde, Earl of Clarendon, she married the Duke of York in 1660; this portrait dates from the early 1660s, and is a fine example of Lely's opulent style.

Plate 15.   The Advancement of Learning. Title-page to the 1640 edition. This image of the spirit of enquiry shows a ship sailing beyond the pillars of the known world, represented by the two universities. Above, the intellect reaches out to encounter the visible world. Engraving by William Marshall.

Plate 17. Leviathan, title-page, 1651. A remarkable image of the body politic, accompanied by symbols of civil and ecclesiastical power.

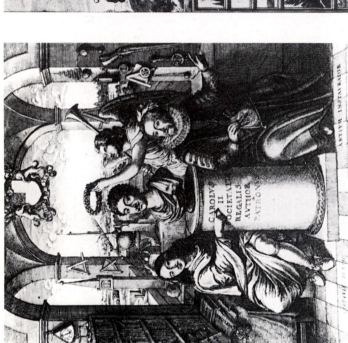

Plate 16. The History of the Royal Society, frontispiece, 1667. The figure of Fame crowns a bust of Charles II for his patronage of the Society. Bacon, whose ideas inspired the formation of the Society, sits on the right. On the left sits Lord Brouncker, the first President. Behind them, a collection of early scientific instruments. Etching by Hollar after a design by John Evelyn.

Plate 18. Edward Pierce, Bust of Wren, 1673. English baroque sculpture at its finest. Pierce was one of Wren's craftsmen, and worked in wood and metal as well as stone.

Plate 19. Wren's Sheldonian Theatre, engraving by Loggan. Modelled on a design for an ancient Roman theatre, the building was a gift to the University of Oxford from Gilbert Sheldon to mark his appointment as Archbishop of Canterbury.

Plate 20. Bethlehem Hospital, designed by Robert Hooke, 1676. A magnificent institution for the relief and cure of the insane.

and a train of like-minded debauchees have this urge to burn themselves out in a flare of dissipation, to fling away their fortunes by
gambling and drink, to ruin their marriages by endless fornications,
and risk their lives in fights and duels? This was not just the thought-
less high spirits of a privileged group, it was more like a deliberate
choice of a style of living that bordered on nihilistic hedonism. Their
behaviour may well be seen as a reaction to the earnestness of the
previous generation: 'Utterly disgusted with the endless discussion of
questions of principle and conscience, they had reverted to a purely
pagan attitude, and proclaimed that intellectual and sensuous pleasures
were the only aim of a sensible man.'[5] But the outrageousness of Rochester was more than the revulsion of a young man against the pretentions of the social code: his libertinism seems to be that of a highly
intelligent cynic, haunted by a sense of the utter futility of life. In such
poems as his 'Satire against Mankind' and 'On Nothing', this terrible
emptiness is glimpsed; he expressed it most succinctly in a translation
he made of a chorus from Seneca:

> After Death nothing is, and nothing Death;
> The utmost Limits of a gasp of Breath.
> Let the ambitious Zealot lay aside
> His hopes of Heaven; (whose Faith is but his Pride)
> Let slavish Souls lay by their Fear,
> Nor be concern'd which way or where,
> After this life they shall be hurl'd:
> Dead, we become the Lumber of the World;
> And to that Mass of Matter shall be swept,
> Where things destroy'd, with things unborn are kept;
> Devouring time swallows us whole,
> Impartial Death confounds Body and Soul.[6]

The 'Satire against Mankind' sceptically dismisses man's pretentions
to be guided by reasonable principles or by generous ideals: Rochester
is incredulous that any serious claim can be made for consistent intelligence, let alone for the immortality of the soul. Man's reasoning
capacity leads him into perverse conflict with the instincts of his nature,
and human nature itself seems utterly depraved. He would desire to
believe otherwise, but in this darkly pessimistic poem he finds no aid
from philosophy or religion. Man is nothing more than a self-deluding
beast, cursed with a maddening rational faculty, faced with extinction.

> Huddled in dirt the reasoning Engine lies,
> Who was so proud, so witty and so wise.
>
> (ll. 29–30)

Loathing himself for being such a creature, Rochester's reaction was to fling himself into sensual gratification as a kind of crude existential test, a cynical verification of his selfhood. Rochester's poetry flickers with a tragic self-awareness as he describes his repeated degradations in the rage for pleasure, when 'drunkenness relieved by lechery' drives this most brilliant of Restoration wits into the most sordid of courses. In his 'Conference with a Postboy' he makes the facetious enquiry:

> Son of a Whore God damn thee, canst thou Tell
> A Peerless Peer the readiest Way to Hell?
> I've Outswill'd Bacchus, Sworn of my own Make
> Oaths, Frighted Furyes, and made Pluto quake:
> Swived Whore more ways than ever Sodoms Walls
> Knew, or the Colledge of the Cardinals, . . .
> But hang't, why do I mention these poor Things,
> I have blasphem'd God, and libell'd Kings;
> The readiest way to Hell, Boy; Quick!
>   (*Boy*) Ne're stir
> The readiest way, my Lord's by Rochester.

But hell was a fable anyway, and the only punishment for Rochester's vices was to remain himself. Apparently, however, he made a deathbed conversion to the Church of England, an incident related in great detail by Gilbert Burnet, the minister who received him, and who tried to use it to show that the Church was still the last repository of truth and comfort in scandalous times, and that even the most besotted sinner would ultimately come home to it. But Burnet's sober contrived narrative of his conversion cannot diminish the force of the energetically obscene poems that Rochester wrote in the 1660s and 1670s to praise his salacious days and nights, and amuse his friends. Copulation thrives, or on occasion fails to thrive, and wit aids and abets. From time to time, in the midst of this obsessive sensuality, a lyric of unusual charm and grace appears, but only too often the scathing verse is motivated by an impulse to defile.

Rochester's poetry has an imaginative vitality which is only intermittently present in the verse of his fellow wits, Buckingham, Sedley, and Dorset, though they too can turn out an effortless lyric on occasion. These titled Restoration poets were the heirs to the Cavalier tradition of Lovelace, Suckling, and Carew, but now the old nobleness of manner has been lost. The Cavaliers could be witty and flippant in love, changeable in affections, cynical or resigned in misfortune, and were not unacquainted with lechery, but the Restoration writers lacked the generosity of spirit and vision of an ideal love that gave such assurance and gallantry to the Cavaliers. The grosser life-style of the later poets must account for some of the difference, but the character of the court reinforced the change. At the court of Charles I the cult of platonic love patronized by the King and Queen exercised a refining influence over the imaginative expressions of that culture; by contrast, after the Restoration, it was virtually impossible to maintain an elevated or generous tone in the poetry of love when licentiousness was the norm at a court whose king could be satirized in lines such as these:

> Nor are his high desires above his strength:
> His sceptre and his prick are of a length; . . .
> Restless he rolls about from whore to whore,
> A merry monarch, scandalous and poor.
> (Rochester; 'A Satyr on Charles II'.) ll. 10–11, 20–21

The King's taste and example were not always so deleterious. He exercised an encouraging influence over the drama which revived most remarkably in his reign. Unlike his father, Charles II did not foster a delicate court drama based on the theatre in Whitehall Palace, but patronized the public theatre. Shortly after his return, Charles issued a royal warrant for two companies to perform in London, one directed by Sir William Davenant under the patronage of the Duke of York, playing first at Salisbury Court, then at Dorset Garden; the other, the King's Company, headed by Thomas Killigrew, eventually established itself in the Theatre Royal, Drury Lane. These two companies enjoyed a monopoly of theatrical performance throughout the period, and Davenant's presence ensured a continuity of acting experience that went back to the days of the Jacobean theatre. He had also been directly involved in the production of Caroline masques and of Cromwellian opera; his productions in the new reign were predictably accomplished, and noted for their use of music, lavish scenery, and stage effects. With the King and the Duke of York as constant patrons, and an audience composed mainly of the nobility, gentry, and prosperous citizens, the theatres were soon furnished with new plays that reflect the stylish, pleasure-seeking society that was transforming London life. A fresh sprightliness of language was one of the most striking features of the new comedy of manners. Dryden believed that the King was directly responsible for this improvement in the language of society, for he had acquired a French manner of witty speech during his exile.

> If any ask me whence it is that our conversation is so
>   much refined, I must freely, and without flattery, ascribe it
>   to the Court, and in it, particularly to the King, whose
>   example gives a law to it. . . . The desire of imitating so

great a pattern first awakened the dull and heavy spirits of
the English from their natural reservedness, loosened them
from their stiff forms of conversation, and made them
easy and pliant to each other in discourse. Then,
insensibly, our way of living became more free, and the
fire of the English wit, which was being stifled under a
constrained melancholy way of breeding, began first to
display its force, by mixing the solidity of our nation with
the air and gaiety of our neighbours.[7]

The Restoration playwrights made the most of the new style of
conversation: the brisk 'sparkish' exchanges between the wits, the
tingling language of flirtation, the elegant observations on the beau
monde and the arch asides gave a lasting vitality to the scenes of social
life. Epigrammatic exchanges were much in favour, partly as a display
of polished wit, and partly, it has been suggested, out of a desire to
expose the patterns of behaviour at work in society.[8]

This interest in the operations of emerging codes of social behaviour
is a hallmark of Restoration comedy, and it links the theatre with the
pervasive curiosity that was a characteristic of the Restoration spirit,
which expressed itself also in the spheres of science and philosophy.
There was an eagerness to understand inner workings which gave rise
to a new literary self-consciousness (most fully developed in Dryden)
leading to sustained critical activity in English about the nature of
comedy or satire and about the construction of plays or the purity of
language. The philosophic curiosity displayed by Locke, who wanted
to understand plainly the processes of thought and sensation by which
men acquired their ideas and understanding, was another aspect of the
same investigative mentality. In all these areas there is a common desire
to observe clearly and without prejudice or prejudgement the operations of some process or other.[9] Hobbes had liberated men's minds
for frank objective criticism in his disturbingly honest study of political
power, *Leviathan*, with the effect that, in the intellectually open mood
of the Restoration, an enquiring habit of mind flourished vigorously
without fear of censure. Samuel Pepys comes across as a representative
man here, for his Diary expresses an immense curiosity about his
world. He is intensely interested in his own reactions to experience,
observant about manners and social behaviour, fascinated by the intellectual advances of the times. He experiments with the more liberated
life-style now opening up, takes advantage of the freer relations
between the sexes, and has a vast relish for speculative conversation;
not surprisingly, he is a dedicated theatre-goer.

Restoration comedy dramatized in particular the experiments in
sexual relationships that were possible in the upper reaches of society,

where women were allowed a high degree of independence, where men wanted spirited female company, and where traditional attitudes to marriage were changing fast. Fashionable gentlemen assumed sexual freedom to be a natural right, and they were also inclined to be fairly indulgent to their wives' infidelities, yet they wanted as well the settled affections of marriage. For their part, women of the same class were beginning to feel that they had the right to arrogate the freedoms of the male sex. All these tendencies were reflected on the stage. Intrigues, pursuits, and compromise, conducted with the maximum of style and wit, form the habitual material of the comedies of Etherege, Wycherley, and Dryden. The entertainment they offered was heightened by that deeply appreciated innovation of the Restoration theatre, the presence on stage of actresses, who gave an additional sexual charge to the action, and who tantalized the noble spectators as prospective mistresses.

King Charles, who took great pleasure in comedy (and in the actresses of comedy), cast an approving eye over these scenes, suggesting plots to dramatists and making sure his preferences were observed. But his taste also promoted the rise of heroic tragedy in the theatre of the 1660s and 1670s. Charles wished to encourage an English equivalent to the French heroic drama, with its elevated sentiments concerning the rival claims of love and duty, or the crises of political allegiance. Initially he requested the Earl of Orrery to write a play in heroic couplets, resulting in *The General* of 1663; thereafter the genre enjoyed a remarkable vogue until the mid-1670s. Usually with a classical or exotic setting, such as the India of Dryden's *Areng-Zebe* or the Africa of Settle's *Empress of Morocco*, these plays had an abundance of bombast and flamboyant gesture, but little ethical or political intelligence. One need only try to find some English play to stand comparison with Corneille's tragedies to understand how ineffectual was the 'serious' drama of the Restoration. Yet the King had a passion for these plays. Perhaps their autocratic monarchs and their unrestrained magniloquence appealed to the latent despot in Charles.[10] These plays deserved to attract parody, and Buckingham's *The Rehearsal* (1671) caught many of the preposterous features of the genre in his ridiculous presentation of the rival kings of Brentford and their mystifying intrigues entangled in the stage conventions and the stylized language of heroic drama. Buckingham also struck at the complacent superiority of the 'serious' authors through his figure of Bayes, who resembles John Dryden, the creator of many of these noble confections. Bayes admits the narrow appeal of this kind of drama: 'I write for some persons of quality and peculiar friends of mine that understand what flame and power in writing is; and they do me the right, Sir, to approve of what I do.' He boasts of his intellectual powers:

'When I have a grand design in hand, I take physic, and let blood, for, when you would have pure swiftness of thought and fiery flights of fancy, you must have a care of the pensive part.' (Act II, Sc. i.) It was indeed 'the pensive part' of these plays that was most wanting, for the enforced poetic justice and the sententious moralizing often weakened any achievement of plot and character. Buckingham's attack did much to deflate the pretensions of heroic drama, though it by no means killed off the genre, the prolonged popularity of which should remind us that many of the Restoration nobility did hold an exalted idea of their historical importance and power, and approved of a drama that comp- lemented the heroic image they favoured when in serious mood. However, the new drama was pitched too high to have much genuine relevance to society, the prevailing character of which, with its licence and political jobbery, was too clearly at odds with the noble and elev- ated models that the theatre proposed. In practice, the only area in which Restoration society was able convincingly to project its heroic aspirations was in architecture (see pp. 70–71).

The vogue for heroic drama was one strain in a complex of French influences that came in at the Restoration as a consequence of the court's exile in Paris. French taste then as now seemed more sophis- ticated than English, and social life was conducted more stylishly; in intellectual matters, French methodology had the appeal of clarity achieved by reasonable procedure. In ways both superficial and profound, French practice had a considerable impact on English fash- ionable life and attitudes of mind. Costume altered rapidly, with men of social ambition adopting the long embroidered coat, waistcoat and lace cravat, offset with a full wig, while women wore cascading silk dresses cut low on the shoulders and breast. The easy morals of the upper ranks were encouraged by the example of Parisian society, as was the brighter style of conversation. The royal system of mistresses followed that of the French court, although in most other respects the informal style of Charles II's court was quite unlike that of Louis XIV. As we have noted, Charles had acquired a taste for music in the French style, introducing an orchestra of twenty-four violins into the Chapel Royal in imitation of Louis's practice, to enliven the services with 'brisk and airy' interludes, and a similar orchestra provided music at court. Familiarity with the modern townscape of Paris and the lofty dignified apartments of the Louvre prompted the King and his archi- tecturally minded friends to consider how London might be improved by enlightened planning and handsome design, especially for public buildings and noble residences. Among the arts, poetry was particu- larly attentive to French models. The growing adoption of the heroic couplet owed more to the example of Boileau and the French dram- atists, who had shown how effective it was for pointed, judgemental verse, than to the modest English precedents provided by Waller and Denham. Discussions of literary genre and of the criteria of correctness in language (such as we find in Dryden's essays on 'Dramatic Poesy' and on the 'Origin and Progress of Satire', and in the many prefaces to plays and poems), were stimulated by the critical reflections of Corneille and Boileau, which were part of the neo-Classic impulse to impose rules and limitations on modern literary forms. The French preference for academies as a way of promoting communal investigation of a subject probably conditioned the formation of the Royal Society for the purpose of scientific research in 1660. In philosophy, the logical method of Descartes provided Locke with the systematic techniques that he used to explore the nature of knowledge. The adoption of French styles and ideas was one of the clearest ways in which the new order of society distanced itself from the character of Cromwellian England.

Beyond the fashionable circles touched by these new influences, the earnest Protestant cast of mind that had dominated the Interregnum period persisted. The most enduring imaginative works of the Restoration period, those of Milton and Bunyan, arose out of the traditions rejected by the new establishment. For both men the experience of adversity proved the forcing ground of their work. Milton led a secluded life after 1660, having narrowly escaped execution in the brief purge of the surviving regicides. Bunyan endured a great deal of persecution under the laws against Dissenters. Yet for both of them, the struggle to understand God's purposes towards men caused them to look far beyond their contemporary disabilities to the point where the timeless intersects with time. When *Paradise Lost* appeared in 1667, it must have seemed to many readers to have been published 'an age too late', as Milton feared. Its grand design of universal history and its imaginative colour (which owe much to Spenser and to the Italian writers of epical romance) declare it to be a late work of Renaissance humanism; its theological scheme revives issues that were at their height in the 1640s. *Paradise Lost* was in fact published in the same year as the *History of the Royal Society*, and Milton's cosmology with its attendant angels and devils coincided with Newton's early research into the mathemetics of celestial motion that would be formulated in *Principia Mathematica*. *Paradise Lost* had to attract attention in a literary world distracted by comedies of manners, bombastic tragedies, satires, and erotic verse, but slowly its power was recognized. Although its imaginative scheme is typical of an older age, the poem also bears on recent events: the need to justify God's ways must have been particularly strong after the failure of the Puritan revolution, when Milton, like so many Protestant activists, sought reassurance that the cause was not hopeless, that in spite of their inability to realize the godly state now, the long designs of providence would ultimately bring about the only restoration that mattered, that of the kingdom of Christ.

The same concern with justification persists strongly in *Samson Agonistes* (1671). Samson may be taken as a type of the faithful servant of God who has been cast down by the turn of political events – and indeed has contributed to his own downfall by his weakness of spirit – but who now experiences a regenerative impulse which leads him to the destruction of the enemy and to a spiritual triumph which coincides with his death. God does not desert his chosen people, even though in the fluctuations of history he may appear to do so: it is the end that shows the design complete, and in concentrating on the final phase of Samson's life, Milton can assert the purposeful workings of providence, long delayed but sure. It may be that Milton had in mind Restoration society when he characterized the Philistines as a vain, idolatrous people, given to festivity and licence, whose temple was described as a theatre.[11] Certainly, Samson's destruction of the theatre has a powerful symbolical suggestiveness, and the crushing of the Philistines in the midst of their entertainments hints at Milton's hopes that the bondage endured by the Puritans, like that of the Israelites, might not long continue. Even at the height of its triumph, the new society lay under a threat of doom, and the persevering saint, like Milton, could rest on his faith,

> With God not parted from him, as was feared,
> But favouring and assisting to the end.
>
> (ll. 1719–20)

Bunyan shared this conviction. He spent much of his time in bondage, imprisoned as a Nonconformist to prevent him preaching what the authorities regarded as a troublesome doctrine, Conscience forbade him to obey the civil law, and in his determination to preach the gospel freely he saw himself as a successor to the Apostles in their struggle against unrighteous power. He was not, however, so strictly confined that he could not write or publish. In 1665 he brought out *The Holy City*, an interpretation of the symbolism of the celestial city in the Book of Revelation, which encouraged the belief that 'in time of oppression the Saints can think of triumph',[12] a sentiment close to Milton's in *Samson*. In this book Bunyan looked forward in holy fear and anticipation to the apocalyptic year 1666, the year that engrossed the Number of the Beast. All Christians were apprehensive of this date, which promised some momentous revelation,[13] and for many Puritans it promised to be the climax of the Christian era when the prophecies of Christ's return would be realized and the saints called to his presence, their struggle justified at last. The Great Plague of 1665 and the Great Fire of 1666 were strictly in line with apocalyptic expectations – God punishing a wicked generation before showing his mercy to his saints. However, chastened yet unchanged, England survived the fatal year, and Bunyan, instead of triumphing with the just, published his spiritual autobiography *Grace Abounding to the Chief of Sinners*. Here the pattern of conversion that countless Puritans had experienced receives its clearest and most memorable expression in our literature. The careless early life, known in retrospect to be sinful, the apprehension of a divine light in some sermon or passage of the Bible, signs of God's providence glimpsed in commonplace happenings, phases of temptation and doubt, the urgent desire to be saved, the fear that one is not, the final overwhelming conviction of one's calling – all is communicated with a rare directness in clear, moving English lit by the phrases and cadences of the Bible.

The stages of that experience were universalized in *Pilgrim's Progress*, which was published in 1678, though apparently begun in prison a decade earlier. 'What shall I do to be saved?' cries Christian. The City of Destruction where he lives is also a place of Philistines, but unlike Samson, whose wise passivity awaits the divine impulse to act, Christian is an activist, who urgently seeks the pathway to heaven, overcoming all temptations of earthly pleasure in his singleminded quest for grace. Bunyan's dream takes us into a realm of allegory which is easily penetrated by anyone well read in the Bible and aware that the terrain of spiritual life is rough and hazardous. The clue to understanding is always there in the biblical references, but what prevents *Pilgrim's Progress* from being just another manual to salvation is the detailing of ordinary life and manners, and the earnest colloquial discussions that prove that common men can grasp the difficulties of religion and enjoy its promise as effectively as any learned divine. The plain convictions of Bunyan and the vast imaginative power of Milton meet in the Bible, which would remain the strength and refuge of the Nonconformists during their long period in the wilderness. When the bishops of the restored Anglican Church joined with the politicians in the long process of excluding the Dissenters from the national life and of trying to suppress their activities, they scarcely understood the energies they were attempting to control.

The re-established Church of England showed itself to be socially conservative and lukewarm in faith. Its leading bishops, Sheldon, Tenison, Tillotson, and Stillingfleet, were moderate, secular men who favoured a cool tone and a plain style in sermons. Gilbert Burnet, Bishop of Salisbury, described what he considered to be the appropriate manner for preaching in the Restoration Church:

> As to the style, sermons ought to be very plain; the
> figures must be easy, not mean, but noble, and brought in
> upon design to make the matter better understood. The
> words in sermons must be simple, and in common use;
> not savouring of the Schools, nor above the understanding
> of the people. All long periods, such as carry two or three
> different thoughts in them, must be avoided, for few
> hearers can follow or apprehend these.[14]

The mild tone of Burnet's recommendation exemplifies the restored
Church's mistrust of enthusiasm in religion, that is, emotive preaching
and the outpouring of spiritual experience such as sustained Bunyan
and the sectaries. The whole character of Anglicanism became increasingly polite and civil, a matter more of good taste than of deep
convictions, and Wren's city churches of the 1670s convey the mood
well, with their plainly lit, distinguished interiors. This politeness
tended to discourage the writing of devotional verse, which had been
one of the distinctive exercises of the Anglican spirit for much of the
century, but which became unfashionable after 1660. Just as the decline
of love-poetry after the Restoration was due in some measure to the
tone of the highest ranks of society, communicating itself downwards,
so devotional verse failed because the prevailing character of the upper
classes grew too secular. Both the earlier Stuart kings had had a high
respect for religious verse, and in their courtly circles and far beyond
it was assumed that gentlemen wrote social and religious verse as
complementary expressions of a balanced character. The life of the
spirit was valued then at every level of society, and the wide circulation
of devotional verse was an aid to Christian community among Anglicans, Puritans, and Catholics alike.

The manifest impiety of the upper reaches of Restoration society
soon caused this tradition to lapse. The King again set the tone: 'His
sense of religion was so very small that he did not so much as affect
the hypocrite; but at prayers and sacraments let everyone, by his
negligent behaviour, see how little he thought himself concerned in
these matters.'[15] That was Bishop Burnet's opinion, and most of the
leading figures of society were equally neglectful of religion. In the
churches, as we have seen, there was a preference for plain sermons
and for the public statement of a Christian's duty, but little evident
interest in the intimate spiritual experiences that had so absorbed earlier
generations of Englishmen and had provided the impetus for so much
devotional poetry. Moreover, the fashion for a plainer style in
language, which was aided by the admiration for French practice and
furthered by the Royal Society's recommendations of clear, informative English, discredited the complex, allusive, metaphor-dominated

poetry that had been so favourable to religious meditation. Given the notably cynical and profane character of the court and city circles that dominated the literary worlds in this period, it is hardly surprising that when religion is the subject of poetry, the mode is satirical, with religion regarded as a branch of politics, as with Butler's *Hudibras*, Dryden's *The Hind and the Panther*, and Oldham's *Satires upon the Jesuits*. Butler's unremitting contempt for all forms of religious profession helped to make *Hudibras* one of the best selling books of the time (and one that King Charles liked to carry round in his pocket). Its popularity was an ill omen for devotional verse in the fashionable world.[16]

If one looks at the uncomfortable career of the leading man of letters of the age, John Dryden, one can appreciate how difficult it was to follow the serious calling of a poet. By temperament a celebratory, idealizing, constructive poet, he found plenty of material in the early years of Charles's reign, but after 1666 there was notably less to celebrate in the national life, although elegies still exercised his skills in panegyric. Meeting the demand for tragedies and comedies occupied his middle years, but the tragedies 'exhibit a kind of illustrious depravity, and majestic madness', thought Johnson, and the comedies were good but lacked the ease and sparkle of the best. Later, in the 1680s, he discovered a talent for satirical verse on political and religious subjects which brought him great acclaim, but which also entangled him in the embitterments of factional politics. Never did Dryden find a large subject worthy of his poetic abilities, but instead he invested his talents in the many translations from the classics that make up well over half of his collected verse. A man whose work is so largely composed of translation must surely have been short of real subjects. Criticism attracted him, and allowed him an authority he could not achieve in his poetry. The generations of the eighteenth century were inclined to appreciate him less for his subject-matter than for his advances in poetic technique, his strength and variety of expression, and his smoothness of metre.

In fact, the society of the later seventeenth century never found a poet who succeeded in transmitting the central energies of his time. Milton was a survivor from a quite different society, Rochester and the wits were too extreme and clearly not part of a society that was in the process of renewing itself, Dryden was unsure of his stance. Poetry in fact no longer closely engaged with the main intellectual achievements of the age, which belonged now to the men associated with the Royal Society, figures such as Wren, Hooke, Boyle, Newton, and Locke, whose importance is such that it requires a separate consideration.

Notes

1. Dryden, 'To his Sacred Majestie: a Panegyric on his Coronation' l. 48.

2. 'Volvenda dies . . .': 'Circling time has brought unasked that which no god had dared to promise' (*Aeneid*, IX, 9). Also used by Cowley as the epigram to his 'Restoration Ode'.

3. Gilbert Burnet, *A History of His Own Times*, Everyman edition (n.d.), p. 37.

4. Ibid., p. 102.

5. Vivian de Sola Pinto, *Sir Charles Sedley* (1927), p. 52. Pinto perceptively notes the association of Sedley and other Restoration wits at Oxford with the experimental philosopher John Wilkins, Warden of Wadham, and suggests that 'the excesses of these young men in the reign of Charles II may be regarded as a sort of distorted application of the experimental view of life taught by such men as Wilkins' (p. 41).

6. Translation of Seneca's *Troades*, II, Chorus, ll. 1–12.

7. Dryden, *Essays*, edited by W. P. Ker (1926), I, 176.

8. See Bonamy Dobrée, *Restoration Comedy*, second edition (1962), pp. 37–38.

9. Ibid., pp. 10–11, for the suggestions I have developed here.

10. See James Sutherland, 'The Impact of Charles II on Restoration Literature', in *Restoration and Eighteenth-Century Literature: Essays in Honor of A. D. McKillop*, edited by C. Camden, (Chicago, 1963), pp. 259–60.

11. See the interpretation of *Samson Agonistes* in terms of contemporary politics, offered by Nicholas Jose in *Ideas of the Restoration in English Literature, 1660–71* (1984), pp. 142–63.

12. Roger Sharrock, *John Bunyan* (1968), p. 45.

13. The mysterious number of the second Beast of Revelation 13 is made known in verse 18: 'Here is wisdom. Let him that hath understanding count the number of the beast: for it is the number of a man; and his number is six hundred threescore and six.' The year 1666 had long been anticipated as a critical date in the apocalyptic scheme, when Antichrist would arise and the final struggle of history would begin. Vast ingenuity was expended on discovering who was the man whose number was that of the. Beast. The history of this obsession is given in Christopher Hill, *Antichrist in Seventeenth-Century England* (1971).

14. Gilbert Burnet, 'A Discourse of Pastoral Care', in *The Clergyman's Instructor* (1692).

15. Gilbert Burnet, *A History of His Own Times*, p. 33.

16. One must remember that Thomas Traherne was probably writing his visionary verse in the early 1660s, but he was secluded in Herefordshire and his work remained unknown until this century.

John Evelyn

A man who was always close to the centres of activity in the cultural
and intellectual life of Restoration society was John Evelyn.

John Evelyn exemplifies to perfection that distinctive Restoration
type, the virtuoso. The virtuoso tended to be a well-travelled gentleman of almost limitless curiosity, professing a certain connoisseurship in the arts and aspiring to be something of a collector. He
would hope to obtain some sixteenth-century Italian paintings or some
fragments of antique sculpture, and almost certainly he would form
a collection of engravings. His library would be a magazine of miscellaneous learning. His pride, however, would be his cabinet of curiosities, where his collection of rarities would be on display, probably
consisting of some well-preserved oddities of natural history (shells,
fossils, bits of coral, etc.), archaeological bric-à-brac (a spearhead or
a fragment from the Temple of Diana), and a few items of a semi-
precious nature (such as cameos or intaglios). Although the virtuoso,
especially after the Restoration, tended to take an intelligent interest
in scientific experiments (in some cases making observations or
collecting data himself), the appeal of his own collections was more
to the faculty of wonder than to any fundamental scientific instinct.
He inclined also to an interest in antiquities, expecially local ones, such
as earthworks, Roman remains, and the ruins of medieval abbeys.
Evelyn had all these tendencies, plus a practical sense of application that
enabled him to rise above the amiable trifling that afflicted too many
virtuosi, so that his interests were made to serve the public good and
contribute to the general intellectual advance.

Evelyn came from a landed family in Surrey (whose wealth derived
from the manufacture of gunpowder), and after his studies at Oxford
in the late 1630s he had the good fortune to become acquainted with
the Earl of Arundel, who was the leading art collector among the
Stuart aristocracy. When Evelyn set out on his European travels,
prudently avoiding the Civil War, he met Arundel again in Padua,
where the Earl conducted him around the antiquities and gave him
instructions for further studies to perfect his taste. He spent some time
in Paris before returning to England in 1645 to manage his estates. As
a royalist, he kept out of public life during the 1650s, devoting himself
to laying out the gardens on his estate at Sayes Court near Deptford,
and reflecting on projects that he would carry out in later years.

The Restoration transformed Evelyn's life. He had published a
pamphlet urging the return of the King and had intrigued on his behalf;
he had made many contacts among the exiled royalists in France, so
in 1660 he was instantly *persona grata*, with access to the King. In the

next few years he was extraordinarily active, responding to the invigorating atmosphere of the new reign. Civic improvement was his first concern. His years of travel in Italy and France had shown him how handsome and distinguished a great city could appear; in contrast London was a dim, smoky huddle, quite lacking the nobility appropriate to a metropolis of international significance. In his pamphlet *Fumifugium or The Smoak of London Dissipated* (1661), he proposed to purge London of its filthy air by removing all the great polluters – the soapworks, breweries, lime-kilns, and dyeing works – out of the city and relocating them several miles downstream. In addition, he proposed to plant a great aromatical hedge to the west of London, so that the air would be filled with fragrant odours. Vast plantations of lavender, rosemary, juniper, bays, and other scented herbs, and fields of beans and hops would tinge and refresh the air and restore the spirits of those who had been 'long in city pent'. In a more immediately practical move, Evelyn got himself onto the commission for sewers and drains. In 1664 he published a translation from the French of Fréart's *Parallel between Ancient and Modern Architecture*, finely illustrated with details of every kind of Classical pillar, cornice, and ornamentation, and dedicated to King Charles, in the hope that he would be a true Augustus, raising princely buildings and giving a harmonious order to new construction in the capital. The King was disposed to undertake great works, both royal and civic. Evelyn was nominated to the commission for the rebuilding of St Paul's, and he records in his Diary how, late in August 1666, the commission, which included Wren, surveyed the cathedral and recommended that it should be demolished, 'for that the shape of what stood was very mean, and we had a mind to build it with a noble cupola, a form of church-building not as yet known in England, but of a wonderful grace'. A few days later, the Great Fire implemented their recommendation by burning down St Paul's and most of the City of London. Within a week Evelyn presented the King with a survey of the ruins and a plan for rebuilding the City on spacious continental lines, with wide avenues, squares, circuses, and a fine embankment as a promenade, but this imaginative project, like the similar ones submitted by Wren and Hooke, came to nothing because of the tenacity of local property owners, who could not be dislodged.

Evelyn was involved with the Royal Society from its inception, finding there a congenial intellectual circle that gratified his unfailingly curious mind. 'Hence to the Royal Society, to refresh among the philosophers', reads a typical entry in his Diary. He had already, in 1659, proposed the foundation of 'a philosophicall college' whose members should pursue experiments along Baconian lines (another of his projects for the public good), so the Royal Society was to some extent a realization of his scheme, although it was more informal than his scholarly collegiate plan. Within the vast operation of the ordering of knowledge that the Society undertook, Evelyn addressed himself to matters of horticulture and to the fine arts, as befitted his character as a virtuoso; he had relatively little to do with the research carried on by the serious scientists, although he was an admiring observer of their achievements. His major work was *Sylva, or A Discourse of Forest Trees*, dedicated to the King and presented to the Royal Society in 1664. This was one of those encyclopaedic treatises of a kind beloved of seventeenth-century polymaths that carries a great freight of classical learning to a modern destination. His aim was to encourage new plantations of hardwood trees throughout the kingdom, to restock the country after the immense loss of trees during the Civil Wars, to provide a long-term supply of timber for naval and architectural purposes, and to improve the appearance of gentlemen's estates by fine woody prospects. Part of the book is a practial account of the propagation of forest trees and of their different properties, but the book culminates in an elevated discourse on 'The Sacredness and Use of Standing Groves', wherein Evelyn evokes the sanctity and mysteriousness of trees, their role in spiritual history, and their benevolent influence on mankind, until his English woods become indistinguishable from the groves of paradise itself. Evelyn's combination of horticultural treatise and spiritual meditation belongs to the transitional phase in the intellectual world of the seventeenth century, between the leisured humanist display of learning and piety and forthright scientific enquiry. The balance between the old and the new sensibility, as one encounters it in Evelyn or in his friend Sir Thomas Browne, was productive of a deeply imaginative expression, wherein the factual content is glorified by association with some lofty theme. So, Evelyn's mind can rise from practical advice about planting trees to the consideration that

> the sum of all is, Paradise itself was but a kind of
> Nemorous Temple, or Sacred Grove, planted by God
> himself and given to man, tanquam primo sacerdoti . . . a
> place consecrated for Sober Discipline, and to contemplate
> those mysterious and sacramental Trees which they were
> not to touch with their hands; and in memory of them, I
> am inclined to believe Holy Men (as we have shew'd in
> Abraham and others) might plant and cultivate Groves,
> where they traditionally invoked the Deity. . . . They
> were reputed so venerable, because more remote from
> Men and Company, more apt to compose the Soul, and
> fit it for divine Actions and sometime Apparitions.[1]

Evelyn followed up the success of *Sylva* with *Terra, or A Philo-sophical Discourse of Earth*, which was a systematic study of types of soil and a survey of what crops and plants are best suited to different soils, with suggestions to improve fertility. He presented this work to the Royal Society in 1675, together with *Pomona*, a tract encouraging the development of the cider industry in England, a project then exercising several members of the Society. In addition to the economic possi-bilities of a flourishing cider trade, the drink was thought to promote health and longevity. Similar concerns prompted Evelyn's wonderful discourse on salads, *Acetaria*, an enraptured account of the healthful qualities of 'the tribe of Sallets', which he esteemed to be rich in moral and philosophic virtue. One's opinion of lettuce is vastly improved by the assurance that

it allays Heat, bridles Choler, extinguishes Thirst, excites
Appetite, kindly nourishes; and, above all, represses
Vapours, conciliates Sleep, mitigates Pain; besides the
Effect it has upon the Morals, Temperance and Chastity.
Galen (whose beloved Sallet it was) from its pinguid,
subdulcid, and agreeable Nature, says it breeds the most
laudable Blood. No marvel then that they were by the
Ancients called Sana, by way of eminency, and so highly
valu'd by the great Augustus, that attributing his Recovery
of a dangerous Sickness to them, 'tis reported, he erected a
Statue, and built an Altar to this noble Plant.[2]

Transported by such excellent thoughts, Evelyn becomes an enthusi-astic proponent of vegetarianism. In the beginning, in paradise, Adam and Eve were salad folk, and 'fed on Vegetables and other hortulan Productions before the fatal Lapse', and the extraordinary longevity of man in the first age was due, he believes, to his temperate diet of fruit and herbs.

Evelyn's imagination, so concerned with gardens, frequently reverts to man's original garden state. Gardening for him is a spiritual exercise in which he can faintly recover the condition of innocence, and it is perhaps not surprising that the great work of his lifetime, begun in the 1650s, was called 'Elysium Britannicum'. The manuscript runs to nearly a thousand pages, dealing with every conceivable aspect of gardens, their 'natural, divine, moral and political' qualities, their ordering and ornamentation, terminating in 'Garden Burial' and 'Paradise'. It is a plan for life lived entirely within a garden state, a vision of an innocent existence shared with other 'garden heroes', as he called them, that he secretly cherished as an alternative to his busy public preoccupations.

Evelyn's Diary is the record of a man who remained in the main-stream of intellectual and social life until the end of the century. He is constantly going about among his illustrious friends to view their houses and estates, to observe the latest experiments, or to savour the latest novelties, and to read his Diary for a sustained period is to be reminded of the amazing surge of activity across the whole spectrum of society that the Restoration, with its promise of a stable future, had released. Consider for example Evelyn's day in Oxford in October 1664:

> I went to visit Mr. Boyle, whom I found with Dr. Wallis
> and Dr. Christopher Wren, in the tower of the Schools,
> with an inverted tube, or telescope, observing the discus
> of the sun for the passing of Mercury that day before
> it. . . . We went to see the rareties in the Library. . . .
> Thence to the new Theatre, now building at an exceeding
> and royal expense [the Sheldonian]. The foundation had
> been newly laid, and the whole designed by that
> incomparable genius Dr. Christopher Wren, who showed
> me the model, not disdaining my advice in some
> particulars. Thence to see the picture on the wall over the
> altar at All Souls, being the largest piece of fresco painting
> in England, not ill designed by one Fuller. . . . It seems
> too full of nakeds for a chapel.
>
> (Diary, 24 October, 1664)

Two days later, 'Being casually in the Privy Gallery at Whitehall, his Majesty gave me thanks before divers lords and noblemen for my book of Architecture and again for my Sylva. . . . He then caused me to follow him alone . . . asking my advice.' Evelyn records many conversations with the King, which show both men to advantage, with their wide-ranging curiosity about the new developments of the time.

Throughout his life Evelyn was sustained by a deep Anglican faith, which he practised clandestinely during the Commonwealth. His faith reconciled him to the death of several children and many close friends, including the young Margaret Godolphin, with whom he enjoyed a religious friendship which was the most intense emotional experience of his life. The temperate moral code that was allied to his religion caused him to deplore the libertinism of the court, but it did not prevent him from frequenting that court for the sake of the many interests that were concentrated there. All in all he was representative of the most civilized tendencies in Restoration society. He cultivated both mind and spirit with equal attentiveness in an entirely beneficial career, which continued until the very end of the century.

Notes

1. *Sylva*, fourth edition, (1706), pp. 329–30.
2. *Acetaria*, second edition, (1706), p. 154.

Part Two

Chapter 6
The Scientific Milieu

The spirit of scientific enquiry in seventeenth-century England flourished to a quite remarkable degree, and commanded admiration throughout Europe in a way that the literary or artistic achievements of the country never did. The impulse to engage in research was already evident at the beginning of the century, when Gilbert described his work on magnetism (1600), and before the turn of the next century Newton had published his unified theory of celestial dynamics in *Principia Mathematica* (1687). The reasons why this spirit of enquiry and inventiveness operated to such effect in England have been much explored. A major but unquantifiable influence must have been the impatience with ancient authority that had already shown its strength in the enactment and defence of the Protestant Reformation, and would exert itself again in the rejection of monarchy and in the political experiments of the mid-century. Practical aims too were a factor. In a seafaring nation like England, there was always pressure to improve navigational aids and to adopt technical advances of all kinds. Then there was the impetus towards constructive enquiry provided by the work of Francis Bacon, whose writings called for a general advancement of learning in the interests of human welfare and as a vindication of man's intellectual dignity. His conviction that the men of his age were capable of raising a vast edifice of knowledge relating to the natural world, greater than anything that antiquity had constructed, gave the necessary confidence and direction to research. In ideological and practical ways, there was throughout the century a slow, fluctuating development of a scientific culture in England.

Bacon articulated the sense that his age was alive with new ideas, discoveries, and improvements, which gave it a completely unprecedented character. He understood too the international dimension of change, and the need to circulate and co-ordinate information. The astronomical observations of Kepler, Tycho Brahe, and Galileo were altering man's understanding of the cosmic system; voyages of exploration were enlarging knowledge of the earth's surface; experiments by Paracelsus and his followers were beginning to develop a science of chemistry that was moving away from alchemy and magic; Vesalius and the Italian anatomists were opening up the human body to inspection; and Harvey had described the circulation of blood in a book that overthrew 2,000 years of error. New light was being directed to the dark places of the macrocosm and the microcosm, but Bacon saw that the illumination was intermittent and lacking in power. In *The Advancement of Learning* (1605) he called for a co-ordinated movement of investigation across the entire frontier of knowledge. He wrote in response to what he felt to be innumerable quickening impulses in intellectual life, and he attempted to justify this immense programme of enquiry as timely, the particular duty of his generation in history, a work conformable to the will of God, and beneficial to mankind. It is a rousing, exhilarating book, an appeal in the noblest terms to men of intelligence to co-operate in the most sustained enlargement of knowledge ever undertaken. When Bacon came to identify the original cause of man's lamentable ignorance of his world, he looked back to the Fall, for he was typical of his age in inclining to set all problems in a framework of biblical history. Adam in paradise had enjoyed a godlike completeness of understanding as part of his perfection; he had possessed 'that pure and immaculate Natural Knowledge, by the light whereof Adam gave names unto the creatures according to the propriety of their natures'.[1] His naming of the creatures was conventionally interpreted as a sign of Adam's total mastery of the created world, but his disobedience to God had caused him to forfeit that instinctive wisdom, and retain only fragmentary recollections of truth confused by tangles of error. So, argued Bacon, learning needed to be restored to a state as near as possible to that first perfection, and he termed his programme of recovery 'The Great Instauration', a term that conveys the idea of renovation and renewal. The advancement was also a reversion to an imagined original unity of knowledge.

Contemporaries acknowledged the validity of this concept: one of the testimonies printed in the 1640 edition of the *Advancement* praised Bacon as one 'who may seem to have learned his knowledge even in the school of the First Man'. The endemic ignorance of man about his natural environment and his own constitution could be dispersed, Bacon believed, if only 'the Commerce of the Mind and of Things . . . might by any means be entirely restored; at least brought to terms of nearer correspondence'. But, he advises, 'a far different way than has been known to former Ages must be opened to Man's understanding, and other aids procured, that the Mind may practice her own power upon the nature of things'.[2] A good deal of the book is given over to a discussion of the obstacles that have impeded the exercise of the mind's power over things: the supine acceptance of received opinions, a belief in the unchallengeable superiority of Graeco-

Roman learning, the centuries-old domination of theology over the
intellectual scene, and the almost irresistible fascination of unprofitable
controversies about words to the exclusion of things. What is now
needed is the humbling of the mind to the primacy of ascertainable
facts in 'a sincere and solid enquiry' into the phenomena of the physical
world. The method that Bacon recommends is induction, which he
contrasts with the traditional mode of proceeding in scholastic argument by syllogism. Syllogisms consist of propositions of generalities
from which deductions about particulars are made, and are a word-
dominated device for arriving at verbal definitions; induction,
conversely, begins with observations of particular instances from
which general principles may be inferred, so that preconceptions are
avoided and primacy is given to specifics; it is, in fact, the conceptual
structure of the experimental method, and is an agent of discovery, not
simply of confirmation. The experimental temper is everywhere
encouraged in the *Advancement*, not only to clarify the mind's compre-
hension of the physical world and improve its mastery over it, but also
actively 'to promote the good of mankind' by improving the circumstances of life and health. He warns, however, that men of science
should not be content with the practical consequences of their
experiments, but should seek to know the principles that produce those
consequences, for 'experiments of fruit and use' as he calls them are
less significant than those of 'light and discovery', which expose principles that open the way to further progress.

   The Advancement of Learning is a remarkably optimistic book, clear
in purpose, free from nationalistic sentiment and prejudices of religion.
It was translated into Latin so that it might reach the intelligentsia
of Europe, and it not only invited the present generation to participate
in the work of enlightenment, but engaged posterity as well in the
immense design. It brims with confidence in the genius and proficiency
of modern minds. Bacon firmly but tactfully argues against the well-
rooted assumption that the Greek and Roman philosophers had
attained all the accessible summits of knowledge; we must honour their
achievements, but not be servile in our respect. Some authors 'have
usurpt a kind of dictature in Sciences' – he is thinking of figures such
as Aristotle, Galen, Ptolemy, and Pliny – but a change of attitude can
dispel their authority: it may be that they flourished 'in the Child-hood
of Knowledge' and not in its prime. Bacon is especially circumspect
when he counters the suspicion that he is subverting the authority of
religion by setting so high a value on scientific enquiry. Once again
going back to the Fall, he insists that knowledge of the creation is
intrinsically good, and indeed should contribute to one's worship of
the Creator. The Fall, according to Bacon, occurred not through any
desire to penetrate the secrets of nature, for Adam was already in full

possession of them, but through 'that proud and imperative Appetite of Moral Knowledge, defining the laws and limits of Good and Evil, with an intent in man to revolt from God, and to give laws unto himself, which was indeed the project of the Primitive Temptation'.[3] The secrets of nature were intended to be uncovered by the power of human reason, and were in fact a challenge to the exercise of our highest faculties. 'The Divine nature took delight to hide his works, to the end that they might be found out',[4] and there were indications in the Bible that enquiry into the Creation met with God's approval, notably in the figure of Solomon, whose wisdom was reputed to have sounded many of the mysteries of the natural world. The Proverbs of Solomon are much the most quoted book of the Bible in the *Advancement.*

Bacon's optimism is the greater as he believes that Providence is on his side. It may well be, he suggests, that his epoch is the one foretold by Daniel in his prophecy concerning the growth of knowledge that will be a sign of the revival of man's condition in the last age of the world: 'Plurimi pertransibunt et augebitur scientia' – 'many shall run to and fro, and knowledge shall be increased' (Daniel 12. 4). The mysterious phrase 'plurimi pertransibunt' was understood by Bacon to refer to the great voyages of trade and discovery which were so spectacular a feature of the times, and which had transformed the whole context of Western thought. The ancient limitations had been broken, new information was pouring into Europe, and that information would help to raise a more complex structure of intelligence than the ancients had contrived. So Bacon dared to hope that he lived in auspicious times, as he marvelled at

> our voyagers, to whom it hath been often granted to
> wheel and roll about the whole compass of the earth, after
> the manner of heavenly bodies. And this excellent felicity
> in nautical art, and environing the world, may plant also
> an expectation of farther proficiencies and augmentations
> of sciences; especially seeing it seems to be decreed by the
> divine counsel, that these two should be coaevals, for so
> the prophet Daniel speaking of the latter times foretells,
> *Plurimi pertransibunt et augebitur scientia*: as if the through
> passage or perlustration of the world, and the various
> propagation of knowledge were appointed to be in the
> same ages; as we see it is already performed in great part;
> seeing our times do not much give place for learning to
> the former two periods, or returns of learning, the one of
> the Grecians, the other of the Romans, and in some kinds
> far exceed them.[5]

Daniel's prophecy reappeared on the engraved title-page to the English translation of the *Advancement* in 1640, in conjunction with a ship representing the mission of exploration and the unbounded freedom of the new age, as if to demonstrate that the venturesome spirit of enquiry enjoys divine sanction (Plate 15). Overhead, emblems show the interaction of the intellectual world with the visible world, with a phrase that proclaims the coming together of reason and experiment. The title-page also depicts the banner of learning upheld by Oxford and Cambridge, but here Baconian confidence was misplaced, for these institutions did little to further the cause of the sciences before the establishmant of the Commonwealth. Both were too conservative, too deeply committed to the teaching of rhetoric, divinity, and Aristotelean philosophy to be responsive to an experimental outlook. The conviction that Aristotle was magisterial and definitive in matters of natural philosophy was one of the most enduring legacies of the Middle Ages in the universities. Book learning and a prodigious respect for classical authority dominated the system, and the modernist spirit expressed itself mostly in religious controversy, a subject also heavily dependent on the citing of authorities. Oxford did appear to be moving towards an acknowledgement of modern developments when the Savilian Professorships of Geometry and Astronomy were founded in the 1620s, along with lectureships in natural philosophy and anatomy, but these were endowments made to the university from without, not instituted from any internal desire for modernization, and, as Christopher Hill has pointed out, the university actively discouraged the holders of these posts from lecturing on recent advances in their subject.[6] The anatomy lecturer, for example, was not allowed to dissect, and Laud's new university statutes in 1636 required that he lecture on Galen and Hippocrates, but not on the work of Vesalius and Fallopius, the pioneers of modern anatomical science. It is hardly surprising that serious students of medicine should go abroad, to Padua, Leyden, or Montpellier, for their instruction. Cambridge showed little disposition to develop an experimental ethos in anything except modes of worship. One need not be too censorious of the universities' attachment to the traditional curriculum, for we should remember that their principal functions were the training of ministers for the Church of England and the social education of the gentry.

Bacon had appreciated at an early stage that his scheme would be best served by the establishment of some institution especially for research into the sciences. He described such a college in his Utopian fragment *New Atlantis*, which gives an imaginary account of an enlightened society discovered in the Pacific Ocean by a storm-driven English ship. The island of Bensalem is Christian, and distinguished for the wisdom of its social and political arrangements, and above all for its mastery of the natural world for the benefit of its citizens. The source of their power is 'Solomon's House' or 'the College of the Six Days' Works', which is the ideal Baconian institute for scientific research, with a mission to search after 'the knowledge of causes and secret motion of things, and the enlarging of the bounds of human empire'. The extensive range of experiments carried on there corresponds very closely to the programme of investigations suggested by Bacon in his *Sylva Sylvarum* as the foundation for an empirical study of the properties of the natural world.[7] The thousand experiments proposed in *Sylva* touched on such matters as acoustics, optics, the physics of motion, the properties of metals, the generation of plants and animals, the improvement of soils and crops, and the development of medicines.[8] Bacon's mind was extraordinarily fertile in envisaging sequences of tests that would yield useful information and also build up an interlinked chain of theoretical knowledge. In vain Bacon appealed to King James to found a college of experimental philosophy, a Solomon's House for England, dedicating book after book to him with eloquent pleas to earn the gratitude of posterity by some far-sighted, munificent endowment, but James was convinced that the urgent issues of the age were theological, with the result that the only institution that he raised by patronage was Chelsea College, established to train scholars in polemical divinity.

The nearest approximation to a Baconian centre was Gresham College, founded by the London merchant Sir Thomas Gresham in the 1580s. Here the teaching was resolutely modern, with an emphasis on practical application. The college housed laboratories and employed instrument makers. Astronomy, navigation, mathematics, anatomy, physics, and pathology were on the curriculum, and lecturers presented instruction in the different subjects that was as up to date as anything to be had in England. The 'students' tended to be adult London citizens who expected to be given serviceable information and taught effective skills that could be applied to their own callings. The names of the early professors at Gresham – Gwynne, Gunter, Briggs, Gellibrand – do not have much resonance in the annals of science, but these men and their fellows gave an impetus to teaching and experimentation that kept up through the 1630s when there was little encouragement from court or church or from the old universities. Neither King James nor King Charles had any scientific curiosity, and Laud, who long dominated church and university affairs, generally discouraged scientific interests, but Gresham College survived, governed by a body of merchants whose concerns were secular and melioristic. When Oxford came under Puritan control in the later 1640s, it would be primarily from Gresham that the first generation of 'natural philosophers' would be recruited.[9]

It was the onset of the Puritan revolution that improved the prospects of Baconian science, for the expectations of reform in society that accompanied the Parliament that met in 1640 raised the hopes of the radicals that a Baconian programme of research might be encouraged. As Charles Webster has commented in his important book on the intellectual climate of Baconianism in the seventeenth century,

> Bacon gave precise and systematic philosophical expression
> to the anti-authoritarianism, inductivism and utilitarianism
> that were such important factors in the puritan scale of
> values. The metaphysical aspect of his philosophy avoided
> the atheistic tendencies which eventually rendered so much
> of the new philosophy anathema to protestants.
> Furthermore Bacon's philosophy was explicitly conceived
> in the biblical and millenarian framework which was so
> congenial to the Puritans.[10]

Bacon, although dead, was one of the men of the hour in 1640. Schemes for educational reform proliferated, as did Utopian projects that were intended to realize the happy commonwealth of the *New Atlantis* with its beneficent college of natural philosophy working for the universal good.

One of the busiest projectors was Samuel Hartlib, a German exile living in London. Fired by the conviction (derived from his lifelong study of the Apocalypse) that the reformed Protestant cause was moving the world towards an era of spiritual and physical regeneration, Hartlib persistently lobbied influential Englishmen to adopt a Baconian outlook. He clamoured for reforms in education and for research into medicine, technology, and agricultural science that would serve as means towards the improvement of society. In 1641 his close disciple, Gabriel Plattes, published a description of an ideal commonwealth incorporating the progressive schemes of the Hartlib circle; it was entitled *Macaria* (The Blessed Land) and dedicated to Parliament, the one agency capable of realizing such schemes. In it, the island of Macaria enjoys a controlled economy regulated in the public interest by a council of state. Landed estates have been much reduced in size and are intensively cultivated and there is a fairness in the distribution of goods; an efficient system of medical care exists and education has become almost universal. The chief agency of progress is the 'college of experience' that concentrates the skills of the most ingenious Macarians on utilitarian research after the fashion of Solomon's House.[11] The Long Parliament showed many signs of favour to Hartlib in 1640–41, regarding him as a useful constructive philosopher, and at the beginning of 1641 Parliament encouraged him to invite to England two other Protestant Utopians to help in the planning of a scheme of reformation in education and science, John Dury, who was half English, half German, and Jan Amos Comenius, the prophetic sage of Bohemia. Dury had a vision of Protestant unity and a passion for Baconian pragmatism. Comenius was the herald of the 'pansophic enlightenment' which he had already urged on several European Protestant leaders.[12] Pansophia was a programme for the advancement of learning on all fronts that required radical reform of the existing educational structure, with a vast extension of instruction throughout all the ranks of society. At the top of the system, the most acute spirits of the age should be engaged in well-funded research to clear the forests of ignorance that grew so thickly around the areas of civiliz- ation. Comenius hoped that the new enlightenment would be co- extensive with the domain of Protestantism. He foresaw natural philosophers and technicians in different countries communicating with each other so that there would be a 'universal college' of European intellectuals co-operating in the common cause of riddling out the secrets of nature, inventing instruments and machines that would increase man's control over the physical world, and improving medicine and agriculture. The centre of this ambitious enterprise would be in England, which Comenius, in common with large numbers of Englishmen, believed to be the nation most favoured by God, the country where his foremost designs would be enacted and where the regeneration of the human spirit seemed already to be taking place in the ferment of Puritan activism.[13]

Hartlib, Comenius, and Dury were all motivated by a fervent millenarianism, which provided the grounds for their optimistic belief that they were on the edge of a new and final phase of history, cloudily glimpsed in the Book of Revelation. They believed that God would intervene in human affairs, directing them through the turbulent times that would culminate in the return of Christ to reign over his true followers. The rough course of the Reformation and the terrible wars of religion that were sweeping Europe could be accommodated into this apocalyptic scenario as signs of the desolations and turmoil that would mark the latter days of history. The courage and persistence required to extend the reform of religion intensified the zeal of the faithful and hardened their resolve (an attitude that explains much of the stubbornness of the Puritan groups in the confrontations with auth- ority that preceded the Civil War). The faithful were charged not to wait on events, but to hurry them forward by their activism. It was held that the saints of the Protestant Reformation needed to meet God half-way in these providential times: men must demonstrate to God that they were making the utmost efforts to fulfil the divine will by preparing the way for the return of Christ, and that meant fighting sin and error in every quarter and trying to undo the effects of the Fall.

Hence it was that the restoration of learning took on a particular urgency at a time when so many Protestants anticipated some momentous emanation of the divine spirit in history, for by this endeavour they could show their desire to raise human nature towards its lost prelapsarian perfection, and prepare themselves to be worthy to receive Christ. So, behind the demand for educational reform and the founding of colleges of science lay this metaphysical cause: increased knowledge was an aspect of the Reformation and a component of the ideology of the latter days. Those latter days might last an age or only a few years. In either case, the knowledge raised would be useful to man and pleasing to God. No man could read the mind of God to determine the timing of events, but there were clues hidden in the Book of Revelation and also in the prophecies of Daniel and Isaiah. Comenius, Hartlib, and their followers were avid students of the Apocalypse. The millenarian tendency of which they were part persisted as an undercurrent of the scientific movement throughout the seventeenth century, and it should come as no surprise to discover that Isaac Newton, later in the century, spent as much time on research into the Apocalypse as he gave to his work on mechanics.

Many Members of the Long Parliament shared these millenarian beliefs and were anxious to help the pansophic scheme. Plans were in train to make over Chelsea College or the Savoy Hospital as the nucleus of a universal college, when the Civil War broke out and turned attention away from the schemes of peace. Comenius left the country, but Hartlib and Dury stayed on, proselytizing and hoping that their time would come. The distinguished character of their ideals remained influential, however, and provided a context for Milton's *Tractate of Education* (1644), which was addressed to Hartlib and evidently arose out of conversations they had had together.

Milton repeated the commonplace of Baconian ideology that the present age must attempt to roll back the consequences of the Fall by an enlargement and reintegration of knowledge: 'The end then of learning is to repair the ruins of our first parents by regaining to know God aright.' He accepted that education should fit a man to engage with the affairs of his time, and should not be a cloistered, self-gratifying exercise as it so often was in universities. He came out emphatically in favour of a modern curriculum, running through a lifetime's study in a couple of sentences:

And having thus passed the principles of arithmetic,
geometry, astronomy and geography, with a general
compact of physics, they may descend in mathematics to
the instrumental science of trigonometry, and from thence
to fortification, architecture, enginery or navigation. And

in natural philosophy they may proceed leisurely from the history of meteors, minerals, plants and living creatures, as far as anatomy.

Although fortification does not seem in the spirit of 'repairing the ruins of our first parents' (unless with the intention to keep out Satan), it is evident that in the *Tractate*, the general drift of Milton's views is in line with Baconian and Comenian ideals.

A new intellectual phase began after the capture of Oxford in 1645, when the parliamentarians weeded out the Laudians and their associates and replanted the university with fresh stock. In this changed atmosphere men of a scientific cast of mind began to prosper. A group of active mathematicians emerged, most of whom had been trained up under the teaching of the Gresham Professor of Geometry, Henry Briggs, or were pupils or friends of William Oughtred. Oughtred was probably the most influential mathematician in England at this time. He held no university post, but was chaplain to the Earl of Arundel: his book *Clavis Mathematicae* (1631) helped to train up a new generation of scholars competent in advanced algebra, trigonometry, and the use of logarithms.[14] Oughtred was conscious of the practical implications of his subject, working on close terms with instrument makers, surveyors (who found his improved slide-rule of great value), and navigators. Among his friends were Seth Ward, the mathematician and astronomer, John Wallis, who was a mathematician as well as an expert on ciphers, and Christopher Wren. The invention of logarithms by the Scotsman John Napier opened the way to much more sophisticated advances in mathematics, notably the differential calculus, which was partially worked out by Wallis and ultimately resolved by Newton. Napier is another example of an important scientific figure who had no university affiliation; he was also a millenarian, who wrote *A Plaine Discovery of the Whole Revelation of St. John*, which was often reprinted during the seventeenth century. (To what extent he developed logarithms as an aid towards computing the Number of the Beast or calculating the chronology of the Apocalypse remains an open question. To the interweaving of scientific and apocalyptic interests in the mid-century one might apply Dryden's lines: 'All, all of a piece throughout:/The chase had a Beast in view' *The Secular Masque*, 11. 92–3.)

At Oxford the mathematicians began to join forces with the experimental scientists, who were beginning to congregate there in the 1650s. Robert Boyle was at the centre of this group, a scientist and a theologian who through his sister had close contacts with Hartlib. Boyle set up his laboratory in Oxford about 1655, and operating on the Baconian principle of cumulative experiment, began his researches that were to establish chemistry as a scientific subject distinct from alchemy. His reading of the pre-Socratic philosophers encouraged him to investigate the theory of the atomic structure of matter, and it was largely owing to his work that the concept of matter as 'corpuscular' or 'mechanical' gained acceptance in England, following a trend already set in France by Descartes and Gassendi. Such a theory was sharply opposed to the underlying principles of alchemy that assumed occult influences or secret sympathies to be the vital cause of motion or change in matter. Boyle rapidly established an interest in pneumatics, studying the mechanical properties of air and gases – their density, elasticity, and behaviour under pressure. He published his *New Experiments Physico-Mechanical on the Spring of the Air and its Effects* as early as 1660. Boyle recruited the brilliant technician and future virtuoso Robert Hooke as his research assistant in the late 1650s. He was also closely associated with Christopher Wren, who was then working, along with Seth Ward, on astronomical observations and problems of geometry. (We should remember that Wren succeeded Ward as Savilian Professor of Astronomy in 1661.) Medical research was also being pursued effectively at Oxford during the 1650s, as pupils of Harvey obtained positions there and conducted experiments in the liberal atmosphere of the Interregnum. Some of the most significant work was carried on in the areas of physiology, embryology, and the feasibility of blood transfusion.

The co-ordinating figure behind all these Oxford scientists seems to have been John Wilkins, the Warden of Wadham College (and incidentally the brother-in-law of Oliver Cromwell). He was a Baconian, inspired by the idea of an interlinking of the sciences across a broad experimental front, and eager to see new developments that would benefit man's estate. The gardens at Wadham were used for medical and botanical research and also for experiments in husbandry and horticulture. The college installed its own laboratories in the 1650s. Among Wilkins's many books was *Mathematical Magic* (1649), which offered designs for mechanical devices that included flying machines and submarines.[15] 'His head ran much upon the Perpetuall Motion', Aubrey noted in his brief life of Wilkins. Evelyn gave an engaging account of a visit to Wilkins in 1654 that also conveys the excitement that the emerging scientific culture aroused in a lively minded observer:

> We all dined at that most obliging and universally-curious
> Dr. Wilkins's at Wadham College. He was the first who
> showed me the transparent apiaries, which he had built
> like castles and palaces, and so ordered them one upon
> another, as to take the honey without destroying the bees.
> These were adorned with a variety of dials, little statues,

vanes, etc.; and, he was so abundantly civil, finding me
pleased with them, to present me with one of the
hives. . . . He had also contrived a hollow statue, which
gave a voice and uttered words by a long concealed pipe
that went to its mouth, whilst one speaks through it at a
good distance. He had, above in his lodgings and gallery,
variety of shadows, dials, perspectives, and many other
artificial, mathematical, and magical curiosities, a way-
wiser, a thermometer, a monstrous magnet, conic and
other sections, a balance on a demi-circle, most of them of
his own, and that prodigious young scholar Mr.
Christopher Wren, who presented me with a piece of
white marble, which he had stained with a lively red, very
deep, as beautiful as if it had been natural.[16]

Wilkins's enduring concern was the reform of the language in the
interests of precision and objectivity, so that the vocabulary of
educated men, whether in theology, science, politics or business,
would have a fixed value, so that the confusions caused by sectarian
meanings, verbal evasions, colourful and affected phrases might be
ended. He worked on his scheme from the mid-1650s, eventually
publishing in 1668, under the auspices of the Royal Society, *An Essay
towards a Real Character and a Philosophical Language*. This huge book
contains an immense classification of 'things and notions to which
marks or values ought to be assigned according to their respective
natures' (Preface), so that all the principal nouns are ranged in cat-
egories that define and clarify their range of reference. Then, after a
survey of comparative philology, to establish what he takes to be the
principles of a universal grammar, Wilkins goes on to propose a system
of symbolic notation, which he calls a 'Real Character', that will enable
learned men of any nation to communicate with a high degree of
specificity about 'things and notions'. The 'Real Character' is intended
to function rather like Chinese characters, which can be read and
understood by men whose different dialects would give many mutually
incomprehensible pronunciations to these ideograms. Wilkins seems to
have derived the impulse for his universal language from Bacon (he
acknowledges the *Advancement*, Book VI, Chapter 1), and in his desire
to subjugate words to things, he is thoroughly in the Baconian spirit.
Yet the ambition for a universal reform of the discipline of thought
and expression, so that men of all nations can share a common value
system for words as they relate to ideas and objects, suggests an
indebtedness also to the pansophic vision of Comenius. The concept
of universally accepted language values is, one need hardly point out,
a prerequisite for effective communication within an international

scientific community, though Wilkins also hoped it would 'contribute much to the clearing of some of our modern differences in religion'.[17] Wilkins's stimulating intellectual influence, exercised from a position of considerable authority, was invaluable in encouraging and drawing together the lines of scientific activity in Oxford, so that his election as the first Secretary of the Royal Society in 1660 was in effect a continuation and extension of his earlier role.

The overall impression that one has of Oxford in the 1650s is that here for the first time is an effectively functioning scientific community that could draw on an abundance of talent. The intellectual ethos of Commonwealth Oxford was liberal and progressive, congenial to research. The activity there was complemented by similar but less notable groups of experimental philosophers at Gresham College and at the College of Surgeons in London. Beyond these institutional circles were the instrument makers associated with shipping, and the network of gentlemen virtuosos spread over the country. The entries in Evelyn's diaries for the later 1650s record a widespread passion for ingenious devices of a mechanical kind as well as for horticultural improvement, as if educated gentlemen were responding to the fashion for experiment. It is difficult to distinguish between virtuoso entertainment and serious scientific purpose in this period. The glass beehives that Evelyn mentions in connection with Wilkins may have been a significant advance in beekeeping methods, but they also afforded a good deal of entertainment to curious observers, and no doubt provided the occasion for extempore discourses on political organization or for moral fables. A sense of wondering pleasure accompanies most accounts of new inventions, for the desire to hear of novelties was a passion of the times. One cannot, however, read far in contemporary diaries without being convinced that there was a steadily rising interest in systematic scientific research, and that such research was beginning to produce important results.

Amid such evidences of profitable activity, the old design for a college of natural philosophy along the lines of Solomon's House surfaced again. Evelyn was corresponding with Robert Boyle in September 1659 about a project for a small college where a group of speculative men might retire (with their wives) to pursue researches into horticulture, medicine, and chemistry. 'There should likewise be one laboratory, with a repository for rareties and things of nature, aviary, dovehouse, physic garden, kitchen garden and a plantation of orchard fruit.' 'The promotion of experimental knowledge shall be the principal end of the institution.'[18] Evelyn was also in correspondence at this time with Samuel Hartlib, who was still promoting his philanthropic schemes, so that one can see that the idealistic impulses that touched the generation of 1640 were still strong at the end of the

Commonwealth. Evelyn's friend Abraham Cowley also came up with a proposal for a philosophic college in 1659, which he seems to have addressed to the members of Gresham College. Cowley envisaged a more ambitious foundation than Evelyn's (although be observes that it cannot be as comprehensive as Bacon imagined Solomon's House to be). It should house twenty professors, and have a chapel, a library, an anatomy theatre, a mathematical chamber with instruments, laboratories for chemical experiments, an observatory, and gardens for experiments concerning plants. For inspiration, there would be 'a gallery to walk in, adorned with the pictures or statues of all inventors of anything useful to human life, as printing, guns, America, etc.'. In order to transmit a knowledge of natural sciences to a new generation, there would be a school attached to the college. Publication of research would be required, and 'if the thing be very considerable, his statue or picture, with a eulogy under it, shall be placed in the gallery, and made a denizen of that corporation of famous men'.[19]

Proposals such as these of Evelyn and Cowley, as well as renewed activity by Hartlib, must have aided the formation of the Royal Society in 1660. The Royal Society in effect magnetized all the particles of scientific matter and drew them in one direction. Its initial phase was so vigorous because there was already so much productive work being done in the Puritan period. Although propagandists for the Royal Society in the 1660s such as Sprat and Glanville tended to present it as a glorious new development that drew its inspiration directly from Bacon and owed its success to royal encouragement, in fact the Society emerged from and continued the scientific activity of the Commonwealth that had been energized by the mixture of Utopianism and practical recommendation from Hartlib and his circle at the beginning of the Puritan revolution. The Restoration was self-evidently another time of renewal, this time with a sure prospect of peace, and scientifically minded men responded rapidly by uniting in a society for the universal improvement of knowledge that would contribute to the progressiveness and enlightenment anticipated in King Charles's reign.

Bishop Burnet was typical of those who liked to think that true civilization dated from 1660:

> The truth is, a spirit of learning came in with the
> Restoration, and the laity as well as the clergy were
> possessed with a generous emulation of surpassing one
> another in all kinds of knowledge. Mathematics and the
> new philosophy were in great esteem; and the meetings
> that Wilkins had begun at Oxford were now held in
> London too, and that in so public a manner that the King
> himself encouraged them much, and had some experiments
> made before him.[20]

But it would have been more accurate to say that learning became fashionable with the Restoration, largely because King Charles, the Duke of York, and Prince Rupert were actively interested in experimental philosophy, and attended the meetings of the Royal Society from time to time. The King even had a laboratory installed in Whitehall where he could observe chemical experiments. Royal interest caused a number of lords, gentlemen and virtuosos to become members of 'the philosophic assembly' which soon took on the character of a social club, where the more searching and speculative minds of the time came together. In keeping with the character of the new dispensation, the dominant religious tone was now Anglican, with a number of bishops enrolling as evidence of the new religious establishment's favourable disposition towards scientific enquiry. They were evidence too that society had accepted the Baconian belief that such enquiry did not tend towards atheism but led to a heightened awe of the Creator's wisdom.

The foundation of the Royal Society was facilitated by the movement to London of many of the Oxford group who were drawn there by the opportunities offered by the new administration. Many country gentlemen moved into London at this time too, attracted by the re-establishment of the court and by the world of fashion and novelty that suddenly opened up. There have been several recent attempts to clarify the circumstances leading to the formation of the Royal Society, but here it is sufficient to know that by the end of 1660 a small group of friends was meeting for the purpose of scientific discussion, and suggesting names of others who might be invited to join in these talks.[21] The original nucleus included Robert Boyle, Lord Brounker (who became the President of the Society), John Wilkins, Christopher Wren, Lawrence Rooke, John Evelyn, and William Petty. Within a few weeks another forty members had been drawn in, among them Robert Hooke, Kenelm Digby, Walter Charleton, John Wallis, and John Winthrop. The membership grew in a few years to around two hundred, with perhaps half this number taking some active part in the proceedings. Meetings were held in Gresham College, except for a period after the Great Fire when they were moved to Arundel House. In 1662 the long dream of royal patronage for a formal society of experimental philosophy was realized when Charles II granted the Society a charter. Bacon had courted James I and Charles I in vain for such a display of approval and support, Hartlib and Comenius had seen promised parliamentary patronage swept away by the war, and the Oxford group had operated informally. At last the scientific movement was progressing with official sanction, and was rapidly becoming an illustrious feature of English society.

The confident aspirations of the members were expressed in Thomas Sprat's *History of the Royal Society*, begun in 1663 shortly after its incorporation and published in 1667. Sprat had been a pupil of

Wilkins at Wadham, and Wilkins as Secretary of the Society presumably oversaw the writing of the *History*, which had been commissioned as a propagandist exercise. The fact that such an exercise was thought necessary, however, indicates that there was still a large body of educated men who needed to be convinced that rational scientific investigation was a worthwhile activity.

The *History* is prefaced by an ode 'To the Royal Society' by Abraham Cowley who insisted on seeing the foundation as the fulfilment of Bacon's design, and ignored the intervening developments of the century. In this respect, Cowley's poem complements the engraved frontispiece of the book, which honours Bacon as the Society's intellectual founder (Plate 16). Cowley praises Bacon for breaking the idols of ancient authority that kept men ignorant and prevented them from gathering the fruit of knowledge in nature's great orchard. That orchard, we perceive, is a type of the Garden of Eden, for Cowley imaginatively follows Bacon's motivating idea that the advancement of learning is also a return to a state of knowledge approximating to that enjoyed by Adam before the Fall. That fullness of knowledge might be recovered, Cowley reflects, but the old problem of presuming to be like god reappears. Where do the limits on knowledge lie? Where do delight in knowledge and control over nature turn into hubristic excess and trespass onto the prerogatives of divinity? Cowley sounds a cautionary note amidst the triumphal strains of his ode:

> The Orchard's open now, and free;
> Bacon has broke that scare-crow Deitie;
>   Come, enter, all that will,
> Behold the rip'ned Fruit, come gather now your Fill.
>   Yet still, methinks, we fain would be
>   Catching at the Forbidden Tree,
>   We would be like the Deitie,
> When Truth and Falsehood, Good and Evil, we
> Without the Senses' aid within our selves would see;
>   For 'tis God only who can find
>   All Nature in his Mind.
>   (ll. 58–68)

These lines might remind us that *The History of the Royal Society* was published in the same year as *Paradise Lost*. Both works accept that the transactions in paradise up to the Fall exert a defining influence over the events of modern history. Although the scientific movement could be presented as a sign of the regeneration of human nature, Milton's indifference to that cause in his epic, after his early sympathy, might be taken as a measure of his pessimism in the years after the Restoration.

Cowley's ode proceeds to interpret the advance of science in modern times in term of Israelitish history: Bacon was the Moses who brought his followers within sight of the promised land after long years of wandering and error; the members of the Royal Society are like Gideon's small band of warriors chosen by God to fight the huge forces of ignorance. Throughout the ode, Cowley inclines to a belief in the providential guidance of the scientific quest. When he turns to assess the character of the Society's work, he singles out for special praise the commitment to plainness of speech and clear definition in the uses of language, essential if the mind is to observe and report the behaviour of things: 'The real Object must command/Each Judgement of his Eye, and Motion of his Hand' (ll. 87–88). Sprat's own achievement in this respect is exemplary: 'His candid Style like a clear Stream does slide.'[22]

The reform of language is a major theme in the *History*. A rational discovery of nature cannot proceed unless the instrument of communication is clean and sharp. Sprat restates Bacon's arguments from the *Advancement* with the refinements developed by his own teacher, Wilkins, in his *Essay towards a . . . Philosophical Language* about the need to have a universally received vocabulary with a consistently focused meaning. Obfuscation caused by the national fondness for metaphor, imagery, ambiguity, and verbal embellishments of all kinds should be avoided as more proper to the childhood of the language, and unsuited to the age of reason that it has now attained.

> If we observe well the English Language, we shall find,
> that it seems at this time more than others, to require
> some such aid, to bring it to its last perfection. The Truth
> is, it has been hitherto a little too carelessly handled; and I
> think, has had less labour spent about its polishing, than it
> deserves.[23]

The distortions of meaning inflicted by political passion and the wild enormities of religious zeal in the Civil War have set back the cause of lucidity most damagingly. 'Now, when men's minds are somewhat settled, their passions allayed, and the peace of our country gives us the opportunity . . . if some sober and judicious men would take the whole mass of our language into their hands' and correct it, a great service would be rendered to the intellectual life of the nation. Sprat evidently had in mind the success in regulating and formalizing the French language achieved by the Académie Française; he certainly expects this task of reform to be one of the duties of the Royal Society.

An assumption underlying Sprat's *History* is that a new era charac-terized by rationalism has opened with the Restoration. The aber-ration of the Republic has ended, the enthusiasm that inflated the sects and caused such distortions in religion has subsided, and now a calmer, more enlightened age is setting in. An important part of his strategy for reconciling religious opinion to scientific enquiry is to suggest that in a rational age the Church should be progressive and avoid the odium of being thought reactionary or a defender of ignorance and supersti-tion, an oppressor of men's minds rather than an agent of liberty. Sprat argues that the scientific movement, like the Church of England, grew out of the challenge to decayed authority that was the cause of the Reformation. 'The present Inquiring Temper of this Age was at first produced by the liberty of judging, and searching, and reasoning, which was used in the first Reformation.'[24] Since the same spirit of fresh judgement animates both movements,

> I will farther urge, that the Church of England will not
> only be safe amidst the consequences of a rational age, but
> amidst all the improvements of knowledge, and the
> subversion of old opinions about Nature, and introduction
> of new ways of reasoning thereon. This will be evident,
> when we behold the agreement that is between the present
> design of the Royal Society, and that of our Church in its
> beginning. They both may lay equal claim to the word
> Reformation; the one having compassed it in Religion, the
> other purposing it in Philosophy. They both have taken a
> like course to bring this about; each of them passing by
> the corrupt Copies, and referring themselves to the perfect
> Originals for their instruction; the one to the Scripture, the
> other to the large volume of the Creatures. They are both
> unjustly accused by their enemies of the same crimes, of
> having forsaken the Ancient Traditions, and ventured on
> Novelties. They both suppose alike, that their Ancestors
> might err; and yet retain a sufficient reverence for them.
> They both follow the great Praecept of the Apostle of
> trying all things. Such is the harmony between their
> Interests and Tempers. It cannot therefore be suspected,
> that the Church of England, that arose on the same
> method, though in different works; that heroically passed
> through the same difficulties, that relies on the same
> Sovereign's Authority, should look with jealous eyes on
> this Attempt, which makes no change in the principles of
> men's consciences, but chiefly aims at the increase of
> Inventions about the works of their Hands.[25]

His concluding plea has the assurance of a man who feels that history is on his side:

> The universal disposition of this Age is bent upon a
> rational religion. And therefore, I renew my affectionate
> request, that the Church of England would provide to
> have the chief share in its first adventure; that it would
> persist, as it has begun, to encourage Experiments, which
> will be to our Church as the British Oak is to our
> Empire, an ornament and defence to the soil wherein it is
> planted.[26]

So Sprat clears the way for a final vision in his *History*, that of a new golden age brought about by the harmony of science and religion. The millenarian strain that had accompanied the case for science ever since Bacon's *Advancement* has now been modified by the rationalist outlook of Sprat to produce a more secular image of the future:

> But if our Nation shall lay hold of this opportunity, to
> deserve the applause of mankind, the force of this example
> will be irresistibly prevalent in all countries round about
> us; the state of Christendom will soon obtain a new face;
> while this Halcyon Knowledge is breeding, all Tempests
> will cease: the oppositions and contentious wranglings of
> Science falsely so called, will soon vanish away: the
> peaceable calmness of men's Judgments, will have
> admirable influence on their Manners; the sincerity of their
> Understandings will appear in their Actions; their
> Opinions will be less violent and dogmatical, but more
> certain; they will only be Gods one to another, and not
> Wolves; the value of their Arts will be esteemed by the
> great things they perform and not by those they speak:
> While the old Philosophy could only at the best pretend to
> the Portion of Nepthali, to give goodly words, the new
> will have the Blessings of Joseph the younger and the
> beloved son; it shall be like a fruitful Bough, even a
> fruitful Bough by a Well whose branches run over the
> wall: It shall have the blessings of heaven above, the
> blessings of the deep that lies under, the blessings of the
> breasts and of the womb: while the Old could only
> bestow on us some barren Terms and Notions, the New
> shall impart to us the uses of all the Creatures, and shall
> inrich us with all the Benefits of Fruitfulness and Plenty.[27]

Much of *The History of the Royal Society* is given over to an account of the designs and projects entertained by the Society, and reports of investigations already undertaken. These reveal a remarkable range of interests. Among them we find observations of the satellites of Jupiter, ballistic studies, a proposal for a system of meteorology, a chemical analysis of saltpetre with a history of gunpowder, accounts of the natural history of Sumatra and Tenerife, improved methods of wine-making and of the cultivation of oysters, and an account of the vivisection of a dog undertaken by Robert Hooke. There are descriptions too of many improved instruments that have been designed to facilitate the work of recording data. As the Secretary of the Society wrote in 1667 to John Winthrop, the Governor of Connecticut and a corresponding member of the Society: 'Sir, you will please to remember that we have taken to task the whole universe, and that we are obliged to do so by the nature of our design.'

Overall, the intellectual forces of the Royal Society were capable of meeting this challenge, as the work of Newton pre-eminently shows. The first thirty years of the Society's existence was a time of outstanding achievements in many fields, pioneered by a group of exceptionally talented men, in a setting that gave every encouragement to success. The Society was considered by the highest social circles to be a national ornament, there was a stimulating audience to communicate results to, and there were unprecedented facilities for experiment.

The pivotal figure in the whole scheme was Robert Hooke, who was appointed Curator of Experiments in 1662. He was, in effect, the first salaried scientist. Hooke was a universal man of Restoration England. As a young man he had been apprenticed to Peter Lely the painter, he was a musician of talent, and he eventually became a highly successful architect who was employed extensively on the rebuilding of London after the Great Fire. He had a genius for mechanical invention, producing instruments indispensable to scientific research. He designed an air-pump for Boyle when he was his assistant, which enabled Boyle to carry out his work on pneumatics and combustion. He invented the barometer in furtherance of his 'history of the weather', as well as devices for measuring the temperature, pressure and moisture of air, and the direction of wind. He improved the thermometer and made many contributions to more accurate timekeeping, notably the balance-spring and new forms of escapement. He developed the universal joint for the free movement of machinery, a tracking mechanism for telescopes, and the iris diaphragm for lenses. Hooke is probably best known today for his work on the microscope, an instrument which he brought to a fully operational state and described in his exquisitely illustrated book *Micrographia* (1665), with its many observations of hitherto unseen worlds. Minute animalculae in drops of water came swimming into view for the first time in history, the cellular structure of plants was revealed, the miraculous design of insects discovered, and the phenomena of crystallization and refraction accurately described. The Preface contains a plea to 'the gentlemen of our nation' to engage in experimental science as a more noble pursuit than philosophy, offering 'high rapture and delight of the mind in an unsurpassed degree'.[28] Besides extending the power of sight, Hooke also applied himself to enlarging the sense of hearing: he devised an 'octacousticon' for the amplification of sound as well as various forms of hearing-aid, and he also investigated the transmission of sound along wires. He tried to analyse the nature of sound, just as in optics he proposed a theory of colour and explored the nature of light in ways that prefigured Newton's better-known and more fully formulated findings.

Hooke's versatility involved him in the work of most of the active members of the Society, although his closest relations seem to have been with Sir Christopher Wren, whose interests ran close to his own. Wren's early inclinations were towards mathematics and astronomy. He was made Professor of Astronomy at Gresham College in 1657, and he held the Savilian Chair of Astronomy at Oxford after 1661. Like Hooke, he had a passion for practical inventions. A list of designs communicated by Wren to the Royal Society includes a model of an artificial eye, instruments for duplicating writing and for writing in the dark, engines to raise water, a formula for a composite stone, 'harder, fairer, cheaper than marble', a speaking organ that articulated sounds, 'probable ways for making fresh water at sea', an instrument for measuring time at sea, systems of cipher, and new weapons of defence and attack, including a submarine.[29] Many of the papers that he read to the Royal Society concerned astronomy, and showed a particular interest in the mechanics of celestial motion and gravitational phenomena. (Wren had a boundless admiration for Gilbert: 'This man would I have adored, not only as the sole inventor of Magneticks, a new science to be added to the bulk of learning, but as the father of the new Philosophy.' Gilbert, he continued, was the cause 'of introducing Magneticks into the Motions of the heavens, and consequently of building the elliptical Astronomy'.[30]) He demonstrated to the Society 'the effects of all sorts of impulses, made between two hard, globulous bodies, either of equal or of different bigness and swiftness, following or meeting each other, or the one moving, the other at rest', and worked on the mathematics of planetary motion, contributing to the data that Newton would eventually synthesize. Architecture, towards which Wren was almost accidentally drawn, became the dominant activity of his life after 1661, and his practice owed much to his scientific skills, for behind his elegant solutions to the challenge of spires and domes lay his mastery of mathematics, solid geometry, and mechanics.

Robert Boyle continued his chemical researches throughout the Restoration period, diversifying them with philosophical discourses on issues raised by science, and with works that asserted the compatibility of religion with the new philosophy. The spirit of enquiry and the ordering of information were yielding results on all sides, which were fed back to the Royal Society at its meetings, recorded in books published under its licence, or entered in the *Transactions*. One of the great virtues of the Society was that it could organize and retain information, and so maintain a continuity in research and collaborative activity. For example, Nehemiah Grew did basic research on plant anatomy, and his work overlapped with John Ray's, who worked on the classification of plants; Flamsteed and Halley were able to use the resources of the Royal Observatory at Greenwich, founded in 1673 and associated with the Royal Society, for their astronomical observations. William Petty's economic survey of Ireland, carried out under Cromwell, with its accurate surveying and ordered assessment of land values, population, and resources, became a model for John Grant's pioneering work on demography, *Natural and Political Observations upon the Bills of Mortality*, presented to the Society and published in 1662. Grant's statistical approach to population studies enabled him to establish patterns of population growth and life expectancy, and like Petty, he could demonstrate that laws of statistics existed which operated under the confusing mass of social data.[31]

The greatest elicitor of principles out of dense information was Isaac Newton. He became a member of the Society in 1672, at the age of twenty-nine, some two years after his appointment as Lucasian Professor of Mathematics at Cambridge. He immediately submitted to the Society his theory of colours, involving a corpuscular notion of light, and also an account of the reflecting telescope he had constructed. During the 1670s, his engagement with the new science gave way to a passion for alchemy and to a fascination with detailed historical research aimed at an interpretation of the Apocalypse. It was the appearance of the great comets of 1681 and 1682 (the latter now known as Halley's comet) that focused his mind upon the question of orbital mechanics and the dynamics of planetary motion that ultimately led to the formulation in *Philosophiae Naturalis Principia Mathematica* of the theory of universal gravitation and the laws of motion and force. The work was presented to the Royal Society in 1686. The memorandum regarding it notes simply that 'he gives a mathematical demonstration of the Copernican hypothesis as proposed by Kepler, and makes out all the phaenomena of the celestial motions by the only supposition of a gravitation towards the centre of the sun decreasing as the squares of the distances therefrom reciprocally'.[32] Such a synopsis catches something of the remarkable economy of Newton's conceptions, but scarcely hints at the complexity of the mathematics that validates the theory. With the *Principia*, Newton had offered an account of the behaviour of objects in motion that had a universal application, uniting the fall of an apple with the movements of the planets in space, and had shown that the key to the code of nature was mathematics, which had a unique relationship with natural laws, and by extension, divinity. If the universe was consistent in the operations of matter and motion throughout its extent, then the Creator's ordering of it was entirely rational and expressed through unvarying natural laws. In understanding those laws, Newton was in effect offering a new revelation to mankind, and proved that the scientific method, as Bacon had foretold, would confirm the perfections of the Creator to 'the purified Intellect'.[33]

But what of the alchemy and the apocalyptic chronology? Fascination with the latter subject, as we have seen, was an almost conventional adjunct of the scientific movement, based on the assumption that the increase of learning and the fulfilment of the prophecies relating to the last age of the world were related events in the scheme of Providence. In Newton's case, he believed that the prophetic books of the Old Testament and the Revelation of St John, being divinely inspired, might, like the divinely created universe, contain a code that was decipherable by human reason, perhaps even by the aid of mathematics. Spiritual events should yield an order and discipline analogous to events in the natural world. As for alchemy, Newton's attachment to it shows how deeply alluring was the idea of a vital spirit in minerals and acids, a spirit which could be controlled by occult knowledge and fire. Other members of the Royal Society were drawn to alchemy – Kenelm Digby and Elias Ashmole, for example – but the arcane character of the subject was essentially incompatible with the new open scientific mentality encouraged by the Society. According to this new philosophy, all the operations of nature were held to be ultimately explicable by reasonable investigation, and such knowledge as was gained should be freely available for the benefit of all interested persons, not locked up as secret information in the cabinets of a few magi.

The persistence of alchemy should remind one that it took a long time to distinguish between the fabulous and the real, between a belief in a supernatural, astral, or providential influence over the material world, and a conviction that laws of nature existed and operated impartially. This was particularly true in matters of medicine, where the treatment by sympathetic magic continued to be very popular well into the century. At the time of the Restoration the great majority of the people at large probably believed in the significance of omens, premonitions, and astrological influences as determining factors in their life. The growth of a scientific mentality was very gradual, but the remarkable attainments of the Royal Society in its first three decades ensured that the new philosophy would prevail.

Notes

1. Francis Bacon, *The Advancement of Learning* (Oxford, 1640), Preface, p. 18.
2. Ibid., Preliminaries.
3. Ibid., Preface, p. 18.
4. Ibid., Preface, p. 18.
5. Ibid., Book II, Ch. x, p. 10. Bacon was not alone in his conviction that Daniel's prophecy related to his own age and to the world voyages. For a discussion of the widespread application of this prophecy in the early seventeenth century, and its use to justify scientific enquiry, see Charles Webster, *The Great Instauration* (1975), pp. 1–31. Webster draws attention (p. 24) to a passage in Bacon's Latin treatise *Cogitata et Visa* which bears strikingly upon the section I have quoted from the *Advancement*:

   It would disgrace us, now that the wide spaces of the material globe have been broached and explored, if the limits of the intellectual globe should be set by the narrow discoveries of the ancients. Nor are those two enterprizes, the opening up of the earth and the opening up of the sciences linked and yoked together in any trivial way. . . . Not only reason but prophecy connects the two. What else can the not at all obscure oracle of the prophet mean which, in speaking about the last times says: *Multi pertransibunt et multiplex erit scientia*? Does he not imply that the passing through or perambulation of the globe of the earth and an increase or multiplication of the sciences, were destined to occur in the same age and century?

6. See Christopher Hill, *Intellectual Origins of the English Revolution* (1982 reprint), pp. 54 and 309. Cambridge did not have a chair of mathematics until 1663.
7. *New Atlantis* and *Sylva Sylvarum* were published together, posthumously, in 1627.
8. Related to *Sylva* were *A History of Winds*, which opened up the science of meteorology, and *A History of Life and Death*, which dealt with the pathology of the body and considered what measures might be taken to increase health and extend the term of human life.
9. Webster is inclined to regard Gresham College as in decline during the 1630s; in his opinion the vital scientific discussions of the time were taking place privately among mathematicians, surgeons, apothecaries, and navigators. See *The Great Instauration*, pp. 52–53.

10. Ibid., p. 514.

11. *Macaria* was long thought to have been written by Hartlib himself until recent investigations assigned it to Plattes. The name is taken from More's *Utopia*, and means 'land of the blessed', but Macaria had also featured in Jonson's masque *The Fortunate Isles and their Union* (1625) as an island where the enlightened spirits of the Jacobean court were feigned to live.

12. For an account of Hartlib, Dury, and Comenius in England, see H. R. Trevor-Roper. 'Three Foreigners', in *Religion, the Reformation and Social Change* (1967), pp. 237–93; G. H. Turnbull, *Samuel Hartlib. A Sketch of his Life and his Relations to J. A. Comenius* (1920); Charles Webster, *Samuel Hartlib and the Advancement of Learning* (1970); Webster, *The Great Instauration*, pp. 44–51. For Protestant Utopian schemes in Europe, see Frances Yates, *The Rosicrucian Enlightenment* (1972).

13. The programme of Comenius is described in *Pansophiae Prodromus* (English translation, 1642), *A Pattern of Universal Knowledge* (1651) and in his *Via Lucis*, composed in England but not published until 1668 in Amsterdam.

14. Oughtred, almost predictably, shared the millenarian expectations of the age. See Evelyn's record of a conversation with him on 28 August 1655: 'He had strong apprehensions of some extraordinary event to happen the following year, from the calculation of coincidence with the diluvian period; and added that it might possibly be to convert the Jews by our Saviour's visible appearance, or to judge the world.'

15. See Webster, *The Great Instauration*, pp. 163–64.

16. Evelyn, Diary, 12 July 1654. (A way-wiser was a wheeled instrument for measuring distances along a road.)

17. Wilkins's *Essay* is available in a modern facsimile edition published by the Scolar Press (Menston, 1968).

18. John Evelyn to Robert Boyle, in *The Diary and Correspondence of John Evelyn*, edited by W. Bray (1854), III, 116–20.

19. Both quotations from Abraham Cowley, *A Proposition for the Advancement of Experimental Philosophy* (1659).

20. Gilbert Burnet, *A History of His Own Time*, Everyman edition (n.d.), pp. 46–47.

21. For detailed accounts of the earliest phase of the Royal Society, see Webster, *The Great Instauration*, pp. 88–99; Michael Hunter, *Science and Society in Restoration England* (Cambridge, 1981), pp. 21–58; Margery Purver, *The Royal Society: Concept and Creation* (1967).

22. Cowley, 'Ode to the Royal Society,' l. 176. Sprat repaid the compliment later by writing a life of Cowley.

23. Thomas Sprat, *The History of the Royal Society* (1667), p. 41.

24. Ibid., p. 372.

25. Ibid., pp. 370–71.

26. Ibid., p. 374.

27. Ibid., pp. 437–38.

28. Quoted by Margaret 'Espinasse, *Robert Hooke*, second edition (1962), p. 48. This book provides a valuable account of Hooke's career.

29. See *Parentalia* (1750), pp. 198–99. This volume, compiled by Wren's son Christopher, is the indispensable account of Wren's life and career.

30. From Wren's inaugural speech at Gresham College, printed in *Parentalia*, p. 204. This speech is an important statement of Wren's scientific opinions, and of his sense of the heroic age of science that he is living in. There is much about the relation of science to biblical matters, including a plea for the establishment of an accurate chronology for sacred history, and an appeal for astronomy to confirm certain critical events in the Old and New Testaments.

31. For Petty and Grant, see Webster, *The Great Instauration*, pp. 433–46.

32. In Thomas Birch, *The History of the Royal Society*, (1756–7), IV, 479–80.

33. An excellent account of the evolution of Newton's *Principia* may be found in Richard S. Westfall, *Never at Rest: A Biography of Isaac Newton* (Cambridge, 1980), Chapter 10.

Sir Kenelm Digby

We have seen how the modern scientific method slowly emerged from confusion of beliefs about how the natural world functioned. Most men interested in natural philosophy in the mid-seventeenth century held a mixture of opinions, some backward-looking, some advanced, and to typify this condition we look here at the career of Sir Kenelm Digby.

Digby stands as a good example of an intermediary between the traditions of magic and the experimentation of the new science. The son of one of the leading conspirators in the Gunpowder Plot, he was born in 1603, and in spite of the disadvantages of that notoriety and of his Catholic faith, he made his way in society by the irresistible brilliance of his character, so that by 1634 Henry Peacham in his *Compleat Gentleman* could account him the perfect virtuoso of the age. As a courtier, he had all the graces, as Aubrey acknowledged in his brief life of Digby: 'He was such a goodly handsome person, gigantique and great voice, and had so gracefull Elocution and noble addresse, etc., that had he been drop't out of the Clowdes in any part of the World, he would have made himself respected.'[1] He led a flamboyant life as a privateer or pirate (with royal approval) in the Mediterranean for some years in the 1620s, his exploits culminating in a victory over the Venetian and French fleets at Scanderoon in 1628.

A dominant passion of his intellectal life was astrology. Like most men and women of the time, he believed in astrology as an exact science capable of determining the character, career, medical history, and fortune of an individual. The many different influences and qualities that were attributed to the sun, moon, and the five known planets were thought to affect all living things, even metals and rocks; the innumerable combination of forces produced by these bodies as they moved through the signs of the zodiac worked continually on the sublunary world. For many people, these influences provided a comprehensive explanation of the otherwise randomly diverse incidents of life. Astrology was disliked by the Church for providing an independent, naturalistic alternative to the divine ordering of events, and because it could be interpreted by skilful men free from church control; official opposition, however, did little to counter the immense enthusiasm for the subject on the part of those who believed that the heavens shed their influences purposefully upon the earth.[2] An extension of his astrological studies was his interest in alchemy, the pseudo-science in which metals, minerals, and acids were made to interact with close regard to their astral affinities. Alchemy in the sevententh century was as much concerned with spiritual refinement as with the transmutation of metals, and still attracted distinguished practitioners eager to penetrate the secrets of nature with the aid of magic. Digby conducted his experiments in company with his friend Van Dyck during the 1630s, seeking to extract the *prima materia*, the fundamental component of all matter, which, if ever discovered, could in principle be built up by experiment into whatever the alchemists desired, usually gold. Digby and Van Dyck were no more successful than others, but alchemy impelled Digby towards the fringes of the new scientific movement, even though his reluctance to separate spiritual from physical phenomena prevented him from making any enduring contribution to research.

In the mid-1630s, he associated himself with Gresham College, where he set up a laboratory in which to carry out experiments in physics and botany. In particular, he was tantalized by the possibility of reviving a flower from its ashes by means of a gentle heat, an experiment which might demonstrate the indestructibility of seminal matter, and which had too a spiritual corollary. Sir Thomas Browne, who was also fascinated by this experiment for many years, explained in a letter to a friend in 1647 why he was so anxious to succeed with this 'so high and noble a piece of chemistry, viz, the re-individualling of an incinerated plant':

> 'Tis not only an ocular demonstration of our resurrection, but a notable illustration of that Psychopannchy which Antiquity so generally received, how these Formes of ours may be lulled, and lye asleep after the separation (closed

up in their Ubi's by a surer than Hermes his seale,) untill
that great and generall Day, when by the helpe of that
gentle heat, which in six dayes hatch'd the world, by a
higher chymistry it shall be resuscitated into its former
selfe.[3]

In the social world of the Caroline court, Kenelm Digby was much
envied for his possession of an extraordinary wife, 'a most beautiful,
desireable Creature', Lady Venetia Stanley, the nonpareil of her time.
Celebrated by poets, adored by Ben Jonson as his Muse, gossiped
about avidly for her amours, Venetia gave an electric lustre of erotic
fame to Kenelm's reputation, which was long remembered. She died
in 1633, possibly as a result of Digby's experiments with homoeopathic
medicine, for he had prescribed her viper wine to drink as a cordial.
In his unbounded grief at her death, he poured out letters of affectionate reminiscence to his friends, creating for her an unprecedented
epistolary monument. He had Van Dyck paint her shortly after her
death to preserve the memory of her exquisite beauty, and he also
commissioned a large allegorical portrait from the same artist showing
Lady Venetia as Prudence, as a vindication of her blameless life as his
devoted wife and companion.

In 1635 Digby removed to France to pursue his studies and
perhaps change his religion in a fresh setting. He soon became friendly
with Hobbes, who was then in Paris, and before long with Descartes,
with both of whom he shared the new mechanistic view of the physical
world that had been propounded in the 1620s by the Frenchman Pierre
Gassendi, who held that all the properties of matter were the effect of
the shape, size and motion of its component particles. This corpuscular
theory of matter later received considerable support from the experiments with the microscope carried out by Robert Hooke, from the
analysis of light and colour undertaken by Hooke and Newton, and
from Boyle's work on chemistry and the properties of gases, but in
the 1630s and 1640s it was still in a largely speculative state. Hobbes
was a thoroughgoing materialist, declaring all the operations of the
physical world to be mechanical, even in the case of the human body,
where he found no trace of a soul. Descartes was desperate to maintain
a spiritual presence in the material body, and came up with his notorious theory of the pineal gland as the seat of the soul, the point of
interaction between the physical and the spiritual. Digby embraced the
corpuscular system, finding in the basic particles the *prima materia* that
he believed to be the indestructible principle of matter, the existence
of which he had tried to demonstrate in his experiments with plants.
But he also needed to prove that matter was responsive to spirit, that
the human body was a machine containing a ghost. He followed

Descartes fairly closely, but lacking the Frenchman's spacious philosophic conceptions and expository skill, Digby's works have never
received much attention or praise after their initial success. His *Two
Treatises* of 1644 put forward his summation of the human condition.
The first, *Of Bodies* describes the human machine: the five senses are
all activated by the pressure or motion of atoms, blood is corpuscular
and circulates, bones and tissue are composed of particulate matter.
The emotions are also caused by mechanical action, by different kinds
of particles travelling in the blood to the heart to cause it to expand
or contract in different ways. The process of generation intrigued him
greatly, but he thought that the 'formative characters' resided in the
blood. Beneath the modernism of his opinions, however, Digby
retained a belief in the ancient idea that all forms of matter have associations with the four basic elements, earth, air, fire, and water. The
second treatise, *Of Man's Soul*, argues passionately for the penetration
of physical matter by spirit. Consciousness is the guarantee of our spiritual being, and the process of thought is understood to be an operation
of the soul. Digby does not attempt to distinguish between mind and
soul, and soon the inconveniences of analysis are left far behind as he
soars into a panegyric of the soul and its immortality.

His attraction to metaphysics led him to a famous encounter with
Sir Thomas Browne, when he composed a long series of *Annotations*
on *Religio Medici* immediately after its publication, complaining that
Browne had not effected a sufficient synthesis of physics and metaphysics in his discussion of the soul. His tract is a notable attempt to
balance the methodology of the new science with the metaphysical
preoccupations of the old.[4]

Involvement in Henrietta Maria's affairs and in the Catholic interest
occupied Digby for a decade, and it was not until 1658 that he
published an account of the most sensational discovery of his 'scientific'
career, *The Powder of Sympathy*. This renowned medicament purported
to cure wounds by treating the object that had caused them or the
bloodstained bandage that had covered them, and operated on the principle of sympathetic magic. Digby narrates how his friend James
Howell had had his hand so badly cut by a sword that it would not
heal. By steeping a bandage in a solution made from the powder of
sympathy, Digby caused the wound to heal in a few days, and he
explains how. The explanation is in part atomistic: the action of the
volatile salts and the balsam that compose the powder causes the
particles of blood on the bandage to fly on atoms of air back to their
natural residence in the body of the victim, and they carry with them
the lighter atoms of healing balsam that help to make the wound
whole. Sympathetic attraction of like to like serves to draw the lost
blood home together with the healing ingredients. The powder of

sympathy that Digby so enthusiastically recomends has much in common with the weapon salve that Francis Bacon had described in *Sylva Sylvarum* (1627) where he suggested that its efficacy should be investigated, though he admits that he is half inclined to believe its virtue because he suspects there is a sympathetic interaction over distance between kindred creatures or analogous objects. Among the ingredients mentioned by Bacon are 'the moss upon the skull of a dead man, unburied' and 'the fats of a boar and a bear, killed in the act of generation', items that ensure that the ointment will always be in short supply and not readily available for experiment. Bacon notes, however, that while one is applying the precious salve to the weapon or instrument of harm, 'the wound must be at first washed clean with white wine or the party's own water, and then bound up close in fine linen, with no more dressing renewed till it be whole',[5] a point of hygiene that might well explain the ultimate cure. Digby's powder could be made much more readily than Bacon's salve, and the twenty-eight editions of his lecture suggest that it was extensively tried in the seventeenth century, perhaps even with successful results upon those with a strong imagination.

With the foundation of the Royal Society, Kenelm Digby was rapidly enrolled as 'courtier and chemist', but his contributions did not greatly advance the cause of science. 'He presented a sympathetic cure for indigestion that was made of toad ashes',[6] and gave reports on wolf-children, on a petrified foetus, and on a magical stone called 'oculus mundi'. More significantly, he gave a paper on the vegetation of plants that had sound observations on plant germination and reproduction, and by proposing that 'there is in the air a hidden food of life', he came close to understanding that plants take in nourishment in the form of carbon dioxide.[7] But Digby never really belonged with the rising school of scientists. He was too enmeshed in the quasi-magical explanations of phenomena to be capable of benefiting from the new methodology; although he was attracted to the atomistic view of physics and chemistry, he could never bring himself to exclude the occult from his study of processes in the physical world – but in this respect he belonged with the majority of his contemporaries, for the principles of scientific method took hold very slowly. He died in 1665.

Notes

1. John Aubrey, *Brief Lives*, edited by O. L. Dick (1949), pp. 97–99,

2. For an excellent introduction to the importance of astrology in seventeenth-

century England, see Keith Thomas, *Religion and the Decline of Magic* (1971), pp. 282–385.

3. Sir Thomas Browne to Dr Henry Power, in *The Letters of Sir Thomas Browne*, edited by Geoffrey Keynes, second edition, (1946), p. 280. 'Psychopannchy' means the sleep of the soul between death and Day of Judgement.

4. See Patrick Grant, *Literature and the Discovery of Method in the English Renaissance* (1985), pp. 102–88, for a discussion of Digby's *Annotations upon Religio Medici*.

5. Francis Bacon, *Sylva Sylvarum*, Century X, Experiment 998.

6. R. T. Petersson, *Sir Kenelm Digby* (1956), p. 297. This is the most extensive recent biography in English of Digby.

7. Ibid., p. 299.

Chapter 7
Antiquarianism: The Relevance of the Past

One consequence of the strong current of patriotic feeling that flowed through late Elizabethan England was the rise of antiquarian studies concerning the origin and character of the nation. The powerful sense of national pride and achievement and the intimation of a peculiar destiny highlighted by the success of the Reformation (and demonstrated most dramatically in the victory over the Spanish Armada) found its most enduring literary expression in Shakespeare's long run of history plays, and the same chauvinistic ardour provoked a curiosity about the germination and growth of Britain's genius that gave a new prominence to antiquarianism. Evidently so vigorous and favoured a nation must have had illustrious beginnings. Elizabeth, James, and Charles were all content to be associated with the old legends of the Trojan foundation of Britain which had been gathered together by the twelfth-century chronicler Geoffrey of Monmouth, and which had served as the standard account of British antiquity throughout the Middle Ages. Imitating Virgil's description of the foundation of Rome by the Trojan Aeneas, Geoffrey's version had Aeneas's great-grandson Brutus fulfilling a divine prophecy by sailing with his followers to this island, which he named Brutayne, after himself. 'A race of kings will be born there of your stock, and the round circle of the whole earth will be subject to them', ran the prophecy.[1] According to Geoffrey, the line of kings descended from Brutus extended through Lear and Cymbeline, survived the Roman Conquest, and eventually culminated in Arthur, from whom both Tudor and Stuart monarchs claimed, by an imaginative exercise in genealogy, to be derived. Spenser's *Faerie Queene* had embroidered this legendary line for Elizabeth's benefit, and Jonson, as we have seen, immediately involved King James in it at the celebrations for his entry into London. Poets found the Brutus myth a fertile source of compliment to the Stuarts: it lay behind several of the masques, including *Oberon* for Prince Henry, and *Albion's Triumph* and *Britannia Triumphans* for King Charles, and it permeated Drayton's patriotic survey of the kingdom *Poly-Olbion* (1612).

A distinct advantage of the myth was that it presented Britain as the offshoot of a high civilization renowned for its military spirit, enterprise, and chivalry. However, the desire for a better-authenticated history was to prove stronger than the charms of a fabulous national ancestry. A more critical historiography, of the kind that had emerged in sixteenth-century Italy with Machiavelli and Gucciardini, began to make headway in England, inspired in fact by Polydore Vergil, the historian from Urbino who worked in England during the reigns of Henry VII and Henry VIII. His *Anglica Historia* brushed aside the Trojan story as an unacceptable imposition, and suggested a Germanic, even an Iberian source of settlement for Britain. Educated Englishmen in Tudor times were not over-eager to accept this dismissal of a cherished national myth by an unfeeling foreigner, but Polydore's critical views were reaffirmed by the researches of a native historian, William Camden, whose *Britannia* was first published in 1586.[2] *Britannia* set the model for antiquarian studies for the next century, and sustained an enduring interest in the early history of Britain. This became a fresh area of curiosity for gentlemen of the Stuart era, who, if not greatly exercised by the mythological origins of the nation, at least began to feel obliged to know about the antiquities of their own county. 'It was a sort of learning, that was then but just appearing in the world, when the heat and vehemence of Philosophy and School-Divinity (which had possessed all hearts and hands for so many hundred years) began to cool.'[3]

Camden politely turned his back on the old fables as incapable of proof, and proceeded to build up a picture of Celtic settlement from Gaul, drawing on Greek and Roman accounts of Britain and British customs, and supplementing the written record with philological material that showed the connections between place-names in England, Wales, and Scotland and in Celtic France. Primitive Britain was relegated to barbarian status, culture and civil order being the consequence of the Roman occupation. Camden's principal concern in *Britannia* was to describe the topography of Roman Britain in as much detail as possible, with an account of surviving remains and antiquities, so that Britain could be seen to be formed and stamped by Roman greatness.[4] As Britain had been moulded by the high civilization of ancient Rome, that original character might well reassert itself in a Britain grown great again in the seventeenth century, now independent and with imperial aspirations of her own. Such ideas fired the imagination of Camden's pupil at Westminster School, Ben Jonson, whose lifelong mission in poetry and criticism was to revive Roman values in manners and morals[5]: Jonson addressed an admiring poem to Camden, published in his *Epigrams* (1616) which praised the antiquary's gravity, scholarship, and scrupulous commitment to truth: Camden's learning and impartial judgement were in Jonson's eyes examples of the

Classical balance of intellectual powers that were beginning to give a Roman weight to Jacobean society. Certainly, Camden's postulation of a strong, civilized, and flourishing Roman Britain lay behind the ambition, which persisted as a cultural feature throughout the century, to impose a Classical style on the façade of English society.

Camden was not just a propagandist for Roman Britain, however. As he enlarged his *Britannia* through successive editions, his admiration for the Saxons increased. This barely known race had reinvigorated a declining nation, and superimposed their terse, firm language on the failing Latin of their predecessors. Their customs and their political arrangements spoke of a greater liberty than the Romans had allowed. 'This warlike, victorious, stiffe, stout and vigorous nation, after it had taken root here . . . and spread its branches far and wide, being mellowed and mollified by the mildness of the soil and sweet air', extended its admirable characteristics to produce a distinct new civilization, with a hardy independence and with representative political assemblies. Above all, it was warmly receptive of Christianity. Camden slights the old stories of Britain being evangelized shortly after the Crucifixion by Joseph of Arimathea, and he has little to say about the effects of early Roman Christianity in the island. He emphasizes instead the later flowering of Christianity among the Anglo-Saxons, following its reintroduction by St Augustine at the end of the sixth century.

> As soon as the name of Christ was preached, the English shewed so much eagerness to dedicate themselves to his service, that with incredible diligence in spreading his name they set about the several duties of piety, building and endowing churches, so that no part of the Christian world could shew more or richer monasteries. Some of their kings forsook their thrones for a religious life. And it produced so many holy men, who for their steadfast profession of the Christian religion, unwearied perseverance, and sincere piety, were ranked among the saints, that in this respect it yielded to no other province in Christendom; and as Britain was called by the prophane writer Porphyry 'a province productive of tyrants', so England might justly be called, 'an island fruitful of saints'.[6]

Camden was enlarging the interest already taken in the Anglo-Saxon Church by the Tudor Protestant apologists, the chief of whom was Elizabeth's first archbishop, Matthew Parker, who had seen the advantage of arguing that the reformed Church of England had its origins in the Anglo-Saxon Church, from which it derived its legitimacy and much of its doctrinal purity, untainted by Rome and its errors. Parker and his associates had done much to preserve Anglo-Saxon manuscripts, and had retrieved the Anglo-Saxon language from oblivion. Camden now opened up the study of Saxon antiquities and offered a far broader appreciation of that culture than had hitherto existed, one that would have increasing political reverberations as the seventeenth century advanced.

The reputation of the Anglo-Saxons was further enhanced by an influential little book published in 1605, *A Restitution of Decayed Intelligence in Antiquities* by Richard Verstegan. In the dedication to King James, Verstegan ignores the conventional flattering genealogy of the King from Brutus and Arthur, and plainly asserts that 'your majestie is descended of the chiefest blood-royal of our ancient English-Saxon kings'. (James would probably have flatly denied any such affiliations.) Verstegan offered a convincing theory of the Teutonic origin of the British people which he buttressed with sensible evidence from Tacitus and other Roman historians, supplemented with philological material astutely used. He also introduced evidence of cultural and religious similarities with the ancient Germanic tribes encountered by the Romans. He acknowledged that his theory of Teutonic settlement lacked the glorious appeal of the far-fetched derivations from Troy or Greece or Scythia, but none the less he maintained there was a peculiar virtue in the Nordic line that was every bit as admirable as any Mediterranean inheritance. The repossession of Britain by the Saxons after the Roman occupation was a reinforcement of the old Teutonic strength. Verstegan admired the hardiness and energy of what he called the English Saxons (whom we would term the Anglo-Saxons) in their military and political affairs, just as he admired the spiritual brightness shown by their eager reception of Christianity. Above all, the vigour of the race was characterized by the English language, which overcame the Latin of the Romans and resisted the French of the Normans. A terse, witty, and sinewy language, it expressed the plain forthrightness of the English spirit. Although it showed the scars of its battles with Latin and French, it needed no meretricious ornaments from modern languages, and Verstegan was hostile to any new borrowings from Europe, or neologistic inventions, for 'our tongue is most copious if we please to make our most use thereof'.

These were exactly the same sentiments as Camden had put down in his essay on languages in *Remains Concerning Britain* (1605).[7] In both Camden and Verstegan, an admiration for the Saxon accompanies a linguistic nationalism, which together would develop a political edge as the century evolved. Little by little the Anglo-Saxon liberties as reconstructed by the antiquarians came to be seen as the lost rights of free-born Englishmen. The simple and direct form of trial by a jury of 'twelve good men and true', backed by clear and comprehensible laws, had been replaced by a bewildering legal system dominated by obscurantist lawyers and tyrannic justices operating according to a complicated body of laws written in Norman-French that only the initiated could understand. Independent Saxons who had owned and tilled their own lands had, under the Normans, become English small-holders subject to the laws of copyhold, entangled by fees and rents and dues. The Saxons had benefited from truly representative assem-blies; in their local moots any man could state his case; now Parliament was elected by a small number of freeholders and gentlemen, and represented only their interests. The Anglo-Saxon Church had had a plain creed and an intense simplicity of faith, since lost under the confusing doctrinal accretions of the Middle Ages and the superstitious practices of Roman Catholicism, and only partially recovered after the Reformation. The fall from this state of liberty and faith had been caused by the Norman Conquest, which had subjected the free English to the Norman yoke and to the full domination of the Roman Church. The line of kings that had succeeded William, and the aristocracy that he had set up over the English, had enjoyed privileges and immunities at the expense of all those below the rank of gentleman, protected by the tangle of laws and feudal rights. As the Stuart kings showed increasing signs of absolutism, so an increasing number of examples of Anglo-Saxon liberties was cited against them.[8]

A significant spokesman for these Saxon liberties was Sir Henry Spelman, who produced discourses on Saxon law and land tenure, and on the structure of Saxon society, that made Stuart England seem like a country of eroded rights, and subject to an excessive bureaucracy. The formidable jurist and antiquarian, John Selden, also mined the records to produce results that the establishment found uncomfortable. He was obliged to retract his *History of Tithes* (1618) because it suggested that the equitable system of Saxon law had been broken by the Norman Conquest. His *Titles of Honor* (1614) described the layers of aristocracy that had accumulated over the English people since the Normans came in, and in trying to determine the origin and meaning of the gradations of rank he conveyed the impression of a growing burden of privilege and oppression. Selden's sympathies lay with parliamentary rights, and with the common law as a defender of civil rights; many of his antiquarian researches were to strengthen those causes and to provide material against royal prerogative and arbitrary power. His bias was made plain in the notes he contributed to Michael Drayton's *Poly-Olbion*, where he advised the reader not to believe the stories of Brutus and Troy and Arthur, the fables and conceits that the royal family wrapped around themselves: instead, we should respect the more mundane evidences of our history. The emphasis should be more on the achievements of the English people and their institutions than on the deeds of legendary heroes.

A view of national history in keeping with Selden's criteria was provided by John Speed in his *History of Great Britain* (1611), which drew much on Camden, emphasizing the shaping influence of the Roman occupation, but seeing the Saxons as admirable exemplars of hardy independence and political liberty. He dwelt on the different periods and reigns in order to extract useful axioms of statecraft. He was inclined to see the establishment of good laws as one of the best preservatives of national vigour, and when the realm was governed by able monarchs respectful of the law and advised by counsellors chosen for their intelligence and integrity, England was likely to flourish. Speed's *History* is full of political implications favourable to the policies of Queen Elizabeth and critical of those of James, who was too dependent on his personal minions and was disposed to bypass Parliament.

In fact, the study of antiquities rapidly became politicized in the reign of James I. The Society of Antiquaries, which had been founded about 1586, around the time of the first publication of Camden's *Britannia*, and whose members read and discussed papers on antiquarian topics, found itself coming under royal censure about 1608. Its members tended to belong to the parliamentary opposition to the King, and when they began to discuss the origins, liberties, and privileges of Parliament, they moved on to dangerous territory. Arguments that the Anglo-Saxons had enjoyed popularly elected parliaments were too liberal for the time, as were debates on land tenure and rents. The Society broke up around this time, and when it attempted to re-form in 1614, it determined to avoid political issues, but as Spelman recorded: 'We had notice that His Majesty took a little mislike to our Society, not being informed that we had resolved to decline all Matters of State. Yet hereupon we forbare to meet again, and so all our labours lost.'[9]

The figure around whom all these antiquarian issues revolved was Sir Robert Cotton, once a pupil of Camden and in time the possessor of an incomparable library of manuscripts and books, charters and codices, deeds and statutes. This was the arsenal and magazine of antiquarian studies to which all scholars resorted for information and advice, for Cotton seems to have been an exceptionally generous patron of scholarship. In an age when ancient authority and precedent were more compelling than reason or practicality, a repository of such richness as Cotton's library was an invaluable resource. It could be used to determine anything from the order of entry into dinner at a mayoral banquet to the King's right to exact taxation by arbitrary

power. The library was used most effectively by lawyers and antiquaries disposed to thwart the expansion of royal authority, so it is not
surprising that the Duke of Buckingham, whose power owed nothing
to historical antecedent, tried to close it in 1626, and that in 1629 King
Charles ordered it to be locked up as a place of sedition. The royal
decree was a fair indication of how a study that had begun as a scholarly form of patriotism had become a hostile instrument of political
investigation. Selden thought that the most useful service of antiquarian enquiry was to 'give necessary light to posterity in matters of
state, law and history',[10] but the court world preferred to conduct its
affairs in darkness.

Perhaps as a result of royal disapproval, antiquarian studies declined
during the 1630s, the decade of Charles's personal rule. The following
decade of revolution and war was hardly favourable to research. The
more settled years of the 1650s saw a resurgence of activity, much of
it by royalists who were staying out of public life and devoting themselves to the past as a tolerable alternative to the distress of the present.
The Warwickshire gentleman William Dugdale emerged as the
dominant figure in antiquarian research, occupying a position comparable to that of Camden two generations earlier. (Both incidentally
became heralds, a position that greatly facilitated their access to state
and local records.) Dugdale turned his attention to county history,
publishing in 1656 his *Antiquities of Warwickshire*, which was in effect
a vast enlargement of Camden's earlier treatment of the county in
Britannia, now supplemented with a mass of tightly handled information about county families and their genealogy, the histories of the
churches and monastic foundations, records of tombs and inscriptions,
descriptions of buildings, details of landownership and a survey of
every kind of topographical feature. It is a wonderful work of scholarship, stripping back layer after layer of county history down to the
Roman foundations. It received a most enthusiastic reception, best
exemplified by Anthony Wood's note in his diary of how his 'tender
affections and insatiable desire of knowledge were ravished and melted
down by the reading of that book'. For Wood, as for most other
antiquaries, *Warwickshire* became the model of the in-depth county
history, and it would act as the inspiration for a succession of similar
books: Robert Plot's Oxfordshire and Staffordshire, Robert Thoroton's
Nottinghamshire, Elias Ashmole's Berkshire, and John Aubrey's
Surrey.[11] The genre was rapidly becoming a gentleman's recreation,
and before long the gentry of England would be counted the best
informed in Europe about the history and antiquities of their region.

Dugdale's most impressive achievement was the *Monasticon Angli-
canum*, a monumental compilation in three volumes (1655, 1661, and
1673) that brought together the surviving documents relating to the

monastic establishments of England, and built up a comprehensive picture of the great network of monasteries that had once covered the country. The pages are crowded with accounts of the rules of the different orders and the circumstances of their foundation, with their charters, possessions, and valuations. All this was accompanied by the delicate etchings of Wenceslaus Hollar and the crude illustrations of Daniel King which conveyed the magnificence of the surviving churches of the monastic orders. For all its scholarly objectivity, the *Monasticon* showed considerable sympathy towards the pre-Reformation ecclesiastical world. The book celebrated not only the extent and vigour of the Church in Saxon days, when most churches had their foundation, but also expressed admiration for the ever-expanding religious commitments of the Middle Ages. Hollar's illustrations brought home to the reader the daring and exquisite beauty of medieval architecture, and for the first time showed an accurate awareness of the different phases of Gothic as it had evolved from Norman to Tudor times. There was no denunciation of the corruption or laziness or doctrinal errors of the monastic system, but a record of centuries of Christian worship, building, and expanding economic activity on the part of the Church. There is a strong sense of lost beauty and lost holiness about the book, but it does not amount to nostalgia. Above all, Dugdale has a passion to preserve an inheritance in danger of being swept away by ignorance, prejudice and violent accident. There can be no doubt that the *Monasticon* marked a turning-point in attitudes towards the medieval Church, so that instead of being reviled or denounced as an abomination, it could be admired for its achievements, and its remains counted as part of the imaginative wealth of the realm.[12]

Dugdale made an even greater retrieval of antiquities in his *History of St. Paul's*, a splendid folio of 1658, again illustrated by Hollar; the value of the documentation and of the plates was to become evident when the cathedral was burned to rubble eight years later. Dugdale exemplifies here the antiquary at full stretch in the race against time. In the 1650s men were able to take stock of the latest round of devastations: during the Civil Wars castles had been destroyed, great houses burned down, churches vandalized, tombs mutilated, and a world of documents destroyed. The monarchy, the House of Lords and the church courts had all been abolished, and all this only a century after the the Dissolution of the Monasteries. So much of old England was sliding into oblivion, and there were few people to record the loss. John Aubrey and Anthony Wood, both friends of Dugdale, were scurrying around the country in the 1650s, indefatigably taking notes of inscriptions on monuments or of the details of stained glass windows, sketching ruins, snatching documents out of careless hands, even interviewing old men and women before they took their memories to the grave. The Puritan ethos was hostile to relics of paganism such as standing stones and many rituals and ceremonies that were still enacted in English villages. Aubrey, in particular, took it upon himself to note the sites of megaliths and preserve the folklore of southern counties, often detecting just what the Puritans suspected, survivals of Roman or Celtic practices, which to Aubrey showed a satisfying continuity of popular beliefs which had withstood so many changes of authority in the land.[13] 'How these curiosities would be quite forgot, did not such idle fellows as I am put them down', was his deprecating comment on his activities, but he was none the less aware of the value of his jottings, as we may judge by the care he took to preserve them at Oxford.

Research into the distant past frequently induced a mood of sadness in the enquirer. So much had been lost and destroyed, and one was always being reminded of the vanity of ambition and of the hopeless struggle against time. This melancholy, which was almost inseparable from antiquarian studies in the 1650s, became almost a requiem for mankind when Thomas Browne ventured into the field with his *Urn-Burial*, or 'A Discourse of the Sepulchral Urns lately found in Norfolk' (1658). Browne knew that antiquities were in fashion, and formed an acceptable topic of communication between country gentlemen, but he had the genius to enlarge a local incident into universal history, transforming 'these sad and sepulchral Pitchers' into 'Theatrical Vessels' that resound with the mournful tones of old mortality, and speak of 'the ruins of forgotten times'. He was careful to describe the urns that occasioned his discourse, even including an illustration which shows them to be Saxon (not Roman, as Browne assumed); he displayed a detailed acquaintance with recent archaeological discoveries in Norfolk, a region he knew as well as anyone, yet his intention was to use the dull discovery of some broken pots as the subject for a meditation on man's obsessive desire to perpetuate his identity against the deluge of time, and to reflect on the fantastic ambitions that strove to deny the finality of the grave. The learning accumulated to this end is prodigious. The funerary customs of ancient nations, the varieties of burial, the rituals of mourning, and the beliefs of afterlife, together with innumerable sherds of curious information and speculation – all are poured out of the anonymous urns from a Norfolk field. Browne is not so much interested in the advancement of learning as he is in the summing up of all that is known, and the inconsistencies and gaps in human knowledge are all resolved in the sublime reflections on 'the iniquity of oblivion' (Ch. 5). If Browne gave grandeur to antiquarian thought, he did not extend the boundaries of the subject: he was essentially a contemplative antiquary.

Far more practical and innovatory was John Aubrey, who was the most imaginative antiquary of the century, but who suffered from a sad inability to get his works into print.[14] Growing up in Wiltshire, he had become fascinated with the vestiges of prehistoric culture that were so numerous in that county. Apart from Stonehenge, they had attracted little attention, usually being described as Roman or Saxon burial sites when they were noted, but Aubrey, by close observation, comparison, and the gift of insight, recognized that they were the very extensive remains of the Ancient British people. The great discovery of his life was the prehistoric complex of Avebury, which he came across while out hunting in 1649, and which had never before been noted by scholars. The great circle of standing stones and the long avenue of megaliths with the protective earthworks excited his imagination and made him look eagerly for more signs of the unrecorded past. The publication in 1655 of Inigo Jones's posthumous book *Stone-Henge Restored* caused Aubrey to put his own opinions into some order. Jones had proposed, after having measured the site and studied the geometry of the monument, that Stonehenge was a Roman temple, for he insisted that its design agreed with the ground-plan of a temple described by the Roman architectural authority Vitruvius. Its ruinous state had prevented it from being recognized as a Roman work, but its geometry, Jones argued, was conclusive. Aubrey knew that Jones was wrong, and suspected that he had rigged the geometry to suit his theory: 'that is, he framed the monument to his own hypothesis, which is much differing from the thing itself. This gave me the edge to make more researches', and he speculated that Stonehenge had been built by the Ancient Britons, possibly as a temple of the Druids.[15] In the section he headed 'Templa Druidum' in a large work on antiquities entitled *Monumentum Britannicum*, he was able to relate Stonehenge to Avebury and to other circular monuments, and evoke a primitive culture that had extended all across south-west England, with links to similar cultures in Wales and Scotland. Aubrey was really the first man in England to think in archaeological terms. He had little interest in the documents and literary records that had been the foundation of the older antiquarian tradition. He relied instead on field-work and observation, measurement, comparison, and deduction. Particularly in the matter of prehistoric remains, he saw the importance of what other men had dismissed as insignificant: earthworks, ditches, barrows. standing stones, and circles, and the marks of old tracks. He understood that a new kind of history could be made out of stones, sherds, and hollows in the earth. In the introduction to *Monumentum Britannicum* he wrote:

> This enquiry, I must confess is a groping in the dark: but although I have not brought it into a clear light, yet I can affirm, that I have brought it from an utter darkness to a

> thin mist: . . . These antiquities are so exceeding old, that
> no books do reach them, so that there is no way to
> retrieve them but by comparative antiquity, which I have
> writ upon the spot, from the monuments themselves.

He believed that, 'being but an ill orator' himself, he should 'make the stones give evidence for themselves'.[16]

In fact, Aubrey went further than associating monuments with a function and a meaning: he attempted to re-create a society around them and to see the remote past as a human place. As early as 1590 Thomas Harriot in his *Brief and true Report . . . of Virginia* had suggested 'that the inhabitants of the Great Britain have been in times past as savage as those of Virginia'. To give point to the comparison, he had published engravings showing naked and painted Picts and slightly better-clad Britons which portrayed them as more primitive than the Virginia Indians. These engravings had been re-used by John Speed in his *History* of 1611 to portray Ancient Britons. But no one before Aubrey had enlarged on this analogy to produce a credible scheme for primitive British society. Aubrey had the imagination of a historical novelist, and soon peopled the prehistoric landscape. In his preface to *Wiltshire Antiquities* he mused:

> Let us imagine then what kind of country this was in the
> time of the ancient Britons, by the nature of the soil,
> which is a sour woodsere land, very natural for the
> production of oaks especially. One may conclude that this
> north division was a shady dismal wood, and the
> inhabitants almost as savage as beasts, whose skins were
> their only raiment. They were 2 or 3 degrees I suppose
> less savage than the Americans.

He brought together in *Monumentum Britannicum* many accounts from Greek and Roman authors from which he tried to re-create the ceremonies which might have been enacted around the stones and in the oak groves, and he drew up a map of ancient Wessex showing the roads and camps and earthworks as they would have been known to the Romans after the invasion. He imagined the warfare of the Britons, and their domestic life. He sensed too that the past continues into the present, and that there are innumerable customs and practices that have hardly changed since ancient times. When he wrote, ''Tis likely that the Britons did mix the poppy with their cakes when they did bake on their hearth-stones. In Wales the poor people do use hearth-stones still', (vol. I, p. 432), he was testifying to the human continuity of history. Just as place-names often contain the distorted memory of their first foundation (Aubrey actually compiled a book on place-name derivations), so present habits may preserve some shadowy reflexes of the past.

It is refreshing to find that Aubrey had no ideological designs on the past. His Britons have no descent from Brutus, his Romans are not the conveyors of instant imperial civility, his Saxons are not the enlightened exponents of civil liberties. (Indeed, Aubrey's Saxons are a tumbledown lot: 'Here was a mist of Ignorance for 600 years. They were so far from knowing Arts, they could not build a wall with stone. They lived sluttishly in poor houses, where they ate a great deal of beef and mutton, and drank good ale in a brown mazard; and their very Kings were but a sort of farmers.')[17] His antiquarianism was not coloured by patriotic feeling or by political motives. He achieved an unusual degree of objectivity by letting the archaeological evidence control his thoughts instead of serving as an accessory to some theory. For Aubrey, history was a process of change and development, not a succession of ages each with a distinctive character. Typical of his approach to the past was his attempt to describe the different phases of Gothic in his unpublished work, 'Chronologia Architectonica', where he was the first to suggest that buildings might be datable from their style. He also found that alterations in heraldic escutcheons offered a reliable clue to the dating of buildings and monuments. He tried to clarify the historical changes undergone by handwriting to provide a basis for the study of palaeography and he recorded the development of costume throughout the Middle Ages as displayed in effigies and monumental brasses. In all these ways he was a pioneer of modern methods of research, and a worthy member of the Royal Society, for which body most of his compilations were intended. It was his profound misfortune that he could never organize his materials to the point where they could be published, but his manuscripts circulated freely among his many friends and were consulted by most of the active enquirers into antiquity in the latter part of the century.[18]

In the post–Restoration ethos, antiquarian studies developed steadily under the impetus of professional scholarship and amateur excavation. The subject had a broad appeal to the gentry, who enjoyed digging around on their estates, and it benefited considerably from the growth of Anglo-Saxon studies that flowered after the publication of the first dictionary of that language in 1659. Philological, literary, and ecclesiastical studies, associated especially with the names of Francis Junius, Thomas Gale, and George Hickes, made possible an intelligent, well-informed view of the Saxon centuries that would be acceptable to a student of today.[19] Roman Britain never lacked enthusiastic enquirers, although no major breakthroughs occurred in this area after the comprehensive survey of the subject made by William Burton in his

Commentary on Antoninus his Itinerary in 1658. Welsh and Gaelic studies did advance importantly in the later seventeenth century, thanks to the pioneering work of Edward Llwyd and Robert Sibbald in Celtic philology and field antiquities. Medieval studies remained dominated by documentary research in the tradition of Dugdale, with Elias Ashmole's *History of the Garter* (1672), Francis Sandford's *Genealogical History of the Kings of England* (1677), and Henry Wharton's *Anglia Sacra* (1691) on the history of cathedrals and bishops, being among the most notable productions. Medieval archaeology, however, remained a neglected subject. There were occasional outbreaks of old-style theorizing by antiquaries with bees in their bonnets: Walter Charleton, in his *Chorea Giganthum* (1663), insisted that Stonehenge had been built by the Danes as a place for the election of their kings (the electors stood on the lintels to proclaim their choice), and in 1676 Aylett Sammes published his engaging thesis that Britain had been originally settled by the Phoenicians, in his lengthy *Britannia Antiqua Illustrata*.

How far antiquarian studies had advanced in the seventeenth century can be gauged from the revised edition of Camden's *Britannia*, which came out in 1695. It was prepared by Edmund Gibson (a clergyman who would later become Bishop of Lincoln and then London), who assembled a team of thirty antiquaries – the species had now grown numerous – charged with retranslating the work into English and making very considerable additions that reflected the new state of the art. Vast quantities of recent data were incorporated: the prehistoric ages were adequately represented (thanks mainly to Aubrey), there was much information about Celtic remains, and the remains of Roman and Saxon periods were amply documented. A detailed, uncontroversial summation of Britain up to the Norman Conquest was achieved. The work reflected the importance of field-work and of the empirical approach that characterizes modern archaeology. Collection and collation of evidence had become the approved method of progress. The aids to historical understanding had multiplied considerably, with numismatics and philology, comparative mythology and folklore, all contributing new forms of specialized information. By the end of the century, the past had been liberated from fable and depoliticized. The rich depths of national history attracted the imagination of most educated Englishmen, but the appeal was no longer to discover noble ancestors or to identify dynamic racial energies or to mourn over the decay of the world, but to enjoy the past as an area for civilised recreation.

Notes

1. Geoffrey of Monmouth, *The History of the Kings of Britain*, Penguin edition (Harmondsworth, 1966), p. 65.

2. There were five more editions in Latin. An English translation by Philemon Holland came out in 1610.

3. From the 'Life of Camden', translated by E. Gibson, prefacing the 1695 edition of *Britannia*.

4. See Stuart Piggott, 'William Camden and the *Britannia*', in *Ruins in a Landscape* (Edinburgh, 1976). Piggott's chapter 'Antiquarian Thought in the 16th and 17th Centuries' in the same volume should also be noted.

5. See G. Parry, 'Ben Jonson: Britain's Roman Poet', in *Seventeenth Century Poetry: The Social Context* (1985), pp. 17–41. Jonson described Camden as 'the glory and light of our Kingdom' in his *King's Entertainment* of 1604.

6. *Britannia*, edited by Richard Gough, 4 vols, (1806), pp. clvi–clvii.

7. 'Our tongue is as copious, pithy and significative as any other tongue in Europe. . . . [It] is as fluent as the Latin, as courteous as the Spanish, as Court-like as the French, and as amorous as the Italian.' Camden also claims that the resistance of English to French after the Norman Conquest is 'a notable argument for our ancestors' steadfastness'. 'In all that long space of 300 years they intermingled very few French-Norman words, except some terms of law, hunting, hawking and dicing.' See also the chauvinistic essay on 'The Excellency of the English Tongue', by Richard Carew, included in Camden's *Remains*.

8. This phase of political antiquarianism is dealt with in detail by Christopher Hill in the chapter 'The Norman Yoke', in *Puritanism and Revolution* (1958).

9. Quoted in Joan Evans, *History of the Society of Antiquaries* (Oxford, 1956), p. 13.

10. John Selden, *History of Tithes* (1618), Dedication to Sir Robert Cotton.

11. One should also note Aubrey's two compilations on Wiltshire not published until the nineteenth century, *Wiltshire Antiquities*, edited by J. E. Jackson, (1862), and *A Natural History of Wiltshire*, edited by John Britton, (1847).

12. A book which complements Dugdale's work, published in the same year as the *Monasticon*, was Thomas Fuller's *Church History of Britain* (1655), which gave a narrative rather than a documentary account of the Church in Britain, but also presented the medieval Church without rancour or prejudice.

13. See Aubrey's *Remains of Gentilism and Judaism*, edited by J. Buchanan-Brown (Fontwell, 1972).

14. A stimulating discussion of Aubrey as an antiquarian appears in Michael Hunter, *John Aubrey and the Realm of Learning* (1975), especially in Chapter 3, to which I am indebted here.

15. At the beginning of his book, Inigo Jones had speculated that Stonehenge might have been built by or for the Druids, but he rejected the possibility in favour of his Roman theory.

16. *Monumentum Britannicum* has only recently appeared in print, edited by J. Fowles and R. Legg (Boston, 1981).

17. Preface to *Wiltshire Antiquities*, quoted in Hunter, p. 176.

18. Of Aubrey's antiquarian works, only the 'Templa Druidum' section of *Monumentum Britannicum* (on Stonehenge and prehistoric stone circles) reached print in the seventeenth century, being extensively cited in Camden's *Britannia* edited by Edmund Gibson (1695).

19. For an account of this great period of Saxon studies, see David Douglas, *English Scholars* (1939), Chapters 3 and 4.

Chapter 8
Varieties of Religious Experience

Private fears for the state of one's soul and public concern about the health of the Church caused turbulence that endured throughout the century. The two anxieties were interrelated. Salvation depended upon God's grace, and the individual Protestant sought his God through the study of the Bible, appealed to him in prayer, and moved towards him in meditation. He scrutinized his daily life for signs of favour or disfavour, and lived as best he could a godly life informed by conscience. Every Englishman was by law a member of the Church of England, which was responsible for formal worship and the care of souls, but what if a conscientious member believed that the Church was not entirely pure in doctrine or justified in its practices? The Church then became a danger to souls rather than a preservative, and the conscientious Christian could maintain that it stood in need of further reform. With literate Englishmen able to make their own judgements about matters of doctrine, ceremony, and church government, the potential for dissent was remarkably high. Even as King James journeyed down to London in 1603, he was presented with the Millenary Petition, supposedly signed by a thousand ministers, which requested certain modest modifications in church ritual. As a skilled theologian who enjoyed controversy, James used the petition as an opportunity to convene a conference at Hampton Court in January 1604 so that he could settle the affairs of the Church at the beginning of his reign. He was inclined to use the conference as a forum to display his own wisdom and judiciousness, but in the course of the debates he came increasingly to dislike the representatives of the Puritans and to side more with the bishops who upheld the status quo. In fact the King was not averse to the Puritan requests, which included the encouragement of a more learned preaching ministry, less emphasis on the Prayer Book in services, greater prominence to be given to the doctrine of predestination, and the abandoning of the rite of confirmation. But, most unfortunately for the later peace of the realm, James became convinced that the English Puritans were no different from the Scottish Presbyterians, who wished to abolish the hierarchies of the Church and dissolve its ceremonies in the acid of private opinion.

> Then Tom and Dick shall meet and at their pleasure
> censure me and my Council and all our proceedings. Then
> Will shall stand up and say 'It must be thus', and Dick
> shall reply and say 'Nay, Marry, but we will have it thus'.
> . . . I know what would become of my supremacy. No
> Bishop, No King. When I mean to live under a
> presbytery, I will go into Scotland again, but while I am
> in England I will have bishops to govern the Church.[1]

It is unlikely that the Puritans at this time had any such disruptive ambitions. They were all members of the Church of England, and most of them were willing to abide by the system of episcopal government. Their desire, as their name suggests, was to achieve a greater purity in the doctrines and practices of the Church, conformable to what they imagined had been the state of the Church in the early centuries before the Papacy emerged as the dominant authority. The Elizabethan settlement had retained too many traces of popery that still needed to be purged. Hence the Puritans' insistence on plainness, on doing away with vestments and music and ceremonies, and on avoiding gestures that seemed idolatrous, such as making the sign of the cross or kneeling or bowing. They wanted to reduce the number of the sacraments – only two, baptism and communion, were thought to be essential – and they wished also to demote the importance of the Prayer Book, which they saw as a survival of the old Catholic mass book that gave services a mechanical character. Instead they looked for more intensive preaching to move the spirit, and for greater spontaneity of prayer. Inward power was preferable to outward show. James's rejection of the Puritan case at Hampton Court and his favour thereafter to middle-of-the-road bishops tended to set the Puritans in opposition to the King and his episcopal bench. Certain hard-line Puritans, particularly some groups from East Anglia and Lincolnshire, who found the Church of England practices totally unacceptable, were now moved to separate themselves from a church they regarded as impure, emigrating to Amsterdam from 1606 onwards, where they believed they would be able to enjoy freedom of worship. It was from this community of separatists that the voyage of the Pilgrim Fathers would originate in 1620, as they attempted to found a godly commonwealth in the wilderness of the New World, uncomplicated by any interventions of state.[2]

The idea that many varieties of opinion and practice could be tolerated within one church had little currency in the early seventeenth century. The Church of England with the monarch as its head was an instrument of state as well as a system of religion: conformity was an act of political allegiance as well as an acceptance of rules and beliefs.

Catholicism was prohibited not only for its doctrines, which Protestants judged erroneous and likely to impede salvation, but also because its adherents owed their allegiance to a foreign prince, the Pope, who was committed to the recovery of England and the destruction of Protestantism. The Gunpowder Plot of 1605, which came so close to exterminating the King and Prince and much of the aristocracy, demonstrated beyond question the reality of the Catholic threat, and immediately the Plot's anniversary was given institutional status as an occasion to denounce Catholicism, praise the King, and thank God for his watchful providence towards the Stuarts.[3] Among members of the Church of England, divergencies of belief were strongly discouraged as productive of civil disobedience and liable to weaken the Church's authority, and by implication, its credibility. Dissent also called into question the spiritual judgement of the governors of the Church, a matter which was seen in a hierarchical age as a type of rebellion. Once the principle of individual conscience is admitted in the religious sphere, there is no limit to the forms of belief, behaviour, and community structure that might develop, and the Stuarts were more concerned with maintaining clear lines of authority and a stable state than they were with granting liberty to tender consciences.

In one important respect the Church of England was prevented from splitting apart in the reign of James I by the fact that almost all the parties shared the same basic theology, that of Calvinism, with its central belief in predestination. The Thirty-Nine Articles that were the Elizabethan statement of the Church of England's creed are Calvinist in character, and they contain a fundamental affirmation of the doctrine of predestination, based on Romans 9. Article XVII reads:

> Predestination to Life is the everlasting purpose of God,
> whereby (before the foundations of the world were laid)
> he hath constantly decreed by his counsel secret to us, to
> deliver from curse and damnation those whom he hath
> chosen in Christ out of mankind, and to bring them by
> Christ to everlasting salvation, as vessels made to honour.

Whatever the role of the sacraments, there was agreement over this cardinal principle. The archbishops and the great majority of the bishops of the Jacobean Church maintained it, as did all the Puritan leaders. What would irreparably crack open the cohesion of the Church was the emergence of a rival doctrine that was alluringly formulated by the Dutch theologian Arminius.[4] He argued that man possessed a will that was free to seek salvation through Christ, that grace was freely available to all men through the sacraments, as long as they sought it with faith and honesty, and that good works were efficacious and smoothed the path to salvation. In short, an individual might contribute to his salvation by the exertion of his will and by his complete faith in Christ. Arminius denied that all men are irreversibly predestined to glory or perdition, although he conceded that certain were indeed the elect of God from before the beginning of time. In spite of its more generous conception of God's mercy and man's faith, Arminian theology did not make much headway against the well-established position of Calvinism. It appealed most to the sacerdotalists among the Anglican ministers who valued the greater redemptive powers attributed to the sacraments they administered. The challenge of Arminianism to Calvinism caused great perturbation in the Netherlands, leading to the convening of a synod at Dort in 1618, to which the English Church sent a formidable contingent of Calvinist divines. King James, who feared the spread of a doctrine he regarded as heretical because it impugned 'the Eternity and Omnipotency of God', and subversive because it was productive of religious faction, had already made his own views clear by ordering a bonfire of Arminian books in St Paul's Churchyard. The conclusions of the Synod of Dort vigorously reaffirmed the Calvinist position, which can be neatly summed up in a mnemonic suitable to the Dutch setting: TULIP. T stands for Total Depravity, the result of original sin, whereby human nature is innately corrupt, and incapable of seeking salvation unaided; U for Unconditional Election, God's choice of his saints being absolute and unalterable; L for Limited Atonement, that Christ died to redeem only the elect, not all mankind; I for Irresistible Grace, that an individual cannot frustrate God's intentions towards him; P for Perseverance of the Saints, that one cannot lose one's election. These were the harsh tenets of a rigorous creed.

During James's reign, Arminianism was blocked. It had some eminent representatives, notably Richard Neile, who became Bishop of Durham in 1617, John Overall, Bishop of Lichfield, and Lancelot Andrewes, advanced to Bishop of Winchester in 1618. Andrewes was the most gifted of the Jacobean divines, in whom outstanding qualities of scholarship, leadership, and personal piety were combined, but he failed to become Archbishop of Canterbury because James recognized that his theology would be at odds with the great majority of churchmen, and ultimately divisive. The apostle of Arminianism who would eventually realize all of King James's fears was William Laud. His progress was retarded by James, who permitted him to reach only the insignificant see of St David's, Llandaff. Laud attracted the patronage of the Duke of Buckingham, becoming his chaplain, and thereby gaining access to Prince Charles. Charles already had Arminian sympathies, which Laud consolidated, and when he succeeded to the throne he immediately showed the bias of his favour and his theology by selecting Laud to be in charge of the arrangements for his coronation, which was a more devoutly ceremonial affair than his father's. From then on, Charles advanced Laud at every opportunity, finally making him Archbishop of Canterbury in 1633. In turn, Laud set about advancing men of his own persuasion in the Church, and enforcing conformity to practices that he believed enhanced the reverence of services and accentuated the role of the sacraments: greater use of the Prayer Book was enjoined, divine service should he conducted by ministers wearing a surplice, communion should be received kneeling, not sitting.

Particular acrimony was aroused by the question of where the communion table should be placed, and whether it was really an altar. From early Elizabethan times it had usually been set lengthwise in the nave or just inside the chancel so that the congregation was around it. Laud thought this disrespectful, indicative of an indifferent attitude towards the sacrament of communion.

> For should [the Holy Table] be permitted to stand as
> before it did, churchwardens would keep their accounts on
> it, parishioners would despatch the parish business at it,
> schoolmasters will teach their boys to write upon it, the
> boys will lay their hats, satchels and books upon it, many
> will sit and lean irreverently against it in sermontime, the
> dogs would piss upon it and defile it.[5]

Laud wanted the table to become an altar, railed off at the east end of the chancel in an area of sacred space where only the minister entered, and it should be covered with a decent cloth, with a crucifix placed upon it.

'The beauty of holiness' may sound an attractive ideal, but to most Englishmen in the 1630s it was anathema. The emphasis on ritual and ceremony seemed idolatrous; Laud seemed bent on reintroducing the priestcraft and magic associated with popery, and abandoning the Protestant priorities of preaching and earnest prayer. The Arminian doctrine of free will grated on the spirits of those for whom Calvinistic determinism was the crucial article of belief. Certainly, Laud's theology was more reconcilable with Catholic doctrine than with the traditional tenets of the Church of England. Then again, Laud's attempts to suppress the lecturers who were maintained by many corporations and guilds to act as edifying preachers of Puritan attitudes, often in competition with the parish clergyman, gave deep offence to many groups who regarded these lecturers as the mainstay of their spiritual lives. Laud too continued to promote the authority of bishops within the Church, requiring them to impose conformity throughout their dioceses, so that to many of the laity they came to appear as spiritual tyrants, careful to suppress zealous preaching and obstructing 'the plain man's pathway to heaven'.

Nothing is so bitter as religious division and frustration. Laud provoked intolerable strains within the nation, and it was no wonder that he was one of the first targets of the Long Parliament when it assembled in 1640, or that the Church of England fragmented into scores of sects when his authority was removed.

Before we survey the confusion that followed, we should reflect on the ways in which the intense religious emotions in the time of the first two Stuarts found literary expression. Overarching everything was the new translation of the Bible. Of all the suggestions from the Puritan side at the Hampton Court conference, the only one that James effectively responded to was the request for a more scholarly and authoritative translation of the Bible to replace the two competing versions then in use, the Bishops' Bible, officially adopted by the Church of England, and the Geneva Bible, preferred by the laity. Some fifty translators were employed, working in six groups and consulting frequently among themselves. The King kept in close touch with the work, providing instructions concerning the guiding principles: the Bishops' Bible should serve as a model as far as possible, the established ecclesiastical words should be kept, and the proper names familiar to the people should be retained. Above all, the language of the translation should be simple and clear and direct, avoiding ambiguity and consequent doctrinal confusion. The work was completed in six years, published in 1611, and deservedly dedicated to King James who had presided over the project and moved it forward. The quality of the translation testifies to the excellence of Greek and Hebrew scholarship at this time, as well as to the health of English prose. That committees should be able to express themselves in a fairly uniform style that has dignity, clarity, and terseness, that achieves gravity but does not lose touch with the popular image, all harmonized by noble and moving cadences, seems a linguistic miracle to us who are only too accustomed to language thinned by abstractions and bleached by clichés, but such was the power of Jacobean prose.

The religious poetry, which is so memorable a feature of this period, owed much to the constant practice of meditation and prayer. Poetry was often the product of meditative hours; it helped to give form to religious musings, to relate a particular incident or insight to the universal scheme, and to discipline the excitement or dismay of spiritual discovery. On the whole, devotional formality in verse tended to indicate a conservative position within the Church of England, sympathetic to ritual and order, wary of the spontaneous spiritual impulse. It is understandable that John Donne, who had converted from Catholicism, should retain traces of Catholic attitudes in his verse, as in his devotional sequences 'The Litanie', which celebrates the hierarchies of the Church and the mercy of God, and 'La Corona', with its belief that 'Salvation to all that will is nigh'. As a highly intellectual man with a Catholic upbringing, Donne was drawn to the idea of a God who was approachable through reason, whose purposes were comprehensible, and whose mercy was infinite; the Calvinist acceptance of an utterly unknowable God, whose scheme appeared arbitrary and beyond all grasp of human reason, he found difficult to share. Yet in his 'Holy Sonnets', which are his most intimate and tortured self-examinations, his hope of salvation cannot rest on prayer and petition as in those earlier poems. The deep consciousness of sin and the almost desperate hope for grace given not for any personal merit, for he has none, but by an arbitrary act of mercy, suggest that Donne might have been turning to a Calvinistic interpretation of spiritual events.[6] But Donne's theological position is difficult to chart in a developing career: he was willing enough to engage in controversy, he preached often and learnedly, and he wrote verse about the wars of faith and sin within him, but he cautiously concealed the groundwork of his theological beliefs.

Not so George Herbert. His Arminian disposition is evident throughout *The Temple*, from his reverence for the altar (to which we are immediately led as the most important object in the church) to his celebration of the Eucharist in the final poem, 'Love'. His poems transmit a deep feeling of the redemptive forces operating through the eucharist. Throughout there is a sacramental note, as Herbert reassures the reader that the antidotes against sin and the benefits of Christ's sacrifice are available to all men of faith through baptism and communion. Herbert strives for a congregational inclusiveness in *The Temple*, whose door stands open to all believers as a refuge and a place of prayer and hope. The fateful separation of the sheep from the goats that Calvinists acknowledge is an irrelevancy in Herbert's world: Christ died for all mankind and established the Church as the sanctuary for all who seek him. But Herbert believes in a decent order of service, conducted by a minister who is a priest of the mysteries, not just a godly preacher with a power to move the spirit.

> Holiness on the head,
> Light and perfections on the breast,
> Harmonious bells below, raising the dead
> To lead them unto life and rest:
> Thus are true Aarons drest.
> ('Aaron' ll. 1–5)

The altar at which Herbert ministers is clearly, almost provoca-
tively, a declaration of his High Church Arminian sympathies. It is
made of stone (in contrast to the wooden communion tables preferred
by the Calvinists, who set no value on objects of worship), and it is
obviously fixed in a place of sanctity, not movable. To make his point
more forcibly, Herbert shapes the poem so that it appears as an ancient
stone altar.

The ceremoniousness of worship enacted in *The Temple* speaks of
Herbert's care for 'the beauty of holiness'. There are many echoes of
the liturgy in the poems to remind the reader of the formal patterns
of the Anglican service that Herbert loved. The language of the Eucharist is also prominent, for the bread and wine of communion are
always available to the sinner. 'Sure there was wine, before my sighs
did dry it: there was corn/Before my tears did drown it.' ('The Collar',
ll. 10–11). Christ's offerings are there for all. Neatness and order prevail
in the world of these poems. The church year has its festivals that must
be observed, and Herbert's imagination dwells most on the season of
the Passion as the critical time of spiritual history. There is little
emphasis on preaching in *The Temple*. Most of Herbert's poems were
written before Laud rose to power, so it would be inappropriate to
represent him as a poet of the Laudian ascendancy. It is most likely
that he derived the character of his worship from Lancelot Andrewes,
who had been Herbert's headmaster at Westminster School, and who
had instituted there a highly decorous order of service a generation
before Laud came in. In the churches where Herbert ministered, he
insisted on refurnishing them with decent plain woodwork that
provided a handsome setting for the services, as Laud would later
require by order.[7] Yet although the mode of Herbert's worship was
in harmony with Laudianism, his devotional commitment was so
entire, his sifting of experience so fine, that the poems appealed to
Christians of all shades of belief.

> Doctrine and life, colours and light, in one
>   When they combine and mingle, bring
> A strong regard and awe.
>   ('The Windows', ll. 11–13)

Herrick's religious poems, *Noble Numbers*, written for the most part
in the 1630s, exemplify a characteristic Laudian concern for ceremony
and decency in devotion, even to excess. Herrick takes such pleasure
in ritual and ceremony, the long continuity of which links him to the
ancient world, to both Christian and pagan practices, that he hardly
pays any attention to the doctrinal content of his verse:

With golden Censers, and with Incense, here,
Before thy Virgin-Altar I appear,
To pay thee what I owe.
                        ('To God', ll. 1–3)

There is an engaging modesty about Herrick's ministrations, but he avoids contemplation of the gulfs of sin or the infinity of heaven, and does not presume to search God's purposes towards man, being assured only of an ultimate benevolence.

Much more fully representative of the Laudian moment was Richard Crashaw. This 'bird of paradise,' as Cowley called him, was hatched at Pembroke College, Cambridge, where Lancelot Andrewes had once been Master, and from 1635 to 1644 roosted in Peterhouse, which was in effect a Laudian seminary, the Master being John Cosin, who was the most cultivated exponent of high-Anglican modes of devotion, not only before the Civil War but also after the Restoration, when he became Bishop of Durham. Crashaw was not a thoughtful poet; he was rhapsodic, at times ecstatic, attaining an astonishing power through an unremitting contemplation of a devotional subject, assailing it with a strenuous play of pious wit and paradox until it dissolves into some radiant preview of heaven. Adoration was the element he lived in. His poetry tells one much about the confident spirit of the Anglican Church under Laud, moving to repossess rich areas of piety that had been abandoned at the Reformation. Religious images were returning to help stimulate and concentrate meditation (Crashaw helped to beautify the chapel at Peterhouse with images); the veneration of the saints was again permitted for their perfect faith and exemplary piety; the figure of the Virgin could again be contemplated as a 'transcendant creature' who inspired a special kind of tender affection long denied to Protestants; angels reappeared in the Anglican heavens. To the Puritan elements in the Church, these developments were an encroachment into Catholic territory, but to Laudians such as Crashaw they were a proper expansion of the Anglican Church into the traditional domain of Christian worship, undertaken in a fresh spirit of a pure faith. Many of Crashaw's subjects were borrowed from the Counter-Reformation Catholic Church: Mary Magdalene and the cult of tears, St Teresa and the ecstasies of divine love, the preoccupation with saints and martyrs, the mysteries of the Holy Blood and the sacraments, and the adoration of the Holy Name. The high artifice of his style and the emblematic habit of mind also derive from the same source, yet he exercised his art in the setting of the Anglican Church for most of his life, and his poetry preserves a style of worship which was still unfolding when it was destroyed in the mid-1640s.[8]

Puritan-inclined readers had less accomplished poetry to sustain them. George Wither and Francis Quarles provided the most popular fare for plain Protestants. Like most of the poets with Puritan sympathies, they had little interest in transmitting a record of their intimate spiritual experience, preferring rather to outline the scheme of things, as they saw God's hand everywhere in the shaping of lives and events. They speak of Providence rather than personality. Since God's decisions had been cast before the beginning of time, it was instructive to observe their gradual disclosure in time. As a result, their poems abound in moral instruction. Quarles, who was a Calvinist, rose to success on his *Emblems* (1635) and its sequel *Hieroglyphics of the Life of Man* (1638), both of which are full of schematic pictures that show the moral law at work in the world, illustrating the snares of this world and the obstacles that block the way to heaven. They urge the reader, by way of biblical quotation and poetic commentary, to live according to godly precepts, and trust in hope. The verses shine with bright truisms, which together with the ingenious and often amusing engravings, must have given much pleasure to earnest readers. Quarles himself was a moderate man. He deplored Laudianism for being too popish and authoritarian, but he also disapproved of the separatist tendencies of the extreme Puritans. He was very much a middle-of-the-road Protestant trying to maintain the moderate attitudes of King James's Church in the reign of Charles I, when the movement to extremes was accelerating.[9]

Wither was a more aggressive writer, several times jailed for his attacks on the establishment; titles such as *Abuses Stript and Whipt* and *Halleluja* give some sense of his ebullient character. He liked to think that his verse had a prophetic power, or, after an event, a retributive force, but either way he sang – or shouted – of God's judgements. In *Britain's Remembrancer* (1628) he warned at great length that the plague of 1625 (which had ominously coincided with Charles's accession) was a sign of further judgements to come, unless more reformation was seen in the Church, and corruption rooted out.[10] He was patriotic, noisily anti-Catholic, hostile to the court and to episcopal power. In common with perhaps most religious dissidents, he believed he was living in the last age of the world, and that Christ would return before long to judge and to gather in his elect, a conviction that lent urgency to his writings.[11] The milder Quarles had pleaded with God to intervene in history and put an end to the iniquities of the time:

> Unlock thy clouds, great Thund'rer, and come down;
> Behold whose temples wear thy sacred crown;
> Redress, redress our wrongs; revenge, revenge thy own. . . .

> Lord, canst thou be so mild and he [the Devil] so bold?

> Or can thy flocks be thriving, when the fold
> Is governed by the fox? Lord, canst thou see and
>   hold? . . .
> Lord, rise and rouse, and rule, and crush their furious
>   pride.
>
> (*Emblems*, i. 15.)

Both Wither and Quarles, like most opposition poets, looked back to Spenser as the model Protestant poet, whose sympathies lay with the Puritan side. Spenser had been associated with the Puritan champion Sir Philip Sidney, and *The Faerie Queene* had prophesied the victory of the reformed religion of England, personified in Red Cross Knight. The apocalyptic events of Book i of *The Faerie Queene* that foreshadowed England's key part in the last scenes of history exercised a particular influence over radical religious poets in the seventeenth century, as did Spenser's pastoral religious complaints with their call for more reformation, in *The Shepheardes Calendar* and *Colin Clouts Come Home Againe*. Michael Drayton, William Drummond, and William Browne maintained the Spenserian tradition of writing pastoral verse that contained covert political and religious criticism; the two Fletchers, Giles and Phineas, kept up the line of epic in the Spenserian mode, with a Puritan bias.[12] The grand design of providential history is their prominent theme, lit by flares of apocalyptic anticipation. Phineas Fletcher's *The Locusts* (1621) is an allegorical treatment of the Gunpowder Plot, violently anti-Catholic, dramatically illustrative of God's preservation of his Englishmen, and calling for Apocalypse now.

> Oh is not this the time, when mounted high
> Upon thy Pegasus of heavenly breed,
> With bloody arms, white armies, flaming eye,
> Thou vow'st in blood to swim thy snowy steed,
> And stain thy bridle with a purple dye?
> This, this thy time; come then, Oh come with speed,
>   Such as thy Israel saw thee, when the maine
>   Pil'd up his waves on heaps; the liquid plaine
> Ran up, and with his hill safe wall'd that wandring traine.
>
> (Canto v. 34)

The margins are strewn with references to the Book of Revelation and to Daniel. Giles Fletcher's *Christ's Victory and Triumph* (1610) retold the history of the Fall and Christ's death and resurrection, and rehearsed the redemptive scheme that operated in favour of the faithful Protestant.

One can sense Milton's affinities with this group of poets. He too looked back to 'our sage and serious Spenser' as the exemplary modern poet, and he loved to expound God's providential designs, even in his earlier verse. (It is instructive, in this respect, to contrast Milton's 'Nativity Ode' with Crashaw's: Milton's concern is to explore the significance of the Nativity in the spiritual history of the world; Crashaw writes about the affective presence of the Christ-child and the devotional ardour he experiences in contemplation of the scene.) Milton always regarded poetry as a vehicle for prophecy, and he took satisfaction in reminding his readers that he was often right: he notes, for instance, in the headnote to the 1645 edition of 'Lycidas' that the poem 'by occasion foretells the ruin of our corrupted clergy then in their height'. 'Lycidas' is in fact a notable example of pastoral exploited for political and religious criticism in the manner of the Spenserian opposition poets who were dissatisfied with the condition of the Church or concerned about turpitude in affairs of state. Milton also shared the millenarian expectations that were characteristic of the reformist party, but not so common among the Laudians who held power in the 1630s. But Milton had not always been aligned with the opposition. He had written an extravagant poem in memory of Lancelot Andrewes, and shown a sympathy for the aesthetics of ceremonious worship at the close of 'Il Penseroso', and had intended to take holy orders himself before he became alarmed at the direction of church government under Laud. Milton's developing views about church politics will be looked at later in this chapter, but here it is worth noting that Milton adhered to an Arminian position in theology, believing profoundly that man could exercise his free will to desire and attain salvation, and rejecting a complete divine determinism in the fate of the soul. George Wither also came to adopt an Arminian position in spite of his steady hostility to the Laudian party that was its principal support.[13] Such alignments should remind us that Puritanism was not always synonymous with Calvinism, nor was a Laudian always going to be Arminian in theology. Men like Milton and Wither desperately wanted to see the Reformation advanced in the Church of England, with simpler services, more zealous preaching, much more freedom for the individual to seek his God in the way he chose, according to his own conscience; they deplored the fact that bishops should have authority over the spiritual domain of another free Christian, but they chose, by study and conviction, the theological system of their opponents in preference to the Calvinism that had long been associated with reform. The complexities of religious belief in this period are such that generalizations do not readily stick; in the end each individual evolved his own combination of beliefs and prejudices, and in the 1640s the choice became much wider and the combinations more confusing than ever before. Even opposition to the church establishment in the 1630s did not always mean that a man would side with Parliament when the chips were down. Quarles supported the King, Wither fought for Parliament, and Milton did not fight at all but poured out pamphlets in the cause of reformation.

To revert briefly to the doctrine of Calvinism, it may be that its most popular and enduring literary expression was in the drama of this period. It could be argued that the operative theology behind much Elizabethan and Jacobean tragedy was Calvinistic and that in many plays the tragic hero makes the discovery that he is destined to damnation. As tragedy has always had links with religion, and deals habitually with the operations of fate upon the individual, it would not be surprising to find that English tragedy reflected the dominant theology of the time. Dr Faustus, for example, is a man whose fate is damnation, and even though he repents of his actions and calls on Christ to seek to save his soul, it is all in vain. Christ's blood streams in the firmament, but there is not a drop for Faustus, though it is his consuming desire at the end, because Faustus is predestined to be damned, and Christ died to redeem only the elect, not all mankind. *Macbeth* is another tragedy of damnation, written for King James, whose own creed was Calvinist. The language of the play teems with references to heaven and hell, and as the action unfolds, Macbeth discovers that he is fated to be a creature of the devil and is marked for damnation, experiencing its desolations even in life. *Hamlet* too may be the tragedy of a man who, for all his nobility of thought and virtue of principle, finds himself numbered among the rejected. 'There's a divinity that shapes our ends/Rough-hew them how we will' (V. ii. 10–11) is a thoroughly Calvinist observation. Characters appear to have free will to choose their course of action, but that freedom is an illusion, because the actions chosen only lead them to an end that has been predetermined. At the climax of a tragedy the hero recognizes that while he has believed he has been in control of his destiny, he has in fact been realizing a fate that has been unalterably allotted him by God. 'Flights of angels sing thee to thy rest', (V. ii. 371) bids Horatio, but the action of the play suggests that Hamlet's nature is malignant and depraved, and that his soul will sink. Part of the function of Jacobean tragedy is to reveal the true character of the soul to its possessor through action that moves to a climax of self-knowledge. Vindice, in *The Revenger's Tragedy*, comes to realize that he is not superior in virtue to the palpably damned inhabitants of the court, but is as depraved as they are; he recognizes that his fascination with lust and vengeance is a sign of a polluted soul. Beatrice, in *The Changeling*, believes she is, as her name suggests, blessed, and cannot be infected by the contagion of vice, but the action reveals to her that far from being one of God's elect, she is one of the damned; her affinity with the devilish De Flores was a sign of her true nature. Webster's tragedies portray a world almost totally inhabited by a race of damned people. Ford's heroes too act in a Calvinistic world, where their destinies are pre-ordained, and the pattern of action shows them moving nobly, stoically, towards an end they know is inevitable, even as they go through the motions of choice and self-assertion. If a major preoccupation of ordinary men and women in this period was to search for signs of their souls' destination after death, then part of the appeal of tragic drama might be its clear demonstration of how the most eminent men are brought to understand that, despite their prosperity and greatness in life, they carry within them a soul marked for damnation. If tragedies are cautionary tales, could it be that Shakespeare's late romances are histories of the elect, whose final revelations of felicity are anticipations of a greater bliss to come?

In personal terms, the zealous Christian with Calvinist convictions spent much time and anxiety in searching his life for evidence of God's mercy towards him. In this process prayer, preaching, Bible-reading, and godly conversation were important for releasing sudden impulses of responsiveness, which were signs of the working of the spirit. The classic Puritan autobiography is Bunyan's *Grace Abounding to the Chief of Sinners*, which records his progress from sinful indifference in matters of religion through years of anxious hope and doubt about his calling to the climactic experience of conversion, which assured him he was truly one of God's elect. Although it was written about 1665, its account is broadly representative of the religious life of innumerable people throughout the century. The book is 'a relation of the work of God upon my own soul'. Bunyan describes his unregenerate youth, 'careless of mine own salvation', during which he is none the less struck by several lucky escapes from death that might be providential. His spirit is awakened by a sermon that touches him, and he is persuaded that the preacher 'made me that sermon on purpose to show me my evildoing'. He falls into despair, but then sets about 'outward reformation' in his life. A new stage opens when he overhears some poor women of Bedford 'talking about the things of God'.

> I heard but I understood not, for they were far above, out
> of my reach; for their talk was about a new birth, the
> work of God on their hearts, also how they were
> convinced of their miserable state by nature; they talked
> how God had visited their souls with his love in the Lord
> Jesus, and with what words and what promises they had
> been refreshed, comforted and supported against the
> temptations of the devil. (para. 37)

Their conversation fires Bunyan to a new attentiveness. Constantly reading the Scriptures, he finds certain passages that excite him, seeming to be intended especially for him. He realizes that the critical question is this:

> I evidently saw, that unless the great God, of his infinite grace and bounty, had voluntarily chosen me to be a vessel of mercy, though I should desire, and long and labour until my heart did break, no good could come of it. Therefore this would stick with me, How can you tell you are elected?

He fears that the number of the elect may be already made up, yet he perseveres, and is particularly encouraged by a 'painful preacher'. The Bible keeps on yielding new promises to him, but even so he is seized by a fit of temptation to abandon the whole enterprise as foolish. He recovers, and continues reflecting on the Scriptures, developing an extraordinary love for Christ. One night, as he is sitting by the fire, a Bible verse starts to ring in his head, insistently.

> Wife, said I, is there ever such a scripture, I must go to Jesus? She said she could not tell, therefore I sat musing still to see if I could remember such a place. I had not sat above two or three minutes but that came bolting in upon me.

Hebrews the twelfth is the source.

> Then with joy I told my wife, O now I know, I know! But that night was a good night to me, I never had but few better; I longed for the company of some of God's people that I might have imparted unto them what God had showed me. Christ was a precious Christ to my soul that night; I could scarce lie in my bed for joy, and peace, and triumph, through Christ; this great glory did not continue upon me until morning, yet that twelfth of the author to the Hebrews (ver. 22–24) was a blessed scripture to me. (para. 263)

That was the experience of his conversion, the knowledge that he was saved. It is not surprising that the crucial verse comes from St Paul, whose conversion was the archetype for so many Puritans. Thereafter, Bunyan is at pains to share his experience by preaching and speaking of it wherever be can. One can sense why this type of enthusiasm had no time for the formal structures of a regulated church, and why the only kind of authority it would respect would be that of people who had similar knowledge.

The rising of the spirit was one of many factors that combined to overthrow Church and State in the 1640s. After the Long Parliament ordered the arrest of Laud in 1641, there followed a struggle in the House of Commons between those who wanted to do away with the whole system of church government by bishops, the Root and Branch party as they were called, and the more moderate group who wished to retain the Elizabethan church settlement but stripped of the Laudian innovations. The issues were still being debated when the slide into civil war accelerated events. With the faltering of the Church of England's authority, the sects quickened into independent life. The abolition of censorship in 1640, and of the church courts shortly afterwards, removed the main obstacles to their growth. Soon every kind of conviction was preaching its own kind of truth and refuting the claims of others, all fanned by a high sense that now was the time for a general reformation and given acute urgency by the wide prevalence of millenarian beliefs.

Among all these bewildering developments, Milton provides a guide of sorts through his avid engagement in the controversies of the 1640s. For several years he had expressed opposition to episcopal government in the Church, arguing that bishops had no basis in the Bible, that their power was a relic of papal ways and an unwarrantable intrusion into the private sphere of belief where men should seek the truth by their own conscience. Moreover, in England bishops were the appointees of the State, their status compromised by political considerations. As Laud tottered, Milton fired off several tracts against episcopacy. *Of Reformation in England* in May 1641 urged that the Reformation begun under Edward VI be pushed through to its severe conclusions, which included the abolition of the order of bishops. This he followed a month or two later with *Of Prelatical Episcopacy* and *Animadversions* in which he banged the heads of the bishops with learned relish. Sensing the enemy in disarray, he then threw at them *The Reason of Church Government Urged Against Prelaty* at the beginning of 1642, just after the bishops had been excluded from Parliament. Here he rehearsed the biblical and historical arguments against the legitimacy of bishops, and insisted on the separation of religious matters from state control. Against the bishops' argument that their authority prevented the fragmentation of the Church into an anarchy of sects, Milton asserted that the rise of these sects was caused by a zeal for reformation, each group seeking truth in its own way. The clash of opinions he found exhilarating, not frightful, and out of this free contention a finer sense of the essentials of Christian belief would emerge. 'No wonder then that in the reforming of a church, which is never brought to effect without the fierce encounter of truth and falsehood together . . . there fall from between the shock many fond errors and fantastic opinions, which, when truth has the upper hand and the reformation shall be perfected, will easily be rid out of the way.'[14] Optimism indeed.

The sects that Milton looked on tolerantly at this stage occupied positions all across the religious spectrum, with most crowded into the radical end. Familists denied the divinity of Christ, some believing that Christ was not a real person or heaven or hell real places, but all states of mind; Baptists insisted that only after adult baptism could one hope to find the true way, Ranters followed the impulses of the spirit wherever they led, some of them holding the belief that the operations of grace made it impossible for them to sin, a belief also held by the reviled Antinomians. The Brownists were an old-established separatist group that followed the complex doctrinal specifications of their leader, and in the early 1650s the Muggletonians would emerge as another follow-my-leader group, this one with strong apocalyptic expectations. At this distance in time it is difficult to characterize the sects with any hope of accuracy, for their boundaries and beliefs were so fluid and they were too often defined by their enemies rather than themselves.[15]

Milton himself in the early 1640s favoured the Presbyterian system of church government, with a minister chosen by the congregation, and lay elders appointed too by vote; minister and elders would all be entitled to attend various councils, which in turn contributed to a General Assembly where doctrine and discipline would be established. But Milton came to feel that the Presbyterian system itself admitted too much authority from above, and he moved later in the decade to the Independent position, whereby congregations should elect their own ministers and remain independent, self-determining groups free from all outside interference. Parliament tried unsuccessfully to introduce a full Presbyterian church in 1646, but no real order came into the religious scene until Cromwell managed to set up a broad and tolerant national church after 1653.[16]

The very fact that men and women could now choose their religious standpoint was a profound novelty, for conformity to the State Church had been the universal obligation hitherto. Equally new were the democratic ideas that were now released. As many of the sects preached the complete equality of all men and women before Christ, regardless of rank, conviction hardened in many men's minds that such equality should be reflected in political rights too. The consequences of this line of thought are followed up in this book in Chapter 9, but here one need note that changes in ideas about religious rights inevitably affected one's sense of political rights, and one's relationship to the law of the land. As the bishops lost their powers of jurisdiction in 1642, Milton turned his thoughts to the reformation of the law that might follow in the wake of church reformation. Divorce was the issue he picked on, partly for personal reasons, but also because he saw marriage as an area in which the liberties of the individual might be much improved. Parliament did not listen. Worse still, Parliament showed that it still had an inherently conservative grain – for its membership was recruited from the gentry – when it voted to bring back licensing for the press in 1644. *Areopagitica* was Milton's response to that development, the most eloquent plea for freedom of speech in the English language. Again, Parliament was not moved. Milton's radicalism in his campaigns against authority was so fervent that he made the Long Parliament appear a very cautious body. Parliament in turn found Milton an excessively active man, and his name was mentioned unfavourably in sermons at Westminster. His radicalism derived from the Bible, which made it all the more incontrovertible: biblical justification strengthened by lines of reasonable argument made Milton a formidable antagonist. His large dream of reformation in religion was extended to reformation in society, a throwing off of the checks and controls that inhibited the growth of a nobler type of Englishman free from the religious, legal, and political constraints that had accumulated over the centuries. Here Milton's ideal scheme of education constructed according to the most ambitious Renaissance models and described in his tractate *Of Education* (1644) bears on the scene, because the recipients of this liberal instruction would be young men of the purified religion; the result would be a more regenerate, finer-minded generation, superior even to the best of antiquity.

Behind all this ferment of mind lay Milton's millenarian hopes that looked to the Second Coming of Christ as a rapidly approaching event. The revolutionary turmoil in England coupled with the new spirit of reformation abroad seemed to indicate that the predictions concerning the return of Christ that had been growing more insistent ever since the Reformation of the sixteenth century were soon to be fulfilled. Scores of commentaries on the Book of Revelation and on the prophetic books of Daniel and Isaiah had been published, and innumerable sermons based on them preached.[17] Many of the commentaries attempted to fix a specific date for Christ's return, others preferred to demonstrate that almost all the necessary preconditions were now present. Joseph Mede, one of the fellows at Christ's College, Cambridge, had published an important Latin commentary in 1627, when Milton was a student there. His book was ordered by Parliament to be translated into English and republished in 1643: *The Key to the Revelation* expected the end to come in the course of the century, with

1654 and 1670 prophesied as the critical dates. Milton was caught up in this excitement, which lent added urgency to his plans, for the advent of a gospel-like simplicity in religion and a waking spirit in pious Englishmen would hasten the much desired consummation of history. In *Of Reformation in England* he had written of 'the Eternal and shortly-expected King'; in *Animadversions* he had prayed:

> Come forth out of thy royal Chambers, O Prince of all
> the Kings of the Earth, put on the visible robes of thy
> imperial Majesty, take up that unlimited Scepter which thy
> Almighty Father hath bequeathed thee; for now the voice
> of thy Bride calls thee, and all creatures sigh to be
> renewed.

But the final obstacles, the horns of Antichrist, had to be removed. At first for Milton these were the bishops, then King Charles, whose execution he believed was a necessary act which he justified in his two *Defences of the English People*. After Charles's death, his hopes lay with Cromwell as the reformed Christian Prince who would prepare the way for Christ. When an earthly not a heavenly monarchy was restored in 1660, Milton incorporated his search for an explanation of the failure of all his hopes into *Paradise Lost*. After the collapse of the English revolution, Milton felt a great need to 'assert Eternal Providence,/And justify the ways of God to men'. The reasons for failure, why God's kingdom on earth had been deferred, and why the new paradise so nearly attained had been lost, lay in the very origins of human nature. Disobedience to God's primal laws had let our nature be perverted by sin. Adam, according to Milton, possessed free will, his most precious faculty and the sign of God's highest trust, but he had misapplied it. After the Fall, right reason which should accompany free will had been blurred by sin, and could no longer know God aright. The generations of men wander in the mazes of error, but always there is the one, or the few, the saving remnant, who retain their faith in God's justice. Christ's kingdom will come, but in God's own time. Satan's power is a blocking power dedicated to the frustration of God's purposes, and it is perpetual in history. Recent critics have been inclined to point out how in the debates in hell and in Satan's strategies there are reminiscences of both monarchical and parliamentary-Cromwellian error, for Milton believed that the revolution, besides being impeded by its opponents, had also been betrayed by its supporters who failed to push through reforms when they had time by the forelock.[18] In the dismal preview of history that the Archangel Michael offers to Adam at the end of the epic, there is only the assurance that Satan's power will finally be defeated and that Christ will gather in the just, but the emphasis is now on inward reformation, on obedience to conscience and to the known laws of God, on the achieve- ment of 'A Paradise within thee, happier far', (XII. 587) rather than on the paradise that had been lost at the beginning of time.

Milton's counsel that inward perfection was now to be sought for, in preference to outward reformation of Church or State, continued in *Paradise Regained* (1671) in which Christ rejects the temptations of power, fame, even learning, as distractions from a composure of mind achieved by faith in God and in his ultimate care for the true believers. A similar attitude can be discerned in the much more moving drama of *Samson Agonistes* that was published together with *Paradise Regained*. Patience in adversity, enduring faith in the God who showed so many signs of favour now withdrawn, spiritual composure after temptation – the mood is that of 'They also serve who only stand and wait'. Samson waits, and is rewarded with 'some rousing motions in me which dispose/To something extraordinary my thoughts', (ll. 1382–83) the impulse from God that sends him out to fulfil his destiny. That destiny may be violent, as in Samson's case, or it may be a silent knowledge of divine approval. Looking for some analogy with Samson in the post-Restoration religious scene, one might think of the situation of the Quakers, who had been one of the most radical groups during the Commonwealth, fiercely resistant of any kind of secular authority, responsive to the will of God as they perceived it acting through the conscience, and willing to fight to defend their cause; after 1660 they adopted pacifism, endured civil disabilities, withdrew to the fringes of society, and cultivated the inner life, at their meetings waiting on the impulse of the spirit before they spoke. They had no desire to wreak vengeance on their enemies, but in other ways their accommodation to a changed world was not wholly dissimilar to what Milton had described in *Samson*.

At the Restoration there was a brief promise of toleration for all kinds of Christian belief, but soon the new Parliament and the King imposed the Act of Uniformity in 1662 (ironically on St Bartho- lomew's Day), that reintroduced conformity to a High Church liturgy that was laid out in a new Prayer Book. Some two thousand ministers of the Cromwellian National Church were dispossessed for refusing to accept the new dispensation, which was in effect a return to Laudianism in ritual and doctrine, and the sectarian groups that had enjoyed freedom of worship during the Commonwealth were loaded with penalties and driven into the wilderness of nonconformity. The great failure of the Restoration settlement lay in its inability to find a comprehensive solution to the problem of diverse religious opinions. Instead the nation was divided into Church and Dissent, a rift that would endure for centuries.

Not all religion was conflict, however. A small group of theologians did try to rise above the contentiousness of the times, hoping to distance themselves from the 'enthusiasm' or headstrong private conviction that powered the sects in so many different directions, and, at the other extreme, from Catholicism with its idolatry and its disposition to submit to canonical authority. The Cambridge Platonists, active from the 1650s to the 1670s, have an air of sweet if at times bland reasonableness about them. The leading members, Benjamin Whichcote, Ralph Cudworth, John Smith, Nathaniel Culverwel, and Peter Sterry were all associated with Emmanuel College, Cambridge, generally regarded as the seminary of Puritanism in the seventeenth century; Henry More spent most of his life at Christ's. They attempted to graft Platonism onto the essentials of Christianity in order to escape from credal differences and issues of ritual and the endemic nit-picking that went on in churches. The faculty that discovered the presence of God within the creation was Reason, the spark of the divine mind that every human mind contained. Reason took priority over the Bible, whose general truths were often occluded by accidentals. Whichcote remarked that 'The written word of God is not the first or only discovery of the duty of Man. . . . Clear principles of truth and light, affirmed by the natural reason and confirmed by the law and purpose of the Gospel, are above all particular examples and texts of Scripture.'[19] (By 'above all' he means 'more important than'.) The demonstrable possession of a clear faculty of reason involves accepting that man has free will to choose between better and worse courses of action, and the exercise of reason at its highest level will seek the utmost knowledge of what is good and true, aspiring to know its own source in the Creator. This faculty of Reason that was the centre of the Cambridge Platonists' discourse was, as Basil Willey well observed,

> neither the logical faculty of the philosophers nor the good
> sense of the man-of-the-world; it began in the ordering of
> life according to the highest hypothesis about the divine
> nature, and ended in mystical union with God.

> Nothing is the true improvement of our rational faculties
> but the exercise of the several virtues of sobriety,
> modesty, gentleness, humility, obedience to God, and
> charity to men. (Whichcote, Aphorism 541)

> Divine Truth is better understood as it unfolds itself in the
> purity of men's hearts and lives, than in all those subtle
> niceties into which curious wits may lay it forth. (John

Smith, *The True Way or Method of Attaining to Divine Knowledge*, Section 1).[20]

Central Christian tenets were argued away as incompatible with a reasonable deity: the total depravity of man after the Fall, the inheritance of sin, the doctrine of predestination were in particular unacceptable to the Cambridge Platonists, for these theological propositions seemed 'to save God's absolute power at the expense of his Wisdom'.[21] Sin was a vice contracted in society. In general the Platonists had little to say about the nature of Christ, applying their thought more to the characteristics of the Creator as revealed in the light of Reason. It may be imagined that such abstract and rarefied debate had little popular impact, though it did help to form the outlook of some leaders of the Church in the later seventeenth century, such as Tillotson and Stillingfleet. The Platonists' ideas found some kind of enduring literary expression in the poetry and meditative prose of Thomas Traherne, whose luminous delight in the Creation and in the penetrative power of the mind was sustained by theories of Christian neo-Platonism.[22] The long-term significance of the Cambridge movement would be found in the changed temper of religious belief in the next century, for these religious philosophers initiated a shift away from the theological in-fighting that had bedevilled Christianity since the Reformation towards a deistic view of the Creation that would prevail widely among the more pensive classes of the eighteenth century. They were moving away from the concept of special truths enshrined in Christianity alone towards a broad justification of man's spirituality in nature. They look forward to the cool persuasions of John Locke's *The Reasonableness of Christianity* (1695) and to the hard-edged rationalism of John Toland's *Christianity Not Mysterious* (1696), although they still insist that God must ultimately 'be known, not by demonstration, but by spiritual sensation'.[23] Their presentation of a benevolent Divine Reason at the source of creation reduced the levels of terror and wild hope in religion, and made the tormented struggles with a personal God that had been the vivid experience of so many contemporary Christians seem already like the emotional residue of a more primitive age.

But the Cambridge Platonists recognized a more insidious enemy than enthusiasm or sectarian division, and that was the slow but inexorable rise of materialist theories, advanced by men of formidable intellect, notably Descartes and Hobbes. Bishop Burnet, writing the *History of his Own Times* at the end of the century saw the Cambridge group as an antidote to 'that very wicked book with a very strange title, The Leviathan, that Hobbes in the late times of confusion had ventured to publish'. He synopsized Hobbes's views succinctly and with a degree of unfairness: 'That the universe was God, our souls material, and thought nothing else but subtle and imperceptible motion; that fear and interest were the chief instruments of society; that all morality consisted in following our private will and advantage; that religion had no other foundation than the laws of the land; and that all law was the will of the prince, or of the people.' Hobbes's demonstration of the materialism of the universe, space, and mind, which were all to be explained in atomistic terms of matter and motion, left no place for a soul, and it was to assert the inadequacy of this view of life that the Cambridge Platonists campaigned. The most energetic refutations came from Henry More in his *Antidote against Atheism* (1653) and *The Immortality of the Soul* (1659) and Ralph Cudworth in his *True Intellectual System of the Universe*, (1678).[24] More applied much skill to denouncing Descartes's separation of the material from the spiritual world, which More considered to be a discreet way of relegating spirit to an undiscussable abstraction, leaving materialism with its probable consequence of atheism to dominate the attention of philosophers. More himself celebrated an atomistic universe permeated by spiritual energy in works of dazzling obscurity such as his *Democritus Platonissans* of 1646.

The tendency of religion to become a department of philosophy, and for faith to become an aspect of conduct, was confirmed by the immensely influential writings of Locke at the end of the century. Locke demonstrated the necessary existence of 'an intelligent being' as the author of the universe in a series of propositions in the *Essay Concerning Human Understanding*. If the existence of a God is entirely demonstrable by the process of human reason, what then is the need of revelation through the Bible, and why should Christianity have a unique status among the religions of the world? In *The Reasonableness of Christianity* he suggested that scriptural revelation was God's way of impressing his designs on 'the illiterate bulk of mankind' as 'the greater part of mankind want leisure or capacity for demonstration', and are impervious to reason. Christ was indeed the Messiah – and here Locke accepts the miracles of Christ's birth – whose life and example confirmed a morality that was consonant with reason and justice, and whose resurrection taught what could not otherwise be known by reason, the certainty of an afterlife. Locke puts forward his view that faith in Christ and a righteous life are preconditions of salvation among those whom revelation has reached, but among men beyond Christendom, God's goodness and mercy will favour those who live honourably and well. The calm and tolerant arguments of Locke provided an acceptable model of belief for educated men for the next few generations, and strengthened the secularist character of the Anglican Church. Dissenters, however, preferred the heat of their convictions to the lukewarm assurances of Lockean Christianity.

Notes

1. William Barlow, *The Summe and Substance of the Conference at Hampton Court* (1604).

2. The Pilgrim Fathers sailed from Amsterdam in 1620, going first to Southampton where they picked up another shipload of dissidents. Both parties were forced to crowd into the *Mayflower*, the other ship having become unseaworthy. The separatists had intended to settle in Virginia, and they sailed under a patent from the Virginia Company. But accidents of tide and tempest drove them to Massachusetts instead.

3. See for example the prayer for the Fifth of November in the 1662 Prayer Book: 'We yield thee our unfeigned thanks and praise for the wonderful and mighty deliverance of our gracious sovereign King James the First, the Queen, the Prince, and all the Royal Branches, with the nobility, clergy and Commons of England, then assembled in Parliament, by Papish treachery appointed as sheep to the slaughter, in a most barbarous and savage manner, beyond the example of former ages.'

4. A very clear account of the rise of the Arminian faction in England is provided by Nicholas Tyacke, 'Puritanism, Arminianism and Counter-Revolution', in *The Origins of the English Civil War*, edited by C. Russell (1973).

5. Peter Heylyn, *Cyprianus Anglicanus* (1668), p. 289.

6. A view that John Carey inclines towards in his discussion of Donne's religious position in *John Donne: Life, Mind and Art* (1981), pp. 236–44

7. It is typical of Herbert's conciliatory spirit that when he refurnished his church at Leighton Bromswold, Huntingdonshire, he gave equal prominence to pulpit and lectern, so that 'they should neither have a precedency or priority of the other, but that prayer and preaching, being equally useful, might agree like brethren, and have an equal honour and estimation'.

8. Crashaw did not convert to Catholicism until the Church of England was in ruins and could no longer provide the institutional shelter that he needed. Laudianism was kept from falling into the Roman Church by the safeguards of the Thirty-Nine Articles, by deep division of doctrine over such questions as the intercession of the saints, purgatory, indulgences and the status of the sacraments, and also by vigorous anti-papal sentiments. It should be remembered that Laud was offered a cardinal's hat if he would convert, in the mid-1630s, but he had no interest in the temptation. For Laud, the Church of England should be apostolic, episcopalian, and firmly independent of Rome.

9. Quarles's position is neatly discussed in Christopher Hill's essay 'Francis Quarles and Edward Benlowes', in *Collected Essays* (Brighton, 1985), I, 188–207.

10. Hill's essay on 'George Wither and John Milton', in *Collected Essays*, I, is recommended for its brisk account of Wither as a Puritan 'pseudo-prophet'. Hill reminds us that Wither shared with Milton 'a passionate anti-clericalism, a hatred of ambitious clergymen, of simony and the patronage system, of the

state church, its tithes, its courts, its excommunications, its fees, its superstitious ceremonies and uneconomic observation of saints' days' (p. 135).

11. See Hill, 'George Wither and John Milton', pp. 140–42 for examples of Wither's millenarian beliefs.

12. David Norbrook provides a revealing account of the religious and political criticism that lies camouflaged in the Spenserian poetry of the early seventeenth century in *Poetry and Politics in the English Renaissance* (1984), Chapter 9.

13. See Hill, 'George Wither and John Milton', pp. 143–44.

14. John Milton, *The Reason of Church Government* (1642), Chapter 7.

15. The most memorable guide to the sects is Thomas Edwards's *Gangraena* (1646), which vilifies almost all of them.

16. Cromwell maintained a system of committees that vetted ministers for their suitability to serve in the parish churches, where preaching now composed much of the service, but he also tolerated the existence of separatist groups, and of groups that had gathered round a charismatic leader. A most helpful account of the conditions at this time is by Claire Cross, 'The Church in England 1646–1660', in *The Interregnum*, edited by G. E. Aylmer (1972).

17. For an account of millenarian convictions in the seventeenth century, see especially Christopher Hill, *Antichrist in Seventeenth-Century England* (1971), and Kathleen Firth, *The Apocalyptic Tradition in Reformation Britain, 1530–1645* (1979).

18. See in particular Christopher Hill, *Milton and the English Revolution* (1977), especially Part VI.

19. Quoted by Basil Willey in *The English Moralists* (1965), p. 185. His chapter on the Cambridge Platonists in this book is a clear and brief introduction to the group and their significance. See also his chapter in *Seventeenth Century Background* (1934). For a more recent exposition of their tenets, see *The Cambridge Platonists*, edited by C. A. Patrides (1969). Whichcote's Aphorisms printed as an appendix to Patrides' book are a useful guide to the group's articles of belief.

20. Willey, *English Moralists*, p. 186.

21. Ibid. p. 185.

22. See the chapter on the Cambridge Platonists in Gladys Wade, *Thomas Traherne* (Princeton, N.J., 1944).

23. Willey, *Seventeenth Century Background*, p. 277.

24. For the argument between Hobbes and the Cambridge Platonists, see particularly S. Mintz, *The Hunting of Leviathan* (Cambridge, 1962), Chapter 5.

A number of seventeenth-century autobiographies allow us to scrutinize the religious content of their author's lives. Here follow brief sketches of the position and beliefs of Sir Thomas Browne, a moderate Anglican, and Richard Baxter, a moderate Puritan.

Sir Thomas Browne

Browne was born in 1605, the son of a fairly prosperous London
mercer. He attended Pembroke College, Oxford, and then studied
medicine at Montpellier, Padua, and Leiden. He wrote *Religio Medici*,
the famous account of his intellectual and spiritual life, about 1635,
primarily for the benefit of himself and his friends, and nominally to
refute the common suspicion that doctors were inclined to atheism
because in their examination of the body they found no trace of the
soul and were likely to take an entirely materialistic view of man. His
travels had given him an unusual tolerance for Roman Catholicism –
'We have reformed from them, not against them' – and for the many
varieties of Protestantism. He confesses himself a faithful member of
the Church of England, and we may assume by his fondness for
demonstrative piety that he was sympathetic to the ritual tendencies
of Laudianism: 'I love to use the civility of my knee, my hat, and hand,
with all those outward and sensible motions which may express or
promote my invisible devotion.' He speaks feelingly of baptism and
communion. Being an exceptionally speculative man with a penchant
for metaphysics, he has compiled an exotic portfolio of beliefs, but his
basic theological position would appear to be that of a moderate
Calvinist. He is convinced that God in his eternity has predestined all
who shall live: predestination 'is a definitive blast of his will already
fulfilled, and at the instant that he first decreed it; for to his eternity
which is indivisible and all together, the last trump is already sounded,
the reprobates in the flame, and the blessed in Abraham's bosom'
(Section 11). He thinks it presumptuous to speculate about who is
saved or damned: 'There will appear at the Last Day, strange and
unexpected examples both of his Justice and his Mercy; and therefore
to define either, is folly in man.' Even so, he ventures to declare 'I am
confident, and fully persuaded, yet dare not take my oath of my
Salvation'. He believes, as the Scriptures suggest, that the number of
the elect will be comparatively small, but the mercy and wisdom of
God are such that the elect will be drawn from all mankind, not
exclusively from the Christian world. 'I do desire with God that all,
but yet affirm with men, that few shall know Salvation; that the bridge
is narrow, the passage strait unto life; yet those who do confine the
Church of God, either to particular nations, churches or families, have
made it far narrower than our saviour ever meant it' (Section 35).
Upon the necessity of faith in Christ as an essential for salvation he
is silent, but he does observe that good works as well as faith may be
a mark of salvation. He admits that earlier in his life he believed 'that
God would not persist in his vengeance for ever, but after a definite

time of his wrath, he would release the damned souls from torture',
but now he acknowledges this was an error and a personal heresy of
his.

Heaven and hell are spiritual states, not places, and Browne has
much to say about the hierarchies of angels and their knowledge, and
of the legions of devils that trouble the earth. Among those that the
latter subvert are witches, of whose existence he has no doubt; but
good angels too work upon the world:

> I do think that many mysteries ascribed to our own
> inventions, have been the courteous revelations of Spirits;
> for those nobles essences in Heaven bear a friendly regard
> unto their fellow Natures on Earth; and therefore believe
> that those many prodigies and ominous prognosticks,
> which fore-run the ruins af States, princes, and private
> persons, are the charitable premonitions of good Angels,
> which more careless enquiries term but the effects of
> chance and nature. (Part i, Section 31)

Browne insists that both reason and faith are faculties that reach out
to God. Reason works over the realm of nature and will always pay
homage to the great designer: 'Those highly magnifie him, whose
judicious enquiry into his Acts, and deliberate research into his Creation, return the duty of a devout and learned admiration.' Faith, in
Browne's case, is nourished by the higher mysteries of Christianity,
when reason stands confounded, and faith rapturously accepts. Trini-
tarian enquiries, riddles of the Incarnation and the Resurrection, the
miracles of the Old and the New Testament, why, 'methinks there be
not impossibilities enough in Religion for an active faith . . . I love to
lose myself in a mystery, to pursue my Reason to an O altitudo!'
Browne was perhaps exceptional in his unabashed gaping after the
paradoxes and inconceivables of Christianity, but in his stress on
wonder as a vital agent of faith he was typical of his age. At a lower
level, he was fascinated by omens, coincidences, and significant incidents, all of which he regarded as infallible signs of Providence: 'Sure
there are in every man's life certain rubs, doublings and wrenches
which pass a while under the effects of chance, but at the last well
examined, prove the mere hand of God.' In his last moments of
consciousness, Browne must have been deeply pleased to realize that
he was to die on his birthday, as he had speculated in *Religio Medici*:
his mortal, right-lined circle was closed with great exactitude.

He believed that the world was in its last age, and would not long
survive. 'I believe the world grows near its end, yet is neither old nor
decayed, nor shall ever perish upon the ruin of its own principles.' It

will be destroyed prematurely by the will of God, as a man may die before he has completed his natural span. Browne refuses to join in the solemn game of calculating the date of the Apocalypse, and thinks it an impious speculation. Nor will he name the Pope Antichrist, or propose any other candidate: 'I am half of opinion that Anti-Christ is the Philosophers' Stone in Divinity.' But he expected a judgement soon.

He did not leave his opinion of the sectarian divisions in religion, but he must have found the sects' lack of charity for each other deplorable, as also their claims to the exclusive possession of truth. He shows no eagerness to hear a sermon, and seems to have had few clergymen among his friends. One feels he would have attended church regularly before the Civil Wars, and shown sympathy with the Laudian desire to make services more decorous; he would have complied with the austere services of the Cromwellian Church, and was probably glad to see the restoration of the Church of England, although unhappy to see it impose conformity after 1662. But for Browne, the particular character of his faith was ultimately a private affair, and he sought to impose it on no one.

Richard Baxter

Richard Baxter was born in 1615 to a Shropshire family of moderate means. His autobiography, *Reliquiae Baxterianae*, was written in the 1680s and looks back over a turbulent lifetime of religious commitment. He opens with a memory of the unsatisfactory conditions of the Church in his part of Shropshire in his youth: virtually no preaching, the ministers old and barely literate, who could just manage to recite the common prayer and the psalms, and who led idle, indulgent lives. When he was fifteen, his soul was awakened by reading a devotional book (written by a Jesuit), and he experienced an uncomfortable conviction of sin after robbing an orchard. His regeneration began when he developed consumption, for this affliction brought him into the presence of death, and 'I was yet more awakened to be serious and solicitous about my soul's everlasting state' (p. 8.).[1] He tried for a while to make his way at court, but seeing a stage play on a Sunday scandalized him, and he determined to become a minister. This was about 1635. The men in Shrewsbury 'whose fervent prayers and savoury conference and holy lives did profit me much' would not conform to the Laudian service order and ritual innovations, 'and when I found they were people prosecuted by the bishops, I found much prejudice arise in my heart against those that persecuted them, and thought that those that silenced and troubled them could not be genuine followers of the Lord of Love' (p. 16). He examined his own attitudes to conformity, and found he could accept most requirements, but he would not administer communion to people known to be immoral, nor use the sign of the cross in baptism, nor subscribe that there was nothing contrary to the word of God in the Prayer Book. He now began to have doubts about the legitimacy of bishops as governors of the Church, for he could find no biblical justification for their institution. In 1641 he was invited by the congregation at Kidderminster to be their minister, for they had heard of his preaching and desired a good Puritan. Baxter was attracted by the challenge 'because it was a full congregation and most convenient temple; an ignorant, rude and revelling people for the greater part, who had need of preaching, and yet had among them a small company of converts . . . to assist their teacher' (p. 25).

Baxter exercised his ministry at Kidderminster for nearly three years – preaching once against the sound of cannon from Edgehill field – but then, alarmed by the growth of extremist sects in the army, he joined up to serve as a chaplain on the Parliament side, hoping to counsel moderation. Certain sects caused him particular distress. The Seekers 'taught that our Scripture was uncertain; that present miracles are necessary to faith; that our ministry is null and without authority and our worship and ordinances unnecessary or vain; the true Church, ministry, Scripture and ordinances being lost, for which they are now seeking' (p. 73). The Ranters 'set up the light of nature under the name of Christ in Men. . . . They taught as the Familists, that God regardeth not the actions of the outward man, but of the heart, and that to the pure all things are pure (even things forbidden).' They were all susceptible to libertinism. Then there were the Quakers

> who were but the Ranters turned from horrid profaneness
> and blasphemy to a life of extreme austerity on the other
> side. Their doctrines were mostly the same with the
> Ranters. They make the light which every man hath
> within him to be his sufficient rule, and consequently the
> Scripture and ministry are set light by; they speak much
> for the dwelling and working of the spirit within us, but
> little of justification and the pardon of sin, and our
> reconciliation with God through Jesus Christ; they pretend
> their dependence on the Spirit's conduct, against set times
> of prayer and against sacraments, and against their due
> esteem of Scripture and ministry; they will not have the
> Scripture called the Word of God. (pp. 73–74)

After the war, Baxter returned to Kidderminster, where he was much in request for preaching. He was not enthusiastic about Cromwell, whom he suspected of too much state ambition after he became Protector, a role that compromised his religious integrity, in Baxter's opinion. But he approved of the system of Triers that Cromwell instituted to examine the fitness of candidates to minister in the National Church that was Cromwell's way of bringing order to the confusion of the later 1640s and early 1650s.

> The truth is . . . to give them their due, [the Triers, the
> men appointed to vet candidates for the ministry] did
> abundance of good to the Church. They saved many a
> congregation from ignorant, ungodly, drunken
> teachers. . . . So that, though they were many of them
> somewhat partial for the Independents, Separatists, Fifth
> Monarchy Men and Anabaptists, and against the Prelatists
> and Arminians, yet so great was the benefit above the hurt
> which they brought to the Church, that many thousands
> of souls blessed God for the faithful ministers whom they
> let in, and grieved when the Prelatists afterward cast them
> out again. (p. 71)

At the Restoration, which he considered a providential event, Baxter worked to effect a reconciliation between the ministers of the Cromwellian National Church and the hierarchy of the newly restored Church of England, trying to keep open the gates of toleration for diverse opinions: 'The churches must be united upon the terms of primitive simplicity, and that we must have unity in things necessary and liberty in things unnecessary and charity in all' (pp. 90–91). In the generous and accommodating mood of the first year of the Restoration, Baxter was made a royal chaplain and offered the bishopric of Hereford in the new Church, but his strong doubts about episcopal rule caused him to reject this offer. As the mood changed in 1662 with the Act of Uniformity that required ministers to conform to the services of the revised Prayer Book (that was full of sticking-places for tender consciences), Baxter found himself driven into opposition as a Dissenter. He could not subscribe. He continued to preach unlicensed and the last two decades of his life were a history of conflict with the magistracy, with arrest, trials, and periods of imprisonment which show in a very unpleasant light the harshness of the bigoted church policy maintained under Charles II and James II. During this time, Baxter came to feel more and more admiration for the Quakers as the chief resisters to the power of magistrates to enforce conformity in matters of religion. He agreed with them that the practice of religion should be entirely a matter of conscience between man and God, and the secular power should have no authority therein.

Richard Baxter is an example of a Puritan who managed to stay out of sects. He was a middle-of-the-road, liberty-of-conscience man. Preaching was his life: it was for him the essential means of awakening souls to the spiritual life. He was at first a Calvinist in theology, and had 'doubts of my own salvation which exercised me many years' (p. 10), though in the Commonwealth years he began to concede to the Arminian position, accepting that one might achieve salvation through the exercise of free will, and not be totally dependent on arbitrary grace. He was a committed millenarian, although he did not proclaim his views loudly, and his belief in the imminence of Christ's kingdom strengthened his resolve to act according to his conscience. All his life he confronted the problem of interference with an individual's right to freedom of worship, either by the hierarchy of the Church or by the magistracy. The most absolute enemy of the freedom he desired was the Papacy, and he was always hard against the Roman Church. Above all, he desired to see the establishment in England of a godly society in which Christians agreed on the simple essentials of their religion and lived in tolerance and charity, avoiding extremes of authority or licence and the plague of sectarianism. He would be content for this Christian state to be governed by a limited monarchy and by a magistracy that had no powers over matters of religion; this ideal he put forward in his *Holy Commonwealth* of 1659, which he dedicated with misguided optimism to Richard Cromwell. But human nature was too perverse to follow an enlightened guide.

> Had it not been for the faction of the Prelatists on one side that drew men off, and the factions of the giddy and turbulent sectaries on the other side . . . England had been like in a quarter of an age to have become a land of saints and a pattern of holiness to all the world, and the unmatchable paradise of the earth. Never were such fair opportunities to sanctify a nation lost and trodden underfoot as have been in this land of late. (p. 84)

Note

The quotations in this section are taken from the Everyman edition of *The Autobiography of Richard Baxter* (1931, reprinted 1987). The most recent commentary on his ideological position is by William M. Lamont, *Richard Baxter and the Millennium* (1979).

Chapter 9

Political Theory

When the century opened, a theory of power that was involved with magic prevailed; at the end of the century an ideal of a social contract had emerged that was based on a pragmatic balance of forces within the realm. Almost exactly at the mid-point of the century, the axe that severed the King's neck struck an emphatic political blow: it demonstrated that the King was under the law, not above it; that divine right had to give way to the sovereignty of Parliament, and that henceforth the initiative in political matters lay with Parliament. The sudden cease of majesty in 1649 was the signal for an excited debate about what form of government might best succeed monarchy, and how authority might be reconciled with personal rights. A form of republicanism was experimented with, and failed. The Stuart monarchy returned, but the nation had become so accustomed to discuss and criticize the political scene during the Interregnum that thereafter the structure of power would remain under continuous scrutiny, so that the monarchy's attempt to recover its former authority would soon meet a firm check.

When James I occupied the throne of England, he was prepared to justify his tenure to the world. He enjoyed political theory as much as he did religious debate. He had already demonstrated his commitment to the concept of the divine right of kings in his treatise *The True Law of Free Monarchies* (1598), which was designed to strengthen his position in Scotland against opposition from the Kirk and possible rebellion by his subjects, by investing his authority with a supernatural sanction that owed nothing to the Church. As was normal, James looked to the Bible for justification. The critical texts were II Samuel 7. 8–6, where God instituted kings to rule over Israel, Proverbs 8. 15, where God's word is 'By me Kings reign, and Princes decree justice', and John 19. 11, where Christ tells Pilate, 'Thou couldest have no power at all against me, except it were given thee from above'. Kingship had been instituted by God and was protected by God, and the King was responsible only to God for his actions, not to any human tribunal. The concept of divine right had acquired its modern form in the reign of Henry VIII, when the King was extricating himself from any dependence on papal authority or indeed any religious authority for his title to the crown. In England the subjection of the Church to the crown was an aspect of the King's desire for a right to his throne that derived only from God, and not from the ministrations of clerics who wished to use the coronation rite as a mystery that conferred magical powers via the priesthood. Elizabeth had ordered a modest coronation and the coronations of James I and Charles I were subdued ceremonies; only Charles II had encouraged a lavish celebration in which the Church was seen to bestow divine authority on the King – but even in 1661, Charles was a crypto-Catholic disposed to respect ecclesiastical authority. James I believed that a King's majesty was not dependent on a coronation, which merely confirmed his title, but on hereditary succession and legitimate descent. Majesty, he held, was inalienable. Since James's claim to the English throne was only by descent from Henry VII, it is not surprising that he stressed the hereditary principle.[1] For James there could be only one legitimate king, even if he did not actually occupy the throne, and that was the rightful heir. He imparted this conviction to his dynasty, and it retained sufficient force in the nation at large to bring in Charles II after the collapse of the Protectorate, to secure the defeat of the Exclusion Bill aimed at barring James II, and ultimately to give remarkable vitality to the Jacobite cause in the eighteenth century, the cause of 'the true king over the water'.

James defined the duties of the monarch that fell to him by virtue of his divine appointment, duties that also derived from biblical example: to establish the laws and enforce them, to administer justice, to reward and punish, to seek peace and to concern himself with the religious welfare of the nation. The King had also to act as father of his people, and again the Bible provided the model. Samuel had warned the Israelites that kings may be troublesome and harsh, but their authority, like paternal authority, must not be resisted. The will of Providence determines the way in which men are governed, and even a tyrant must be endured, because a people must submit to God's design, which they may not comprehend. The King may be above man's law, but he is subject to the inescapable law of heaven. The historian of divine right, J. N. Figgis, quotes a document of 1640 drawn up by the clergy who wished to express their loyalty to the crown that brings together most of these elements:

> The most high and sacred order of kings is of Divine
> Right, being the ordinance of God Himself, founded in the
> prime laws of nature, and clearly established by express
> texts both of the Old and New Testaments. A supreme
> power is given to this most excellent order by God

Himself in the Scripture, which is, that kings should rule and command in their several dominions all persons of what rank or estate soever, whether ecclesiastical or civil. . . . For any person or persons to set up, maintain or avow in any their said realms or territories respectively, under any pretence whatsoever, any independent coactive power, either papal or popular, (whether directly or indirectly,) is to undermine their great royal office, and cunningly to overthrow that most sacred ordinance which God Himself hath established; and so is treasonable against God as well as against the king. For subjects to bear arms against their kings, offensive or defensive, upon any pretence whatsoever, is at least to resist the powers which are ordained of God; and though they do not invade, but only resist, yet St. Paul tells them plainly they shall receive to themselves damnation.[2]

James's formulation of the theory of divine right, which was completely accepted by his son Charles, had some notable areas of weakness, such as the status of royal power that was obtained by conquest, and the question of the power of the King as limited by Parliament. James would maintain that acceptance of Parliament's right to participate in legislation and government was a concession made by virtue of the King's grace, not an absolute division of power. The theory, however, did have its own integrity and consistency, and provided the Stuarts, as it had the Tudors in a less specific way, with a serviceable principle of monarchic rule which had its basis in the unchallengeable ground of the Bible. Understandably, it was popular with Stuart monarchs and the Anglican clergy that supported them, but had no appeal to Puritans or parliamentarians, the injunction to unquestioning obedience being particularly distasteful. Yet the principle of divine right survived the execution of Charles I, and flourished again under his son. The growth of secular rationalism as much as the force of events eventually put an end to it, and after the expulsion of James II, the Act of Settlement of 1689 would firmly revise the idea of who could be king and what was the scope of his power.

The theory of divine right was a natural ally of royal absolutism in politics, for it placed the King legally, morally, and magically above all human law and restraint. In the case of James I and Charles I, it undoubtedly strengthened their confidence in the exercise of royal prerogative, the right of the monarch to assert his authority without interference by Parliament or the law. The King had no obligation to summon Parliament, and in practice Parliaments were only called when the King needed them to vote supplies. The King and his ministers could make policy and impose it by proclamation, relying on the magistracy for enforcement. Foreign policy was the special preserve of the monarch, who exercised here the secret wisdom with which God endowed his kings. Against such claims of divinely guided policy, Parliament made slow but persistent headway. Opposition to acts of royal prerogative was a feature of all the Parliaments of the two reigns, personified in the time of James by the legal conflicts between Francis Bacon, the Lord Chancellor, who was disposed to uphold royal prerogative, and Edward Coke, the Chief Justice, who was determined to use all the resources of common law to defeat the King's desire to rule by proclamation and prerogative. During the ten years of Charles's personal rule without Parliament, there was a protracted legal challenge against prerogative, culminating in the Ship Money case of 1637, when John Hampden was tried on an action brought by the King before all twelve common-law judges for refusal to pay taxes levied by royal prerogative, and was found against by a majority of seven to five, a judgement regarded as a moral victory for Hampden. A system of common law that had a fine sense of precedent and a concern for individual rights, and a parliamentary system that had accumulated well-defined privileges over the centuries, together formed a barrier that would limit and eventually stop the exercise of prerogative, and neither system had respect for the King's claim to authority by divine right: both believed that right was something vested in law and confirmed by Act of Parliament. King Charles's sense of being above the law helped him to go to war against Parliament, and even at the very end of his career he still denied the right of any court to try him. 'Remember I am your King, your lawful King, and what sins you bring upon your heads, and the judgement of God upon this land; think well upon it, I say, think well upon it, before you go from one sin to a greater. . . . I have a trust committed to me by God, by old and lawful descent, I will not betray it to answer a new unlawful authority.'[3] The conflicting attitudes were entirely incompatible, and the loser had to go.

The Civil War made people think hard about the type of government that was desirable for England, though at the end of the fighting it was clear that Parliament would impose the settlement. But Parliament traditionally represented only a sectional interest of the nation, i.e. the gentry, and now its representation had become even narrower, for it had been purged until only a Puritan rump remained. For the first time, however, there was a broad representative force drawn from all the people, gathered together for a political end – the army. They had done the fighting and they wanted not only their pay but some voice in the new Constitution. The army bred radicalism, because the men were risking their lives for a cause and they were not bound by the customary restraints of Church, magistracy, and the social hierarchy. The religious sects flourished most vigorously in the army, ideas and passions spreading rapidly in the responsive ranks. As Parliament and the leaders of the army were negotiating with the King in 1647, the movement known as the Levellers began to make headway among the soldiers, following the lead given by the pamphlets of John Lilburne, Richard Overton, and William Walwyn, all radical Puritans in London. At a time when it seemed as if the negotiations might result in the restoration of the King and the institution of a Presbyterian system of church government, the Levellers began to demand the abolition of the monarchy and the state-organized Church, and universal toleration of religious beliefs. The Leveller leaders insisted that power should belong to the people, and as Parliament wanted to disband the army in 1647 on terms that were unacceptable to the soldiers, the Leveller arguments had an immediate appeal, since the soldiers demanded recognition of their achievements and a stake in the new settlement. 'We are not a mere mercenary Army, hired to serve any arbitrary power in the State, but called forth and conjured by the several declarations of Parliament to the defence of our own and the people's just rights and liberties.'[4]

The rank and file of the army elected representatives whom they called Agitators, who met with the spokesmen of the army chiefs of staff at Putney church in October and November 1647 to debate what form the constitutional settlement should take. General Ireton, Cromwell's son-in-law, acting for the army chiefs, or grandees, as they were known, drew up the Heads of Proposals, which aimed to establish a constitutional monarchy with the King under the control of Parliament. There would be broad religious tolerance. Members of Parliament would still be elected on a property basis, but there would be a redistribution of seats to match the actualities of power and population. The Levellers' programme was outlined in *The Agreement of the People*, which declared in favour of dissolving the present Parliament and electing a new one with a greatly enlarged electorate every two years; total freedom of conscience, no military conscription; the laws of the nation to be binding on all men equally. The Levellers' position was implicitly republican with no mention of a king or a supreme governor; it envisaged too a form of social democracy, with suffrage being extended to all heads of households, with no property qualification required. The Putney Debates provided a rare spectacle of free expression of political ideas, uninhibited by rank or threat of legal reprisals, at a critical historical moment. The Levellers were pushing for radical reform while the army grandees were trying to hold a moderately conservative line. The grandees insisted on the property basis for the vote, thus keeping power in the hands of the few; they feared the scarcely imaginable prospect of a democracy which they viewed as a prelude to anarchy.[5] Ireton firmly maintained the traditionalist line: 'I think that no person hath a right to an interest or share in the disposing of the affairs of the Kingdom . . . that hath not a permanent fixed interest in the Kingdom.' Colonel Rainsborough, a gentleman and a republican, sympathetic to the Levellers' case, objected: 'I think that the poorest he that is in England hath a life to live, as the greatest he; and therefore truly, sir, I think it's clear, that every man that is to live under a government ought first by his own consent to put himself under that government; and I do think that the poorest man in England is not at all bound in a strict sense to that government that he hath not had a voice to put himself under.'[6] Cromwell, as chairman of the debate, backed Ireton, and managed to frustrate the Leveller arguments before they were launched as an effective programme, and the debates fizzled out. The army leaders fed the Levellers with false hopes for a while longer, but when the proceedings for the trial of the King got under way, the popular movement was less and less consulted as the grandees and the Rump Parliament took control of national affairs. For a short time however, the significant issues of the sovereignty of the people, as it might be expressed through a non-repressive republican form of government, received a serious hearing.[7] Republicanism, though with narrow social foundations, would soon be instituted, but the democratic tendencies of the Levellers would withdraw into the political underground, to be summoned up by later revolutions.

There can be no doubt that the Levellers' democratic impulses were generated by Puritanism. If men considered themselves equal before God regardless of rank, if they believed in the individual's right to read and interpret the Bible in his own way, and to conduct unaided a colloquy with God, then it is hardly surprising that these egalitarian ideas should spill over from religion into politics. The activism that was part of Puritan ideology – the belief that one should be socially active to promote the kingdom of Christ on earth and work against iniquity, injustice, and ungodliness wherever found – the activism that made Puritanism such a force for change and reform, also helped to give edge to this political desire for participation in the workings of the new Commonwealth.

A similar Bible-based activism gave rise to the short-lived movement of the Diggers, those exponents of a seventeenth-century communism who urged the common people of England to take over the common lands and cultivate them for the benefit of all. Their case was most forcefully put by Gerrard Winstanley, a failed clothier whose experience of social degradation during the 1640s probably contributed to his radical views. His own plight sharpened his sympathy for the

poor and dispossessed, and developed in him a fierce dislike of property rights and ownership which he saw as the source of all division
and exploitation in society. He adopted the character of a prophet,
claiming that 'many things were revealed to me which I never read in
books . . . and among those revelations was this one: that the earth
shall be made a common treasury of livelihood to whole mankind,
without respect of persons; and I heard a voice within me bade me
declare it all abroad . . . that the earth must be set free from entan-
glements of lords and landlords, and that it shall become a common
treasury to all, as it was first made and given to the sons of men'.[8]
England contained vast areas of waste lands and commons which
remained uncultivated, yet were in private ownership or under legal
restraint; why should they not be worked by the poor for the good
of all? Winstanley declared: 'When the Lord doth show unto me the
place and manner, how he will have us that are called common people
to manure and work upon the common lands, I will go forth and
declare it in my action, to eat my bread with the sweat of my brows,
without either giving or taking hire, looking upon the land as freely
mine as another's.'[9]

In April 1649, Winstanley and a group of comrades began 'to plant
and manure the waste land' at St George's Hill in Surrey, and
continued digging there for about a year, provoking all manner of
retaliation from local landowners, who brought suits for trespass and
called in bailiffs and eventually troops to break up the squatter camp
that had developed on the site. The usual forces of repression prevailed
and the Diggers were dispersed. Elsewhere in England similar colonies
that had sprung up were likewise crushed. The brief experiment
collapsed, but the legacy of pamphlets put out by Winstanley remains
to preserve a revolutionary spirit which prefigures much modern
ideology.

Winstanley fetched his political theory from the Bible, from
Genesis:

> In the beginning of time, the great creator Reason made
> the earth to be a common treasury, to preserve beasts,
> birds, fishes and man, the lord that was to govern this
> creation: for man had domination given to him, over the
> beasts, birds and fishes; but not one word was spoken in
> the beginning, that one branch of mankind should rule
> over another.
> And the reason is this, every single man, male and
> female, is a perfect creature of himself; and the same spirit
> that made the globe dwells in man to govern the globe; so
> that the flesh of man being subject to reason, his maker,

hath him to be his teacher and ruler within himself,
therefore needs not run abroad after any teacher and ruler
without him; for he needs not that any man should teach
him, for the same anointing that ruled in the Son of Man
teacheth him all things.

But since human flesh (that king of beasts) began to
delight himself in the objects of the creation, more than in
the spirit reason and righteousness . . .; then he fell into
blindness of mind and weakness of heart, and runs abroad
for a teacher and ruler. And so selfish imagination, taking
possession of the five senses and ruling as king in the
room of reason therein, and working with covetousness,
did set up one man to teach and rule over another; and
thereby the spirit was killed and man was brought into
bondage, and became a greater slave to such of his own
kind, than the beasts of the field were to him.

And hereupon the earth (which was made to be a
common treasury of relief for all, both beasts and men)
was hedged into enclosures by the teachers and rulers, and
the others were made servants and slaves: and that earth,
that is within this creation made a common storehouse
for all, is bought and sold and kept in the hands of a
few, whereby the great creator is mightily dishonoured, as
if he were a respecter of persons, delighting in the
comfortable livelihood of some and rejoicing in the
miserable poverty and straits of others. From the
beginning it was not so.[10]

Winstanley's use of the Bible shows a strong secularizing tendency.
God the Creator has become Spirit, Reason which dwells within every
man and woman; but in most men and women reason is darkened by
covetousness, which is the serpent within the Eden of the mind. In
Winstanley's mythical scheme, the Fall of Man took place when one
man first engrossed a piece of the common land and declared it his;
that Fall repeats itself endlessly in every act of possession and exclus-
iveness. 'The public preachers have cheated the whole world by telling
us of a single man called Adam that killed us all by eating a single fruit,
called an apple'; but more truly, 'you are the man and woman that hath
eaten the forbidden fruit'.[11] 'When self-love began to arise in the earth,
then men began to fall.' Men are born naturally good, but contract
sinful habits from the institutions of society. Christ was not so much
a historical and theological figure as the symbol of love and fellowship
that had power to restore the pristine simplicity and contentment of
mankind. In Fire in the Bush, the most graphic of Winstanley's tracts,

in which he gave his sense of the Bible as spiritual and economic allegory, Christ is described as 'the true and faithful Leveller', who will create a world of brotherhood and freedom from bondage through universal love. Christ's death and ascension tell allegorically of the rising of the spirit of divine reason 'from under the earthy imagination and lusts of the sons of men, for mankind is the earth that contains him buried'.[12] The return of Christ will not be the return of a heroic individual, but would be an internal event as the Christ-spirit arises in the faithful. Heaven is the state of consciousness of the regenerate, and the watch-cry of the Diggers was, 'Glory now!' for they believed in the imminent victory of the saints. Winstanley and his fellows shared a novel kind of millenarianism in which there would be no spiritual leader in the person of Christ, but a communistic state of righteousness. Antichrist would be overthrown, but for the Diggers the forces that were hostile to the Christ-spirit and impeded its rising were fourfold. First was the state-maintained ministry, the 'book-studying, university-divinity, which indeed is Judas's ministry'. Then there was kingly power, that thrives by treading men underfoot, 'that takes ease, honour, fulness of the earth to himself by the sword, and rules over the labours and bodies of others at his will and prerogative'. The law, 'which is but the declarative will of conquerors, how they will have their subjects to be ruled', is another head of Antichrist. And finally, 'buying and selling of the earth, which breeds discontent and divides the creation, and makes mankind to imprison, enslave and destroy one another'.[13]

Winstanley's secularized Christianity had striking political implications. 'The old world is running up like parchment in the fire', he wrote in 1649, shortly after the King's execution. The new world he wished to see emerge purified from the flames was a kind of communist Utopia. Property must be abolished as the cause of division and as the fundamental impediment to universal freedom and equality. Property necessitated the law and ultimately the State; property underwrote rank. The Levellers in their plea for democracy still recognized the right to property, and seemed to accept that those who were economically dependent, at the bottom of society, would be excluded from the political process; they accepted too the inevitability of the State and its institutions. Winstanley and the Diggers went further, towards a condition of Christian anarchy, in which the State would fade away as the spirit of Christ began to exercise dominion. Coupled with Winstanley's notions of primitive community was a passion to destroy 'the Norman Yoke', the combination of monarchical and aristocratic authority, feudal relations, and the system of law that sustained the whole edifice of post-Conquest oppression. 'The reformation that England now is to endeavour is not to remove the Norman yoke only and to bring us back to be governed by those laws that were before William the Conqueror came in . . . but . . . according to the word of God, and that is the pure law of righteousness before the Fall.'[14] Once the yoke was shaken off, there was hope for a society of fraternal egalitarianism. The execution of the King and the abolition of the House of Lords made a good beginning. But every sort of class rule would have to go too, in order to restore the levelled state of the uncovetous world before the Fall. Winstanley and the Diggers welcomed the Republic as the first step towards their Utopia, but it was immediately clear that their idealism was not going to prevail against the modified social order. After 1652 nothing more was heard from them.

At the centre of Winstanley's writings was a myth of the unfallen earth as a common treasury with men working and living together without oppression. In 1651 'a strange new book' was published, describing another political myth, this time a myth of absolute power: *Leviathan*. The myth here is of the State as a gigantic 'artificial man', constituted of the myriad individuals who are the atoms of the body politic. Although the title has a biblical resonance, referring to the huge creature of incomparable power of Job 41, Hobbes's book is a totally secular view of the State. Both the myth and its secular character are given vivid figurative expression on the title-page (Plate 17). The sovereign power towers immense above the landscape in an attitude that is both threatening and protective. His body is literally made up of a multitude of men who have merged their individual identities in his corporate person; he wields the symbols of civil and ecclesiastical power which are represented as the instruments of the State. This striking image was to the English audience as unprecedented as the thought.[15] There is no return to a primitive golden age in Hobbes, no prelapsarian common good, no trace of divine right, no paternalism derived from Adam; the early world for Hobbes was a state in which the life of man was 'solitary, poor, nasty, brutish, and short', and where there was 'no place for industry, because the fruit thereof is uncertain, and consequently no culture of the earth; . . . no commodious building; no instruments of moving . . .; no knowledge of the face of the earth; no account of time; no arts; no letters; no society; and which is worst of all, continual fear and danger of violent death'.[16] Hobbes raised his theory of the State not on the basis of an imaginary past, but on his study and analysis of human nature. For him there was no Fall nor original sin: man is naturally vicious. But he does not accuse man's nature: 'The desires, and other passions of man, are in themselves no sin. No more are the actions that proceed from those passions, till they know a law that forbids them.' But he does believe that as men in a state of nature are endowed with comparable physical powers, so they should enjoy equal natural rights. As a result of his strength, passions, and desires, the natural condition of man 'is a condition of war of every one against every one', where the 'general inclination of all mankind [is] a perpetual and restless desire for power after power, that ceaseth only in death'. In order to escape from this condition, Hobbes postulates that men have entered into a social contract 'to confer all their power and strength upon one man, or upon one assembly of men, that may reduce all their wills, by plurality of voices, unto one will . . . and their judgements to his judgement. This is more than consent, or concord; it is a real unity of them all, in one and the same person, made by covenant of every man with every man.' Such is Hobbes's mythic explanation of how man advances from a state of nature to the establishment of a commonwealth; this is 'the generation of that great Leviathan, or rather of that mortal god, to which we owe under the Immortal God our peace and defence'.[17]

The timeliness of *Leviathan* is emphasized in Hobbes's Introduction, where he equates concord in a commonwealth with health in a body, and sedition and civil war with sickness and death. At the first signs of trouble in 1640, Hobbes had withdrawn to France, from where he watched with fascinated horror the disintegration of the English State. His political theories were evolved during the 1640s, and he published his book in 1651, when it was not certain what kind of new authority would be established. At that time the Rump Parliament ruled, but it would hardly endure. The subtitle of *Leviathan*, 'The Matter, Form and Power of a Commonwealth Ecclesiastical and Civil' had an immediate relevance. The state of stability and peace that Hobbes projected as his political *summum bonum* was an urgent national priority. Hobbes was able to demonstrate by a process of relentless methodical reasoning that a single sovereign power was essential to the maintenance of stability, and that the need for such a power grew out of the very nature of human beings. They desire safety, and fearing their fellows, wish to be defended against them: to secure these benefits they are willing to surrender their rights to individual freedom for a common security under a power with absolute sovereignty. Hobbes's uncompromising propositions overturned much conventional wisdom; the sovereign is not bound by obligation to his subjects; his will is law and should be above the law; his power should be without limits. His authority should be supreme over ecclesiastical matters as well as civil, for the churches have an infinite potential for discord if allowed free rein. By far the most threatening of these religious bodies is the Roman Catholic Church, with its special demands of allegiance and its claims to protect its adherents against damnation and to mediate their salvation. Hobbes treats the Roman Church with considerable scorn, yet the space he devotes to it indicates how dangerous a challenge to the sovereign power he considers it to be. Throughout *Leviathan* Hobbes emphatically argues the Erastian position, that the State must be supreme in ecclesiastical affairs. 'It belongeth therefore to him that hath the sovereign power, to be judge or constitute all judges of opinions and doctrines, as a thing necessary to peace, thereby to prevent discord and civil war.'[18] If one kind of worship is ordained by law, there should be conformity to it, though Hobbes recognizes that thought is free, so a man may believe whatever he likes as long as he obeys the outward forms of prescribed religion. In general, the tone of the long sections dealing with a Christian commonwealth and 'of the Kingdom of Darkness' is sceptical, as he insists that matters of religion should be subject to enquiry by natural reason. Hobbes passes through the metaphysical palace of divinity in a mood of cynical hostility. There is much anti-clericalism in his book, and much condemnation too of the universities, which he sees as breeding grounds for those notorious parasites upon a commonwealth, the students of divinity.

Hobbes's political theory is as applicable to a monarchy as to a republic, and he makes no preference in the book (although his private inclinations were in favour of monarchy). His only criterion is the successful exercise of authority; legitimacy is irrelevant. Rebellion may occur if the ruler is ineffective, and a usurper may succeed. Once the ruler loses the ability to protect his subjects, he risks being deprived of power. In contemporary terms, that suggested that if the King could not rule effectively, then Parliament should assume the sovereignty; if Parliament could not master the nation, they might have to yield power to a prince – or to a 'Protector'. The idea of a mixed monarchy finds no favour with Hobbes; checks and balances are out, for they impede the efficient exercise of authority. Hobbes is the most reasonable apostle of absolutism. He also did much to dispel the mystery that surrounded the operations of government by discussing so openly the means by which princes keep men in awe of their power. The pulling down of veils from so many sanctuaries of state affairs guaranteed that the book would be widely disliked and feared; indeed there was probably more contentious matter in *Leviathan* than in any other book published in the seventeenth century, and for the next forty years it would be denounced, refuted, and attacked for its immoral and atheistic doctrines.[19]

What disturbed Hobbes's critics more than the cynical view of man's political arrangements was the material upon which his whole system rested. In the preliminary account of man, his faculties and his capacity for knowledge, Hobbes had plainly expressed his conviction that man and the universe were composed of matter in motion. Sense impressions form the basis of human knowledge, and those impressions are carried by the interaction of atoms, 'by the pressure, that is by the motion, of external things upon our eyes, ears, and other organs'. Thought itself is a mechanical operation. There is no place for spirit or soul in Hobbes's analysis: 'The world (I mean not the earth only, but the universe, that is, the whole mass of all things that are) is corporeal, that is to say, body, and hath the dimensions of magnitude, namely length, breadth and depth; also every part of body, is likewise body, and hath the like dimensions, and consequently every part of the universe is body, and that which is not body, is no part of the universe: and because the universe is all, that which is no part of it, is nothing, and consequently nowhere.'[20] Spirit, which has no dimension and no location, is excluded by Hobbes's rigorous definitions, and relegated to the status of imaginary words that deceive the mind but are truly 'the names of nothing'. Hobbes does admit that matter and motion must have a source in an unmoved mover, which he denominates God, a word that signifies the unknowable: the name is used 'not to make us conceive him, (for he is incomprehensible, and his greatness and power are unconceivable;) but that we may honour him'.[21] Honouring God could hardly be considered a feature of *Leviathan*, nor does Hobbes express any felt regard for Christ. Although the book is thickly peppered with biblical quotations, these seem intended to deflect accusations of atheism rather than to display any active Christian faith. His low views of the origins of religion reinforce the impression of a man resolutely rational and secular: 'In these four things, opinion of ghosts, ignorance of second causes, devotion towards what men fear, and taking of things casual for prognostics, consisteth the natural seed of religion.'[22] Predictably, Hobbes was fulsomely denounced as an atheist, some critics even declaring that the prevalence of his opinions had helped to bring down the Great Plague and the Great Fire upon the nation; yet true to his own principles, Hobbes showed outward conformity to the religion of the State, receiving the sacraments as he lay dying, though keeping his beliefs to himself. On his gravestone he wished to have carved words that indicated his deep scepticism about metaphysics and about the hopes that inspire religion: 'This is the true Philosopher's Stone.'

Hobbes believed he had constructed his political system on scientific principles. He cherished the analogies with geometry that he laid out at some length: he drew out his system from a number of axioms about human nature, he made his propositions and worked them out to conclusions by the application of a rational methodology that owed much to Bacon's disciplined progressions; (one should remember that Hobbes had once been a secretary to Bacon). It was indeed the systematic framework that he raised that made *Leviathan* so formidable a work; its opponents disliked it intensely, but they were unable to dismantle it, and it towered over the political scene to remind men that the secure solution to the present instability was absolutism of one sort or another. In practice, what emerged from the shaky republican order of 1649–53 was the Protectorate of Oliver Cromwell, a form of government with a prince responsible to Parliament, and the whole Commonwealth being regulated by the Instrument of Government passed in 1653.[23] This settlement with its shared powers, checks and balances, and constitutional restraints would not have satisfied Hobbes, but it found favour with the most scrupulous of republican theorists, James Harrington, who published his book *The Commonwealth of Oceana* in 1656, dedicated to Cromwell, in which he demonstrated the historical necessity of republican government in England, praised the excellence of Cromwell as Protector, and advised what measures might be adopted to improve the system of government to near perfection.

Harrington was a gentleman who had travelled extensively, spending much time in Venice, where he developed a great admiration for the Venetian model of government, an admiration that coloured his own proposals in *Oceana*. His experience of Venice made him a republican, in spite of the personal friendship that he developed with Charles I at the end of the King's life. His reading of history consolidated his experience, and in assessing the settlement under Cromwell he was able to bring to the illustration and defence of the English republic an exceptional knowledge of other political systems both ancient and contemporary. Like most seventeenth-century theorists, Harrington found the early passages of the Bible deeply relevant to his purposes. The kinds of government that prevailed among the Israelites were endlessly instructive because of that nation's special relationship with God; 'the legislator must in some sense, mediate or intermediate, be God himself'.[24] In particular, Harrington is drawn to the theocracy established by Moses which was continued by the succession of high priests, judges, and prophets. In agreeing to the terms of the Covenant, the Israelites had made themselves into a republic under God; the later institution of kingship, Harrington argued, was a deterioration from that first state of relative harmony to the divine will. As we shall see, Harrington believed that a similar harmony should prevail in the state in the final phase of history, when the mysterious reign of Christ would fulfil the cycle of God's purposes as revealed in the Bible. He links with the State of Israel another example of what he calls 'ancient prudence', the early Roman republic with its vigorous interplay between senate, people, and magistracy, so that he may establish a broad range of virtues to which a commonwealth may aspire. He then surveys the degeneration of these 'classical' republics into various forms of monarchy, oligarchy, and despotism.

The political development of England receives particular attention, with Harrington commenting on the different phases through which the government of the nation has passed. Harrington does not believe there was any liberal 'ancient constitution' in Saxon times that should be the object of modern restoration; rather he sees a powerful feudal state dominated by the monarch and a small aristocracy that monopolized power until the reign of Henry VII. Here Harrington is indebted to Bacon's *History of King Henry the Seventh* that had pointed out the decline in the military power of the aristocracy under this King, a process which, when coupled with the enormous redistribution of land under Henry VIII at the Dissolution of the Monasteries, had changed the character of England from a feudal monarchy to a nation in which power was spread across a broad band of independent freeholders, whose obligations to the King were weak. The breakdown of feudal lordship meant that the King could no longer rely on the support of his nobility, whom Henry VII had effectively disarmed to prevent internal conflicts, nor could he control the gentry, who were independent. Queen Elizabeth walked on the waters of this unstable scene, by sheer force of personality: she succeeded by her glamorous affectations, 'converting her reign through the perpetual love tricks that passed between her and her people into a kind of romance, wholly neglected the nobility'.[25] An English monarch had no real protection against Parliament, nor against a disaffected people. Harrington sees that the collapse of the Stuart regime was inevitable, once Parliament and people understood their power. The House of Commons has raised its head, 'which since hath been so high and formidable unto their princes that they have looked pale upon those assemblies. Nor was there anything now wanting to the destruction of the throne but that the people, not apt to see their own strength, should be put to feel it, when a prince, as stiff in disputes as the nerve of monarchy was grown slack, received that unhappy encouragement from his clergy which became his utter ruin.'[26] The House of Lords, which might have mediated, was elbowed out as powerless (and actually abolished in 1649), and 'a monarchy divested of her nobility hath no refuge under heaven but an army'. Yet royal finances cannot maintain an army, nor will an army necessarily remain loyal. Harrington presents England as a nation where one system of government has utterly burnt out, and asks, 'What is there in nature that can arise out of these ashes?'

Political power, he insists, must be related to the distribution of property. In a nation with a very broad distribution of property, this essential condition can only be met by a republic, which includes all property owners among its functioning members, and respects and safeguards their rights. The office of hereditary king and the House of Lords have been abolished because they are no longer historically necessary. The House of Commons in its purged condition as the Rump Parliament of 1649–53 is too narrow and unrepresentative to govern, and lacks the stimulus of a counteracting authority. All this time, Harrington has been telling the story of recent events in a lightly fictionalized way, with Oceana as England, Alma as Whitehall, Pantheon as Westminster Hall, etc.; now he brings forward a victorious general, Olphaus Megalator, alias Oliver Cromwell, who takes the initiative, dissolves Parliament and with the help of the army has himself installed as Lord Archon, the architect of the New Republic. Here Harrington begins to leave the straightforward presentation and analysis of events that has been his manner up to this point, and begins to develop Megalator's role as an idealized ruler in an idealized commonwealth. *Oceana* becomes a design for the perfect republic, a series of recommendations to Cromwell about the improvement of the State. The proposals have a Venetian flavour: the Lord Archon establishes a council of 'fifty select persons to assist him by labouring in the mines of ancient prudence, and bringing her hidden treasures unto new light'. They acted also as legislators, 'and sat as a council whereof he was the sole director and president'.[27] The property–owning electorate are represented by an assembly which debates, accepts, or rejects the proposals of the wise council. The magistracy, to which the execution of laws is entrusted, is also elected. Throughout the model of the Commonwealth there is insistence on the advancement of merit by election, and Harrington grows eloquent in favour of the system of the ballot, which he explains in handsome terms as a noble constitutional instrument. From the Lord Archon, or Protector, down to the humble officers of state, all are appointed by election. Harrington also proposes that the membership of the various bodies should be constantly renewed by rotation to prevent faction, turpitude, or corruption. It should be remarked that Harrington, unlike Hobbes, had an optimistic view of human nature, believing that the nation contains a rich supply of talent and civic virtue that can be brought to serve the Commonwealth, and in order to maintain that supply he gives a high priority to the education of the citizenry in Oceana. The detailed account of the ordering, defending, and financing of the State provides a complete working model of a republic which is a participatory democracy based on property qualifications, offering full religious tolerance. Cromwell's Protectorate came sufficiently close to the Oceanean model for Harrington to celebrate it as an approximate ideal.

In *Oceana* Cromwell is seen to have seized the initiative at a moment when a long cycle of government has run its course and collapsed. He has the opportunity to institute a new order, which will have many similarities with the pristine Roman republic and with the republic of Sparta. But because *Oceana* was compiled in the middle of the seventeenth century, Christian eschatology had to be taken into account. The English republic now in being may not decline, but may extend into the Millennium. A republic, Harrington reasoned, was the form of government best suited to prepare the way for the reign of Christ and his saints: it reflected politically the equality of true believers, and also, since a republic fostered a general spirit of civil virtue among its members, it helped to refine human nature to a condition more susceptible to grace. 'Now if you add unto the propagation of civil liberty, what is so natural unto this commonwealth that it cannot be omitted, the propagation of the liberty of conscience, this empire, this patronage of the world, is the Kingdom of Christ. For as the Kingdom of God the Father was a commonwealth, so shall be the Kingdom of God the Son; *the people shall be willing in the day of his power.*'[28] The final Commonwealth of Oceana shall restore the Mosaic Commonwealth of the Israelites. Harrington does not necessarily expect a physical reappearance of Christ at the end of time; rather he understands this kingship as a metaphor for the mystical prevalence of Christ's spirit in the chosen people, and he does not exclude the possibility that the chosen people might be coextensive with the English republic. Harrington's enthusiastic acclaim of Cromwell in *Oceana* is close to Marvell's characterization of him in 'The First Anniversary' (1655), where he shows him as the Christian prince building the Commonwealth wherein 'the great designs kept for the latter days' will be fulfilled.[29]

When the Protectorate broke down after Cromwell's death in 1658, and it was evident that his son Richard was incapable of sustaining it, the debating society that Harrington had founded, called The Rota (which met in a London coffee-house), became the centre for vigorous discussion of ways to regenerate the Commonwealth, but 'upon the unexpected turn of General Monk's coming-in, all these aerie models vanished. I well remember, he several times said, "Well, the King will come in. Let him come in, and call a Parliament of the greatest Cavaliers in England so they be men of Estates, and let them sit but seven years, and they will all turn Commonwealth's men"'.[30]

Harrington resigned himself to the death of the republic. The only vigorous argument for its preservation came from Milton, desperate to prevent the return of monarchy and the Anglican Church. He rushed out *The Ready and Easy Way to Establish a Free Commonwealth* in March 1660, just as the Parliament that would soon invite back the King was being called, upbraiding the people of England for throwing away the hard-won achievements of the Revolution, creeping back 'to their once abjured and detested thraldom of kingship' and abandoning the cause of reformation and liberty of religion. He proposed instead the idea of a perpetual Parliament: 'The ship of the Commonwealth is always under sail; they sit at the stern and if they steer well, what need is there to change them, it being rather dangerous?' Milton reluctantly makes the Harringtonian confession that the membership of Parliament might be rotated, 'to prevent their settling of too absolute a power', but he remains insistent that 'a free Commonwealth' is the State most expressive of Christian values, and he repeats his conviction that the English republic, composed of godly men, would 'continue (if God favour us, and our wilful sins provoke him not) even to the coming of our true and rightful, and only to be expected King', Jesus Christ.

Charles returned to reign in conjunction with Parliament and the Church of England was restored, but it was not long before Milton's fears were realized, as conformity was enforced, liberty of worship denied, royal prerogative exercised once more, and Charles's tendencies towards absolutism strengthened. The theory of the divine right of kings enjoyed a revival and had sufficient strength to help the crown's case in the great constitutional crisis of the reign, the Exclusion crisis of 1679–81, when a significant portion of Parliament tried to exclude James Duke of York from the succession on the grounds of his Catholic faith. The Tories, newly formed to support the King and Duke, brought out a book written around the middle of the century by the royalist Sir Robert Filmer entitled *Patriarcha, or the Natural Power of Kings* (1680). Filmer's argument was basically that the State was essentially a family over which the monarch had absolute paternal authority. Once again we make the long journey back to Adam to take a new prospect of the primitive social scene. Filmer denies that there was ever any primeval liberty, nor were men free to choose one kind of government over another; from the beginning men have been subject to paternal authority which is the only inalienable natural right.

Unlike earlier defenders of the divine right theory, Filmer does not quote biblical chapter and verse to establish his case; instead he regards the Bible as the only authentic account of the earliest state of mankind, and on this evidence argues that the idea of kingship is founded in human nature and is a natural development from paternal authority. There is no possibility of a social contract, as Hobbes theorized, for men have always lived in families, out of which tribes and then nations emerged:

> Not only Adam, but the succeeding patriarchs had, by
> right of fatherhood, royal authority over their children.
> . . . I see not then how the children of Adam, or of any
> man else, can be free from subjection to their parents. And
> this subjection of children being the fountain of all royal
> authority, by the ordination of God himself; it follows,
> that civil power . . . in general is by divine institution.

. . . This lordship which Adam by command had over the whole world, and by right descending from him the patriarchs did enjoy, was as large and ample as the absolutest dominion of any monarch which hath been since the creation.[31]

Filmer continues to pursue the evolution of Adam's paternal power:

By manifest footsteps we may trace this paternal government unto the Israelites coming into Egypt, where the exercise of supreme patriarchal jurisdiction was intermitted, because they were in subjection to a stronger prince. After the return of these Israelites out of bondage, God, out of a special care of them, chose Moses and Joshua successively to govern as princes in the place and stead of the supreme fathers; and after them likewise for a time He raised up Judges to defend His people in time of peril. But when God gave the Israelites kings, He re-established the ancient and prime right of lineal succession to paternal government.[32]

Some consequences of Filmer's argument were that the origins of property were by divine grant to Adam, who possessed a property in the world, as he possessed the right of government, which he passed on to his heirs, just as after the Flood Noah had passed on the proprietary rights of the world to his sons. The King, as supreme father of a country, possesses at the outset (e.g. as at the Norman Conquest) all the property of the country, which he may devolve to individuals by his will. In the matter of government, Filmer maintains that monarchies precede Parliaments, and that the role of Parliament should be to advise and petition the King. The King is above the law; ideally he is the maker and the interpreter of the law. But the king has duties too: 'As the father over one family, so the King, as father over many families, extends his care to preserve, feed, clothe, instruct, and defend the whole commonwealth.'

The constant referring back of all issues to Adam and his family gives Filmer a naïve and at times preposterous air, yet his arguments did have some substance. His notions of the familial origins of authority and property have more credibility than Hobbes's invention of fearful individuals in a state of nature contracting together for a ruler for their mutual protection. In general, Filmer's appeal to biblical precedent was more congenial to seventeenth-century ears than Hobbes's argument by reason and logic. Both men arrived at the conclusion that absolute authority was natural and essential in a state, but to Filmer that authority was unequivocally monarchical.[33] Filmer's views in *Patriarcha* had too an application that was especially appropriate to the cause of Charles II, for which they were recruited, for no English monarch made a greater paternal contribution to his country. As Dryden admiringly described him in *Absalom and Achitophel*, published in the year after *Patriarcha*:

> Then Israel's Monarch, after Heaven's own heart,
> His vigorous warmth did, variously, impart
> To Wives and Slaves: And, wide as his command
> Scattered his Maker's image through the land.
>
> (ll. 7–10)

Dryden in fact contrives the argument of *Absalom and Achitophel* so that King David (i.e. Charles) expounds his rights of royal paternalism as the concluding triumphant speech of the poem.

The success of *Patriarcha* provoked a response from the most sophisticated political theorist of the age, John Locke, who in 1689 published *Two Treatises of Government*, in the first of which 'the False Principles of Sir Robert Filmer and his followers are detected and overthrown'. Probably written in the early 1680s to justify his patron Shaftesbury's opposition to Charles II, the *Treatises* when published were ideally designed to vindicate the Revolution of 1688, where James II had been deposed. (Shaftesbury was the Achitophel of Dryden's poem, so the Locke–Filmer debate engages with the constitutional issues that run through the satire.) Locke was eager to dispose of arguments that favoured monarchical absolutism, and to support the mixed constitutions framed for William and Mary, where Parliament became the dominant partner in sovereignty. In the 'First Treatise', Locke undoes Filmer's argument stitch by stitch, questioning the construction that he puts on biblical social arrangements, pointing out the convenient jumps Filmer made over awkward obstacles, particularly the identification of paternal power with kingship, which is essential to Filmer's plan. What proof is there of Adam's royal authority? Locke accuses his deceased opponent of loose language and loose logic: a claim such as 'By God's appointment, as soon as Adam was created, he was monarch of the world' is scrutinized until its vagueness and lack of evidence are so exposed that one blushes for poor Filmer. His skills of deduction are made to seem thoroughly inept. Locke does, however, agree with Filmer that there did exist a state of nature, and that political principles can be deduced from that state. He cannot accept, however, that the authority of the father is the one natural and inalienable right, finding many reasons to discredit this view and expose its limitations; instead he asserts that men are 'by nature all free, equal and independent'.

Locke's imagination is swayed much more by what he has heard of the American Indians as a people living close to a state of nature than by the biblical accounts of Adam and his offspring, though, conservative and prudent as he is, he still dwells at length on the scriptural social scene. Like Hobbes, he envisages primitive men as entering voluntarily into a social contract for their better protection, and surrendering some measure of their liberty to a civil government in order to preserve the remainder.

But, as Locke makes clear in the 'Second Treatise', in which he erects his own notion of the origin and purpose of civil government, property predates government, and the latter is instituted to protect the former. In primitive society, 'every man has a property in his own person', and in addition he acquires property by the admixture of his own labour with 'whatsoever he removes out of the state that Nature hath provided and left it in'. Locke defends the acquisition of property as a basic natural right. Man is also by nature a social animal. God having created him such 'that in His own judgement, it was not good for him to be alone', and naturally he enters into conjugal society, 'a voluntary compact between man and woman', so developing the extended society of the family. The desire to protect what they have gives rise to political society,

> which is done by agreeing with other men, to join and
> unite into a community for their comfortable, safe, and
> peaceable living, one amongst another, in a secure
> enjoyment of their properties, and a greater security
> against any that are not of it. . . . When any number of
> men have so consented to make one community or
> government, they are thereby presently incorporated, and
> make one body politic, wherein the majority have a right
> to act and conclude the rest.[34]

Locke has no doubt that 'the great and chief end of men uniting into commonwealth, and putting themselves under government, is the preservation of their property'.[35] Property here subsumes family. Rulers emerge by the consent of the majority – the ruler may be an individual or a council, and is obliged by contract to govern by settled laws and for the good of the people. A ruler who fails in his trust may have his power removed by those acting for the people:

> For all power given with trust for the attaining an end
> being limited by that end whenever that end is manifestly
> neglected or opposed, the trust must necessarily be
> forfeited, and the power devolve into the hands of those

that gave it, who may place it anew where they shall
think best for their safety and security. And thus the
community perpetually retains a supreme power of saving
themselves from the attempts and designs of anybody,
even of their legislators, whenever they shall be so foolish
or so wicked as to lay and carry on designs against the
liberties and properties of the subject.[36]

That lesson both Charles I and James II had painfully to learn.

Locke draws up his system of government on the basis of reason
and utility. Reason is the free gift of God, and to exercise it is a proper
means of honouring the creator. With reason goes a freedom of will
which enables him rationally to choose to engage in a social contract:

> The freedom then of man, and liberty of acting according
> to his own will, is grounded on his having reason, which
> is able to instruct him in that law he is to govern himself
> by, and make him know how far he is left to the freedom
> of his own will.[37]

Reasonableness guides the contractual arrangements that Locke im-
agines must have taken place in the early phases of human society, and
reasonableness now informs the constitutional settlement of 1688 that
Locke defended, with its sharing of power between Commons, Lords,
and King, the King now being invited by Parliament to reign, and now
obliged to swear to obey parliamentary statutes in his coronation oath.
Utility in serving the larger public good becomes the criterion for
acceptable political innovation, but at the heart of that larger public
good was the protection of property: the interests of property holders
had to be defended against the most threatening forces: royal prerogative, the army, and disturbance generated by religious disagreements.
So in 1688 the King was tied down by Parliament, and lost most of
his prerogative rights; the army was put under the control of the
property-owning gentry and the civic oligarchies; and religious
tensions were defused by the Toleration Act of 1689, which gave
freedom of worship to most groups even if it cumbered them with
civil disabilities by excluding them from representative office. The
principles of the Toleration Act were very close to those laid out in
Locke's *Letters on Toleration*. In these he argued that true knowledge
in religion is unattainable – one can only have beliefs, not knowledge,
in this sphere – and therefore men should be free to form whatever
belief they find satisfactory to themselves and should not have a religion imposed upon them. The ruler has no right to promulgate
religious truth, and the dignity and reasonableness of the individual

demand that be should find his own form of faith, so long as this activity does not disrupt the order of the Commonwealth and so impinge on the religious freedom of others.

Locke's own views about *The Reasonableness of Christianity* (1695) offered his own cool beliefs as a model for restraint. By suggesting that the essential articles of belief were very few (they amount to belief in a Creator who had extended a moral law throughout the intelligent creation, and who had sent Christ into the world as the Messiah to effect the salvation of the faithful) and that they were all accessible to confirmation of reason, Locke hoped to shift all the inflammatory issues of religious argument into the marginal area of 'matters indifferent'. Locke's plain, confident prose reasonings took the magic and metaphysics out of religion, just as they took the mystery out of the divine right of kings. Locke had the great good fortune to expound his ideas at a time when they could contribute to the framing of the constitutional settlement after the 'Glorious Revolution' of 1688. He emerged as the spokesman for the Whig Party that had grown up to oppose Stuart absolutism and to exorcize the Catholic spectre that lingered behind the Stuart throne. The competing party of the Tories, who also emerged in the later 1670s, were disposed to hold on to belief in the divine institution of kingship, which made resistance to monarchical authority a religious as well as a political crime. The tide of events was running strongly in the direction desired by Locke, and continued to run that way throughout the eighteenth century.

Notes

1. This emphasis on the hereditary principle helps to explain Shakespeare's concern in *Macbeth*, the play most clearly written for King James, over the escape of Banquo's son Fleance, for Fleance maintains the continuity of legitimate kingship in the Stuart line.

2. John Neville Figgis, *The Divine Right of Kings*, 1965 edition, pp. 142–43.

3. Quoted in C. V. Wedgwood, *The Trial of Charles I* (1964), p. 131.

4. 'Declaration of the Army', 14 June 1647. Quoted in Maurice Ashley, *John Wildman* (1947), p. 27.

5. When Marvell wanted to describe the featureless, unrecognizable landscape that succeeds the mimic battlefield of the Civil War in 'Upon Appleton House', a landscape without order or form, he speaks of 'this naked equal flat,/Which Levellers take pattern at' (ll. 449–50) – a dismissive observation that his patron, the grandee Fairfax, would have appreciated.

6. Quoted in Ashley, pp. 36–37.

7. For a detailed account of the movement, see Howard Shaw, *The Levellers* (1968).

8. *A Watchword to the City of London* (1649), in Gerrard Winstanley, *The Law of Freedom and other Writings*, edited by C. Hill, Penguin edition (Harmondsworth, 1973), pp. 127–28.

9. Quoted by Christopher Hill in Winstanley, Introduction, p. 23.

10. *The True Levellers' Standard Advanced* (1649), in Winstanley, p. 77.

11. Quoted in Christopher Hill, *The World Turned Upside Down* (1972). p. 116.

12. Quoted in 'The Religion of Gerrard Winstanley', in Christopher Hill, *Collected Essays*, (1986), 190. This long article provides a lucid account of Winstanley's complicated religious views.

13. *Fire in the Bush* in Winstanley, pp. 233–34.

14. Winstanley, Introduction, p. 39.

15. Hobbes may have derived the idea for the frontispiece of *Leviathan* from the picture of Richelieu in the Louvre that was described by Richard Fanshawe as 'presenting to the common Beholder a multitude of little faces, (the famous ancestors of that noble man); at the same time, to him that looks through a Perspective, there appears only a single portrait in great of the Chancellor himself'. Fanshawe interprets this piece of illusion as 'demonstrating how the Body Politick is composed of many Natural Ones'. (Richard Fanshawe, *Il Pastor Fido* (1647), Preface, A2v–A3.) Hobbes was in Paris when he was writing *Leviathan*.

16. Thomas Hobbes, *Leviathan*, Penguin edition (Harmondsworth, 1976), p. 186.

17. Ibid., p. 227.

18. Ibid., p. 233.

19. The history of the reaction to Hobbes's work is given by Samuel Mintz in *The Hunting of Leviathan* (Cambridge, 1962).

20. Hobbes, p. 689.

21. Hobbes, p. 99.

22. Hobbes, p. 172.

23. The Instrument of Government, as well as all the significant political measures of this time, may be consulted in S. R. Gardiner, *The Constitutional Documents of the Puritan Revolution*. (Oxford, 1889).

24. *The Political Works of James Harrington*, edited by J. G. A. Pocock (Cambridge 1977), Introduction, p. 47.

25. *The Commonwealth of Oceana*, in *Political Works of James Harrington*, p. 198.

26. Ibid.

27. Ibid., p. 207.

28. Ibid., p. 332. See also Pocock's Introduction, p. 73.

29. Both Marvell and Harrington were anxious to distance themselves from the fanatic sect known as the Fifth Monarchists, who believed that the Kingdom

of Christ was imminent but would have to be brought in by violent military action. There were a couple of small-scale Fifth Monarchy uprisings shortly after the Restoration, which were severely put down.

30. John Aubrey, 'James Harrington', in *Brief Lives*, edited by O. L. Dick (1949) p. 125.

31. Robert Filmer, *Patriarcha* (1884 ed.), pp. 15–16.

32. Ibid., p. 18.

33. For extended discussion of Filmer, see the Introduction to *Patriarcha and other Political Works*, edited by P. Laslett (Oxford 1949) and Figgis, pp. 148–60.

34. John Locke, 'Second Treatise of Government', Chapter VIII, paragraph 95.

35. Ibid., Chapter IX, paragraph 124.

36. Ibid., Chapter XIII, paragraph 149.

37. Ibid., Chapter VI, paragraph 63.

Postscript

In the year 1700, Dryden wrote 'The Secular Masque' to mark the turning of the century. This brief entertainment wittily reviewed the preceding age, represented by the figures of Diana, Mars, and Venus. Diana embodies the time before the Civil War, characterized by Dryden as time devoted to hunting. (Hunting was King James's favourite pastime, and Charles I, in 1633, issued a 'Declaration of Sports' encouraging the practice of games and dancing on Sundays, a declaration which naturally gave great offence to Puritans.) In nostalgic retrospect it was

> A very Merry, Dancing, Drinking,
> Laughing, Quaffing and unthinking Time.
>
> (ll. 39–40)

Mars stands for the era of the Civil Wars, and Venus appropriately for the Restoration years of the lecherous Charles and James. With the confidence that a new beginning inspires, these figures of the past are dismissed, and the seventeenth century written off:

> All, all of a piece throughout:
>   Thy Chase had a Beast in View;
> Thy Wars brought nothing about;
>   Thy Lovers were all untrue.
> 'Tis well an Old Age is out,
>   And time to begin a New.
>
> (ll. 92–7)

What kind of truth lies in these lines? They are lines sung on a festive occasion, they try to project a humorous criticism, and yet they convey a sense of great disillusion. 'All, all of a piece throughout' – yet the consistency Dryden speaks of here is the consistency of failure. 'Thy Chase had a Beast in View' – the cryptic line suggests various interpretations. Is it a comment on some underlying coarseness in early Stuart society? Does it imply that the ends of that society were unworthy in some way? Was the Beast the Civil War that was raised in the thickets of politics and religion? Was it even the Beast of the Apocalypse that so many men pursued in those days? 'Thy Wars brought nothing about' has a certain cynical credibility at first hearing, for kings returned and pursued their autocratic policies as before. But Dryden ignores the Revolution of 1688, when the lessons of the past instructed the firmly Protestant body of Parliament how to attain its ends without bloodshed and civil disruption. The forced ejection of James II and his replacement by an invited monarch, William III, was an achievement of a high political order and a remarkably civilized way of conducting the national business. The Civil Wars had brought a good deal about, in proving that Parliament would have its way, that kings would not impose their will on the nation unchallenged, and that the religion of Protestants would be upheld. 'Thy Lovers were all untrue' sounds like the judgement of an old and disillusioned man who has forgotten the spell of love. The seventeenth century had produced the finest love-poetry in our language, and described the greatest variety of experience in love. Love had heightened the spirit and gallantry of all the generations and had been most fulsomely praised and enjoyed. It is true that increasingly during the Restoration years, in the higher reaches of society and on the stage, love seemed to have given way to promiscuity; Dryden himself had contributed his share to the change, and of course, Dryden is including his own career in this disparaging summary. But the loose morals of the court need not demoralize a whole society. Dryden had only to look at the last royal couple, William and Mary, to find an example of fidelity that redeemed in some measure the example of the previous two kings, James II and Charles II.

The masque is cheerfully dismissive of the departing age, and the entertainment is offered in a spirit of levity. None the less, beneath the humour, Dryden's disenchantment comes across fairly strongly. As a Catholic convert, Dryden had much to be aggrieved about. We could hardly expect him to be enthusiastic about the settlement of 1688, for his sympathies were with the losing side. In any case, that event was too recent to be properly assessed. Perhaps it is, after all, a habit repeated down the generations to feel that one's own age is worse than it is; posterity often comes up with a more approving verdict. Indeed, with the benefit of hindsight, our judgement would be a great deal more favourable. Listening to Dryden's lines, one would scarcely realize that he is writing about the century of Bacon, Milton, Newton, Locke, and Wren. We can appreciate that here was a small country that abounded with inventiveness and genius out of all proportion to its size. In the course of the seventeenth century, England had been the scene of remarkable intellectual advances and of unprecedented political experiment, and now, in 1700, it stood in the first rank of European nations.

Chronology

DATE	VERSE, DRAMA, MASQUE	OTHER WORKS, LITERARY/ARTISTIC	HISTORICAL/CULTURAL EVENTS
1600	Shakespeare *Twelfth Night*		Prince Charles (future Charles I) b.
1601	Shakespeare *Hamlet* (?) Jonson *Cynthia's Revels*	Campion *A Book of Ayres*	Rebellion and execution of Essex Parliament – 1603
1602	Shakespeare *Troilus and Cressida* (?)	Campion *Art of English Poesie* Daniel *Defence of Rhyme*	Bodleian Library opened
1603	Jonson *Sejanus* Drayton *Barons' Wars*	Florio (trans.) *Essay of Montaigne* James I *Basilicon Doron* *True Law of Free* *Monarchie*	Elizabeth I d. Accession of James I Plague
1604	Shakespeare *Measure for Measure* *Othello* Marston *The Malcontent*	Dowland *Lachrimae*	Hampton Court Conference Peace with Spain Parliament – 1610 Bancroft Abp

DATE	VERSE, DRAMA, MASQUE	OTHER WORKS, LITERARY/ARTISTIC	HISTORICAL/CULTURAL EVENTS
1605	Shakespeare *King Lear* Drayton *Poems* Jonson *Masque of Blackness*	Bacon *Advancement of Learning* Camden *Remains concerning Britain*	Gunpowder Plot T. Browne b.
1606	Shakespeare *Macbeth* Jonson *Volpone*		Waller b. Davenant b. Corneille b.
1607	Shakespeare *Antony and Cleopatra* Beaumont *Knight of the Burning Pestle*		Foundation of Virginia
1608	Shakespeare *Coriolanus* Jonson *Masque of Beauty*		Milton b.
1609	Shakespeare *Sonnets* Beaumont and Fletcher *Philaster* Daniel *Civil Wars* Jonson *Masque of Queens*		Suckling b.

DATE	VERSE, DRAMA, MASQUE	OTHER WORKS, LITERARY/ARTISTIC	HISTORICAL/CULTURAL EVENTS
1610	Shakespeare *Winter's Tale* (?) Jonson *The Alchemist* Beaumont and Fletcher *Maid's Tragedy* Daniel *Tethys' Festival*	Camden's *Britannia* trans. by P. Holland Galileo *Siderius Nuncius*	Assassination of Henri IV Prince Henry created Prince of Wales
1611	Shakespeare *The Tempest* Middleton *Chaste Maid in Cheapside* (?) Jonson *Oberon*	Authorized Version of Bible	Abbot Abp
1612	Webster *White Devil* Drayton *Poly-Olbion*		Prince Henry d. Crashaw b.
1613	W. Browne *Britannia's Pastorals*		m. of Princess Elizabeth to Frederick, Elector Palatine
1614	Jonson *Bartholomew Fair* Webster *Duchess of Malfi*	Raleigh *History of the World* Napier invents logarithms	Addled Parliament
1615	Jonson *The Golden Age Restor'd*		Denham b. Baxter b.

DATE	VERSE, DRAMA, MASQUE	OTHER WORKS, LITERARY/ARTISTIC	HISTORICAL/CULTURAL EVENTS
1616	Jonson *Works* (folio) Chapman's *Homer* Jonson *Mercury Vindicated*	James I *Works* Inigo Jones begins Queens House, Greenwich	Shakespeare d. Beaumont d. Cervantes d.
1617	Jonson *Vision of Delight*		Raleigh's Guyana voyage Isaac Oliver d.
1618	Jonson *Pleasure reconciled to Virtue*		Execution of Raleigh Bacon Lord Chancellor Revolt of Bohemia Thirty Years War begins Cowley b. Lovelace b.
1619		Inigo Jones Banqueting House – 1622	Anne of Denmark d. Daniel d. Hilliard d. Frederick accepts crown of Bohemia
1620	Jonson *Pan's Anniversary*	Bacon *Novum Organum*	Campion d. Evelyn b. Pilgrim Fathers sail
1621		Burton *Anatomy of Melancholy*	Parliament Bacon impeached Donne Dean of St Paul's Van Dyck's first visit to England Marvell b.
1622	Middleton *The Changeling* Jonson *Masque of Augurs*	Peacham *Compleat Gentleman*	Molière b.

DATE	VERSE, DRAMA, MASQUE	OTHER WORKS, LITERARY/ARTISTIC	HISTORICAL/CULTURAL EVENTS
1623	Shakespeare *First Folio* Daniel *Whole Works* Jonson *Time Vindicated*		Charles and Buckingham visit Spain Pascal b.
1624		Wotton *Elements of Architecture*	Parliament Charles returns from Spain War with Spain
1625	Jonson *The Fortunate Isles*		James I d. Accession of Charles I m. of Charles and Henrietta Maria Plague
1626			Parliament Attempt to impeach Buckingham War with France Bacon d. Dowland d. Aubrey b.
1627		Charles purchases Mantua Collection	Ile de Rhe expedition Abbot suspended Middleton d.
1628		Harvey *De Motu Cordis*	Assassination of Buckingham Parliament Bunyan b
1629			Dissolution of Parliament (until 1640) Rubens in London – 1630

DATE	VERSE, DRAMA, MASQUE	OTHER WORKS, LITERARY/ARTISTIC	HISTORICAL/CULTURAL EVENTS
1630			Prince Charles b. (future Charles II) Surge of emigration to New England
1631	Jonson *Love's Triumph* *Chloridia*		Donne d. Drayton d. Dryden b.
1632	Townshend *Albion's Triumph* *Tempe Restored*		Gustavus Adolphus d. Locke b. Wren b. Spinoza b. Van Dyck settles in England
1633	Donne *Poems* Herbert *The Temple*	Inigo Jones begins to remodel St Paul's Prynne *Hystriomastix*	Herbert d. Laud Abp Charles visits Scotland Pepys b.
1634	Milton *Comus* Wither *Emblems* Shirley *Triumph of Peace* Carew *Coelum Britannicum*		Chapman d. Marston d. Ship Money introduced
1635	Quarles *Emblems* Davenant *Temple of Love*		
1636		Corneille *Le Cid*	
1637		Descartes *Discours sur la Méthode*	Trial of Hampden Jonson d.

DATE	VERSE, DRAMA, MASQUE	OTHER WORKS, LITERARY/ARTISTIC	HISTORICAL/CULTURAL EVENTS
1638	Milton 'Lycidas' Davenant *Britannia Triumphans* *Luminalia*		
1639			Wotton d. Carew d. Racine b. First Bishops' War against Scotland
1640	Carew *Poems* Davenant *Salmacida Spolia*		Short Parliament Second Bishops' War Long Parliament meets – 1653 Laud and Strafford impeached Root and Branch Petition Censorship breaks down Massinger d. Burton d.
1641		Milton *Of Reformation*	Trial and execution of Strafford Grand Remonstrance Van Dyck d. Lely comes to England
1642	Denham *Cooper's Hill*	Milton *Reason of Church Government*	Outbreak of Civil War Battle of Edgehill Bishops excluded from House of Lords Theatres closed Galileo d. Richelieu d. Newton b.

DATE	VERSE, DRAMA, MASQUE	OTHER WORKS, LITERARY/ARTISTIC	HISTORICAL/CULTURAL EVENTS
1643		Browne *Religio Medici*	First Battle of Newbury Solemn League and Covenant Westminster Assembly of Divines Censorship reintroduced Pym d. Hampden d. Falkland d. Accession of Louis XIV – 1715
1644		Milton *Areopagitica*	Second Battle of Newbury Battle of Marston Moor
1645	Milton *Poems* Waller *Poems*		New Model Army Fairfax Lord General Battle of Naseby Laud executed
1646	Crashaw *Steps to the Temple* Vaughan *Poems* Shirley *Poems*	Browne *Pseudodoxia* Clarendon begins *History of the Rebellion* (pub. 1704)	Charles surrenders to Scots End of First Civil War Episcopacy abolished Leibniz b.
1647	Cowley *The Mistress* Beaumont and Fletcher *Works* (folio)		Scots hand over king to Parliament Declaration of the Army Putney Debates Levellers active King escapes Rochester b.
1648	Herrick *Hesperides*		Second Civil War Pride's Purge

DATE	VERSE, DRAMA, MASQUE	OTHER WORKS, LITERARY/ARTISTIC	HISTORICAL/CULTURAL EVENTS
1649	Lovelace *Lucasta*	*Eikon Basilike* Milton *Eikonoklastes* Winstanley *True Levellers' Standard*	Trial and execution of Charles I Commonwealth declared Abolition of monarchy and House of Lords Cromwell to Ireland Diggers' colonies established Crashaw d.
1650	Vaughan *Silex Scintillans* Marvell's 'Horatian Ode'		Cromwell succeeds Fairfax as Lord General Battle of Dunbar Descartes d.
1651	Davenant *Gondibert* Cleveland *Poems* Vaughan *Olor Iscanus*	Hobbes *Leviathan* Milton *Defensio pro Populo Anglicano*	Battle of Worcester
1652	Crashaw *Carmen Deo Nostro*		Suppression of Irish revolt Dutch War Inigo Jones d.
1653	Shirley *Cupid and Death*	Walton *Compleat Angler*	Rump Parliament dissolved Cromwell declared Lord Protector
1654		Milton *Defensio Secunda*	First Protectorate Parliament Peace with Dutch
1655		Hobbes *De Corpore Politico*	War with Spain Jews readmitted to England

DATE	VERSE, DRAMA, MASQUE	OTHER WORKS, LITERARY/ARTISTIC	HISTORICAL/CULTURAL EVENTS
1656	Cowley *Poems* Davenant *Siege of Rhodes*	Harrington *Oceana* Dugdale *Antiquities of Warwickshire*	
1657			Cromwell refuses crown Harvey d.
1658		Browne *Urn Burial and Garden of Cyrus*	Cromwell d. Richard Cromwell Protector
1659	Suckling *Last Remains*		Collapse of Richard Cromwell's Protectorate Purcell b.
1660	Dryden *Astraea Redux*	Milton *The Ready and Easy Way* Pepys *Diary – 1669*	Restoration of monarchy and House of Lords Bishops restored Declaration of Indulgence Theatres reopen Royal Society founded
1661		Boyle *Sceptical Chymist* Glanville *Vanity of Dogmatising*	Coronation of Charles II Hawksmoor b.
1662		Fuller *Worthies*	Charles m. Catherine of Braganza Introduction of new Prayer Book Act of Uniformity Henry Lawes d.

DATE	VERSE, DRAMA, MASQUE	OTHER WORKS, LITERARY/ARTISTIC	HISTORICAL/CULTURAL EVENTS
1663	Butler *Hudibras*	John Webb K. Charles's block, Greenwich Wren begins Sheldonian Theatre	Declaration of Indulgence withdrawn
1664		Evelyn *Sylva*	Occupation of New York Vanbrugh b.
1665		Hooke *Micrographia* Newton working on calculus	Great Plague Second Dutch War
1666		Bunyan *Grace Abounding*	Great Fire of London
1667	Milton *Paradise Lost* Dryden *Annus Mirabilis*	Sprat *History of Royal Society* Molière *L'Avare*	Dutch in Medway Peace with Holland Fall of Clarendon Cowley d. Swift b.
1668	Denham *Poems and Translations*	Dryden *Of Dramatick Poesy* Wilkins *Real Character*	Davenant d. Dryden Laureate
1669		Racine *Britannicus* Pascal *Pensées*	Henrietta Maria d. Denham d.
1670		Rebuilding of City churches begins	Treaty of Dover Congreve b.

DATE	VERSE, DRAMA, MASQUE	OTHER WORKS, LITERARY/ARTISTIC	HISTORICAL/CULTURAL EVENTS
1671	Milton *Paradise Regained* *Samson Agonistes*	Molière *Le Bourgeois* *Gentilhomme*	
1672	Dryden *Marriage à la Mode* *Conquest of Granada*		Third Dutch War
1673		Rebuilding of St Paul's begins	Test Act Molière d.
1674			Milton d. Herrick d. Traherne d. Clarendon d.
1675	Wycherley *The Country Wife*	Greenwich Observatory opened	Flamsteed Astronomer Royal
1676	Etherege *The Man of Mode* Dryden *Areng-Zebe*	Wren designs Trinity College Library	
1677	Dryden *All for Love*	Racine *Phèdre*	Spinoza d.
1678		Bunyan *Pilgrim's Progress* (I)	Popish Plot Anglo-Dutch Treaty Marvell d.
1679			Exclusion crisis begins Hobbes d.
1680	Rochester *Poems*	Filmer *Patriarcha* Bunyan *Mr. Badman*	Halley's Comet Lely d. Butler d. Rochester d.

DATE	VERSE, DRAMA, MASQUE	OTHER WORKS, LITERARY/ARTISTIC	HISTORICAL/CULTURAL EVENTS
1681	Marvell *Miscellaneous Poems* Oldham *Satires upon the Jesuits* Dryden *Absalom and Architophel* Otway *Venice Preserved*		Exclusion Bill reintroduced
1682	Dryden *The Medal* *Religio Laici*	Wren designs Chelsea Hospital	Browne d.
1683			Rye House Plot Oldham d. Shaftesbury d.
1684		Bunyan *Pilgrim's Progress* (II) Burnet *Sacred Theory of the Earth*	Corneille d.
1685			Charles II d. Accession of James II (1633–1701) Monmouth's Rebellion Battle of Sedgemoor Edict of Nantes revoked
1686			
1687	Dryden *Hind and Panther*	Newton *Principia Mathematica*	Waller d.

DATE	VERSE, DRAMA, MASQUE	OTHER WORKS, LITERARY/ARTISTIC	HISTORICAL/CULTURAL EVENTS
1688			'The Glorious Revolution' William of Orange invited by Parliament James II flees Bunyan d.
1689		Locke *Letter concerning Toleration* Purcell *Dido and Aeneas* Wren begins work at Hampton Court	William and Mary crowned Declaration of Right War with France
1690		Locke *Essay Concerning Human Understanding* *Two Treatises of Government*	Battle of the Boyne
1691		Dryden–Purcell *King Arthur*	Baxter d.
1692		Dryden–Purcell *The Fairy Queen*	Massacre of Glencoe Etherege d.
1693			
1694			Queen Mary d.
1695	Congreve *Love for Love*	Locke *The Reasonableness of Christianity*	Vaughan d. Purcell d.
1696	Vanbrugh *The Relapse*	Toland *Christianity Not Mysterious* Wren at Greenwich	

DATE	VERSE, DRAMA, MASQUE	OTHER WORKS, LITERARY/ARTISTIC	HISTORICAL/CULTURAL EVENTS
1697	Vanbrugh *The Provoked Wife*		Aubrey d.
1698			
1699			Racine d.
1700	Congreve *Way of the World*		Dryden d.

General Bibliographies

Note: Each section is arranged alphabetically. Place of publication is London unless otherwise stated.

(i) Cultural and intellectual history

Butler, M.	*Theatre and Crisis, 1632–42* (Cambridge, 1984). (Antagonism to the policies of Charles I expressed in the drama of the decade before the Civil War.)
Dollimore, J.	*Radical Tragedy: Religion, Ideology and Power in the Drama of Shakespeare and his Contemporaries* (Brighton, 1984)
Fish, S.	*Self-Consuming Artifacts: The Experience of Seventeenth-Century Literature* (Berkeley, Calif., 1972). (Provocative structuralist readings of Bacon, Burton, Browne, Herbert, Bunyan, and Milton.)
Goldberg, J.	*James I and the Politics of Literature* (Baltimore, 1983). (Explores the political dimension of Jacobean literature and art.)
Gordon D. J.	*The Renaissance Imagination*, ed. S. Orgel (Berkeley and London, 1975). (Important essays on masque, emblems, and Stuart iconography.)
Grant, P.	*Literature and the Discovery of Method in the English Renaissance* (1985). (On the tension between the new scientific methodology and the older metaphysical ways of evaluating man's role in nature.)
Heinemann, M.	*Puritanism and Theatre* (Cambridge, 1980). (Opposition politics in the theatre, focusing on Middleton.)
Hill, C.	*Intellectual Origins of the English Revolution* (Oxford, 1965; repr. 1982). (Discussions of the intellectual forces that moved Englishmen towards revolution; changing attitudes towards science, history, and the law as expressed in the ideas of Bacon, Raleigh, and Coke.)
Hill, C.	*Some Intellectual Consequences of the English Revolution* (1980). (Stimulating reflections on the afterlife of revolutionary ideas.)

Hill, C.   *Collected Essays*, 3 vols (Brighton, 1985–87).

Jose, N.   *Ideas of Restoration in English Literature, 1660–71* (1984). (Notable chapters on Cowley and *Samson Agonistes*.)

Lindley, D., ed.   *The Court Masque* (Manchester, 1984).

Martines, L.   *Society and History in English Renaissance Verse* (1985). (Social and economic stresses impinging upon poetry.)

Norbrook, D.   *Poetry and Politics in the English Renaissance* (1984). (Important book on radical Protestant poetry and the influence of Sidney and Spenser on Stuart verse.)

Orgel, S.   *The Jonsonian Masque* (Cambridge, Mass., 1967).

Orgel, S.   *The Illusion of Power: Political Theatre in the English Renaissance* (Berkeley, Calif., 1975). (Brilliant brief introduction to masque.)

Orgel. S., and R. Strong.   *Inigo Jones: The Theatre of the Stuart Court*, 2 vols (1973). (Contains texts of all the masques Jones designed, plus illustrations and commentary.)

Parry, G.   *The Golden Age Restor'd: The Culture of the Stuart Court 1603–42* (Manchester, 1981). (On Stuart iconography, and the role of the arts at court.)

Patrides, C. A., and R. B. Waddington, eds   *The Age of Milton* (Manchester, 1980). (Useful background essays.)

Sherwood, R.   *The Court of Oliver Cromwell* (1977).

Spencer, T. J. B., and S. Wells, eds   *A Book of Masques* (Cambridge, 1967; repr. 1980). (Most varied collection of masques currently available.)

Worden. B., ed.   *Stuart England* (Oxford, 1986). (Wide-ranging essays on culture and politics covering the whole century. Copiously illustrated.)

(ii) Religion

Collinson, P.   *The Religion of Protestants: The Church in English Society, 1559–1625* (Oxford, 1982).

Collinson, P.   *Godly People: Essays on English Protestantism* (1983).

Cross, C.   *Church and People, 1450–1660: The Triumph of the Laity in the English Church* (Brighton, 1976).

Davies, H.   *Worship and Theology in England, 1603–1690* (Princeton, N. J., 1975).

Firth, K. R.   *The Apocalyptic Tradition in Reformation Britain, 1530–1645* (Oxford, 1979). (Describes influence of prophetic texts on religious thought.)

Haller, W.   *The Rise of Puritanism* (New York, 1938). (An influential work, still important.)

Hill, C.   *Antichrist in Seventeenth-Century England* (1971). (Detailed documentation of who believed what about Antichrist.)

Hill, C.   *Milton and the English Revolution* (1977). (Outstanding account of Milton's religious and political thought, emphasizing his radicalism.)

Lamont, W. M.   *Godly Rule: Politics and Religion, 1603–60* (1969). (Concerned with the millenarian strain in Puritanism.)

Martz, L.   *The Poetry of Meditation* (New Haven, Conn., 1954). (Important study of the shaping power of meditative disciplines on seventeenth-century poetry.)

Patrides C. A., and J. Wittreich, eds   *The Apocalypse in English Renaissance Thought and Literature* (Manchester, 1984).

Patrides, C. A.   *The Cambridge Platonists* (1969). (Selection from Whichcote, Smith, More, and Cudworth, with useful introduction and bibliography.)

Stocker, M.   *Apocalyptic Marvell: The Second Coming in Seventeenth Century Poetry* (Brighton, 1986).

Thomas, K.   *Religion and the Decline of Magic* (1971). (A fascinating account of the systems of popular belief in sixteenth- and seventeenth-century England; covers astrology, witchcraft, magic. An indispensable book, reprinted in Penguin.)

Trevor-Roper, H. R.   *Archbishop Laud, 1573–1645* (1940). (The standard biography.)

Trevor-Roper, H. R.   *Religion, The Reformation and Social Change* (1967). (Important collection of essays, including studies of the European witch craze, of Comenius, Hartlib, and Dury, and on the general crisis of the seventeenth century.)

Willey, B.   *The Seventeenth Century Background: Studies in the Thought of the Age in Relation to Poetry and Religion* (1934). (A seminal book, much reprinted.)

Yates, F.   *The Rosicrucian Enlightenment* (1972). (Radical Protestant ideas in Germany and England; alchemy and spiritual illumination.)

(iii) Politics and political thought

Aylmer, G. E.   *The Struggle for the Constitution, 1603–1689* (1963).
                     (A compact political history of the century.)

Aylmer, G. E., ed.   *The Interregnum: The Quest for Settlement, 1646–1660*
                     (1972). (Fine collection of essays on the problems
                     of State and Church in this critical period.)

Cranston, M.   *John Locke: A Biography* (Oxford, 1957; repr. 1985).
                     (The standard life.)

Figgis, J. N.   *The Divine Right of Kings* (1896; repr. 1965). (Still a
                     basic source-book for this subject.)

Gardiner, S. R., ed. *The Constitutional Documents of the Puritan Revolution
                     1625–1660* (Oxford, 1889). Many subsequent
                     editions.

Harris, R. W.   *Clarendon and the English Revolution* (1983).
                     (Biography and study of Clarendon's political
                     ideas.)

Hill, C.   *Puritanism and Revolution* (1958). (Includes important
                     essays on the Norman Yoke, Hobbes, Harrington,
                     and Marvell.)

Hill, C.   *The Century of Revolution 1603–1714* (1961). Dense
                     informative survey.)

Hill, C.   *The World Turned Upside Down. Radical ideas during
                     the English Revolution* (1972). (On populist politics
                     and sectarian aspirations.)

Hutton, R.   *The Restoration: A Political and Religious History of
                     England and Wales, 1658–1667* (Oxford, 1985). (A
                     fluent account of complicated events.)

Lockyer, R.   *Buckingham: The Life and Political Career of George
                     Villiers, First Duke of Buckingham, 1592–1628* (1981).

Macpherson, C. B.   *The Political Theory Of Possessive Individualism:
                     Hobbes to Locke* (Oxford, 1962). (On property and
                     power; Marxist orientation.)

Pocock, J. G. A.   *The Ancient Constitution and the Feudal Law: A Study
                     of English Historical Thought in the Seventeenth
                     Century* (Cambridge, 1957; repr. 1987). (Classic
                     account of legal and antiquarian arguments over the
                     Constitution.)

Prestwich, M.   *Cranfield: Politics and Profits under the Early Stuarts*
                     (Oxford, 1966). (The mercantile and political career
                     of Lionel Cranfield in the reigns of James I and
                     Charles I.)

Russell, C., ed.   *The Origins of the English Civil War* (1973).

Sharpe, K.   *Sir Robert Cotton, 1586–1631: History and Politics in
                     Early Modern England* (Oxford, 1979).

(Antiquarianism, literary relations and court politics.)

Skinner, Q.   *The Foundations of Modern Political Theory*, 2 vols (Cambridge, 1978).

Somerville, J. P.   *Politics and Ideology in England, 1603–40* (1986). (Summarizes the main arguments in political theory in early Stuart times.)

Stone, L.   *The Causes of the English Revolution* (1972).

Tuck, R.   *Natural Rights Theories: Their Origin and Development* (Cambridge, 1979).

Willson, D. H.   *James VI and I* (1956). (Still the most satisfactory biography of James I.)

Wootton, D., ed.   *Divine Right and Democracy: An Anthology of Political Writing in Stuart England* (Harmondsworth, 1986). (A collection of lesser-known tracts with helpful introduction.)

(iv) The scientific movement

'Espinasse, M.   *Robert Hooke* (1956).

Hall, A. R.   *The Scientific Revolution, 1500–1800: The Formation of the Modern Scientific Attitude* (1954). (Still a useful introductory survey.)

Harris, I.   *All Coherence Gone: A Study of the Seventeenth Century Controversy over Disorder and Decay in the Universe* (1949; repr. 1966). (Valuable study of a debate that involved many of the leading intellectual figures in the first half of the century.)

Hunter, M.   *Science and Society in Restoration England* (Cambridge, 1981). (Important book on the ethos of the Royal Society; excellent bibliography.)

Jones, R. F.   *Ancients and Moderns: A Study of the Rise of the Scientific Movement* (1933; repr. 1961).

Keynes, G.   *The Life of William Harvey* (Oxford, 1966). (Much about seventeenth-century medicine.)

Webster, C.   *The Great Instauration: Science, Medicine and Reform, 1626–1660* (1975). (Ground-breaking work on relations between religion and science; outstanding account of the Baconian movement, and of the organization of the scientific community in this period.)

Webster, C.   *Samuel Hartlib and the Advancement of Learning* (Cambridge, 1970).

Webster, C ed.   *The Intellectual Revolution of the Seventeenth Century* (1974). (Essays on science, politics, and religion.)

(v) Art and architecture

Beard, G.   *Craftsmen and Interior Decoration in England 1660–1820* (1981). (Valuable account of commissions of Restoration craftsmen and their working conditions. Excellent illustrations.)

Downes, K.   *Christopher Wren* (1971).

Ede, M.   *William and Mary* (1979). (Informative survey of the arts at the end of the century.)

Edmond, M.   *Nicholas Hilliard and Isaac Oliver* (1983). (Detailed biographies.)

Foskett, D.   *Samuel Cooper 1609–1672* (1974).

Foskett, D.   *Samuel Cooper and his Contemporaries* (1974). (Catalogue of the exhibition at the National Portrait Gallery.)

Harris, J., S. Orgel, and R. Strong.   *The King's Arcadia: Inigo Jones and the Stuart Court* (1973). (Highly informative exhibition catalogue.)

Hook, J.   *The Baroque Age in England* (1976). (Fine analysis of the social implications of the baroque style; much about patronage and politics.)

Howarth, D.   *Lord Arundel and his Circle* (1985). (Impressive study of Arundel as patron and collector.)

Millar, O.   *The Age of Charles I* (1972). (Catalogue of the Tate exhibition.)

Millar, O.   *Sir Peter Lely* (1978). (Catalogue of the National Portrait Gallery exhibition.)

Millar, O.   *Van Dyck in England* (1982). (Catalogue of National Portrait Gallery exhibition; extremely informative.)

Palme, P.   *Triumph of Peace* (1957). (Extended study of Inigo Jones's Banqueting House and its symbolism.)

Parry, G.   *Hollar's England: A Mid-Seventeenth-Century View* (Salisbury, 1980). (Well-illustrated account of Hollar's English career; landscapes, portraits, and scenes of contemporary life.)

Rogers, M.   *William Dobson, 1611–46* (1983). (Catalogue of an exhibition which did much to establish Dobson's *œuvre*.)

Stevenson, S., and D. Thomson.   *John Michael Wright: The King's Painter* (Edinburgh, 1982). (Exhibition catalogue of this artist whose reputation has risen considerably in recent years.)

Strong, R.   *Charles I on Horseback* (1972). (Detailed study of Van Dyck's painting in the Royal Collection.)

Strong, R.   *The Renaissance Garden in England* (1979). (Authoritative account of garden design in this period.)

Strong, R.   *Britannia Triumphans: Inigo Jones, Rubens and Whitehall Palace* (1980).

Strong, R.   *Henry Prince of Wales and England's Lost Renaissance* (1986). (Prince Henry as patron and collector.)

Summerson, J.   *Inigo Jones* (Harmondsworth, 1966).

Whinney, M.   *Sculpture in Britain, 1530–1830* (Harmondsworth, 1964).

Whinney, M., and O. Millar.   *English Art, 1625–1714* (Oxford, 1957).

(vi) Music

Hollander, J.   *The Untuning of the Sky: Ideas of Music in English Poetry, 1500–1700* (Princeton, N. J., 1966).

Lefkowitz, M.   *William Lawes* (1960). (A study of this innovative composer, killed in the Civil Wars, who was the brother of Henry Lawes.)

Le Huray, P.   *Music and the Reformation in England, 1549–1660* (1967).

Mace, T.   *Musick's Monument* (1676; repr. 1958). (Invaluable account of the musical scene in the mid-seventeenth century.)

Poulton, D.   *John Dowland* (1972). (Thorough study of Dowland's music and his social milieu. Second edition (1982) contains important additions.)

Westrup, J. A.   *Purcell* (1965; repr. 1980).

Woodfill, W. A.   *Musicians in English Society from Elizabeth to Charles I* (Princeton, N. J., 1953).

(vii) Social history

Akrigg, G. P. V.

Jacobean Pageant or The Court of King James I (1962). (Well-painted picture of the social world of the Jacobean court.)

Aubrey, J.

Brief Lives, ed. O. L. Dick (1949; repr. Penguin). (Essential reading: vividly preserves the force and idiosyncrasy of so many seventeenth-century personalities.)

Fraser, A.

The Weaker Vessel: Woman's Lot in Seventeenth-Century England (1984). (A broad account of women's experience).

Laslett, P.

The World We Have Lost (1965). (A notable sociological study of the age.)

Stone, L.

The Crisis of the Aristocracy, 1558–1641 (Oxford, 1967). (Contains *inter alia* many memorable descriptions of the aristocratic life-style in this period.)

Stone, L.

Family and Fortune (Oxford, 1973). (Analysis of how leading aristocratic families made their money and spent it.)

Stone, L.

The Family, Sex and Marriage in England 1500–1800 (1977; repr. Penguin). (Much unusual information on this period; Stone's conclusions have proved cententious.)

Wrightson, K.

English Society, 1580–1680 (1982). (A fine, comprehensive social history.)

Individual Authors

Notes on biography, major works, and suggested further reading

Note: Place of publication is London unless otherwise stated.

ANDREWES, Lancelot (1555–1626). Son of a London merchant. Merchant Taylors School and Pembroke College, Cambridge. Fellow of Pembroke, then Master from 1589 to 1605. Chaplain to Queen Elizabeth. 1601 Dean of Westminster. Under James he rose rapidly in the Church: 1605 Bishop of Chichester; 1609 Ely; 1619 Bishop of Winchester. A man of immense theological learning; a great patristic scholar. One of the translators of the 1611 Bible. A man of ascetic habits. He favoured the use of ritual in services, and fine furnishings in his churches. Arminian in theology, he was the patron of such notable High Anglicans as Matthew Wren and John Cosin, and a friend of Laud. Strongly anti-Roman. King James passed him over for Canterbury in 1610 probably because his theology was too Arminian. Buried in Southwark Cathedral.

> *Works*, ed. J. Bliss, in The Library of Anglo-Catholic Theology (1841–54).
> *Sermons*, ed. G. M. Storey (Oxford, 1967).

> See: Eliot, T. S., *For Lancelot Andrewes* (1928).
> Welsby, P., *Lancelot Andrewes, 1555–1626* (1958).

AUBREY, John (1626–97). Born at Easton-Piers, Wiltshire, son of a gentlemen whose fortunes were in decline. Blandford School, Dorset and Trinity College, Oxford. He was at Oxford when the city became the royalist headquarters, with the King and court in residence. 1646 enrolled at Middle Temple to study law. 1646–56 divided time between Oxford and London; 1650s and 1660s Living as a country gentleman in Wiltshire. 1648 recognized that Avebury in Wiltshire was an important prehistoric site. 1656 began to write *Natural History of Wiltshire*. 1663 elected Fellow of the Royal Society. Late 1660s and early 1670s lawsuits and negotiations for his marriage proved disastrous, and ruined him. 1671 Easton-Piers sold; thereafter obliged to live on friends. Endlessly sociable and insatiably curious. His sketches of the lives of interesting men of the seventeenth century, many of whom were or had been his friends, show a genius for biography; tried to put these lives together for publication from the late

1660s onwards, in collaboration with Anthony Wood. Assembled much
material for a life of his particular friend Thomas Hobbes. Compiled
material for his projected work on British antiquities, 'Monumentum
Britannicum', stemming from his interest in Stonehenge and Avebury.
Also gathered information for books on folklore, place-names, dreams, and
nativities. Attempted a chronology of English architecture. Wrote a
comedy, 'The Country Revell', never performed, never published. He
composed an antiquarian survey of Surrey, and wrote a treatise of
education. Full of schemes and plans, eager to preserve all kinds of
evanescent details about men and events, he never brought anything to
completion, and when he died in 1697 he left a mass of manuscripts that
were eventually deposited in the Bodleian Library. Only his *Miscellanies*
(1696) were published in his lifetime. These were mainly speculations
about curious phenomena, many of them psychic. In recent years a
number of Aubrey's manuscripts have been printed, and his varied and
entertaining contributions to the intellectual life of the later seventeenth
century have been widely recognized. He described himself as 'a
whetstone' against which other men sharpened their wits. Buried in the
church of St Mary Magdalene, Oxford.

> *Brief Lives*, ed. A. Clark, 2 vols (Oxford, 1898). (The complete
> collection.)
> *Brief Lives*, ed. O. L. Dick (1949; repr. in Penguin). (Extensive
> selection with excellent introduction.)
> *Three Prose Works*, ed. J. Buchanan-Brown (1972). (Contains
> *Miscellanies, Remaines of Gentilisme and Judaisme, Observation*.)
> *Aubrey on Education*, ed. J. E. Stephens (1972).
> *A Natural History of Wiltshire* (Newton Abbot 1969).
> *Monumentum Britannicum*, ed. J. Fowles and R. Legg, 2 vols (1980).
> (Photo-plates of the original manuscript with some transcription
> and notes.)
> *A Perambulation of the County of Surrey*, 5 vols (Dorking, 1975.)

> See: Hunter, M., *John Aubrey and the Realm of Learning.* (1975).
> (Fascinating study of Aubrey's intellectual life.)
> Powell, A., *John Aubrey and His Friends* (1948; repr 1963). (A
> biography written in the spirit of Aubrey's own *Lives*.)

BACON, Francis (1561–1626). Born at York House, London, son of Sir
Nicholas Bacon, the Lord Keeper. Nephew of Lord Burghley. Educated at
Trinity College, Cambridge, and Gray's Inn. MP 1584–1618. Associated
with the Earl of Essex in the 1590s as friend and adviser, but distanced
himself from Essex's rebellion. Did not enjoy advancement under
Elizabeth, but had a spectacularly successful legal career under James. 1607
Solicitor-General; 1613 Attorney-General; 1617 Lord Keeper; 1618 Lord
Chancellor. Engaged in prolonged judicial disputes with Sir Edward Coke,
Bacon defending the King's exercise of prerogative, Coke attacking it in
the name of the common law. 1618 created Baron Verulam, 1621 Viscount
St Albans. (Bacon's family seat was at Gorhambury, St Albans.) 1621
politically outmanœuvred by Coke and Cranfield, he was accused of
bribery and impeached. Found guilty by the House of Lords, he was fined
and disgraced. He did not regain favour.

His *Essays* the fruits of his political and social observations, were first
published in 1597, enlarged in 1612, and again in 1625. His long attempt
to reform the intellectual habits of the European mind began with the

publication of *The Advancement of Learning* in 1605, which attacked the unprofitable scholasticism that inhibited the growth of knowledge and the mental prejudices that helped to keep men in ignorance. Above all he deplored the poor and confused state of knowledge about the operations of the natural world. *Novum Organum*, begun about 1608, published 1620, called for a systematic study of the natural world and of the causes of things, and proposed the inductive method as the most reliable instrument of enquiry. Bacon worked out the principles of the experimental method in this book, and developed them in *De Augmentis*, 1623. *Sylva Sylvarum*, a proposal of 1,000 experiments to be undertaken, was published posthumously in 1627, together with *New Atlantis*, a Utopian fragment written about 1617 that urged the foundation of a college for scientific research. A short book that enjoyed much popularity in his lifetime was *De Sapientia Veterum*, 1609 (translated as *The Wisdom of the Ancients*, 1619), which tried to demonstrate that the myths of the Greeks were coded accounts of their knowledge of the physical world.

> *The Works of Francis Bacon*, ed. J. Spedding, R. L. Ellis, and D. D. Heath, 14 vols (1857–74).

See: Webster, C., *The Great Instauration* (1975).

BOYLE, Robert (1627–91). Fourteenth child of the Earl of Cork. Educated at Eton and by private tutors. About 1655 Moved to Oxford to join the group of proto-scientists centred on John Wilkins, Warden of Wadham, and which included Wren, Ward, Petty, and Hooke. Early interest in alchemy, but under the influence of Descartes and Gassendi became convinced that the structure of matter was corpuscular and its operations open to rational investigation. His work was instrumental in turning chemistry from an occult art to a recognizably modern science. An early practitioner of the experimental method, and assisted by Robert Hooke, his most rewarding research was into the behaviour of air and gases. 1660 founder member of the Royal Society. 1661 published *The Sceptical Chymist*, attacking the Aristotelian theory of matter and investigating how change occurred in the material world. 1666 *The Origin of Forms and Qualities* offered a defence of the corpuscular theory of matter, falling back to Greek atomic theory for support. His desire to demonstrate the intellectual compatibility between scientific enquiry and revealed religion led him to found the Boyle Lectures. Numerous scientific publications. Promoted the spread of the Gospel in New England, and was a director of the East India Company.

> *Works*, ed. T. Birch, 5 Vols (1744). (Includes an important biography.)
> *Selected Philosophical Papers of Robert Boyle*, ed. M. A. Stewart (Manchester, 1979).

See: Hunter, M., *Science and Society in Restoration England* (Cambridge, 1981).
Maddison, R. E. W., *The Life of Robert Boyle, F.R.S.* (1969).

BROWNE, Thomas (1605–82). Son of a London mercer. Educated at Winchester and Pembroke College, Oxford. Studied medicine at Montpellier, Padua, and Leyden. Practised as physician briefly at Halifax, then for the rest of his life at Norwich. The self-portrait of his mind and beliefs, *Religio*

Medici, composed in the mid-1630s, was published in 1643. His rambling and miscellaneous compilation of the 'Vulgar Errors' that have imposed themselves on the credulity of men, *Pseudodoxia Epidemica*, came out in 1646, an Alexandrian Library of curious learning in itself. The discovery of some ancient urns in Norfolk-inspired *Hydriotaphia or Urn-Burial*, 1658, a discourse on the funeral customs of the nations that becomes a meditation on the vanity of ambition and ultimately an elegy for mankind. It was published together with *The Garden of Cyrus*, a metaphysical discourse on the significance of the Quincunx, artificially and mystically considered. After Browne's death, *Miscellany Tracts* came out in 1684 and the folio of his *Works* in 1686. Later came *A Letter to a Friend*, 1690, and *Christian Morals*, 1716. Browne's learning was prodigious, and he had a greater range of prose styles at his command than any other seventeenth-century Englishman. But he had no art to clarify a subject; on the contrary, he tended to increase the complexity of a topic discussed, and his learning often provides a fortification for a subject instead of a means of access. His singular endeavours to advance learning did not win the approval of the Royal Society, and he did not become a member. Physician, antiquarian, amateur theologian, and moralist, no subject was beyond Browne's interest and all knowledge was interconnected in his mind. He is buried in the church of St Peter Mancroft, Norwich.

> *The Works of Sir Thomas Browne*, ed. G. Keynes, 4 vols (1964).
> *Pseudodoxia Epidemica*, ed. R. Robins (Oxford, 1981).
> *The Letters of Sir Thomas Browne*, ed. G. Keynes (1931).
> *A Bibliography of Sir Thomas Browne*, ed. G. Keynes (Oxford, 1968).
>
> See: Huntley, F. L., *Sir Thomas Browne* (Ann Arbor, 1962).
>   Willey, B., *The Seventeenth Century Background* (1934).

BURTON, Robert (1577–1640). Son of a Leicestershire gentleman. Educated at the Free School, Sutton Coldfield. Brasenose College, Oxford, 1593, then moved to Christ Church, 1599. Spent most of his life in Oxford, living in Christ Church and being vicar of St Thomas's. Apart from a Latin comedy and some minor occasional verse, his contribution to literature consists of one remarkable work, *The Anatomy of Melancholy*, first published in 1621, with later editions in 1624, 1628, 1632, 1638, 1651, 1660, 1676. (The famous engraved title-page showing various victims of melancholy was added to the third and later editions.) In part a fantastical medical treatise, in part a vast survey of life under the sign of melancholy, it aspires to the order and method of a treatise, but collapses under the weight of its learning into a wonderful confusion of anecdote, opinion, and humorous speculation. 'I have read many books but to little purpose, for want of good method; I have confusedly tumbled over divers authors in our libraries with small profit for want of art, order, memory, judgement.' Burton wrote under the name of Democritus Junior, the reincarnation of the Greek philosopher whom he described as immensely learned, solitary, contemplative, and given to laughing at the world. It was as Democritus Junior that he was buried in Christ Church Cathedral in 1640, with a calculation of his nativity upon his monument that showed him to have been born under the sign of Saturn.

> *The Anatomy of Melancholy*, ed. H. Jackson, Everyman's Library, edition (1932).

> *The Anatomy of Melancholy*, ed. F. Dell and P. Jordan-Smith (New York, 1955). (Translates all the Latin quotations.)

See: B. Evans and G. J. Mohr, *The Psychiatry of Robert Burton* (New York, 1944).
W. R. Mueller, *The Anatomy of Robert Burton's England* (Berkeley, Calif., 1952).
S. Fish, 'Thou Thyself art the Subject of my Discourse', in *Self-Consuming Artifacts* (Berkeley, Calif., 1972).

CLARENDON, Earl of (Edward Hyde) (1609–74). Born in Wiltshire, son of a gentleman of Cheshire extraction. Magdalen Hall, Oxford, then Middle Temple. Became a friend of Ben Jonson, John Selden the jurist, and Lucius Cary, Earl of Falkland, the rational theologian. Early 1630s member of the Great Tew circle around Falkland that engaged in religious, philosophical, and moral debate. Practised law, and entered Parliament in 1640. A committed royalist. 1646 went into exile in Jersey, and began to write his *History of the Rebellion*. Later moved to Paris, and became one of Prince Charles's chief advisers. 1660 appointed Lord Chancellor at the Restoration. Introduced legislation against Nonconformists generally known as 'The Clarendon Code'. Built a splendid house in Piccadilly which occasioned much envy among his political opponents. A conservative, traditionalist statesman. The disastrous wars against the Dutch and the unpopularity of his policies brought about his downfall in 1667. Into exile again, in France, where he finished his *History* and wrote his autobiography. Also wrote against Hobbes. Clarendon died in 1674, and was buried in Westminster Abbey. His *History* was published in 1704, and the profits went to found the Clarendon Press at Oxford.

> *The History of the Rebellion* (Oxford, 1704).
> *The History of the Rebellion*, ed. W. D. Macray, 6 vols (Oxford, 1888). (Best edition.)
> *The Life of Edward, Earl of Clarendon* (Oxford, 1759).

See: Harris, R. W. *Clarendon and the English Revolution* (1983).
Wormald, B., *Clarendon: Politics, History and Religion, 1640–1660* (1951).

COSIN, John (1594–1672). Born in Norwich, son of a wealthy merchant. Norwich Grammar School and Caius College, Cambridge. Fellow of Caius, secretary to Bishop Overall, then chaplain to Bishop Neile of Durham. Friend of Laud and Montagu; Cosin's friendships indicate a lifelong disposition to High Church principles. 1634 Master of Peterhouse, Cambridge. (Crashaw was among the Fellows.) Devoted much attention to the adornment of the chapel to enhance its devotional ethos. 1644 ejected from Peterhouse for his High Church practices. Went into exile in Paris, where he became chaplain to the Anglican community surrounding Henrietta Maria. 1660 returned, and was appointed Bishop of Durham. Cosin was one of the chief designers of the 1662 Book of Common Prayer. At Durham he was an outstanding administrator. He also undertook the refurnishing of many churches within his diocese, where he favoured an unusual late Gothic style of decoration. Cosin died in 1672, and was buried in the chapel at Bishop Auckland.

> *Works*, in the Library of Anglo-Catholic Theology (Oxford, 1843–55).

A Collection of Private Devotions, ed. P. G. Stanwood (Oxford, 1967).

See: Osmond, P. H., *A Life of John Cosin, Bishop of Durham, 1660–1672* (1913).

COWLEY, Abraham (1618–77). Born in London, son of a stationer. Westminster School and Trinity College, Cambridge. Published his first volume of poetry while at school. Fellow of Trinity, but ejected by the Puritan commissioners in 1644. Went into exile in Paris, and became a secretary to Henrietta Maria. 1647 published *The Mistress*, a volume of love-poems that enjoyed immense popularity. Engaged in secret service activities for the royalists; eventually captured and imprisoned as a spy. Made his submission to Cromwell and lived quietly in England. 1656 published his *Poems*, containing his epic *Davideis* and his best odes. Turned to the study of medicine and botany. Floated a proposal for the foundation of a college of experimental science in 1659. Elected to Royal Society in 1661, but was an inactive member. Lived a life of rural retreat. Cowley's patrons were Henry Jermyn, Earl of St Albans, and George Villiers, Duke of Buckingham. He died in 1677 and was buried in Westminster Abbey.

The Poems of Abraham Cowley, ed. A. R. Waller (Cambridge, 1905).
Essays, Plays and Sundry Verses of Abraham Cowley, ed. A. R. Waller (Cambridge, 1906).
The Civil War, ed. A Pritchard (Toronto, 1973).

See: Hinman, R. B., *Abraham Cowley's World of Order* (Cambridge, Mass., 1960).
Nethercot, A. H., *Abraham Cowley, The Muses' Hannibal* (Oxford, 1931). (Still the standard life.)
Trotter, D., *The Poetry of Abraham Cowley* (1979).

DAVENANT, Sir William (1606–1668). Born at Oxford, son of a vintner; Shakespeare appears to have been his godfather. Became a page to the Duchess of Richmond, then entered the service of Fulke Greville, Lord Brooke. Began to write plays about 1628. Very productive during the 1630s, writing numerous plays and masques, and publishing a volume of poems, *Madagascar*, in 1638. 1640 *Salmacida Spolia*, the last of King Charles's masques. Also 1640 appointed manager of the Cockpit Theatre. Closely involved in the royalist cause, particularly in the Queen's interest. Left England at the end of 1645, and joined the circle of talented exiles in Paris. 1650–52 employed on missions for Charles II, captured, and imprisoned. 1650 published *Gondibert*, his heroic poem, about which he had a critical debate with Hobbes. 1656 introduced opera into England with *The Siege of Rhodes*. After the Restoration, Davenant became manager of the Duke of York's Theatre. His prominent role in the theatrical world meant that his career was the main line of continuity between the Jacobean and Caroline stage and the Restoration theatre. Davenant died in 1668, and was buried in Westminster Abbey.

The Shorter Poems and Songs from the Plays and Masques, ed. A. M. Gibbs (Oxford, 1972).
Gondibert, ed. D. F. Gladish (Oxford, 1971).
Dramatic Works, ed. J. Maidment and W. H. Logan, 5 vols (Edinburgh, 1872–74).

See: Edmond, M., *Rare Sir William Davenant* (Manchester, 1987).
Harbage, A., *Sir William Davenant, Poet Venturer, 1606–1668* (1935).
Hotson, L., *The Commonwealth and Restoration Stage* (1928; repr.
1968).
Nethercot, A. H., *Sir William D'Avenant. Poet Laureate and
Playwright-Manager* (1938).

DRYDEN, John (1631–1700). Son of a Northamptonshire gentleman.
Westminster School and Trinity College, Cambridge. 1657–58 government
clerk in London. 1659 published poem in praise of Cromwell; 1660 wrote
Astraea Redux in praise of the Restoration of Charles II. 1662 elected to
Royal Society; only attended once. 1663 began writing plays. 1667 *Annus
Mirabilis*, poem on the Great Frost, the Great Fire, and the war with
Holland. 1668 made Poet Laureate. 1681 *Absalom and Achitophel* (Part II in
1682). 1682 *Religio Laici*, expression of his Anglican faith. 1687 *Mac
Flecknoe* (written 1676). 1687 *The Hind and the Panther*, expression of his
Catholic faith. 1688 after James II's expulsion, Dryden was dismissed as
Poet Laureate. Concentrated thereafter on plays and translations. From the
1670s onwards he wrote many pieces that were set to music by
Restoration composers. Dryden died in 1700, received a splendid funeral,
and was buried in Westminster Abbey.

The Poems of John Dryden, ed. J. Kinsley, 4 vols (1958).
The Works of John Dryden, ed. E. N. Hooker, H. T. Swedenberg *et
al.* (Berkeley, Calif., 1956–). (The California Dryden.)

See: Bredvold, L., *The Intellectual Milieu of Dryden's Thought* (Ann
Arbor, Michigan, 1934).
Harth, P., *Contexts of Dryden's Thought* (Chicago, 1968).
Miner, E., *Dryden's Poetry* (Bloomington, Ind., 1967).
Miner, R., ed., *John Dryden* (1972). (Stimulating collection of
essays.)
Ward, C., *The Life of Dryden* (Chapel Hill, N. C., 1961). (The
standard life.)

EVELYN, John (1620–1706). Born at Wotton in Surrey into a prosperous landed
family whose fortune was based on gunpowder. Local schools and Balliol
College, Oxford. 1643–47 travelled on the Continent, with extensive stay
in France and Italy, where he was absorbed by art and architecture. Kept
out of the Civil Wars, although his sympathies were strongly royalist.
1649–52 mainly in the exiled royalist circles in Paris. 1653 acquired Sayes
Court near Deptford, which would be his seat for the rest of his life. Set
about planting the orchards and gardens. Late 1650s began writing
'Elysium Britannicum', a work encompassing all aspects of gardening,
practical, historical, mythological, and spiritual (never published). With the
Restoration, Evelyn moved into the mainstream of English cultural life. A
friend of the King, he was frequently at court. Extremely active in the
affairs of the Royal Society, of which he was one of the earliest members.
The full range of his virtuoso interests and civil projects was now given
public expression: 1661 *Fumifugium*, a proposal to clear the smoke-filled air
of London; 1662 *Sculptura*, a history of engraving; 1664 two works about
neo-Classical architecture on the French model, a translation of Fréart's
Parallel between Ancient and Modern Architecture, and *An Account of Architects
and Architecturu*; Evelyn's most admired work, *Sylva*, a discourse of

gardening and forest trees, was also published in 1664, as was *Kalendrium Hortense*, or the *Gardener's Almanack*. Many pamphlets on matters of politics and taste. 1675 *Terra*, on the improvement of soils. 1697 *Numismata*, a book on coins and medals. Evelyn was active in public affairs in the 1660s, on planning committees, involved in caring for prisoners in the Dutch Wars, and setting up hospitals for the wounded. In 1678 Peter the Great of Russia and his entourage were accommodated at Sayes Court, and virtually wrecked the place. 1685 appointed to an office at the Privy Seal as a well-paid civil servant. For much of his life Evelyn kept the detailed diary of personal and public affairs for which he is famous. This was first published in 1818. Evelyn died in 1706, and was buried at Wotton.

> *The Diaries of John Evelyn*, ed. E. S. De Beer, 5 vols (Oxford, 1955). (The definitive edition.)
> *Sylva* (1664; repr. by Scolar Press, 1972).
> Keynes, G. *John Evelyn: A Study in Bibliophily with a Bibliography of his Writings* (Oxford, 1968).

See: Bowle, J., *John Evelyn and His World* (1981).

HARRINGTON, James (1611–77). Son of a Northamptonshire gentleman. Trinity College, Oxford, and possibly Middle Temple thereafter. Travelled extensively in Denmark, Germany, France, and Italy, with more interest in the political systems of these countries than in their curiosities. Appears to have kept out of the Civil War. Became a close friend of King Charles during the King's captivity, and accompanied him on the scaffold. In spite of his royalist sympathies, Harrington favoured a commonwealth as the most just and effective form of government, and laid out his proposals in *The Commonwealth of Oceana*, 1656, dedicated to Cromwell. Much influenced by his experience of the Venetian Republic. He envisaged a system in which power depends on the balance of property, with a moderate aristocracy headed by a doge-like figure. He proposed that membership of the senate should be rotated, and that decisions be taken by ballot. In the 1650s he was at the centre of a coffee-house club given to the discussion of political theory, called The Rota. 1658 published *The Prerogative of Popular Government*, which contained supporting material for *Oceana* and an enquiry into the forms of government of the ancient Israelites. Arrested at the Restoration and imprisoned for a while; his health deteriorated and he became subject to a whimsical madness.

> *The Political Works of James Harrington*, ed. J. G. A. Pocock (Cambridge, 1977). (The standard edition, with a long, outstanding introduction which is essential reading for students of seventeenth-century political theory.)

HOBBES, Thomas (1588–1679). Born at Malmesbury, son of the barely literate parish minister. 1602–06 at Magdalen Hall, Oxford. Became tutor to the son of William Cavendish, Earl of Devonshire and remained closely attached to the Cavendish family for much of his life. Secretary to Bacon for a short time in the 1620s. Early interest in the classics, leading to his publication of a translation of Thucydides in 1628. Attracted to geometry by the certainty of its reasoning, and determined to establish a science of human nature and political behaviour that would be based on firm laws and demonstrable evidence. During his continental visit of 1634–37 he had extensive discussions with the scientist Mersenne in Paris and with Galileo in Florence, and became convinced that the motion of bodies, or their differences in motion, was the fundamental issue. Motion was the cause of sensation and thought, of growth and decline. This mechanistic view of the world would be the basis of his science of politics. *The Elements of Law* (completed 1640, published 1650), composed of two treatises, *Human Nature* and *De Corpore Politico*, was his first attempt at a systematic study of man and the body politic. *De Cive* (1642) enlarged 'on civil government and the duties of subject'. Hobbes moved to Paris in 1640, anticipating the outbreak of civil war, and was a member of the circle of English *émigrés* there during the 1640s; 1647 became mathematical tutor to Prince Charles; engaged in debate about the critical principles of the heroic poem with Davenant, resulting in the publication of their different views in the preface to *Gondibert* (1650). Knew Descartes and Gassendi. His principal activity in Paris was the writing of *Leviathan* (1651) in which he made his classic analysis of human nature and political power. Returned to England in 1651 and lived quietly as a member of the Cavendish household. Much written against and abused for the materialism and supposed atheism of *Leviathan*. Discouraged from publishing further work. He wrote *Behemoth*, an analysis of the Long Parliament and the Civil War, during the 1660s, but it was not published until 1682. Died 1679; buried at Ault Hucknall, near Hardwick Hall in Derbyshire.

> *The English Works of Thomas Hobbes*, ed. W. Molesworth, 11 vols (1839–45).
> *Leviathan*, ed. C. B. Macpherson (Harmondsworth, 1968).

See: Brown, K. C. (ed.), *Hobbes Studies* (Oxford, 1965).
        Goldsmith, M. M., *Hobbes's Science of Politics* (1965).
        Macpherson, C. B., *The Theory of Possessive Individualism, Hobbes to Locke* (Oxford, 1962).
        Mintz, S., *The Hunting of Leviathan* (Cambridge, 1962). (On the controversy that raged around Hobbes's works.)
        Peters, R., *Hobbes* (Harmondsworth, 1956). (The most helpful introduction to Hobbes.)

HOOKE, Robert (1635–1703). Born in Isle of Wight, son of a minister. Westminster School and Christ Church, Oxford. Briefly an apprentice to the painter Lely. Recommended to Boyle as a research assistant, and began to design scientific instruments, for which he showed a talent amounting to genius. Designed a successful air-pump for Boyle's experiments on vacuums and the compression of air. 1662 appointed Curator of Experiments to the Royal Society: the first professional scientist in England, in effect. Invented the balance-spring for watches, the barometer, and the universal joint. Hooke's claim to have invented the microscope seems to take precedence over the same claim by the Dutch scientist, Huygens. 1665 published *Micrographia*, describing his microscope and many experiments made with it. 1666 appointed one of the commissioners for rebuilding London. Designed the Royal College of Physicians, Bethlehem Hospital ('Bedlam') and the Monument to the Great Fire. 1680 Designed Montagu House in Bloomsbury. Hooke was an important architect, most of whose buildings have been destroyed. 1677–82 Secretary to the Royal Society. Anticipated Newton's work in optics; also did research on the force of gravity; advanced the science of combustion, and laid the foundations of the study of meteorology. Rivalry between Hooke and Newton in several fields led to the eclipse of Hooke's achievements, which have only recently been properly acknowledged; he was in fact one of the most versatile scientists of Restoration England, and without his technical brilliance the work of the Royal Society would have been much impeded.

> *Micrographia* (1665; repr. 1972).
> *Diary, 1672–80*, ed. H. Robinson and W. Adams. (1935).

See: M. 'Espinasse, *Robert Hooke* (1956).
       M. Hunter, *Science and Society in Restoration England* (Cambridge, 1981).

JONES, Inigo (1573–1652). Born in London. Little is known about his family or about his early years. Probably in the service of the Earl of Rutland or his brother, with whom he may have travelled on the Continent; he seems to have had training as a painter. 1603 in the service of Christian IV, King of Denmark, who seems to have recommended him to his sister Queen Anne in England, 1604. Designed the settings and costumes for Queen Anne's *Masque of Blackness*, played on Twelfth Night 1605. Thereafter designed almost all the masques for the Stuart court until 1640, developing a remarkable sophistication in the invention of costumes, scenery, lighting effects, and stage technology. 1608–10 first essays in architecture, apparently for Robert Cecil, for his New Exchange in London and for Hatfield. 1611 appointed Surveyor to Prince Henry. 1613–14 travelled in Italy with the Earl of Arundel, visiting Venice, Vicenza (the location of the majority of Palladio's buildings), and Rome. 1615 Surveyor of Works to the King. 1616 began work on the Queen's House at Greenwich, his first thoroughly Palladian design. 1619–22 The Banqueting House, Whitehall, his masterpiece. 1620 surveyed Stonehenge and engaged in excavations there, concluding that it was a Roman temple. 1623–25 the Queen's Chapel, St James's Palace, Jones's neo-classical design for a chapel for Henrietta Maria. Early 1630s extensive rebuilding and redecorating of Somerset House for the Queen. For the Earl of Bedford he designed the piazza at Covent Garden with chapel and gentlemen's residences, the first exercise in formal civic planning in London. 1633 began to remodel St Paul's Cathedral, giving it a Classical façade and casing, and adding a magnificent portico in the Corinthian style. Davenant's *Salmacida Spolia*, the last Stuart masque, designed by Jones. 1645 taken prisoner by the parliamentarians at the siege of Basing House. Jones died in 1652, and was buried in St Benet's Church, London.

> Harris, J., S. Orgel, and R. Strong, *The King's Arcadia: Inigo Jones and the Stuart Court* (1973). (Catalogue of the quatercentenary exhibition; excellent documentation, well illustrated.)
> Harris, J., and A. A. Tait, *Catalogue of the Drawings by Inigo Jones, John Webb and Isaac de Caus at Worcester College Oxford* (Oxford, 1979).
> Jones, Inigo, *Stonehenge Restored* (1655; repr. by Scolar Press, 1972). (Jones's account of Stonehenge by his assistant John Webb.)
> Orgel, S. and R. Strong, *Inigo Jones: the Theatre of the Stuart Court*. 2 vols (Berkeley and London, 1973). (Indispensable survey of Jones's work for the theatre.)
> Strong, R., *Festival Designs by Inigo Jones* (1969). (Catalogue of the Victoria and Albert exhibition.)

LAUD, William (1573–1645). Born in Reading, son of a clothier. Reading
Grammar School and St John's, Oxford. Fellow of St John's, and from
1610 to 1621, President of the college. Friend and protégé of Lancelot
Andrewes. 1610 appointed one of the royal chaplains. 1621 Bishop of St
David's. Persuaded the Duke of Buckingham of the superior merits of the
Church of England in a debate with a Jesuit priest, and became
Buckingham's chaplain. Enjoyed rapid advancement under Charles I (at
whose coronation he officiated). 1630 Bishop of London and Chancellor of
Oxford. Set about the restoration of St Paul's. 1633 Archbishop of
Canterbury. Immediately began a strenuous campaign to impose
conformity of worship throughout the Church, insisting on a set order of
worship and encouraging ritualistic practices. Strengthened the authority of
bishops and the power of church courts. Favoured the Arminian position
in theology. Had the confidence of the King, and attained considerable
political influence during the years of Charles's personal rule. His policies
provoked intense hostility among those who sought the freedom to
worship how they chose, and alienated the whole spectrum of Puritans. A
great benefactor of the University of Oxford; Laud revised the statutes of
the university, greatly improving government and discipline; he made
several important donations to the Bodleian of Oriental and Patristic
materials, and endowed St John's with a magnificent new quadrangle.
When the Long Parliament met in 1640, Laud was impeached for high
treason, and sent to the Tower in March 1641. His trial did not take place
until 1644; he was found guilty and executed in January 1645. His sermons
in general are not distinguished for their eloquence, the one he preached
before his execution being much the most memorable. After the
Restoration, Laud's body was exhumed and reburied in the chapel of St
John's College, Oxford.

> Works, in The Library of Anglo-Catholic Theology, 7 vols (Oxford,
> 1847–53).

See: P. Heylyn, *Cyprianus Anglicus* (1668). (An admiring biography of
Laud by his chaplain.)
H. R. Trevor-Roper, *Archbishop Laud, 1573–1645* (1940; repr. 1967).

LOCKE, John (1632–1704). Westminster School and Christ Church, Oxford.
Born in Somerset, son of an attorney. Remained as tutor at Christ Church
until 1666, teaching grammar and philosophy. Friendship with Robert
Boyle, the experimental philosopher. Turned to medicine, and became the
physician, then secretary and friend to Anthony Ashley Cooper, later Lord
Shaftesbury. 1668 elected member of the Royal Society. Engaged in much
public business as Shaftesbury rose to be Lord Chancellor; worked for the
Council of Trade. After Shaftesbury's downfall in the imbroglio of
Monmouth's Rebellion in 1681 and his death in 1683, Locke prudently
removed to Holland. About 1681 wrote the *Two Treatises of Government*
(published 1690). Developed his political and philosophical thoughts in
exile. Returned in 1689, after the Glorious Revolution. 1690 published the
Essay concerning Human Understanding, and the *Letters concerning Toleration*.
Won rapid acclaim as the philosophical mentor of the new era. 1693
published *Some Thoughts concerning Education*. 1695 *The Reasonableness of
Christianity*. His clear propositions about the nature of perception and the
operations of the human mind in the *Essay*, his liberal notions of a
balanced constitution in government, and his demystification of religion all

justified his reputation as the philosopher who established the conceptual framework of the 'Age of Reason'. Locke died in 1704, and is buried at High Laver, Essex.

> *An Essay concerning Human Understanding*, ed. P. H. Nidditch (Oxford, 1975).
> *Two Treatises of Government*, ed. P. Laslett (Cambridge, 1960).
> *The Reasonableness of Christianity*, with *A Discourse on Miracles*, ed. I. T. Ramsay (1958).
> *The Locke Reader*, ed. J. Yolton (Cambridge, 1977). (A useful and wide selection of texts.)

See: Aaron, R., *John Locke* (Oxford, 1955).
Ashcraft, R., *Revolutionary Politics and Locke's Two Treatises of Government* (Princeton, N. J., 1986). (Explore's Locke's subversive tendencies as an organizer of insurrection.)
Cranston, M., *John Locke: A Biography* (1957). (Excellent, readable life.)
Dunn, J., *The Political Thought of John Locke* (Cambridge, 1969). (Considers the religious assumptions underlying Locke's political ideas.)
Gough, J. W., ed., *John Locke's Political Philosophy: Eight Studies* (Oxford, 1973).
Macpherson, C. B., *The Political Theory of Possessive Individualism* (Oxford 1962). (Stimulating chapter on Locke with a Marxist interpretation.)
Parry, G. *John Locke* (1978). (Good general introduction.)

MILTON, John (1608–74). Born in Bread St, London, son of a scrivener (money-lender cum solicitor). 1620–25 St Paul's School. 1625–32 Christ's College, Cambridge. 1632–38 years of private study at Hammersmith and Horton. 1634 *Comus* performed, published 1637. 'Lycidas' first printed in 1638. 1638–39 journey to Italy, where he travelled as far as Naples, visiting men of letters and attending meetings of academies. Met Galileo and Cardinal Barberini. Returned home, he threw himself into the acrimonious debates over the need for further reformation in the English Church with a series of powerful tracts in the Puritan cause: *Of Reformation, Of Prelatical Episcopacy, Animadversions*, all 1641, *The Reason of Church Government* and the *Apology for Smectymnuus* in 1642. He married Mary Powell, from a royalist family, in 1642, fell out with her, and next year protested against the illiberality of ecclesiastical law in *The Doctrine and Discipline of Divorce*. 1644 published his tractate *Of Education*, and in the same year came his celebrated plea for freedom of speech, *Areopagitica*, intended to thwart Parliament's attempt to reimpose censorship of the press. More works urging the reasonableness of divorce followed. In 1645 he published his *Poems*, all of which had been written before the Civil War. After the execution of Charles I on 30 January 1649, Milton published (in February 1649) *The Tenure of Kings and Magistrates*, justifying the right of the people to resist tyranny. In March he received official recognition, and was appointed Secretary for Foreign Tongues by the Council of State. His first task was to answer the King's book, *Eikon Basilike*, which he did in *Eikonoklastes*, 1649. In 1651 he produced the *Defensio pro Populo Anglicano*, justifying the Revolution to European onlookers, and followed it up with the *Defensio Secunda* in 1654, a work that includes much autobiographical content. Blindness overtook him about 1652. Around the middle of the century Milton began to compile *De Doctrina Christiana*, the system of his own theological beliefs which he continued to work on for many years, and which remained unpublished until 1825. He remarried in 1656. As the Commonwealth began to collapse Milton tried to halt the slide of events with *A Treatise of Civil Power* and *The Likeliest Way to Remove Hirelings out of the Church* in 1659, and *The Ready and Easy Way to Establish a Free Commonwealth* in 1660. At the Restoration he went into hiding, and feared for his life as the apologist of the regicides. He was imprisoned late in 1660, but released, apparently upon the intervention of Andrew Marvell. Married for a third time in 1663. Keeping out of public affairs, he worked on *Paradise Lost*, published in 1667. *Samson Agonistes* and *Paradise Regained* appeared in 1671. In 1670 he published his *History of Britain*, and in 1672 his *Art of Logic*. Milton died in 1674, and was buried in St Giles, Cripplegate.

> *The Poems of John Milton*, ed. J. Carey and A. Fowler (1968).
> *Complete Prose Works of John Milton*, ed. D. M. Wolfe (New Haven, 1953–).
> *The Works of John Milton*, ed. F. A. Patterson *et al.*, 20 vols (New York, 1931–40). (The Columbia edition.)

See: Empson, W., *Milton's God* (1961). (Provocative; hostile to Milton's theological scheme and to Christianity in general.)
Fish, S., *Surprised by Sin* (Berkeley, 1971).
French, J. M., ed., *Life Records of John Milton*, 5 vols (1949–58).
Hill, C., *Milton and the English Revolution* (1977). (Outstanding account of Milton's place in the political and religious developments of the age.)
Lewalski, B., *Milton's Brief Epic* (1966). (Full-length study of *Paradise Regained*.)
Low, A., *The Blaze of Noon* (New York, 1974). (On *Samson*.)
Parker, W., *Milton: A Life* 2 vols (Oxford, 1968). (The standard biography.)
Wolfe, D. M., *Milton and the Puritan Revolution* (1941).

NEWTON, Sir Isaac (1642–1727). Son of a Lincolnshire gentleman. Grantham Grammar School and Trinity College, Cambridge. Showed an early genius for mathematics. 1667 Fellow of Trinity, 1669 Lucasian Professor of Mathematics. By this time he had already elaborated his theories of colour and gravitation, and had formulated the basis of the differential and integral calculus. 1672 Fellow of Royal Society. Published papers on optics and colour theory in 1672 and 1675. Worked on the laws of motion and evolved the universal theory of gravitation, which were given to the world in *Philosophiae Naturalis Principia Mathematica*, 1687. Mathematics was the key to the understanding of the universe, and all matter from atoms to the planets obeyed consistent and rational laws that could be expressed in mathematical terms. Entered public affairs after 1688 as MP for Cambridge University. 1699 appointed Master of the royal Mint and involved in currency reform. 1703 President of the Royal Society. 1704 *Opticks* published. Throughout his life Newton was deeply interested in alchemy. He also gave much time to the study of biblical prophecy and to working out a chronology of the Apocalypse. Posthumous publications included *The Chronology of the Ancient Kingdoms*, 1728, and *Observations on the*

Prophecies of Daniel and the Apocalypse, 1733. Newton died in 1727, and was buried in Westminster Abbey.

> *Opticks, or a treatise of the Reflections, Refractions, Inflections, and Colours of Light* (1704; repr. 1931).
> *Mathematical Principles of Natural Philosophy*, English translation by A. Motte (1729; repr. Berkeley, Calif., 1947).

See: Butts, R. E., *The Methodological Heritage of Newton* (Oxford, 1970).
Dobbs, B. J. T., *The Foundations of Newton's Alchemy, or 'The Hunting of the Green Lyon'* (Cambridge, 1975).
Nicolson, M. H., *Newton's Demands the Muse* (Princeton, N. J., 1946). (On the consequences of Newton's theories, especially those of colour and light, in poetry – particularly eighteenth-century poetry.)
Westfall, R. S. *Never at Rest: A Biography of Isaac Newton* (Cambridge, 1980). (Very long, very readable, vastly informative; the definitive scientific life.)

PEPYS, Samuel (1633–1703). Born in Huntingdonshire, son of a tailor with good social connections. St Paul's School and Magdalene College, Cambridge. Entered the service of his cousin Sir Edward Montagu, later Lord Sandwich. Accompanied Montagu on the mission to bring back Charles II from Holland in 1660, and returned with the King's party on board the *Naseby*. Montagu secured for Pepys a clerkship in the Navy Office, where Pepys proved a very efficient administrator, rising to become Secretary to the Admiralty in 1672. From 1660 to 1669 kept in cipher his Diary of public and private events that provides a uniquely intimate picture of these years. Pepys had an immense relish for music, theatre, books, business, and women; he attended to work and pleasure with equal energy and spirit. 1665 elected to Royal Society. 1672 imprisoned in the Tower on suspicion of involvement in the Popish Plot. 1684 President of Royal society. 1689 deprived of his office at the Admiralty, and retired to Clapham. Pepys died in 1703, and was buried in St Olave's in the City of London.

> *The Diary of Samuel Pepys*, ed. R. Latham and W. Matthews, 11 vols (1970–83). (A superb edition with excellent notes.)

See: Ollard, R., *Pepys: A Biography* (1974).

ROCHESTER, Earl of (John Wilmot) (1647–80). Born at Ditchley in Oxfordshire, son of a landowner who had been a royalist general; his mother was a member of a well-known Puritan family, the St Johns. Burford Grammar School and Wadham College, Oxford. 1661–64 travelled to Italy, going as far as Naples, and studied at the University of Padua. 1665 to court, where he became a favourite of Charles II, and a close friend of the Duke of Buckingham, the Earl of Dorset, Sir Charles Sedley, Sir George Etherege, and Thomas Killigrew. They formed the pre-eminent group of Restoration wits and rakes. 1665–66 served with distinction in sea-fights against the Dutch. A long career of debauchery followed, during which time Rochester wrote his lyrics of love and lust, and his libertine philosophical poems. Shortly before his death he engaged in a series of religious discussions with Gilbert Burnet, the liberal Anglican divine. Burnet claimed that Rochester underwent a conversion to the Anglican faith (from a position of complete scepticism) just before he died, in July 1680.

The Complete Poems, ed. D. M. Vieth (New Haven, Conn., 1968).

The Poems of John Wilmot, Earl of Rochester, ed. K. Walker (Oxford, 1984).

The Letters of John Wilmot, Earl of Rochester, ed. J Treglown (Oxford, 1980).

See: Burnet G., Some Passages of the Life and Death of The Earl of Rochester (1680). (Modern reprints.)

Farley Hills, D., Rochester's Poetry (1978).

De S. Pinto, V., Enthusiast in Wit (1962).

Treglown, J. (ed.) Spirit of Wit: Reconsiderations of Rochester (Oxford, 1982).

SELDEN, John (1584–1654). Born in Sussex, son of a prosperous yeoman. Chichester Grammar School and Hart Hall, Oxford. 1604 Inner Temple. Practised law at the Temple. Friend of Ben Jonson, Robert Cotton, and Edward Hyde (later Earl of Clarendon). Strong interest in antiquarianism, using the knowledge he gained from these studies to supplement his juridical arguments. Wrote a History of Britain (unpublished), and several other works tracing the laws and customs of the Britons, Saxons, and Normans, e.g. Jani Anglorum Facies Altera and England's Epinomis, (both 1610). 1612 provided learned notes to Drayton's Poly-Olbion. 1614 Titles of Honor, a history of social titles current in England. 1617 De Diis Syris, a treatise of comparative religion, which Milton used and admired. 1617 History of Tithes, dedicated to Cotton, traced tithes from the time of Abraham, and debated their status in law. Selden was one of the great jurists of Stuart England, a supporter of common law against canon law and prerogative. Became an MP in 1621, and engaged in many notable debates, especially those on the liberty of the subject with Coke and Eliot in the Parliament of 1629. Imprisoned in the early 1630s for his hostility to royal prerogative. Remained very active in Parliament in the 1640s as a legal adviser and committee-man, but retired from public life before the trial and execution of Charles I. Among his voluminous works should be mentioned Marmora Arundelliana (1629), an account of the inscriptions and sculptures in the Earl of Arundel's collection, and Mare Clausum (1636) on the legal question of the dominion of the seas. In 1689 his Table Talk was published, a book of sturdy common sense. Selden died in 1654, and was buried in the Temple Church.

Works, 3 vols (1726).

See: Pocock, J. G. A. The Ancient Constitution and the Feudal Law (Cambridge, 1957).

SPRAT, Thomas (1635–1713). Born in Dorset, son of a minister of the Church. Wadham College, Oxford. 1657–70 Fellow of Wadham. Wrote verse in the manner of Cowley, who was his friend. His best-known piece was a poem on 'The Plague at Athens', in the Pindaric mode. 1661 ordained. Became chaplain to the second Duke of Buckingham. 1663 elected Fellow of the Royal Society. 1667 published History of the Royal Society, intended as a defence and a promotion of the Society's activities. 1668 'Life of Cowley' printed with Cowley's Works. As a churchman, Sprat held High Church doctrines and argued for the divine right of kings. 1683 appointed Dean of Westminster, and in 1684 Bishop of Rochester, holding both posts jointly. Suspected of wanting to restore James II after 1688, but proved his innocence. Buried in Westminster Abbey. There is no modern assessment of Sprat, but see:

Hunter, M., *Science and Society in Restoration England* (1981).
Willey, B., *The Seventeenth Century Background* (1934).

WILKINS, John (1614–72). Son of an Oxford goldsmith. Magdalen Hall, Oxford, then took orders. Chaplain to Viscount Say and Sele, Lord Berkeley, then to Charles Louis, Prince Palatine. Devoted to mathematics. 1638 *The Discovery of a World in the Moon*: an ingenious treatise that tried to prove the moon is habitable; second edition included an imaginary voyage there. Wilkins was Oxford based by the mid-1640s; friendly with Boyle and other scientists. 1648 *Mathematical Magick, or The Wonders that may be performed by Mechanical Geometry*. 1648 appointed Warden of Wadham College. Under his mastership, Wadham flourished as an intellectual centre: students included Wren, Seth Ward, Sedley, Sprat, and Rochester. The Oxford group of scientists, the nucleus of the Royal Society, met at Wadham during the 1650s. 1656 married sister of Oliver Cromwell. 1659 became Master of Trinity College, Cambridge. Deprived at the Restoration, and turned to the Church for a living. Centrally involved in the activities of the Royal Society during the 1660s. 1668 *Essay towards a Real Character and a Philosophic Language*, an attempt to formulate a universal language based on symbols. 1668 Bishop of Chester. 1672 Wilkins died and was buried in St Lawrence Jewry, London. 1675 publication of *The Principles and Duties of Natural Religion*.

Shapiro, B., *John Wilkins 1614–72. An Intellectual Biography* (1969).

WINSTANLEY, Gerrard (*c.* 1609–?). Biographical material about Winstanley is very scarce. Probably born in Wigan, son of a mercer. Moved to London and apprenticed in the cloth trade, becoming a freeman of the Merchant Taylors Company in 1637. Failed to establish himself in trade, and *c.* 1643 moved to Walton-on-Thames in Surrey, where he declined to the level of hired labourer, herding cattle. Developed his egalitarian ideas and his religious communism during the 1640s. April 1649 led a group of Diggers to occupy and cultivate waste land near Walton. The colony aroused a good deal of support and survived for about a year, before being broken up by soldiers. 1648–52 he published a large number of pamphlets, of which the most significant are: *The True Levellers Standard Advanced*, 1649, *A Watch-Word to the City of London, and the Armie*, 1649, *Fire in the Bush*, 1650, and *The Law of Freedom in a Platform*, 1652 (dedicated to Cromwell). Winstanley can be traced in and around Walton until 1660, but after that date there is no record of him.

The Works of Gerrard Winstanley, ed. G. H. Sabine (Ithaca, NY, 1941).
The Law of Freedom and Other Writings, ed. C. Hill (Harmondsworth, 1973). (A selection of central texts with excellent introduction.)

See: Hill, C. 'The Religion of Gerrard Winstanley', in *Collected Essays*, II (Brighton, 1986).
Hill, C., *The World Turned Upside Down* (1972).
Petegorsky, D. W., *Left-Wing Democracy in the English Civil War* (1940).

WREN, Sir Christopher (1632–1723). Born in Wiltshire, son of a minister who shortly afterwards became Dean of Windsor. His uncle was Matthew Wren, Bishop of Ely. Westminster School and Wadham College, Oxford. 1653–7 Fellow of All Souls. Early interests in astronomy, mathematics, and geometry. 1657 Professor of Astronomy at Gresham College, London; 1661 Savilian Professor of Astronomy, Oxford. Wren belonged to the Oxford circle of scientists who formed the core of the Royal Society: Wilkins, Ward, Wallis, Boyle, Hooke. Wren turned to architecture about 1662, when his uncle asked him to design a new chapel for Pembroke College, Cambridge. The success of this led to his being invited to design the Sheldonian Theatre at Oxford in 1663. 1665–66 visited France to look at recent architectural developments there; may have met Mansart and Bernini in Paris. 1666 the Great Fire of London provided Wren with a unique opportunity to impose his architectural style on the City. Immediately he produced a formal plan for rebuilding the City, but it was blocked by local interests. Appointed to the rebuilding committee which included Robert Hooke, Hugh May, and Roger Pratt. Of these Wren was the least experienced architect, but he soon came to dominate the committee. 1669 Surveyor of Works. Wren had special responsibility for rebuilding the City churches; by 1672 twenty were under construction, and by the end of the century he had designed some fifty in all. First design for St Paul's 1669; several other designs followed; building began in 1675, and continued until 1710. Wren's interest in interior decoration caused him to assemble an outstanding team of craftsmen, whose legacy of skills would extend all over England: Grinling Gibbons the wood-carver, Jean Tijou in ironwork, Francis Bird the sculptor, Doogood and Goudge the artists in plaster. 1676 Trinity College Library. 1682 began Chelsea Hospital, and also started to build a new palace for Charles II at Winchester (unfinished). For William and Mary he designed the Fountain Court at Hampton Court and the Naval Hospital at Greenwich. Hawksmoor and Vanbrugh worked under him, and Talman, Archer, and Gibbs were all profoundly influenced by him. Wren died in 1723, and was buried in St Paul's Cathedral, with the inscription 'Si Monumentum Requieris, Circumspice' – 'If you seek a memorial, look around you'.

> *Parentalia* (1750), compiled by Christopher Wren, the architect's son, is the indispensable collection of documents for the study of Wren. It contains lives of Wren and his uncle Matthew Wren, and detailed accounts of Wren's scientific interests and his architectural activities. (Reprinted by Gregg Press, 1965, with many illustrations.)
> Downes, K., *Christopher Wren* (Harmondsworth, 1971). (A compact, informative Penguin volume.)

See: Beard, G., *The Work of Christopher Wren* (Edinburgh, 1982).
Downes, K., *English Baroque Architecture* (1966).
Summerson, J., *Architecture in Britain, 1530–1830* (Harmondsworth, 1953).
Whinney, M. D., *Wren* (1971).
Whinney M. D. and O. Millar, *English Art, 1625–1714* (Oxford, 1957).

Index